Henry Louis Baugher

Annotations on the Gospel According to St. Luke

Volume 4

Henry Louis Baugher

Annotations on the Gospel According to St. Luke
Volume 4

ISBN/EAN: 9783337285456

Printed in Europe, USA, Canada, Australia, Japan

Cover: Foto ©Lupo / pixelio.de

More available books at **www.hansebooks.com**

THE LUTHERAN COMMENTARY

A PLAIN EXPOSITION OF THE

Holy Scriptures of the New Testament

BY
SCHOLARS OF THE LUTHERAN CHURCH IN AMERICA

EDITED BY
HENRY EYSTER JACOBS

Vol. IV.

New York
The Christian Literature Co.
MDCCCXCV

ANNOTATIONS

ON THE

GOSPEL ACCORDING TO ST. LUKE

BY

H. LOUIS BAUGHER, D.D.

Late Franklin Professor of Greek in Pennsylvania College at Gettysburg

🕮 New York
The Christian Literature Co.

MDCCCXCVI.

PREFACE.

The Gospel according to St. Luke is the largest book in the New Testament. Having much in common with the other Evangelists, especially Matthew and Mark, far the largest part of the book is peculiar to Luke. Our space being so limited, it has seemed best to us to pass over with slight consideration the portions common to the other gospels, with references to their discussion in the other volumes of this work, and to give our space chiefly to what is peculiar to Luke. And even thus we have overrun the limit of pages allowed by the publishers. Whilst these comments will be found to be popular and practical, we believe they will also satisfy scholarly inquiry and taste. We have not hesitated to incorporate the results of former studies while Editor of *The Augsburg Sunday School Teacher*. If the readers of the following pages get from them the benefit and delight that have come to the Author in their preparation, this book will serve a blessed purpose. May they find God's " wonderful testimonies " in His word " more to be desired than much fine gold; sweeter also than honey and the honeycomb!"

H. L. B.

INTRODUCTION.

1. THE AUTHOR.—In the Greek manuscripts this gospel history is entitled κατὰ Λουκᾶν, that is, according to Loukas, which is easily anglicized into Luke. The best etymologists say this name is not to be confounded with Lucius, found in Acts xiii. 1, and Rom. xvi. 21. The Acts of the Apostles, written also by Luke, and the Pauline Epistles (Col. iv. 14; Philem. 24; 2 Tim. iv. 11,) are the only sources of historical information that we have concerning him. From these he appears to have been a Gentile by birth (comp. Col. iv. ver. 11 with ver. 14), a physician by profession, and a companion of Paul from the time when he joined him at Troas, on that apostle's second missionary journey. At this point in the Acts it is noticeable that the narrative changes from the third to the first person (Acts xvi. 10). As the narrative resumes the indirect third person after the events at Philippi, some conjecture that Luke remained there till the apostle's return, some years later, joining him there again *en route* to Jerusalem, the direct first person appearing there again (Acts xx. 6), from which time he continued with him till the close of the apostle's life (2 Tim. iv. 11). There are no historical data regarding the time or place of his birth or his death: and all that the fathers say about him is legendary. The lan-

guage and style of this gospel history, as well as of the Acts, show that their author was an educated man.

2. SOURCES OF LUKE'S GOSPEL. First, there was oral tradition, distinctly referred to as a source in Luke's preface (i. 1-4). Our author's advantages for getting and sifting this were great. Resident in Judæa, in all probability, during Paul's two years' imprisonment at Cæsarea (comp. Acts xxi.-xxvii.), he would likely come in contact with many who had been eye-witnesses and hearers of Christ, e.g., with some of the apostles, with James the Lord's brother, President of the Church at Jerusalem, and Mary the Lord's mother, and Philip the Evangelist, of Cæsarea; and through Paul he must have learned much which that apostle had received from the other apostles, with whom he must have had frequent communication. (See pp. xvii. and xviii. of Introduction, Vol. III. of this series.)

Secondly, there were written documents, to which also our author refers in his preface. These were numerous, some of them of more value, others, of less; and Luke sought accurately (ἀκριβῶς) to weigh and use them freely, as suited his purpose. The tendency of opinion is, that among these documents was the gospel according to Mark and, possibly, that according to Matthew, although there is no absolute proof either that Luke had or had not these gospels before him. The synoptic problem— of the order in which the first three gospels were written, and which one or ones, if any, each of these writers had before him—is one much speculated upon, but it probably will remain unsettled. The opinion that Marcion's Gospel was the primitive Luke has fallen entirely and criticism has established it that Marcion's Gospel is an abbreviation and variation of Luke.

3. CHARACTERISTICS.—In language and diction Luke

is, for a New Testament writer, unusually pure and correct. This is seen in the Acts as well as in the gospel history. A marked individuality appears in his style and diction.. Schaff (History of the Church, Vol. II. p. 665) says, " The vocabulary of Luke considerably exceeds that of the other evangelists; he has about 180 terms which occur in his Gospel alone, and nowhere else in the New Testament; while Matthew has only about 70, Mark 44, and John 50 peculiar words. Luke's Gospel has 55, and the Acts 135 ἅπαξ λεγόμενα, and among them many verbal compounds and rare technical terms." This shows our author's command of the Greek language, and confirms the opinion of his Gentile origin.

Comprehensiveness is another characteristic. Luke alone gives an account of the Forerunner's birth and the interesting circumstances connected therewith, of the Annunciation to Mary and the circumstances of Jesus' birth and His presentation in the temple. He alone gives an incident of Jesus' childhood, and refers to His youthful years, and closes with an account of the Ascension. Moreover there are twelve parables and six miracles given by Luke that are not found in the other Gospels. From ix. 51 to xviii. 14 most of the narrative is peculiar to Luke, interspersed with some things either the same as or like what is given by the others.

Luke's Gospel is the Gospel of the Gentiles, so considered from Origen down and sufficiently shown by its contents, explaining Jewish customs and localities, introducing so many Gentile personages, to one of whom it is dedicated, and setting forth with so much frequency and earnestness Christ as the Saviour of men, not of Jews only. Moreover our author brings out more than the others the humanity of Christ.

The prominence given to women is another characteristic of this gospel, and this in harmony with the features before mentioned.

Schaff, who calls Luke the proper father of Christian Church History, says, "His is the Gospel of historical development. To him we are indebted for nearly all the hints that link the gospel facts with the contemporary history of the world."

Reuss says, "It is proportionally the richest of the extant Gospels, and the one of the three most carefully worked out."

Weiss says, " It is a doctrinal writing, notwithstanding that it has more the character of historiography."

Renan says, "From a purely literary and humanitarian standpoint, it is the most beautiful book ever written."

4. GENUINENESS AND INTEGRITY.—The genuineness and integrity of the Gospel by Luke have not been successfully impugned. The unanimous tradition of the ancient church, reaching back as far as Irenæus, ascribes it to Luke as author. The most noteworthy objection brought against it is its relation to the Gospel of Marcion, concerning which it may now be considered as demonstrated that Marcion copied and mutilated Luke, having seen in it the Pauline character which suited his teachings.

The portion from ch. i. 5 to end of ch. ii., has been called in question because of its absence in Marcion's Gospel and its Hebraic character. But this contention has been clearly shown by scholars to be without foundation, and that external and internal testimony alike accredit it as a genuine portion of Luke.

5. DATE AND PLACE OF COMPOSITION.—There is no certain evidence where Luke's Gospel was written. Cæsarea, Alexandria, Achaia and Bœotia, Greece, Rome, and other places have been assigned by different scholars.

Dates ranging from A. D. 58 to A. D. 130 have been assigned. The last named is now universally abandoned in favor of an earlier one. Whilst most assign this gospel to the first century, there is a division of opinion as to whether it was written before or after the destruction of Jerusalem. Credner, DeWette, Bleek, Meyer, Holzmann, Weiss, Reuss, Sanday, and others, put the date after that event—we think on insufficient grounds; Michaelis, Lardner, Horne, Guericke, Ebrard and Godet assign A. D. 63 or 64, as the date; Alford, Thomson and Schaff, A. D. 58-60; and Gloag, A. D. 60, at Cæsarea, toward the conclusion of Paul's imprisonment there.

It certainly was written before the Acts of the Apostles, in which it is spoken of as "the former treatise."

CHAPTER I.

1-4. Forasmuch as many have taken in hand to draw up a narrative concerning those matters which have been fulfilled among us, even as they delivered them unto us, which from the beginning were eye-witnesses and ministers of the word, it seemed good to me also, having traced the course of all things accurately from the first, to write unto thee in order, most excellent Theophilus; that thou mightest know the certainty concerning the things wherein thou wast instructed.

The classical beauty of this introduction is noted by all who study it. It is a gem and a model. Luke is more classical in his language and style than the other evangelists; but this characteristic cannot appear in the greater part of his gospel history, where he quotes from others and cannot write after his own style.

This introduction sets forth the occasion and purpose of his writing and the sources of his information.

1. It appears that **many** at that early day had undertaken to **draw up a narrative** purporting to give the gospel history. This shows the interest taken therein, and that writings of this sort were not rare. Luke does not refer to the apocryphal writings, which were later, nor to Matthew's history, and likely not to Mark's, but to writings not included in our canonical Scriptures, and which are no longer extant. That there was abundant material for such writings appears from John xxi. 25.

Matters which have been fulfilled among us. The rendering of the "authorized version" is, "Things which are most surely believed among us." The original allows either rendering, and each comes with about equal authority. It is easy to combine the two and get the full force of the original. The things of which Luke proposes to write had been historically so fully established among them as to be surely believed among them. These were the things concerning Jesus Christ.

2. **Even as they delivered them unto us.** The many writers referred to were not original authorities, and did not profess to be, but had received their information, chiefly orally, but may be sometimes in writing, from those who **from the beginning were eyewitnesses** of what they reported, **and ministers of the word.**

To the latter belonged the Twelve (comp. Acts i. 21, 22), and the Seventy, and to the former Mary, the mother of Jesus, and the women that followed Jesus from Galilee, ministering unto Him (Matt. xxvii. 55, 56).

3. **It seemed good to me also.** Here Luke includes himself among the many who so received their information; but signifies that he thought there was still further need of a treatise on these subjects. That he was inspired of God to prepare such a treatise is here neither affirmed nor denied. His competence for the work appears from his **having traced the course of all things accurately from the first.** Luke therefore felt called upon to undertake the difficult work and improve upon the narratives of the many (ver. 1.) And God has been pleased to preserve to us his accurate history for our study. Let us be thankful.

To write unto thee. So the Acts and most of the Epistles are specially addressed, yet came abroad to all in God's good providence. **In order.** Consecutively; one thing after another, in historical sequence. Who **Theophilus** was, we do not know. He is supposed to have been a Gentile convert, and the address **most excel-**

lent is thought by many to mark him as a man of rank, though not necessarily so.

4. **That thou mightest know** thoroughly, or clearly, **the certainty,** the unshaken and immovable character of **the things,** the doctrines (λόγων not merely πραγμάτων of ver. 1), **wherein thou wast instructed,** catechized (as the orignal word is). Theophilus, it appears, had been, in accordance with early custom, instructed before he was baptized. Luke proposes by his narrative to confirm him in his faith. The assurance of the doctrines is to come from accuracy in the history. "Luke wrote from the dispassionate consciousness that Christianity, as it subsisted for him as the Pauline contents of faith, had its firm basis of truth in the evangelical history of salvation" (MEYER).

In like manner may a careful study of this gospel history increase our knowledge and confirm our faith.

5-7. There was in the days of Herod, king of Judæa, a certain priest named Zacharias, of the course of Abijah: and he had a wife of the daughters of Aaron, and her name was Elisabeth. And they were both righteous before God, walking in all the commandments and ordinances of the Lord blameless. And they had no child, because that Elisabeth was barren, and they both were *now* well stricken in years.

Luke goes further back into the particulars of the history of the development of the plan of salvation than the other evangelists. After the general introduction, in his first four verses, he begins in a manifestly different style, as though copying from records he deemed authentic, kept in the Aramaic dialect of the Jews. The particularity of his statements about persons, places and times is very noticeable.

5. **In the days of Herod.** But as there were several of this name, our accurate author specifies the **king of Judæa** as the one meant. This was the first king of

Judæa of that name; he was son of Antipater, an Idumean, descendant of Esau by birth, but a proselyte to the Jews' religion. He received his authority from the Romans, under whom Judæa was a tributary province. This Herod was commonly called "the Great," from his many warlike exploits and natural gifts and vigorous government. He was great also in barbarity and passion. He reigned from 40 to 4 B. C., dying four years before the year from which the common designations B. C. and A. D. are reckoned, which shows that chronology to be wrong by four years.

A certain priest—not the high priest—came on the stage of the drama Luke is describing, **named Zacharias**, which means *the Lord remembers*. The priests had been divided by David into 24 courses (1 Chron. xxiv., etc.), each of which officiated at the temple one week in each six months. **The course of Abijah**, one of the heads of families in David's time, was the eighth. Although but few of these courses returned from the captivity (Ezra ii. 36-39), those who did return were divided into the original number of courses, with the same names and order as before. These facts enter into the determination of the chronology of the events presently spoken of. This man's **wife**—for there was no priestly celibacy in those days—was **of the daughter of Aaron**, also of priestly descent. Her name—**Elisabeth**—means *God's oath*. Is there not significance in the meaning of these two names, which, taken together, illustrate that God remembers His oath, and will not forget His promises.

6. **Both righteous before God**, who sees the heart as well as the life. They were not sinless, since they were but human; yet their characters were pleasing to God. (Comp. Acts x. 35.) Theirs was a godly walk, **in all the commandments and ordinances of the Lord**, so that they

were **blameless.** Nothing could be said against their characters or lives. They exemplified Psalm i. Such persons were Noah (Gen. vi. 9; vii. 1), Job (Job i. 8; ii. 3), Daniel (Dan. v. 11, 12; x. 11), Simeon and Anna (Luke ii. 25, 36, 37), and Paul (Acts xxiii. 1; Phil. iii. 6), in their times.

7. The great trial of their lives was that **they had no child.** God has implanted in the human heart a desire for offspring, and in those days to be childless was regarded as a judgment of God. As at the time mentioned the wife was **barren, and they both were well stricken,** advanced, **in years,** they no longer had any hope of posterity.

8-12. Now it came to pass, while he executed the priest's office before God in the order of his course, according to the custom of the priest's office, his lot was to enter into the temple of the Lord and burn incense. And the whole multitude of the people were praying without at the hour of incense. And there appeared unto him an angel of the Lord standing on the right side of the altar of incense. And Zacharias was troubled when he saw *him*, and fear fell upon him.

8, 9. The priests' daily duties were assigned by lot (Prov. xvi. 33), as well as the order of service of the several courses; and so nothing of the services was left to any one's fancy, to do or neglect it. Everything was assigned. On this occasion Zacharias' **lot was to enter into the temple of the Lord and burn incense.** The directions concerning the offering and composition of this incense may be seen in Ex. xxx. 7-10, 34-38. It was offered every morning and evening on the golden altar of the Sanctuary before the Holy of Holies. None but priests dared offer it. The fire upon which it was burnt was taken from the altar of sacrifice before the temple. The fumes that ascended from the incense represented the prayers of God's people. (Comp. Rev. viii. 1-4.)

10. None but the officiating priest was in the sanctuary at such a time. But **the whole multitude of the people were praying without,** in the temple court, in silence, **at the hour of incense.** An impressive scene, indeed. Probably David had such a scene in mind when he used the words of Ps. cxli. 2, which again are appropriately found in our "Order of Evening Service," where, all standing, the minister says, "Let my prayer be set forth before thee as incense," and the people respond, "And the lifting up of my hands as the evening sacrifice," and then the closing devotional exercises follow.

Jesus has entered into "heaven itself," there to appear in the presence of God for us. We are waiting without, praying in His name, until He appear with the blessings of full salvation (Heb. ix. 28).

11, 12. The last of the Old Testament prophets that had to do with angels was Zachariah, who lived 500 years before this time; and now to his namesake, the priest, **there appeared an angel of the Lord,** the same that had appeared to Daniel (Dan. viii. 16; ix. 21), Gabriel by name, a prime minister, we may say, of heaven (ver. 19), **standing on the right side** (as the priest faced) **of the altar of incense**; that is, on the north side, between the altar and the table of shewbread. Notice the exactness of statement. No wonder Zacharias was **troubled** and stricken with **fear**; ever since man's conscience was defiled by sin and the knowledge of good *and evil* was gained, he has been afraid of God's glorious manifestation of Himself. And this though Zacharias was a "righteous" man and "blameless." Is it not well, then, that God's word is preached to man by man, and not by angels?

13-17. But the angel said unto him, Fear not, Zacharias: because thy supplication is heard, and thy wife Elisabeth shall bear thee a son, and thou shalt call his name John. And thou shalt have joy and gladness; and many shall rejoice at his birth. For he shall be great in the sight of the Lord, and he shall drink no wine nor strong drink; and he shall be filled with the Holy Ghost, even from his mother's womb. And many of the children of Israel shall he turn unto the Lord their God. And he shall go before his face in the spirit and power of Elijah, to turn the hearts of the fathers to the children, and the disobedient *to walk* in the wisdom of the just; to make ready for the Lord a people prepared *for him*.

13. The heavenly messenger's first words—the first from heaven in the N. T. record—were those blessed ones, **Fear not.** So had the word of the Lord come to Abram nearly 2,000 years before (Gen. xv. 1), and how often it sounds from the sacred word. **Thy supplication is heard.** Some take this to mean his personal prayer for offspring, put up often in years past, and now remembered before God, though he had ceased to offer it. "Prayers of faith are *filed* in heaven, and are not *forgotten*, though the thing prayed for is not presently *given*. Prayers made when we were young and coming into the world, may be answered when we are old and going out of the world" (MATT. HENRY). Others think the prayer referred to was the one just then put up by him and the people for the coming of the Messiah, or for the salvation of Israel and the world. Why should we not include all these objects as the substance of his prayers, both uttered and unexpressed, and now to be realized? **Thy wife Elisabeth shall bear thee a son,** and that will answer thy personal prayer; and that son shall usher in the Messiah, in whom all thy prayers shall find answer.

And thou shalt call his name John. Will any one ask, "What's in a name?" since God thus carefully assigns names to His chosen ones? See Matt. i. 21. "John" means "Jehovah's gracious gift," or, making a sentence of it, "Jehovah is gracious." He remembers ("Zacharias") His oath ("Elisabeth"). See on ver. 5.

14. **And thou shalt have joy and gladness,** exultation. This represents the personal and family joy; but this would expand to a much wider circle, for **many shall rejoice at his birth.** This shows the large extent of the influence of the promised son, which is still further recited in the verses following. See his father's prophecy at the time of the child's circumcision (vers. 67-79).

15. Herod was called "great" by men; John would be **great in the sight of the Lord,** and that is the only real, true greatness! The Lord's opinion of him (Matt. xi. 11) was that among them that are born of women there had not risen a greater personage. His greatness lay in both his character and his office; and it was a gracious gift of Jehovah (John), not the result of ordinary instrumentalities. **Shall drink no wine nor strong drink** made of anything else than the fruit of the vine. He shall be a *Nazarite*, the law of which service is fully laid down in Numbers, chap. vi. "Nazarite means *separated*, and denotes one specially *devoted*. As the leper was the living symbol of sin, so was the Nazarite of *holiness*" (BROWN). Ordinarily the Nazarite's vow was voluntary and temporary; in the case of John, as in those of Samson and Samuel, it was lifelong. **And he shall be filled with the Holy Ghost**—but how soon? **Even from his mother's womb,** from the beginning of his being, a sanctified child growing up into a sanctified manhood and life. (Comp. ver. 41. See Eph. v. 18.) John's development will not be sensual, but spiritual. See Is. xlix. 1, 5; Jer. i. 5; Gal. 15, 16, and consider the divine knowledge, and the possibilities of spiritual impressions on children—even before they are born—and both bring your children to baptism, and train them up *with more faith in the operation of God* who has promised.

16. John's personal mission was to be to **the children**

of Israel, the people through whom God's plan of salvation was to be made known to mankind. **Many** of them he was destined to **turn to the Lord their God.** His preaching would be *repentance*, which is a turning. In chap. vii. 29, 30; Matt. iii. 5, 6; Mark i. 3, we have a record of the fulfilment of this.

17. **And he** (John) **shall go before his face**—that is, before the Lord their God, just before mentioned, when He would, according to the prophecies, become manifest in the flesh, in the person of Jesus—**in the spirit and power of Elijah,** a man of prophetic spirit and influential power, like that greatest of the old-time prophets. In dress (Matt. iii. 4; 2 Kings i. 8), in manner of life, retired from the world (i. 80), in preaching of repentance and reformation to a degenerate people, in zeal and testimony, in effectiveness, in persecution by rulers, John and Elijah were much alike. John was not the person Elijah (John i. 21), but had the "spirit and power" of that prophet, and so was the fulfilment of the prophecy of Malachi (iv. 5, 6) as we learn from our Lord's own interpretation (Matt. xi. 14; xvii. 10–13). It had been 400 years since a prophet had appeared in Israel: now by angelic messenger the beginning of the new era, which is to be the fulfilment of the old, is announced. **To turn the hearts of the fathers to the children.** To restore society, which has its foundation in the home, in right relations between parents and children, and which had become degenerate in the preceding days. John would be one of those spoken of in Is. lviii. 12. He would turn the hitherto **disobedient** so that they would walk in **the wisdom of the just,** the thoughtful ways of the obedient. Others, making this passage more closely interpretative of Mal. iv. 6, make "children" and "disobedient" refer to the same, namely, degenerate Jews and Gentiles, and "the

just" and "fathers" to early and believing Israel, the heroes of faith (Heb. xi.) of old, and explain that John shall be the restorer of the right ways of the fathers, from which the children had degenerated. His ministry is summed up in the clause **to make ready for the Lord a people prepared.** "John *prepares* the people in such a way that they are *disposed* to receive the Messiah. Of course it is the ideal task of the forerunner that is described here. In reality this plan will succeed only in so far as the people shall consent to surrender themselves to the divine action" (GODET).

<small>18–20. And Zacharias said unto the angel, Whereby shall I know this? for I am an old man, and my wife well stricken in years. And the angel answering said unto him, I am Gabriel, that stand in the presence of God; and I was sent to speak unto thee, and to bring thee these good tidings. And behold, thou shalt be silent and not able to speak, until the day that these things shall come to pass, because thou believedst not my words, which shall be fulfilled in their season.</small>

18. **Whereby shall I know this?** Ver. 20 interprets this question as characterized by unbelief, although it seems in form similar to that of Abraham (Gen. xv. 8; xvii. 17), and of Mary (ver. 34). God who knoweth the hearts did not see in Zachariah the simplicity of faith that dwelt in Abraham (Rom. iv. 20), and in the Virgin Mary (ver. 45). That the priest was **an old man** is not contrary to the fifty year limit (Num. viii. 25, 26), which applied only to the Levites.

19. **I am Gabriel.** The priest would recognize this as the name of the angel who appeared to Daniel (Dan. viii. 16; ix. 21), one of the only two angels whose names are given in Scripture, the other being Michael (Jude 9). **That stand in the presence of God.** Rev. viii. 2 speaks of seven such. Are these the archangels? This "man of God" (as the name signifies) **was sent** specially with the

good tidings to Zachariah, and his word was not to be doubted.

20. **And behold** the sign thou askest shall be also a reproof of thy lurking unbelief. **Thou shalt be silent,** not from choice but because **not able to speak**—shut up to thyself, with the compensation of time and opportunity for reflection **until the day these things shall come to pass.**

21, 22. And the people were waiting for Zacharias, and they marvelled while he tarried in the temple. And when he came out, he could not speak unto them: and they perceived that he had seen a vision in the temple: and he continued making signs unto them, and remained dumb.

21. **The people were waiting** till the close of the service, and perhaps for the benediction (Num. vi. 23–26), **and they marvelled** at his delay; for it was customary, as the Talmud declares, for the priests to do their work in the temple with dispatch, in awe of God.

22. Their surprise was increased, when he came out and **could not speak unto them.** All he could do was to keep **making signs** explanatory; from all which **they perceived that he had seen a vision in the temple.**

A symbolic meaning has been given to this moment in the sacred history. BENGEL says: "Zachariah while dumb was excluded from priestly duty. This is a prelude to the end of the ceremonial law at Christ's coming." CHEMNITZ says: "When the voice of the preacher (Is. xl.) is announced, the priesthood of the Old Testament becomes silent. The Levitical blessing is silenced, when the Seed comes, in whom 'all the families of the earth are blessed.'"

23–25. And it came to pass, when the days of his ministration were fulfilled, he departed unto his house. And after these days Elisabeth his wife conceived; and she hid herself five months, saying, Thus hath the Lord done unto me in the days wherein he looked upon *me*, to take away my reproach among men.

23, 24, 25. **The days of his ministration,** the week of service of the course of Abijah (vers. 5, 8, 9), are the timemark in this reckoning. **Elisabeth his wife conceived,** naturally, yet according to the angel's prophecy (ver. 13). **She hid herself** for the reason given in her words quoted in the next verse, because her condition was a special ordering of **the Lord,** whose further direction she awaited; "because with resignation and confidence she awaited the emerging of the divine guidance" (MEYER). Hence the mention of **five months,** which merely prepares the way for the statement of the next verse about what occurred "in the sixth month."

26, 27. *Now in the sixth month the angel Gabriel was sent from God unto a city of Galilee, named Nazareth, to a virgin betrothed to a man whose name was Joseph, of the house of David; and the virgin's name was Mary.*

26, 27. **In the sixth month** of Elisabeth's pregnancy, another message was sent, **from** the same high source, **God** in heaven, by the same messenger, **Gabriel,** unto **a city of Galilee** not named in the Old Testament or by Josephus, among the 204 cities and towns of Galilee that he mentions, or in the Talmud, but here **named Nazareth.** (See on Matt. ii. 23. Comp. John i. 46; 1 Cor. i. 27; 1 Sam. ii. 8, and Ps. cxiii. 7, 8.) **To a virgin.** (See ver. 34.) **Betrothed to,** engaged to marry, **a man whose name was Joseph** and who belonged to **the house,** or lineage, **of David.** She was going to marry a man of David's royal line. Matthew says more about him. (See on Matt. i. 16–20.) Luke says more about her, who is also supposed to have descended from David. Observe Luke's exactness in giving names. **Mary.** Same as

Miriam of the Old Testament (Ex. xv. 20), and means *Exalted*.

<small>28. And he came in unto her, and said, Hail, thou that art highly favoured, the Lord *is* with thee.</small>

28. The divine messenger fulfilled his mission. We are not told of his appearance—angels are everywhere in the Scriptures represented as men, generally young men in white raiment and radiant of countenance. We have his salutation to Mary—**Hail**; this was not unusual, nor the subsequent **the Lord is** (or be) **with you.** But he also called her **highly favoured,** i. e. object of the Lord's favor. The word occurs again only in Eph. i. 6. The Vulgate rendering *gratia plena*, taken actively as "full of grace," is misleading and is misinterpreted by the Roman Catholics. The further address, found in the Authorized Version, "Blessed art thou among women," although found in many ancient authorities, and undoubtedly genuine in ver. 42, is omitted here by the best criticism.

<small>29, 30. But she was greatly troubled at the saying, and cast in her mind what manner of salutation this might be. And the angel said unto her, Fear not, Mary: for thou hast found favour with God.</small>

29, 30. That **she was greatly troubled at the saying** of the angel, was quite natural. How quickly we think! And **she cast in her mind,** was reasoning in herself, before anything more was said, **what manner of salutation this might be** (was). Young, timid, hopeful, Mary said to herself, what does this mean? Quickly the reassuring word (see on vers. 12, 13) **Fear not, Mary,** came from the angelic visitant, with the general explanation, **Thou hast found** (didst find) **favour with God.** The particular instance and illustration of this follows. Notice here and everywhere Mary is spoken of as a recipient, not a source, of favor, of grace.

31-33. And behold, thou shalt conceive in thy womb, and bring forth a son, and shalt call his name JESUS. He shall be great, and shall be called the Son of the Most High: and the Lord God shall give unto him the throne of his father David: and he shall reign over the house of Jacob for ever; and of his kingdom there shall be no end.

31. **Behold.** Marks something notable, perhaps startling. **Conceive . . . and bring forth a son.** She would fulfil one of her functions (Gen. i. 28; 1 Tim. ii. 15), and on her part the result would be natural. **His name Jesus**, divinely given before His conception, was indicative of His mission. (See on Matt. i. 21.) "Jesus" means *Saviour*.

32, 33. **He shall be great**, essentially and not as John (ver. 15) "in the sight of the Lord," **and shall be called**, according to His real nature and being (ver. 35), **Son of the Most High**, i. e. God. History has verified this. (Comp. John i. 34; v. 18; x. 29-36; Matt. xvi. 16; xxvi. 63, 64; xxvii. 54.) Somewhat differently OTTO V. GERLACH says: "It is worthy of remark that the proper divinity of her son was not revealed to Mary; otherwise, neither she nor Joseph could have been in a position to bring up the child; for the submission, which was a necessary condition of His humanity, would have been submission only in appearance. But this promise, while it by no means abolished the parental relationship, would yet direct the reverential attention of the parents toward the Child. From the very beginning of our Lord's incarnation, we see that the knowledge of His divinity was not to be communicated in an external and awe-inspiring manner, but to be gradually manifested by His humanity and His work of redemption."

That He should receive **the throne of his father David**, marks Him as the promised Messiah, whose rule and its duration is still further set forth in the rest of the verse, all according to the prophetic Scriptures (Ps. cx.; Is. ix. 6, 7; Dan. ii. 44; vii. 13, ff.). As He was expressly to have no human father, some think the expression "his father David" must refer to Mary's lineage as from the royal line. (Comp. ch. xx. 41-44.)

34, 35. And Mary said unto the angel, How shall this be, seeing I know not a man? And the angel answered and said unto her, The Holy Ghost shall come upon thee, and the power of the Most High shall overshadow thee: wherefore also that which is to be born shall be called holy, the Son of God.

34. **Seeing I know not a man.** Inasmuch as I am a virgin. Mary's question, unlike that of Zachariah (ver. 18), expresses not doubt or unbelief, but only innocent surprise, and perhaps asks for further instruction. (See ver. 45.) Hence **the angel answered** in the explanation that follows.

35. **The Holy Ghost,** to whom in Gen. i. 2 the entire work of fructifying the earth is ascribed (comp. Job xxvi. 13; Ps. civ. 30; Is. xxxii. 15; Ezek. xxxvii. 9), **shall come upon thee.** Hence we say in the Creed, " Conceived by the Holy Ghost." (See Matt. i. 18, 20.) **And the power of the Most High**—whose Son ver. 32 says the child shall be—**shall overshadow thee.** This is not merely another way of saying the same thing as the former clause declared, but is additional to it. BENGEL says, " The coming of the Holy Ghost upon Mary made her fit to receive the overshadowing of the power of the Highest." By the dogmaticians this clause is referred to the act of the Son of God who became man, the Word who became flesh (John i. 14), taking up the human nature into His own personality. The Father thus sent the Son into the world. HOLLAZIUS says, " Overshadowing denotes the mysterious and wonderful filling of the temple of the body, formed by the Holy Ghost." So

the angel delicately, yet profoundly, tells the virgin of her prospective conception, which was naturally inconceivable. **Wherefore also**—in view of such conception—**the holy thing which is begotten**—(as the American Committee of the Revisers has it, rightly)—**shall be called**—and when thus divinely called, the name always indicates the reality—**the Son of God.** Mary's son would be the Son of God. The eternal Son of God became the Son of man in the womb of the virgin Mary. (See Nicene Creed.)

Our churches teach, "That the divine and human natures in Christ are personally united, so that there are not two Christs, one the Son of God, the other the Son of man, but that one and the same is the Son of God and the Son of man" (FORM. CONC. 545 : 1).

36, 37. And behold, Elisabeth thy kinswoman, she also hath conceived a son in her old age : and this is the sixth month with her that was called barren. For no word from God shall be void of power.

36. **And behold**—another wonder confirmatory of what had just been promised Mary—**thy kinswoman**—what the relationship was is not certainly known ; it does not prove anything concerning Mary's tribal descent—**she also hath conceived a son in her old age,** unexpectedly and by special divine providence (as the following words show). The relation of Elisabeth's conception to Mary's she will learn afterwards. (See what follows.)

37. **No word from God shall be void of power,** but every word shall be effectual and mighty ; Elisabeth is already an illustration of this, and Mary will presently become so. God's word abides, whatever, whenever, wherever, to whomsoever spoken.

38. And Mary said, Behold, the handmaid of the Lord; be it unto me according to thy word. And the angel departed from her.

38. Here is the humble submission of faith: and it is beautiful.

<blockquote>39, 40. And Mary arose in these days and went into the hill country with haste, into a city of Judah; and entered into the house of Zacharias and saluted Elisabeth.</blockquote>

39, 40. It looks as if Mary, who, we know, afterwards "kept all these things in her heart" (ch. ii. 19, 51), said nothing to any one about the angel's appearance to her, but **with haste** made her way to her kinswoman Elisabeth, whose condition the angel had made known to her, and who alone of all living would at this time be most in sympathy with her. Elisabeth lived in **a city of Judah in the hill country**, most likely Hebron (Josh. xxi. 11), or some place in that neighborhood, south of Jerusalem and from eighty to a hundred miles south of Nazareth. Mary probably **saluted Elisabeth** with the Hebrews' usual salutation, " Peace be with thee! "

<blockquote>41-45. And it came to pass, when Elisabeth heard the salutation of Mary, the babe leaped in her womb; And Elisabeth was filled with the Holy Ghost; and she lifted up her voice with a loud cry, and said, Blessed *art* thou among women, and blessed *is* the fruit of thy womb. And whence is this to me, that the mother of my Lord should come unto me? For behold, when the voice of thy salutation came into mine ears, the babe leaped in my womb for joy. And blessed *is* she that believed; for there shall be a fulfilment of the things which have been spoken to her from the Lord.</blockquote>

41. **The babe leaped in her womb.** The inspired mother declares (ver. 44) it was **for joy.** All this was supernatural. Recall, however, that John was "filled with the Holy Ghost even from his mother's womb" (ver. 15) and that the Holy Ghost had come upon Mary (ver. 35), and we have the Holy Ghost thus recognizing His own work and responding to Himself.

42. Further now **Elisabeth was filled with the Holy Ghost.** " Goes forth from the babe and fills the mother

also" (LUTHER). In consequence came her outcry, responsive to Mary's salutation. The knowledge Elisabeth here showed is due to the Holy Spirit within her. This whole passage abounds in illustrations of the supernatural. **Blessed.** "The first beatitude of the New Testament, and, in a certain sense, the root of all the rest" (VAN OOSTERZEE. Comp. ch. xxiii. 29.)

43. **Whence is this to me?** Note Elisabeth's humility amid her joy, and the absence of all envy. And hear her call Mary **the mother of my Lord.** "Turn this as we will, we shall never be able to see the propriety of calling an unborn child 'Lord,' but by supposing Elisabeth, like the prophets of old, enlightened to perceive the Messiah's *divine nature*" (OLSHAUSEN). See above.

44. **For behold.** Another wonder; and putting it with what the angel had said to Zachariah (ver 17), she gives it as "the ground of knowledge, on which she declares Mary the mother of the Messiah. She had the discernment of this connection through the Holy Spirit, ver. 41" (MEYER).

45. Elisabeth commends Mary for her faith, having daily in the dumbness of her husband a striking monitor against want of faith. Faith is always blessed. If we read it **for there shall be a fulfilment,** we have in these words a hopeful encouragement of Mary; if we read it *that there shall be*, etc., it merely marks the object of Mary's faith. Either construction is allowable; we prefer the latter.

>46, 47. And Mary said,
>My soul doth magnify the Lord,
>And my spirit hath rejoiced in God my Saviour.

46, 47. **And Mary said.** Probably not with that "loud voice" (ver. 42) of Elisabeth's salutation; but in the modest quietness of her sweet virgin character. This is one of the most beautiful passages in the Bible, a lyric of exquisite simplicity, worthy of a descendant of the sweet singer of Israel. It is full of Old Testament spirit and expression, and, of course, was uttered before there were any New Testament Scriptures. Mary was no doubt familiar with the Psalms of David and other songs in the sacred word, committed to memory as they were wont to be by Jewish children, and read and sung on various public occasions. See the song of Moses (Ex. xv.), the first song in the Bible, and Miriam's response ; the song of Deborah and Barak (Judges v.) upon the defeat of Sisera ; the song of Hannah (1 Sam ii.) in thanksgiving for Samuel ; also many of the Psalms, for example, Ps. ii. ; xxxi. 7, 8 ; xxxiv. 2, 3 ; xcvii. 1 ; xcix. 3 ; cxiii. ; cxxvi. ; cxlv. 17 ; and the psalms of Zacharias and Simeon, in this and the following chapters of Luke. Mary was divinely influenced to become here at once poetess and prophetess. **My soul** ($\psi\nu\chi\dot{\eta}$)—**My spirit** ($\pi\nu\varepsilon\tilde{\nu}\mu\alpha$). The spirit is "the highest and noblest part of man, whereby he is qualified to grasp incomprehensible, invisible, eternal things ; and is, in brief, the house within which faith and God's word abide" (LUTHER) ; the soul, the mediating organ between $\pi\nu\varepsilon\tilde{\nu}\mu\alpha$ and body. We observe in the Bible (1 Thess. v. 23) a threefold division of man's being into spirit, soul and body ; yet, probably, in this emotional utterance of Mary "soul" and "spirit" are not to be specifically distinguished, but taken to embrace the whole inner and higher nature. (Comp. Ps. ciii. 1.) **Magnify**. In the Latin version this word is *magnificat*, and stands first in the sentence. Hence this song is sometimes called the *Magnificat*. We cannot in any way increase God's greatness ; but we can dwell upon it in thought and feeling, and utter it forth in praise. This is what Mary does. **The Lord** of all, whom she personally calls God, **my**

Saviour. If Mary had been born without sin, as the Romish Church teaches, she would not have needed a *Saviour*. But that false doctrine of modern times is refuted here and wherever Mary appears in the history. **Hath rejoiced.** How much joy had already filled her spirit, since the angel's visit! Pure and holy joy, of a quality and degree vouchsafed to her alone among women. We must look upon Mary as imbued with the Jewish idea of the office of the coming Messiah; yet withal, better instructed through the visit and words of Gabriel, in which her promised Son's nature, "The Son of God," and office, involved in His name Jesus (Saviour), were declared. Still, her view was probably not as clear and distinct as ours. New light has broken forth to us from her words, in view of all that followed them in the sacred narrative, and with the Holy Scriptures of both Testaments in our hands.

> 48. For he hath looked upon the low estate of his handmaiden:
> For behold, from henceforth all generations shall call me blessed.

48. **Low estate.** This denotes humble condition, which evidently was also accompanied by humbleness of mind. Mary was obscure and poor; the house of David had long been in obscurity. Yet was she the Lord's **handmaiden**, a modest, faithful servant of God. **Hath looked upon,** considered, not despised or neglected. Yes; God saw it away back in Eden, when He spoke of the seed of the woman that should bruise the serpent's head! **For, behold, from henceforth all** (the) **generations** (of mankind) **shall call me blessed,** shall count me happy. Elisabeth had done so already (ver. 42); and until to-day Mary stands first among women, as being the mother of our Lord. Eve brought sin 'into the world; Mary brought in the Saviour; through the one the race fell,

through the other the race is redeemed. In Mary woman has regained her position, lost by the fall. But observe that this distinction is altogether from the choice of God and His divine mercy and power, not from any natural superiority of Mary above other women. So, whilst we may, indeed, call her blessed—the blessed virgin Mary— we may not worship her in any sense whatever.

> 49. For he that is mighty hath done to me great things;
> And holy is his name.

49. Throughout, Mary acknowledges the divine power as the cause of her changed estate, and takes nothing to her own credit. **He that is mighty** (compare ver. 37) **hath done to me great things,** as promised in ver. 35. The Almighty, Creator of heaven and earth, through whose breath (Spirit, Gen. ii. 7, compare John xx. 22) man first became a living soul, had by His creative Spirit caused this virgin to conceive. We note here Mary's pious joy. **And holy is his name.** "This feature of holiness which Mary so forcibly expresses, is, in fact, that which distinguishes the incarnation from all the analogous facts (fancies rather) of heathen mythologies" (GODET). Holiness, everywhere in the Scriptures attributed to God, is not a characteristic of man-made divinities.

> 50. And his mercy is unto generations and generations
> On them that fear him.

50. **And his mercy** to herself, personally, already celebrated in ver. 48, **is on them that fear him**—to which class she and Zacharias and Elisabeth belonged— **unto generations and generations,** throughout the ages, is unfailing, will be accomplished. (Comp. Ex. xx. 6.) The "fear," of course, is reverent, worshipful obedience.

So "His mercy endureth forever," and is for us of this generation.

> 51–53. He hath shewed strength with his arm:
> He hath scattered the proud in the imagination of their heart.
> He hath put down princes from *their* thrones,
> And hath exalted them of low degree.
> The hungry he hath filled with good things,
> And the rich he hath sent empty away.

51, 52, 53. **He hath shewed strength with his arm.** God is spoken of as a man; the arm is the instrument and symbol of power. In these verses **the proud, princes,** and **the rich** are one class set forth in three several relations of **their hearts,** their affections, their internal character, their **thrones,** positions of honor and influence, and, finally, their external prosperity and abundance,--**the rich.** Among them we may count Herod and his court, the Pharisees, Sadducees and Scribes, as well as the heathen powers of this world. On the other hand she puts **them of low degree,** like herself, such as would not be chosen by human judgment, **the hungry,** whose poverty has been a chastening of their spirit into meetness for the Spirit's indwelling, the hungry for righteousness, the dissatisfied with themselves, the longing souls. The former are **scattered, put down, sent empty away:** the latter are **exalted,** and **filled with good.** Herein is set forth one of the general laws of God's kingdom. See Matt. xix. 30; Luke xiv. 11; xviii. 14; 1 Cor. i. 26–28; James ii. 5. And herein that kingdom differs entirely from kingdoms of this world.

The tense rendered **hath** in all these verses is the aorist, and properly denotes mere past action finished; but Mary may be regarded with prophetic spirit, as looking upon these past instances of God's working as illustrations of His whole action in the matter.

The law that is to characterize the kingdom finds remarkable illustration in the coming into the world of the King. Mary's pious joy is properly shared by all pious people. Hence the inspired words in which she gave it utterance have for ages been used in public worship, and we have her song in our order of Evening Service, as the canticle of closing devotions. As sinners redeemed by the coming of Jesus into the world to save it, we can enter into the joy of Mary's song, appropriating it to ourselves. Already in this song, and particularly now, at its closing verses, we note Mary's patriotic joy.

54, 55.   He hath holpen Israel his servant,
That he might remember mercy
(As he spake unto our fathers)
Toward Abraham and his seed for ever.

54, 55. She sings as a true Israelite, mindful of her people's heritage guaranteed by God's promise. **He hath holpen** (old English for *helped*) **Israel his servant;** she gathers her whole people up in the name of their illustrious progenitor; together they are called "his servant." She foresees her people's exaltation through the Lord's word and doing to her. **That he might remember mercy . . . toward Abraham,** with whom the covenant was first specifically made (Gen. xii. 3 ; xv. ; xvii. 1–8), **and his seed forever.** LANGE thinks, "This is a remarkable proof that Mary's expectations concerning the Messiah's appearance were not exclusive, but of a universal nature; for the seed promised to Abraham was to be a blessing to the whole world." But it is impossible for us to tell how far the Virgin's insight into the divine plan, and outlook over the world, extended. Presumably, like most of the prophets, she spoke more comprehensively than she understood, the Spirit speaking through her. **As he spake to our fathers** is a parenthetic clause, referring to the prophecies extending from the time of Abram's call. All God's promises of mercy were to have their complete fulfilment in the coming Redeemer.

The Romish doctrine of "The Immaculate Conception" teaches that the Virgin Mary was conceived without the stain of original sin. Although often before broached, it was officially put forth as a dogma of that church only in 1854, by Pope Pius IX. It is entirely a doctrine of men, with no sanction from the Scriptures; and their continual "Mariolatry"—by which term the worship of Mary is indicated—is a gross idolatry. In this, like the heathen, they worship the creature instead of the Creator.

A close analysis of this rapturous song of Mary is like tearing apart a beautiful flower. We may enter into its particular structure and relations; but we are most impressed by it as a whole. Commit it all to memory, and learn its thankful, humble, believing, trusting, waiting, pious spirit; and join heartily in the singing of it in our public worship.

56, 57. And Mary abode with her about three months, and returned unto her house. Now Elisabeth's time was fulfilled that she should be delivered; and she brought forth a son.

56, 57. **About three months** Mary stayed in the hill country of Judah, with her kinswoman. If any one should ask whether the Spirit did not know exactly how long, and why here and elsewhere He says "about" so long, we say, certainly He knew but He was not concerned to state these things exactly.

Elisabeth's time to be delivered was at hand (ver. 36,39), and Mary would not wait for the stir and notoriety of that time, but modestly **returned unto her house** at Nazareth. Some time after this occurred what is written in Matt. i. 18-25.

In due time Elisabeth **brought forth a son,** according to the angel's word (ver. 13). The mother nursed and fondled it in rapturous ecstasy; the father looked at it with silent joy, as he took it in his arms, while in the multitude of his thoughts within him God's comforts delighted his soul (Ps. xciv. 19).

<blockquote>58. And her neighbours and her kinsfolk heard that the Lord had magnified his mercy towards her; and they rejoiced with her.</blockquote>

58. There was the usual, in this case more than usual, report and talk about this among **her neighbours and her kinsfolk.** "Have you heard about Elisabeth?" They counted it all a **mercy towards her, and rejoiced with her.** Zachariah's house was a happier place than ever before and more of a home.

<blockquote>59. And it came to pass on the eighth day, that they came to circumcise the child; and they would have called him Zacharias, after the name of his father.</blockquote>

59. **The eighth day** was the fixed time (Gen. xxi. 4; Levit. xii. 3; Phil. iii. 5) for circumcision, and to this rite even the law of the Sabbath yielded (John vii. 22, 23).

They, the kinsfolk and neighbors, **came to circumcise the child.** "No domestic solemnity," says EDERSHEIM, "so important or so joyous as that in which, by circumcision, the child had, as it were, laid upon it the yoke of the law, with all of duty and privilege which this implied . . . It was, so tradition has it, as if the father had acted sacrificially as High Priest, offering his child to God in gratitude and love; and it symbolized this deeper moral truth, that man must by his own act complete what God had first instituted." **And they would have called** (ἐκάλουν, were calling, began to call) **him Zacharias**—it was customary to name a boy at his circumcision and a girl when she was weaned—**after the name of his father,** it being the only child, and naturally the one to keep his father's name alive.

> 60–63. And his mother answered and said, Not so; but he shall be called John. And they said unto her, There is none of thy kindred that is called by this name. And they made signs to his father, what he would have him called. And he asked for a writing tablet, and wrote, saying, His name is John. And they marvelled all.

60–63. His mother, hearing and noticing this, said, **Not so; but he shall be called John,** no doubt recalling what the angel had told her husband (ver. 13), and he had doubtless told her; but they had probably intimated nothing of his name to any one else. They objected that "John" was not a family name, and **made signs to his father**—whether he was deaf as well as dumb, or they "made signs" merely from habit or convenience, we do not know—**what he would have him called.** Zacharias was not indifferent about the matter, but having **asked for a writing tablet**—a tablet smeared with wax and written on with a stylus—he **wrote** these words (in Hebrew), **John is his name.** There was no doubt or hesitation in his mind; he now obeys the angel to the letter.

BESSER remarks: "Zacharias is the first who has written in the time of the New Testament, and the word which he wrote means *God's grace* [meaning of 'John']. The last word that stands written in the O. T., is *Curse* [Mal. iv.]. Observe here Law and Gospel."

And they all marvelled at this evident fixed determination on the part of both parents to call the child John.

> 64. And his mouth was opened immediately, and his tongue *loosed*, and he spake, blessing God.

64. Now **his mouth was opened,** who for nine months had been dumb, **immediately** upon his testimony to the child's name accordant with the angel's annunciation. The sign is over; the thing has come to pass; Zacharias has learned a lesson of faith. **And he spake** [imperfect, began to speak], **blessing God,** whose last word had been an expression of doubt.

<small>65, 66. And fear came on all that dwelt round about them: and all these sayings were noised abroad throughout all the hill country of Judæa. And all that heard them laid them up in their heart, saying, What then shall this child be? For the hand of the Lord was with him.</small>

65, 66. The effect on all the neighbors of all these events was **fear,** the usual effect of things so extraordinary; "the fear also of a nameless hope" (EDERSHEIM). And in all that neighborhood **all these sayings** at the circumcision of this child **were noised abroad,** everywhere reported and talked about and **laid up in their heart,** while all said, **What then shall this child be?** And all this from the evident fact that **the hand of the Lord,** His peculiar power and leading, **was with him.** Not till thirty years after this did anything occur accordant with this widespread expectancy. (See ver. 80.)

<small>67. And his father Zacharias was filled with the Holy Ghost, and prophesied, saying,</small>

67. Zacharias had been in God's school of discipline not without good effect. It was for chastening that he endured (Heb. xii. 7), and now, with chastened heart and lips, **filled with the Holy Ghost,** and so made an inspired author, he **prophesied**—uttered forth the divine will, whether it regarded past, present or future events—in the following lyric, which, like Mary's song, has passed into the permanent liturgy of the Church, and is able to express the devotion of every pious heart. Concerning it

EDERSHEIM says: "Strictly Hebrew in its cast, and closely following O. T. prophecy, it is remarkable—and yet most natural—that this hymn of the Priest closely follows, and, if the expression be allowable, spiritualizes a great part of the most ancient Jewish prayer, the so-called eighteen Benedictions; rather, perhaps, that it transforms the expectancy of that prayer into praise of its realization. And if we bear in mind that a great portion of these prayers was said by the Priests before the lot was cast for incensing, or by the people in the time of incensing, it almost seems as if, during the long period of his enforced solitude, the aged Priest had meditated on, and learned to understand, what so often he had repeated."

68. Blessed *be* the Lord, the God of Israel;
For he hath visited and wrought redemption for his people,

68. **Blessed.** A word of praise. The Latin for it is *benedictus;* and this song is often called "The Benedictus," as Mary's is called "The Magnificat." The very name **the Lord, the God of Israel**, is a reminder of His covenant faithfulness. Jacob inherited the blessing upon Abram, and became "Israel," and went down into Egypt, there to have fulfilled the prediction of Gen. xv. 5, 13, whence his descendants, under the name of "the children of Israel," were to be brought forth as His (God's) **people**, with the mission to preserve the knowledge of the one living and true God, amid the polytheism of the other nations, and to be the sphere of the development of God's plan of salvation for the world. Now this priest-prophet rejoices that after their so long and varied experience, **God hath visited and wrought redemption for his people.** " Visited " means, *looked upon, considered,* with the idea of helping, doing what was needed. " Redemption " is a ransom, a release.

Vers. 74, 75, 77-79, show that this refers to spiritual redemption from sin and its consequences, whatever other notions of temporal deliverances may have found place in Zacharias' mind. Notice again the past tense "hath" although the prophet saw only the preliminaries, we may say, of what he now rejoiced in.

> 69. And hath raised up a horn of salvation for us in the house of his servant David

69. **A horn of salvation** signifies a strong salvation, or a saving strength, the figure being derived from animals whose strength and defence is in their horns. Kingdoms and great powers are often described as *horns.* See Book of Daniel. **In the house of his servant David.** So we say, "the house of Hanover," "the house of Stuart," "of Tudor," etc. Zacharias belonged to the house of Aaron. His reference here is to the coming Messiah, to be born of the virgin Mary. During those months of Mary's visit to Elisabeth, how much they must have talked over what had been divinely told them, what had occurred to them, and what the Scriptures had before announced! And, though Zacharias was dumb, yet he and they could communicate with one another about the wonderful doings of the Lord.

> 70. (As he spake by the mouth of his holy prophets which have been since the world began),

70. **As he spake.** Zacharias, "taking up the golden thread which had dropped from Mary, ver. 55" (VAN OOST.), recognizes God's keeping to His word spoken prophetically **since the world began,** from the beginning of the age, or "of old," as the Amer. Comm. have it. From the first sound of the Gospel, in Gen. iii. 15, down to the last of Revelation, the testimony of Jesus is the

spirit of prophecy (Rev. xix. 10); and to the two disciples on the road to Emmaus, Jesus expounded in all the Scriptures the things concerning Himself, beginning at Moses and all the prophets (Luke xxiv. 27). " The whole volume of Scripture did prophesy of Him. He was the sum and scope of all their predictions. He was Abraham's promised seed, Abraham's Isaac, Jacob's Shiloh, Moses' Great Prophet, Esaias' Immanuel, Ezekiel's Shepherd, Daniel's Holy One, Zachariah's Branch, Malachi's Angel; all of them predictions to foretell His coming. He was Abel's Sacrifice, Noah's Dove, Abraham's Firstfruits, Aaron's Rod, the Israelite's Rock, the Patriarch's Manna, David's Tabernacle, Solomon's Temple; all these prefigured His incarnation. They were folds and swathing bands of this babe *Jesus*" (BISHOP BROWNING).

71. Salvation from our enemies, and from the hand of all that hate us;

71. **Our enemies** and **all that hate us.** These terms to this patriotic Israelite signified temporal and civil adversaries, whether from heathen or other sources. Zacharias may have thought of the Roman tyranny, or of Herod's usurpation, the galling bondage of the Jewish state. But that his view was not confined to such adversaries is evident from the verses pointed out above (ver. 68), and that for us the reference is to those worst enemies, *our sins*, is certain.

72, 73. To shew mercy towards our fathers,
And to remember his holy covenant;
The oath which he sware unto Abraham our father,

72, 73. All this deliverance is a matter of God's **mercy**, not of man's merit; and, though **our fathers** have long since gone before, their rest is in hope of the mercy promised long, which God's faithfulness is engaged to

shew. Note that Moses and Eljiah came from the spirit-world, at the transfiguration (ch. ix. 30, 31), and spake of the decease which Jesus was to accomplish at Jerusalem: Jesus is to the fathers as well as to us the fulfilment of God's **holy covenant,** called also **the oath which he sware to Abraham our father.** The covenant with Noah was the world covenant, of natural life; that with Abraham was the Church covenant, of Redemption, of spiritual and eternal life.

> 74, 75. To grant unto us that we being delivered out of the hand of our enemies
> Should serve him without fear,
> In holiness and righteousness before him all our days.

74, 75. However politically Zacharias understood the terms **delivered out of the hands of our enemies,** the purpose of such deliverance was the purification and freedom of God's worship, as shown in the next clause— **should serve him without fear.** This is the enfranchisement of true religion; and this is it which we rejoice in in this country—freedom to worship God according to the dictates of our own conscience as enlightened by the opened word of God. And this has come to us through the restoration to the people of that Bible which informs us of our deliverance and teaches us how to use it. To **serve him without fear,** so far as the individual is concerned, is to be delivered from sin, which makes afraid of God's wrath, and, through Christ, to be made sons, no longer left in bondage. See Rom. viii. 15. The characteristics of this free service are **holiness and righteousness before him,** the inward principle and the outward activity of godliness, proper regard for our relations to both God and man. These words fully recognize the spiritual character of the deliverance which the Messiah was to effect.

Note that this father's thanksgiving is based not on his natural affection for the child born to him, but on his spiritual perception of God's mercy, joy at his manifested faithfulness, and faith and hope in one yet to be born.

> 76. Yea, and thou, child, shalt be called the prophet of the Most High: For thou shalt go before the face of the Lord to make ready his ways;

76. Turning to the little babe the inspired father said, **Yea, and thou, child, shalt be called the prophet of the Most High.** The Most High, here as in vers. 32 and 35, refers to God Almighty, who was to be *manifested* in Jesus, the Christ. Such also is the reference of the word **Lord** in the following phrase, **the face of the Lord.** Indeed, Jesus was to be the face of the Lord Jehovah, the manifestation of Himself to men; and John was to go before Him **to make ready his ways.** John's mission as Jesus' forerunner is here set forth, according to the prophecy of Is. xl. 3 and Mal. iii. 1, as also John declared himself afterwards, John i. 19-28, and Jesus testified of him, Matt. xi. 7-15.

> 77. To give knowledge of salvation unto his people In the remission of their sins,

77. **To give knowledge of salvation.** "This word, in fact, throws a vivid light on the aim of John the Baptist's ministry. Why was the ministry of the Messiah preceded by that of another divine messenger? Because the very notion of salvation was falsified in Israel, and had to be corrected before salvation could be realized. A carnal and malignant patriotism had taken possession of the people and their rulers, and the idea of a political deliverance had been substituted for that of a moral salvation. If the notion of salvation had not been restored to its Scriptural purity before being realized by the

Messiah, not only would He have had to employ a large part of the time in accomplishing this indispensable task; but, further, He would certainly have been accused of inventing a theory of salvation to suit His impotence to effect any other. There was needed, then, another person, divinely authorized, to remind the people that perdition consisted not in subjection to the Romans, but in divine condemnation; and that salvation, therefore, was not temporal emancipation, but the forgiveness of sins. To implant once more in the hearts of the people this notion of salvation, was indeed to prepare the way for Jesus, who was to accomplish this salvation, and no other" (GODET). The salvation John was to make known consisted **in the remission of their sins.** So his cry (Matt. iii.) was, "Repent"; and they were baptized in Jordan, *confessing their sins*; and John (John i. 29, 36), pointing to Jesus, the greater One walking among them, said: "Behold the Lamb of God which taketh away the sin of the world!"

78. Because of the tender mercy of our God,
   Whereby the dayspring from on high shall visit us,

This salvation by forgiveness was **because of the tender mercy of our God.** That was its origin. God's mercy came to meet and satisfy man's need. It came from the heart, the love of God. " God so *loved* the world," etc. " God commendeth *His love* toward us," etc. The first attribute of God as declared to Moses was, " *merciful;* " and John the Evangelist says, " God is Love." It was this **whereby the dayspring**, the dawn of the Sun of righteousness (Mal. iv. 2), **from on high** (see vers. 32, 35 and 76) **shall** (many ancient authorities read *hath visited us*) **visit us,** look upon us (as in ver. 68). When sin entered the world, night fell upon it, and men began to grope for the light. A long dark night it was, too! Zacharias saw the first gleams of the rising day, and blessed God for the sight and the hope it awakened.

> 79. To shine upon them that sit in darkness and the shadow of death; To guide our feet into the way of peace.

79. **To shine** with the light of the knowledge of the glory of God in the face of Jesus Christ (2 Cor. iv. 6), the Revealer of Him who is light (1 John i. 5), predicted by Isaiah (ix. 2; lx. 1-3, compare Acts xxvi. 23), **upon them that sit in darkness and the shadow of death.** Darkness and death are the symbols of sin and all evil, and represent the miserable condition of this present evil world, unenlightened by the truth as it is in Jesus. **To guide our feet.** And surely we all need a guide under such circumstances. **Into the way of peace.** There is no peace to the wicked. Christ is the way to and the way of peace! " Being justified by faith we have peace with God through our Lord Jesus Christ." Of this Zacharias prophesied.

> 80. And the child grew, and waxed strong in spirit, and was in the deserts till the day of his shewing unto Israel.

80. The verbs **grew** and **waxed strong** are in the imperfect tense, denoting what was going on. (Comp. 1 Sam. ii. 26; Luke ii. 52.) **The deserts** here referred to were the "wilderness," i. e. less peopled and more wild parts of Judæa, including "the hill country," but extending further north and south, west of the Dead Sea and the Jordan, from which John emerged (Matt. iii. 1) on **the day of his shewing unto Israel**, the time of the declaration of his public office as the forerunner (ver. 17). See ch. iii. 2, 3.

CHAPTER II.

1. Now it came to pass in those days, there went out a decree from Cæsar Augustus, that all the world should be enrolled.

1. **In those days** is a general designation of time, well understood. **Cæsar** is the generic name of the Roman Emperors. The word is reproduced in the German "Kaiser" and the Russian "Tzar." Similarly "Pharaoh" was used in Egypt and "Darius" in Persia. The distinctive name of the first Emperor was **Augustus**, born 691 of the Roman Era, i. e. 63 B. C., died 767, i. e. 14 A. D. Other Emperors also had the "title" Augustus. See Acts xxv. 21 (Greek). The expression rendered **all the world** was commonly applied to the Roman Empire, which is here meant. **Enrolled.** The exact purpose, whether for taxation, military service, or statistics, is not indicated by the word.

2. This was the first enrolment made when Quirinius was governor of Syria.

2. Αὕτη ἡ ἀπογραφὴ πρώτη ἐγένετο ἡγεμονεύοντος τῆς Συρίας Κυρηνίου.

The only variation in the Greek text is the presence or absence of the article before ἀπογραφή. The Auth. Ver. accepts it and translates, "This taxing was first made when Cyrenius was governor of Syria." The Revisers of 1881, rejecting it, translate as above. Quite a number, including Ussher, Calovius, Storr, Tholuck, Huschke and Wieseler, evidently trying to meet a chronological diffi-

35

culty, translate, "This taxation (or enrolment) occurred sooner than (or much earlier than) Quirinius," etc., making πρώτη have the sense of προτέρα—of which construction there are a few examples. Others, among them Lange and Van Oosterzee, read αὐτή for αὕτη, saying, in truth, that the original manuscript was without accents or breathings, and translate "The taxing itself"—or, the enrolment itself—"was made for the first time, when Quirinius," etc.; explaining that the decree was one thing, the execution of it another, and the two were not synchronous.

The difficulty arises from the fact that the time when Quirinius was governor of Syria was about ten years later —6 to 11 A. D.—than the accepted time of Jesus' birth. In view of this, some do not hesitate to say Luke was mistaken and is here in error. Others, more sensibly refer to our author's usual exactness regarding contemporary chronolgy, and seek an explanation of the apparent conflict of statements. The Bible Commentary, following Köhler, Ebrard and others, understand Luke to mean that, though the enrolment was ordered by the Emperor and prepared for and partly carried out by Herod, it was not completed, for reasons it adduces, until the time of Cyrenius, which completion is referred to in Acts v. 37 as "the taxing" which Judas and his followers tried to resist; accordingly Canon Cook translates our verse—"This, a first enrolment, was carried into effect [ἐγένετο] when Cyrenius was Governor of Syria."

Another explanation which the same authority gives as finding acceptance "with many considerable scholars both in England and in Germany," is that Quirinius was twice Governor of Syria, the first time about A. D. 4— which is not without evidence. SCHAFF says, in Lange's Commentary *in loc.*, where he cites authorities, and the whole subject is discussed, "A double legation of Quirinius in Syria has recently been made almost certain by purely antiquarian researches from two independent testimonies," which he goes on to cite.

Secular writers note three times when Cæsar Augustus made a census of the people, viz. in 726, 746 and 767. The one in 746 may have been the one Luke here refers to, delayed for various reasons, or executed slowly in the distant provinces and so still going on in 749 when Jesus was born.

Doubtless our difficulty in determining this chronology arises from our ignorance, not from our author's.

3-5. And all went to enrol themselves, every one to his own city. And Joseph also went up from Galilee, out of the city of Nazareth, into Judæa, to the city of David, which is called Bethlehem, because he was of the house and family of David; to enrol himself with Mary, who was betrothed to him, being great with child.

3, 4, 5. **His own city**, according to Roman reckoning, was the town to which the village or place where one was born was attached; according to Jewish reckoning—and the enrolment was going on in Palestine according to the Jewish rather than the Roman method (Judæa was subject to Rome at this time, though not yet made a Roman "province"),—"his own city" was determined by the tribal and family connection. Therefore, as he belonged to **the house and family**, direct lineage, **of David**, Joseph went up to **the city of David**, where that great ancestor was born (1 Sam. xvii. 11). The clause **with Mary**, etc., may be taken with **to enrol himself**, but it rather belongs to the whole preceding sentence. Mary's presence was not required by law; but it was her will to accompany him, whose legal wife she was (Matt. i. 24, 25), though actually only his **betrothed**, whose condition, **being great with child**, had been satisfactorily explained to him by an angel (Matt. i. 20-23). May we not rightly suppose that Mary, in accordance with what the angel had said to her about God's giving her son "the throne of his father David" (ch. i. 32), and other intimations she had received concerning him while with Elisabeth as well as afterwards in conversation with Joseph (of which we read in Matt.), saw the propriety of this son's being born in Bethlehem, and that she expected that which afterwards came to pass, though without any knowledge of the attendant circumstances? Her condition doubtless exposed her to people's "talk" at Nazareth; nobody understood the situation but Elisabeth, away in Judæa, and herself, and at last Joseph; and we note that, afterwards (Matt. ii. 22, 23), they intended to make their home in Judæa, until divinely directed otherwise.

6, 7. And it came to pass, while they were there, the days were fulfilled that she should be delivered. And she brought forth her firstborn son; and she wrapped him in swaddling clothes, and laid him in a manger, because there was no room for them in the inn.

6, 7. **And it came to pass,** not by any chance or accident, but in the direction of God's providence, **while they were there,** in Bethlehem, the city of David, **the days were fulfilled,** etc. She could have expected this, from natural knowledge. **And she brought forth her son.** The word of the angel (ch. i. 31, 35) was so far fulfilled, a pledge that all he had said would be accomplished (ch. i. 45, 54, 55). **Her firstborn.** The Greek has the article. Whilst this might be said where there was but one child, the presumption from Matt. i. 25 with Matt. xiii. 55, 56 is that Mary had other children whose father was Joseph. See another theory, in exposition of the latter passage, by Dr. Schæffer (Vol. I. of this Commentary)—a view we do not accept.

There is not a particle of proof from the Scriptures of the perpetual virginity of Mary, but just the contrary.

She wrapped him in swaddling clothes, bands wrapped close around the body, as babes are wont to be treated, **and laid him in a manger,** a trough from which the cattle were wont to eat. **Because there was no room for them,** for this family of strangers, **in the inn,** in the caravansary where travellers put up. It was full, in consequence of the large attendance of people, come for a like purpose with Joseph. "The khan (or caravanserai) of a Syrian village, at that day, was probably identical, in its appearance and accommodation, with those which still exist in modern Palestine. A khan is a low structure, built of rough stones, and generally only a single story in height. It consists for the most part of a square enclosure, in which the cattle can be tied up in safety for the night, and an arched recess for the accommodation of travellers. The paved floor of the large khan might contain a series of such recesses, which are, in fact, low small rooms with no front wall to them. They are, of course, perfectly public; everything that takes place in them is visible to every person in the khan. They are also totally devoid of even the most ordinary furniture. The traveller may bring his own carpet if he likes, may sit cross-legged upon it for his meals, and may lie upon it at night. As a rule, too, he must bring his own food, attend to his own cattle, and draw his own water from the neighboring spring. He would neither expect nor require attendance, and would pay only the merest trifle for the advantage of shelter, safety, and a floor on which to lie. But if he chances to arrive late, and the *leewans* were all occupied by earlier guests, he would have no choice but to be content with such accommodation as he could find in the courtyard below, and secure for himself and his family such small amount of cleanliness and decency as are compatible with an unoccupied corner of the filthy area, which must be shared with horses, mules, and camels. . . . In Palestine it not unfrequently happens that the entire khan, or at any rate the portion of it in which the animals are housed, is one of those innumerable caves which abound in the limestone rocks of its central hills. Tradition strongly points to a cave of this kind as the place where our Saviour was born, and over the supposed place there now stands the Church of the Nativity, making in its elegance a sharp contrast with its original condition as a stable" (FARRAR). Travellers in Switzerland are struck with the close connection of the abodes respectively of the human beings and the beasts, they often being under the same roof: and DR. THOMSON (*The Land and the Book*) says of the Holy Land: "It is common to find two sides of the one room, where the native farmer resides with his cattle, fitted up with these mangers, and the remainder elevated about two feet higher for the accommodation of the family. The mangers are built of small stones and mortar, in the shape of a box, or rather of a kneading-trough, and, when cleaned up and whitewashed, as they often are in summer, they do very well to lay little babes in. Indeed, our own children have slept in them in our rude summer retreats in the mountains."

 8. And there were shepherds in the same country abiding in the field, and keeping watch by night over their flock.

 8. **There were shepherds,** whose occupation was a very common one in those days and lands, **in the same country** of Bethlehem, in that neighborhood. Abel was a shepherd, and ever since his day shepherds have been

conspicuous in sacred history. Moses and David both were shepherds once. Under the figure of a shepherd God's care of His people is often tenderly set forth in the Scriptures. Perhaps no text is better known or more loved than that one—" The Lord is my Shepherd ; I shall not want ; " and when we sing, " Saviour, like a shepherd, lead us," we seem to come into relations of tender nearness to our gracious Lord. The Judæan shepherds were a favored few on the occasion set forth in our lesson. **Abiding in the field,** not in houses in the town or city, but living in the open air, and **keeping watch,** probably by turns, **by night over their flock.** EDERSHEIM thinks these were not the ordinary flocks that pastured in the wilderness, in the open country away from human habitations, but those that were intended for the temple service, which lay close to Bethlehem, on the road to Jerusalem, and that these lay out all the year round. He thinks there is no adequate reason for questioning the historical accuracy of Dec. 25th as the date of Christ's birth.

9. And an angel of the Lord stood by them, and the glory of the Lord shone round about them : and they were sore afraid.

9. This was a great surprise and astonishment to them ; but it need not be to us, for we know that God is wont to visit and exalt with His favor the humble, choosing shepherds before kings. **An angel of the Lord** (there is no article in the Greek), not *the* angel of the Lord in the sense of the second person in the Trinity. For this time the message was *about*, not *by*, that adorable second person in the Godhead. **Stood by them,** all at once, probably appearing in the air overhead. **And the glory of the Lord,** such as they had read and heard of in connection with previous sacred history, **shone round about**

them, still further impressing their minds with the supernatural and heavenly character of what was transpiring. No wonder **they were sore afraid** at such a visitation. (Comp. i. 12, 29; ix. 34; xxiv. 4, 5, etc.)

> 10, 11. And the angel said unto them, Be not afraid; for behold, I bring you good tidings of great joy which will be to all the people: For there is born to you this day in the city of David a Saviour, which is Christ the Lord.

10. **Be not afraid.** God does not reveal Himself or His plans, in special glory, for men's destruction, but for their salvation, and when His ministering spirits come near to commune with men, it is not to make them afraid. The time will come when "all the holy angels" will accompany the Judge of all the earth to judgment, but that will be after these days of grace. **I bring good tidings** is the translation of one word in the Greek, and it is Anglicised in the word *evangelized*, and in old English the word *evangel* was used. The same word (evangelium) appears in German and Latin and the languages belonging to the Latin family. The evangel is the good message (angel), bringing tidings which contained **great joy to all the people** (for the article belongs here) of the Jews, and through them to all people that on the earth do dwell. The gospel is the bearer of joy to the world.

11. **For there is born.** Reason for the joy. "The Word became *flesh* and dwelt among us;" "born of a woman;" taking on Him human nature. **To you**, representing Jews first and mankind next. **In the city of David**, the ancestral town where David was born, where the prophecy (Micah v. 2) had said his greatest descendant should first see the light; in Bethlehem, "house of bread," the true bread from heaven is given, that gives eternal life. **A Saviour.** And that in the full sense of the word. Man, fallen, lost, banished from Paradise,

unable by all his efforts to get back, needed just that; man needs that, it is his greatest, his only want—a *Saviour*. This had been promised again and again, with increasing clearness, from the dark hour of the fall, and now the bright and morning star had come, bursting forth on that Judæan night! Joy! Glad tidings! Great joy! Christ, the Messiah, the Anointed, long promised, long expected, has come, Christ, **the Lord.** Even though born in Bethlehem, little town, born of a woman, laid in a manger, wrapped in swaddling clothes, yet that babe is **the Lord,** Jehovah, called by the divinely taught Isaiah (ix. 6), "Wonderful, Counsellor, The mighty God, The everlasting Father, The Prince of Peace." The Word which not only "was in the beginning with God" but also "was God," this Word "became flesh!" "Being in the form of God, he took upon him the form of a servant." In ver. 9 our author uses "Lord" twice in the sense of *Jehovah*, and so it seems used here, as also in the Old Testament constantly.

12. And this *is* the sign unto you: Ye shall find a babe wrapped in swaddling clothes, and lying in a manger.

12. They needed something to certify their being right when they should go to look for the child. The unusual sight of a newborn child **lying in a manger** would, in that little town, be a sufficient sign of the truth of the angel's message. In such and even rude circumstances the long-expected great Messiah, the Saviour of the world, was to be sought and found. The King of kings comes into the world with little of royal surroundings!

13, 14. And suddenly there was with the angel a multitude of the heavenly host praising God, and saying,
    Glory to God in the highest,
    And on earth peace among men in whom he is well pleased.

13, 14. Yet, withal, consider that His humble birth is announced by an angel, and upon its announcement **suddenly there was with the angel a multitude of the heavenly host,** a more than royal retinue, a shining phalanx of heaven's army. This is more than kingly, it is full of glory! **Praising God.** It was the Father that sent the Son to be the Saviour of the world; that little child was His unspeakable gift. **Glory to God.** The end of all things. God's glory cannot be increased by us, but it can be declared, set forth, proclaimed. **In the highest.** In the highest heavens or in the highest strains—excelling glory. **And on earth peace.** This is the second part of the angels' song, and is amplified in the next clause, which, according to the best authorities, reads not **good will toward men,** but to or *among men of good will, men of God's pleasure.* See the connection of this word, as translated "good pleasure," in Eph. i. 5, 9; Phil. ii. 13; 2 Thess. i. 11. The good will is that of God to men, not of men to God or towards one another. The verb in iii. 22, "In thee I *am well pleased,*" has the same root as this noun rendered "good will" or *good pleasure;* only as men are in Christ, the Son of God's love, can they be reconciled, have peace and be objects of God's complacent good pleasure. His peace is not human fellowship, but fellowship between God and man, a subduing of the enmity that came in by the fall. The clauses of this song answer to one another as follows: "Glory" to "peace," "in the highest" to "on earth," "to God" to "to men of good will." The Auth. Ver follows the reading which has εὐδοκία (good will, or good pleasure) in the nominative case, and so there are three clauses in the angels' song, the last being either in apposition with the second or a ground for the first two. Van Oost., Canon Cook, and Edersheim, among others, strongly advocate this reading, and the latter parallels the three clauses with the threefold blast of the priests' silver trumpets at the laying of the sacrifice on the altar before the temple, and with the *Tris-Hagion* (Holy, Holy, Holy) of Isaiah, vi. 3. This hymn of the angels has been perpetuated in the Church by the *Gloria in Excelsis*, which can be traced to the second or third century and has been sung in the Church ever since; it is one of the connecting links with the early church; it is sometimes called the *Greater Doxology*, and finds a place in our beautiful "Order of Service." It is full of the marrow of the gospel. Schaff calls it "a truly catholic, classical, and undying form of devotion, sounding from age to age and from generation to generation."

15, 16. And it came to pass, when the angels went away from them into heaven, the shepherds said one to another, Let us now go even unto Bethlehem and see this thing that is come to pass, which the Lord hath made known unto us. And they came with haste, and found both Mary and Joseph, and the babe lying in the manger.

15, 16. **The angels went away from** this visit to the shepherds very soon. They had accomplished their mission and must needs go **into heaven,** their home, again. Angels' visits have been called "few and far between;" this is rather the language of unbelief than of faith; but their visits, so far as recorded, have always been *short*. **Let us now go . . . and see,** for to this end **the Lord hath made known unto us** the wonderful event. They first believed and afterwards saw. Here, too, as in vers. 9 and 11, "Lord" must mean Jehovah.

Mary is put before **Joseph. In the** (not *a*) **manger.** Everything just as it had been told.

17. And when they saw it, they made known concerning the saying which was spoken to them about this child.

17. **They made known** abroad to whoever were thereabout, what had been told them by the angel visitor, and all about the angels' song. So they became the first human preachers of the gospel.

18, 19. And all that heard it wondered at the things which were spoken unto them by the shepherds. But Mary kept all these sayings, pondering them in her heart.

18, 19. Whilst **all that heard** their story **wondered, Mary kept all these sayings, pondering them in her heart.** Here was much to produce wonder, and much to cause thoughtful persons to ponder. But 'tis easier to wonder than to ponder, to be flushed with excitement than to weigh events. " Mary appears here," says VAN OOSTERZEE, " as well as in ch. i. 29 and ii. 51, richly adorned with that incorruptible ornament which an apostle describes (1 Pet. iii. 4) as the highest adorning of women. Heart, mind and memory are here all combined in the service of faith."

20. And the shepherds returned, glorifying and praising God for all the things that they had heard and seen, even as it was spoken unto them.

20. **Returned, glorifying and praising God.** A new song had been put in their mouths. They go back to their calling; it was there the herald angels found them. VAN OOSTERZEE considers "their experience the best example of the first beatitude."

Read Is. vii. 14; ix. 6; John i. 14; Gal. iv. 4; Phil. ii. 5–7; and compare the statement of the Creed, "Conceived by the Holy Ghost, born of the Virgin Mary." Can you say, "*I believe?*"

See Augs. Conf., art. iii.; Luther's Catechisms, larger and smaller, on art. ii. of Apostles' Creed; Nicene Creed; Form of Concord, ch. viii.; Schmid. Dog., pt. i. ch. 2.; pt. iii. ch. 2.

21. And when eight days were fulfilled for circumcising him, his name was called JESUS, which was so called by the angel before he was conceived in the womb.

21. **Circumcising him.** See on i. 59. "Born of a woman, born under the law, that He might redeem them which were under the law" (Gal. iv. 4, 5), He must thus "fulfil all righteousness" (Matt. iii. 15). "This was the divine arrangement for His appearing as the God-man in necessary association with the people of God (Rom. ix. 5)." (MEYER.) On this occasion first Jesus shed His blood, and it was for us. And **his name was called Jesus,** etc. See on i. 13, 31, 60–63, and on Matt. i. 1, 21.

22–24. And when the days of their purification according to the law of Moses were fulfilled, they brought him up to Jerusalem, to present him to the Lord (as it is written in the law of the Lord, Every male that openeth the womb shall be called holy to the Lord), and to offer a sacrifice according to that which is said in the law of the Lord, A pair of turtledoves, or two young pigeons.

22, 23, 24. **The days of their**—Joseph included here with Mary, the whole family there together—**purification** amounted to forty-one in this case, **according to the law of Moses,** written in Levit. xii. 1–4. In connection with **a sacrifice,** there presented, it devolved on them, in the case of this child as the firstborn, **to present him to the Lord,** to whom the firstborn of all animals as well as men specifically belonged (Exod. xiii. 2), in memory of the deliverance from Egypt. By divine arrangement the Levites as a body took the place of the firstborn of Israel in the temple service (Numb. viii. 17–19), and each firstborn child was to be redeemed by the payment of five shekels (Numb. xviii. 15, 16), amounting to from two-and-a-half to three dollars in our money. They **brought him up to Jerusalem** for this; and we note here our Lord's first visit to the Holy City and the Temple. **A pair of**

turtle doves, or two young pigeons, instead of a lamb and one of either of these birds, one for a burnt offering and the other for a sin offering, was the offering prescribed for the poor (Levit. xii. 6, 8); and this was Mary's offering. Observe how **the law of the Lord** is magnified in all this proceeding and record.

> 25. And behold, there was a man in Jerusalem, whose name was Simeon; and this man was righteous and devout, looking for the consolation of Israel: and the Holy Spirit was upon him.

25. **Simeon.** Although there has been considerable speculation about this man, nothing further than is here given is certainly known about him. VAN OOST. says: "In Simeon and Anna we see incarnate types of the expectation of salvation under the Old Testament. . . . At the extreme limits of life, they stand in striking contrast to the infant Saviour, exemplifying the old covenant decayed and waxing old before the new, which is to grow and remain." This man was **righteous** in his life, upright in character, and **devout** in his spirit, a truly pious Israelite. **Looking for the consolation of Israel.** There was a general expectation in those days of a deliverer, which expectation extended even to the Gentile world, as we see from the visit of the Magi (Matt. iii), and know from other sources. This expectation was part of the preparation of the world for "the fulness of time." "The consolation of Israel" is an expression for the Messiah, whose coming the prophets had held forth as a comfort to the people. Afterwards, in John xiv. 16, Jesus calls the Holy Ghost "another Comforter." **And the Holy Spirit was upon him.** Although the Holy Spirit was not given (John vii. 39) in general and to abide with the whole Church forever until after Jesus was glorified, yet He was in the world and moved at times individual

hearts, especially giving inspiration to prophets and the writers of the Scriptures (2 Pet. i. 20, 21).

26. And it had been revealed unto him by the Holy Spirit, that he should not see death, before he had seen the Lord's Christ.

26. **It had been revealed unto him**—in what manner we do not know, just as we cannot explain how spirit influences spirit: "the wind bloweth where it listeth, and thou hearest the sound thereof, but canst not tell whence it cometh and whither it goeth," and thus undistinguished except by His effects are the workings of the Divine Spirit. **That he should not see death before he had seen the Lord's Christ.** The times were revealed to this good man, and he was assured of *seeing* the Messiah, the Lord's Anointed, before his death. LANGE says, "Simeon is, in the noblest sense, the eternal Jew of the old covenant, who cannot die before he has seen the promised Messiah." "The secret of the Lord is with them that fear Him, and He will show them His covenant!" (Ps. xxv. 14). So Jehovah revealed to Abraham, His friend, the purposed overthrow of the cities of the plain (Gen. xviii. 17 ff.). 'Tis good to *walk with God*.

27. And he came in the Spirit into the temple: and when the parents brought in the child Jesus, that they might do concerning him after the custom of the law,

27. The day of our narrative was when **the parents**— for Joseph stood in the relation of father to the child, and was so regarded, and the historian represents the scene as it appeared to the ordinary observers—**brought in the child Jesus** into the "court of the women," **to do for him after the custom of the law**, that is, to present Him before the Lord, offering Him as the firstborn to the priest, God's representative, and then paying the redemption price. See on vers. 22–24.

4

Now Simeon **came in the Spirit,** under special Divine influence, **into the temple** on this occasion, and found himself confronting Joseph and Mary with her child.

28. Then he received him into his arms, and blessed God, and said,

28. By the same Spirit Simeon was made to know who the child was, and **then he received him into his arms**— it must have been a touching and beautiful sight, the old man's radiant face, enraptured over the child, the little one's sweet, innocent, painless look, and the parents' surprised gaze; and then the remarkable words that followed as he **blessed God** in recognition of His fulfilled promise! The world's Redeemer was once a babe in arms! How infancy is exalted and sanctified by this fact! How the humiliation of the Son of God is here set forth!

29-32. Now lettest thou thy servant depart, O Lord,
According to thy word, in peace;
For mine eyes have seen thy salvation,
Which thou hast prepared before the face of all peoples;
A light for revelation to the Gentiles,
And the glory of thy people Israel.

29 ff. The first verse of this reads like a prayer; but **lettest** is in the indicative mood, and the sentence is an assertion. As if Simeon had said, "'Tis done; the waiting and watching are over; I am dismissed, satisfied!" The word rendered **Lord** here is not the usual one, but that from which we get our English "despot," and similarly **servant** is "slave." The margin renders the former word "Master." MEYER translates it "Ruler"—which is very good. ELLICOTT says, "Simeon speaks as a slave who, through the night of long, weary years, has been standing on the watch-tower of expectation, and is at last set free by the rising of the sun." Somewhat similarly GODET says, "Simeon represents himself under

the image of a sentinel whom his master has placed in an elevated position, and charged to look for the appearance of a star, and then announced it to the world." He sees this long-desired star; he proclaims its rising, and asks to be relieved of the post he has occupied so long. Now my waiting is over: I may **depart in peace,** having attained the expected end. **According to thy word.** See ver. 26.

Note the three terms Simeon uses in reference to the child he holds in his arms. **Thy salvation.** See i. 71, 77. Ever since the fall there has been an expectation of deliverance, to come from God. The divine plan was gradually made plainer, until now Simeon's expectant **eyes have seen** it embodied in this babe. Salvation was to be in and through the person of the Messiah. **Which thou hast prepared before the face of all peoples,** of all the nations or peoples of the world. God works according to infinitely wise plans; He prepares what He designs; and had now made salvation *ready for the world.* The distinctive mission of the people of Israel is now about accomplished. **A light for revelation to the Gentiles.** Simeon had the true Old Testament view of the coming salvation; that, though it was to come *through* Israel, it was to be *for* the world. He takes a more comprehensive view than Zacharias. Every careful student of the prophecies might have seen in them this expansion of the Messiah's work. Take Is. xlix. 6 as one example of the plainness of the Old Testament statements. But the Jews were blinded by pride and prejudice. The after development of the comprehensive plan may be noted in the Acts of the Apostles, and in the work and letters of Paul especially. **The glory of thy people Israel.** Not even yet acknowledged so by them as a people; yet the whole world owes and will owe the Jews eternal gratitude as the bearers, in God's providence, or salvation to the world. "Salvation is of the Jews." The Sun of Righteousness shone over the world from Israel's sky! To Israel we go to find the Way, the Truth, the Life! The late Prime Minister of England, DISRAELI, a Jew, says, "The pupil of Moses may ask himself whether all the princes of the house of David have done so much for the Jews as that Prince who was crucified on Calvary. Had it not been for him, the Jews would have been comparatively unknown, or known only as a high Oriental caste which had lost its country. Has not he made their history the most famous history in the world? Has he not hung up their laws in every temple? Has not he avenged the victims of Titus, and conquered the Cæsars? What successes did they anticipate from their Messiah? The wildest dreams of their Rabbis have been far exceeded. Has not Jesus conquered Europe, and changed its name into Christendom? All countries that refuse the cross wither, while the whole of the new world is devoted to the Semitic principle and its most glorious offspring, the Jewish faith."

The three songs we have in the opening of Luke, partaking so much of the poetical character of much of the Old Testament, form a beautiful connecting link between the two " Testaments."

As one was called the *Magnificat*, and the second the *Benedictus*, so this is called the *Nunc Dimittis*, from the words with which it begins in the Latin version.

"The sweetest canticle is ' Nunc dimittis,' when a man hath obtained worthy ends and expectations" (LORD BACON).

33. And his father and his mother were marvelling at the things which were spoken concerning him;

33. Notwithstanding all that had occurred, the annunciation, the visit to Elisabeth, and the three months' conference of the cousins, each confirming the other's faith, and the visit of the shepherds with their account of the angels Song of the Nativity, we see **his father and his mother** still **marvelling** (wondering) **at the things which were spoken concerning him.** Jesus was the Wonderful, even to His mother.

34. And Simeon blessed them, and said unto Mary his mother, Behold, this *child* is set for the falling and rising up of many in Israel; and for a sign which is spoken against;

34. **And Simeon,** whom now they recognized as evidently a prophet, speaking by the Holy Ghost—for how else would he have known anything about this child, now for the first time brought from the obscure place of His birth, or be able to say such extraordinary things about Him?—**blessed them,** but specially addressed the mother, saying, **This child is set,** appointed, destined, **for the falling and rising up of many in Israel.** The terms here used seem to refer to two classes and two results, rather than to one, as the Revised Version shows in contrast with the "Authorized." According to Is. viii. 14, 15, He would be not only "for a sanctuary," but "for a stone of stumbling." (Comp. Rom. ix. 32, 33; 1 Peter ii. 7, 8.) Moreover, as many in Israel have stumbled and fallen, so there is reason to hope there will one day be a rising in Israel and return to the rejected Saviour. **And for a sign spoken against.** A sign was intended to clear up doubt: but Jesus was to be a sign *spoken against.* Until now this prophecy has been fulfilling; what "contradiction of sinners against himself" (Heb. xii. 3) Jesus and His cause have endured and are still enduring!

35. Yea and a sword shall pierce through thine own soul; that thoughts out of many hearts may be revealed.

35. GODET says, "A carnal satisfaction, full of delusive hopes, might easily have taken possession of the hearts of these parents, especially of the mother's, on hearing such words as these. But Simeon infuses into his message the drop of bitterness which no joy, not even holy joy, ever wants in a world of sin." **Yea, and a sword shall pierce through thy own soul.** She shall be a partaker of the sorrows of her son. Some think this refers to conflicts of unbelief in her own soul; others to sorrow for sin, which she, along with all believers, will experience; but we think it refers to all her womanly feelings as tried by the experience Jesus will meet in the world, ending with His crucifixion and death. Mary has well been called *Mater Dolorosa*. **That thoughts out of many hearts may be revealed.** Christ is the touchstone of hearts, the test of characters. "What think ye of Christ?" is the great test question for all who have heard of Him : and death is a departing in peace, to whoever has seen and accepted Him.

The thoughts of ambitious Pharisees were revealed in scornful enmity; the thoughts of sinful publicans and harlots were revealed in penitent faith; the thoughts of the Centurion were revealed when he said, in view of the testimony before him, "Truly this was the Son of God!" The thoughts of thousands were revealed on the day of Pentecost, when, in view of the crucified, risen, exalted, Spirit-giving Jesus, they cried out, "Men and brethren, what must we do?" And so, throughout the world, the doctrine of Christ is the searcher and revealer of hearts.

36-38. And there was one Anna, a prophetess, the daughter of Phanuel, of the tribe of Asher (she was of a great age, having lived with a husband seven years from her virginity, and she had been a widow even for fourscore and four years), which departed not from the temple, worshipping with fastings and supplications night and day. And coming up at that very hour she gave thanks unto God, and spake of him to all them that were looking for the redemption of Jerusalem.

36, 37, 38. **Anna,** or Hannah, was one well known in those days. **prophetess,** a woman gifted with apocalyptic discourse. (See ver. 38.) Far advanced in years; she had lived a married life of only **seven years,** and since then, up to **fourscore and four years,** she had lived **a widow** indeed, such as Paul refers to in 1 Tim. v. 5. The Revised Version seems to think she had been a widow eighty-four years, which may have been so, but is not likely, and the original allows either view. When it is said she **departed not from the temple** and continued her religious acts **night and day,** we take this to be a popular way of expressing the constancy of her religious life and fervor. Notwithstanding her great age, she was always at the religious services and spent much of the intervening time in the temple precincts. EDERSHEIM says, " Nor, as to the Pharisees around, was it the Synagogue which was her constant and loved resort; but the Temple, with its symbolic and unspoken worship, which Rabbinic self-assertion and rationalism were rapidly superseding, and for whose services, indeed, Rabbinism could find no real basis."

Coming up that very hour, this well-known, godly woman, responded to Simeon's words concerning this child, and first **gave thanks unto God** in response to His goodness and faithfulness, and then **spake of him,** that little child Jesus, **to all them that were looking for the redemption of Jerusalem,** i. e. of Israel. (See vers. 25, 32, and i. 68.) The verbs " gave thanks " and " spake " are in the imperfect tense, from which we gather that Anna continued this sort of discourse among her pious companions. AMBROSE comprehensively and suggestively says, " Christ received a witness at his birth, not only from prophets and shepherds, but also from aged and holy men and women. Every age, and both sexes, and the marvels of events, confirm our faith. A virgin brings forth, the barren becomes a mother, the dumb speaks, Elisabeth prophesies, the wise men adore, the babe leaps in the womb, the widow praises God. . . . Simeon prophesied ; she who was wedded prophesied ; she who was a virgin prophesied ; and now a widow prophesies, that all states of life and sexes might be there."

<small>39. And when they had accomplished all things that were according to the law of the Lord, they returned into Galilee, to their own city Nazareth.</small>

39. If we had only this gospel history we would think this return **to their own city Nazareth** took place directly after Mary's offering and the presentation of Jesus. But Matthew's account gives the interesting events of the visit of the Magi, the slaughter of the little boys of Bethlehem, and the flight of the holy family into Egypt —none of which Luke mentions, and all of which we suppose occurred between the **all things** of this verse and the return to Nazareth. Neither does any one of the Evangelists, nor do all of them together, give everything in the life of Jesus.

<small>40. And the child grew, and waxed strong, filled with wisdom : and the grace of God was upon him.</small>

40. The verbs here are in the imperfect tense, denoting continuance. **The child** developed healthily and strongly. This was in accordance with, and in illustration of, His perfect human nature. Comp. 1 Sam. ii. 26; Luke i. 80; and ii. 52, where Jesus' human progress between His twelfth and thirtieth years is similarly noted. **Filled** is the present participle. See marginal rendering. **With wisdom** of all sorts. He learned in His pious mother's

lap and at her knee; He learned from the righteous Joseph who by Jewish law was bound to teach Him (comp. Eph. vi. 4); He learned from the private and united prayers in the family and from the domestic rites of the weekly Sabbath and of the festive seasons; He learned from the Synagogue; He learned from intercourse with men, by observation and experience; He learned at school—for in all probability there was, as in late days was required in every town, a school at Nazareth. Whether at home or at school the chief text-book was the Bible—in which, in His subsequent ministry, Jesus showed Himself fully versed. If Timothy from a child knew the Holy Scriptures (2 Tim. iii. 15), much more did Jesus. **And the grace of God,** the divine favor, **was upon him.** Then the grace of God can be upon even a little child, even upon your child.

41. And his parents went every year to Jerusalem at the feast of the passover.

41. **His parents,** as devout people, of godly character, **went to Jerusalem,** a long distance of about seventy miles direct, and considerably more by the usual routes, **every year,** regularly, **at the feast of the passover,** one of the three chief festivals of the Jews, instituted at the Exodus from Egypt in commemoration of the passing over by the angel of death of the houses of the Israelites whose doorposts were sprinkled with blood (Exod. xii.). This festival was also called "The Feast of Unleavened Bread;" it lasted a week; our Easter takes the place and time of it. At this and the festivals of Pentecost and Tabernacles, all the males of Israel were required to be present (Exod. xxiii. 14-17); this obligation did not rest on the females, nor was it their general custom to

go. That Mary went each year with Joseph is an indication of her religious character.

<small>42. And when he was twelve years old, they went up after the custom of the feast.</small>

42. **When he** (Jesus) **was twelve years old** He had arrived at that period when He became a "son of the law," passing out of the years of childhood, and was allowed to take part in the celebration of the festival. Accordingly this time Jesus went up with them to Jerusalem.

<small>43, 44. And when they had fulfilled the days, as they were returning, the boy Jesus tarried behind in Jerusalem; and his parents knew it not; but supposing him to be in the company, they went a day's journey; and they sought for him among their kinsfolk and acquaintance,</small>

43. **And when they had fulfilled the days,** from the 14th to the 21st of Nisan (April 8–15, that year), they started on the return to Nazareth. How it happened that **the boy Jesus tarried behind in Jerusalem** we are not told; simply the fact is given. We can imagine some of the circumstances. Most likely Jesus had been thoroughly taken up with the religious exercises of the week, and been a wrapt listener to the instructions of the teachers of the law. D. BROWN says: "As a devout child in company with his parents, he would go through the services, keeping his thoughts to himself; but methinks I hear him, after the sublime services of that feast, saying to himself, 'He brought me to the banqueting house, and his banner over me was love. I sat down under his shadow with great delight, and his fruit was sweet to my taste'" (Song, ii. 3, 4). We may suppose, then, that He was so engrossed as not to think of anything else. The return, His mother and Joseph, entered not into His mind, only the things of God and Himself, as His personal consciousness of His being and mission

now rose within Him as never before. As, long after, at the well, human hunger and thirst were forgotten in that meat and drink which was to do the will of Him that sent Him and to finish His work (John iv. 31–34), so now the lad was *absorbed* in things more than human; and, naturally to Him, He thus tarried in Jerusalem, with never a thought of any impropriety toward His mother. Equally naturally on their part, **his parents knew not** of His thus remaining. Everybody was going home again; companies of neighbors, kinsmen and acquaintance were forming and setting off together, the roads out of the city getting thronged with the returning multitudes. Jesus had never occasioned His parents the least trouble; He was entirely trustworthy and had their perfect confidence, as well as loving admiration, and was able now to look after Himself in a great degree.

44. Therefore, **supposing him to be in the company** moving out toward Galilee, somewhere among the boys or men, taking His coming along for granted, they **went a day's journey.** The first day's journey of such a tour, we are told, was usually a short one, so that anything forgotten or left might be gone after and recovered in time to catch up with the company again the next day. Tradition points to a place only eight or ten miles north of Jerusalem, a three hours' journey, as the very place of this first halt. Other circumstances lead to the belief that the distance was nothing like the regular day's journey of eighteen to thirty miles. Wherever it was, the parents now went to look for this boy, seeking Him among **their kinsfolk and acquaintance** in the company.

45, 46. And when they found him not, they returned to Jerusalem, seeking for him. And it came to pass, after three days they found him in the temple, sitting in the midst of the doctors, both hearing them, and asking them questions:

45. At first they felt no apprehension, they were sure He was somewhere there, they could reckon on such a faithful boy; but after a complete search **they found him not.** Parents only can realize their feelings, particularly Mary's, now. **They returned to Jerusalem** forthwith, **seeking for him,** thinking they would find Him yet somewhere along the road. But fainter and fainter grew their hearts, as they were a long time disappointed in their hopes. A lost child! And such a crowd, and so great a city! Once in the city they probably looked for Him where they had lodged during the festival, and inquired of acquaintances in the city, and perhaps of the authorities.

46. **After three days,** that is, according to Jewish reckoning, on the third day after missing Him, **they found him** where, perhaps, they should have looked for Him sooner, **in the temple,** that is, in some one of the enclosures of the temple court, where the law was wont to be taught, **sitting in the midst of the doctors,** that is, the teachers of the law, the Rabbis, **both hearing them,** listening to what they said, and **asking them questions.** Sitting was the posture of both teacher and scholar; asking and answering questions, the method of instruction, a catechetical Bible class, the right way of teaching and learning.

47. And all that heard him were amazed at his understanding and his answers.

47. **And all that heard him,** whether teachers or pupils, **were amazed at his understanding** of the Scriptures and divine things, His intelligence, manifested in His **answers** as also in His questions. (See on ver. 40.) So much so that they appear to have so gathered about Him as to have Him "in the midst" (ver. 46). **There**

were some celebrated teachers at that time, among them Hillel, Simeon and Gamaliel. There is nothing in this narrative to justify any idea of Jesus' *disputing with* the teachers of the day. He appears in the simplicity of a young learner, who, withal, shows Himself wiser than all His teachers.

<small>48. And when they saw him, they were astonished: and his mother said unto him, Son, why hast thou thus dealt with us? behold, thy father and I sought thee sorrowing.</small>

48. It was an astonished gathering all around. When His parents **saw him** there and thus engaged, **they were astonished** (the word is a strong one), dazed at the sight; their meek, gentle, hitherto reticent boy, in such a presence, and manifestly so engaging their attention. Naturally, it was **his mother** that drew near and spoke to him. **Son, why hast thou thus dealt with us?** There is a mild reproof in her words—perhaps the first time she had ever thought it necessary. **Thy father** (Joseph) **and I.** This method of referring to her husband indicates that the mystery of Jesus' coming into the world had not been spoken of to Him by His mother, who wisely left to God who had told her what should be, to bring to Jesus' knowledge and consciousness what had been. **Sought** (were seeking) **thee, sorrowing,** with burdened hearts.

<small>49. And he said unto them, How is it that ye sought me? wist ye not that I must be in my Father's house?</small>

49. **And he said unto them.** What He said to them are the first recorded words of Jesus, and they are, therefore, attended with special interest. **How is it that ye sought** (were seeking) **me?** Ye might have found me here at first. **Wist** (knew) **ye not** who I am and where to find me, that **I must be in my father's house,** the

things of my Father (ἐν τοῖς τοῦ πατρός μου) which now have their centre here in the temple, my Father's house? Mary had said, "Thy father," referring to Joseph; the boy shows He knows His true origin, and reminds them, with some gentle reproof, that they *ought to know* and reflect on the same! The annunciation, the words of Elisabeth, of Zacharias, and of the aged Simeon, the visit of the shepherds and the Magi, the flight into Egypt, with its occasion—had they forgotten all these? No doubt, twelve uneventful years had served to dull the impression of these things upon their memory. His words remind them that He is not only "Jesus," but also "the Son of the Most High," "the Son of God" (Luke i. 32, 35; Matt. i. 20). These first words are an epitome of our Lord's whole life. The consciousness of His origin and destiny was breaking forth within Him.

50. And they understood not the saying which he spake unto them.

50. His understanding and answers outwitted not only all that famous Bible class in the temple, but now His "parents" also; **and they understood not** His comprehensive reply: there was more in it than they could unravel, closely as they were related to Him according to the flesh! No relationship to Jesus "according to the flesh" can make us understand His words. (See 2 Cor. v. 16.) They must be spiritually discerned.

51. And he went down with them, and came to Nazareth; and he was subject unto them; and his mother kept all *these* sayings in her heart.

51. Still, notwithstanding the divine consciousness that was breaking forth within Him, **he went down with them,** literally and figuratively, **and came to Nazareth,** obscure and despised place, **and was subject unto them,** as though He were but their natural son—yes, with a

submission that was without a fault; and His example to His brothers and sisters, and the families of the place, and to us, is a beautiful and perfect one. Through all the ordinary experiences of this mortal life Jesus passed, that He might be "touched with the feeling of our infirmities," having been made "in all points like unto His brethren." How His boyhood and youth ennobles and sanctifies filial love and obedience! Says STIER: "The mystery folds itself up again in the self-denial of eighteen years, till the time when, on the open assumption of His Messiahship, the mother has become 'Woman,' having no longer any authority, and His 'My Father' publicly resounds in His house and before His people, no more to cease till that *last* word, which coincides with this first—'Father, into thine hands!'"

It was a universal custom among the Jews that every boy must learn a trade; and we have no doubt that Jesus learned and worked in Joseph's carpenter shop at Nazareth. Afterwards they called Him "the carpenter" (Mark vi. 3). Think of Him who built all things (Heb. iii. 4), the great Architect of the universe, working with boards, benches and tools, in Joseph's carpenter shop at Nazareth! Surely He "made himself of no reputation" (Phil. ii. 7); yet how He ennobled labor! As there is no mention of Joseph after this, it is supposed he died before Jesus' public ministry began. **And his mother kept all these sayings in her heart.** "Observe," says DR. BUSHNELL, "that she did not keep them in her memory, or her understanding, or her diary, but in her heart—that well of silence in the bosom of true motherhood, where all freshest, purest waters are kept fresh and pure. Infiltered there and stored by living thought, they were not vaporized and shallowed by much talk. Her family story she cannot carry into the street, or even speak of with her friends ; and things are occurring with Jesus every day, in which the stamps and signatures of His divinity are distinctly and even visibly manifested, but which cannot be advertised without becoming tokens of weakness in the mother and precocity in the child. She sometimes wants to even strike a song of triumph, like Miriam coming up out of the sea, but her loudest, only not absurd, song will be silence, a hymn that she keeps hid in her heart, as she does all the sayings and great acts of her wonderful Son."

52. And Jesus advanced in wisdom and stature, and in favour with God and men.

52. See on ver. 40. Here is development internally and externally. The God-man developed **in fvaour with God and men.** "This perfectly normal human being," says GODET, " was the beginning of a reconciliation between heaven and earth." Of the eighteen subsequent years, ALFORD says, "We are apt to forget that it *was during this time* that *much of this great work of the second Adam was done.* The growing up through infancy, childhood, youth, manhood, from grace to grace, holiness to holiness, in subjection, self-denial, and love, *without one polluting touch of sin*—this it was which, consummated by the three years of active ministry, by the Passion, and by the Cross, constituted '*the obedience of one man*' by which many were made righteous. We must fully appreciate the words of this verse in order to think rightly of Christ. He had emptied Himself of His glory: His infancy and childhood were no *mere pretence*, but the Divine Personality was in Him carried through three states of weakness and inexperience of the sons of men. All the time the consciousness of His mission on earth was ripening; 'the things heard of the Father'

(John xv. 15) were continually imparted to Him; the Spirit, which was not given by measure to Him, was abiding more and more upon Him till the day when He was fully ripe for His official manifestation,—that He might be offered to His own, to receive or reject Him,— and then the Spirit led Him up to commence His conflict with the enemy. As yet He was in favor with man also: the world had not yet begun to hate Him."

CHAPTER III.

1, 2. Now in the fifteenth year of the reign of Tiberius Cæsar, Pontius Pilate being governor of Judæa, and Herod being tetrarch of Galilee, and his brother Philip tetrarch of the region of Ituræa and Trachonitis, and Lysanias tetrarch of Abilene, in the high-priesthood of Annas and Caiaphas, the word of God came unto John the son of Zacharias in the wilderness.

1, 2. **Now.** Luke is now ready to take up what Mark (i. 1) calls "The beginning of the Gospel of Jesus Christ, the Son of God," viz. Jesus' ministry. In accordance with his purpose expressed in i. 3 to "write in order," and according to his habit of carefully marking the times, our author here gives us six chronological data. (1) **The fifteenth year of Tiberius Cæsar.** Tiberius, the second Roman Emperor, was associated on the throne with Augustus two years before the death of the latter, which occurred August 19, A. U. C. 767, i. e. A. D. 14. Reckoning from this co-regency, as EDERSHEIM, following WIESELER, thinks provincials would do, we get here the date 779 A. U. C., i. e. A.D. 26. Taking the date of Tiberius' sole rule would give us a period two years later. (2) **Pontius Pilate being governor of Judæa.** Pilate was procurator of Judæa, then a Roman province, from 779, probably about Easter, A. D. 26, to 789, when he was recalled. (3) **Herod being tetrarch of Galilee.** This was Antipas, who succeeded to this part of his father's government at the latter's death in 750 and continued till his deposition in 792. His rule extended also over

Peræa. (4) **His brother Philip tetrarch of the region of Ituræa and Trachonitis.** This was not the Philip mentioned in Mark vi. 17, but the son of a different mother, Cleopatra, and sometimes designated as Philip II. Ituræa was the northeastern province of Palestine, along the base of Mount Hermon; Trachonitis adjoined it, on the East. Batanæa and Auranitis belonged to this region. Philip was made tetrarch here in 750 and ruled till his death in 786 or 787. (5) **Lysanias tetrarch of Abilene.** There were two rulers of this name and they are sometimes confounded. The elder Lysanias was put to death by Mark Antony in 718 (B. C. 36); there was a later ruler of this name, as is shown from Josephus and an inscription at Abila. The place of his rule was in the region of the Lebanon, eighteen miles north of Damascus.

(6) **In the high-priesthood of Annas and Caiaphas.** The Roman authorities were absolute and even assumed the appointment of Jewish high priests. Annas had been appointed by Quirinius, the first Procurator of Judæa. (See on ii. 2.) After nine years he was deposed and the occupancy of the office changed four times, the fourth incumbent being Annas' son-in-law Caiaphas. "But Annas retained withal very weighty influence (John xviii. 12 ff.), so that not only did he, as did every one who had been ἀρχιερεύς, continue *to be called by the name*, but, moreover, he also partially *discharged the functions* of high priest" (MEYER). "But although the expression 'High Priest' appears sometimes to have been used in a general sense, as designating the sons of the High Priests, and even the principal members of their families, there could, of course, be only one actual High Priest. The conjunction of the two names of Annas and Caiaphas probably indicates that, although

Annas was deprived of the Pontificate, he still continued to preside over the Sanhedrin—a conclusion not only borne out by Acts iv. 6, where Annas appears as the actual President, and by the terms in which Caiaphas is spoken of as merely 'one of them,' but by the part which Annas took in the final condemnation of Jesus" (EDERSHEIM). The author just quoted, remarking on a higher purpose than mere exactness of chronology had in view by Luke in adducing these six chronological data, says: "For, they indicate, more clearly than the most elaborate discussion, the fitness of the moment for the Advent of the 'Kingdom of Heaven.' For the first time since the Babylonish Captivity, the foreigner, the Chief of the hated Roman Empire—according to the Rabbis the fourth beast of Daniel's vision—was absolute and undisputed Master of Judæa; and the chief religious office divided between two, equally unworthy of its functions. And it deserves, at least, notice that, of the Rulers mentioned by St. Luke, Pilate entered on his office only shortly before the public appearance of John, and that they all continued till after the Crucifixion of Christ. There was thus, so to speak, a continuity of these powers during the whole Messianic period."

John was not forgotten **in the wilderness,** where i. 80 left him, but, now that "the day of his shewing unto Israel" had come, a **word of God** came unto him, summoning him to his work. How it came we are not told; but John i. 23, 33 shows that he recognized his mission; "he that sent me to baptize," he says, and disclaims anything as coming from himself.

3, 4. And he came into all the region round about Jordan, preaching the baptism of repentance unto remission of sins; as it is written in the book of the words of Isaiah the prophet,
   The voice of one crying in the wilderness,

> Make ye ready the way of the Lord,
> Make his paths straight.

3, 4. All the region round about Jordan denotes comprehensively the scene of John's ministry. (Comp. John i. 28; iii. 23.) **Unto remission of sins.** This was the end sought by John's baptism through **repentance** leading to faith in Jesus Christ whom John heralded as "the Lamb of God that taketh away the sin of the world" (John i. 29, 36). Apart from faith in the Coming One there would not be any forgiveness of sins. (See Acts xix. 4 and context, and on Matt. iii. 2 ff. in Vol. I of this Commentary.) Repentance is not a something done once for all; but our Christian baptism "signifies that the old Adam, with all sinful lusts and affections, should be drowned and destroyed by daily sorrow and repentance; and that a new man should daily arise, that shall dwell in the presence of God in righteousness and purity forever" (LUTHER'S CATECHISM). **As it is written.** The New Testament Scriptures record the fulfilment of the Old Testament Scriptures, prominent among which was **the book of the words of Isaiah the prophet,** in which there is so much about Jesus Christ and His gospel that Isaiah is called the Evangelical Prophet. (See on Matt. iii. 1-6, and on Mark i. 1-8.)

5, 6. Every valley shall be filled,
And every mountain and hill shall be brought low;
And the crooked shall become straight,
And the rough ways smooth;
And all flesh shall see the salvation of God.

5, 6. Luke quotes the passage from Is. xl. 3-5 more fully than Matthew and Mark *in loc.*, following the Septuagint freely. These additional verses set forth the difficulties to be encountered and overcome by the gospel of Christ. Luke, in accordance with the character of his whole narrative, notes that **all flesh,** and not Israelites only, **shall see the salvation of God.** The LXX. interpret " the glory of the Lord " (Isaiah) as " the salvation of God "—which is correct, since the whole refers to the revelation of God in Jesus, the Saviour.

> 7–9. He said therefore to the multitudes that went out to be baptized of him, Ye offspring of vipers, who warned you to flee from the wrath to come? Bring forth therefore fruits worthy of repentance, and begin not to say within yourselves, We have Abraham to our father: for I say unto you, that God is able of these stones to raise up children unto Abraham. And even now is the axe also laid unto the root of the trees: every tree therefore that bringeth not forth good fruit is hewn down, and cast into the fire.

7–9. See on Matt. iii. 7–10.

> 10. And the multitudes asked him, saying, What then must we do?

10. The general question asked by all classes was, **What then must we do?** If judgment is impending (vers. 7–9), what must we do to avert it? The object of preaching is *action* on the part of the hearer; and when he can be led earnestly to ask this question, the way is open for his conversion. (See Acts ii. 37; xvi. 30; xxii. 10.)

> 11. And he answered and said unto them, He that hath two coats, let him impart to him that hath none; and he that hath food, let him do likewise.

11. Here we have a general answer to the question asked by the multitudes. It is a rule of unselfish love. **He that hath two coats**—two tunics, under-garments; and two of these would be but a poor outfit—**let him,** even though poor, **impart,** give, **to him that hath none,** who is poorer still. So with **food.** This was to "love mercy" (Micah vi. 8), which was everywhere taught in the Old Testament, and set forth as a divine attribute. The Old Testament and the herald of the New taught *mercy,* and *remembrance of the poor.* The New Testa-

ment emphasizes this. Everywhere, in precept and example, is written "*Give.*"

> 12, 13. And there came also publicans to be baptized, and they said unto him, Master, what must we do? And he said unto them, Extort no more than that which is appointed you.

12, 13. To the **publicans**, the tax-gatherers, hateful to the Jews as representing the foreign power (Roman) to which they were compelled to pay tribute, and for their notorious exactions for their individual emolument, he said, **Extort no more than that which is appointed you**; go by your list, as faithful officials. This was to "do justly" (Micah vi. 8). (Comp. Zacchæus' words in chap. xix. 8.)

> 14. And soldiers also asked him, saying, And we, what must we do? And he said unto them, Do violence to no man, neither exact *anything* wrongfully; and be content with your wages.

14. **And soldiers also** came with the same question. Just who these were we cannot affirm. It was a military age. The Romans governed by the sword. **Do violence.** The word signifies to take a man by the collar and shake him. This the soldiers, from the nature of their profession, might be easily provoked to do, or take on themselves to do; but John says, do so **to no man.** This evidently refers to their personal relations to men, and so do the other prohibitions. **Neither exact wrongfully.** Do not levy blackmail, seek to advance yourselves or your wealth by falsehood. **And be content with your wages,** your allowance both of money and rations. In this faithful contentment there is also something of the "walking humbly with thy God" of Micah vi. 8.

Observe that John bade none of his inquirers leave their legitimate business; he interfered not with existing relations, but applied the principles of justice, morality and love to the circumstances of all the various classes who applied to him. His is the Old Testament answer, summed up by Micah (vi. 8) seven centuries and a half before,—" He hath shewed thee, O man, what is good; and what doth the Lord require of thee, but to do justly, and to love mercy, and to walk humbly with thy God?"

John's work was preparatory. Consequently *after* Jesus' work *for* man was finished (Ps. xxii. 41; John xix. 30), and He had sent the Holy Ghost to do His work *in* man, the answer to the sinner's cry, "What must we do?" was more full and clear. (See Acts ii. 37-40; iii. 18; xvi. 30, 31.)

15. And as the people were in expectation, and all men reasoned in their hearts concerning John, whether haply he were the Christ;

15. The state of the multitudes at this time was one of **expectation**. There are evidences of this more widely extended than among the Jews, in the writings of the heathen. Moreover, the "seventy weeks" of Daniel (Dan. ix. 24) were now completed, after which "the Messiah, the Prince," was to come. Now, here was John, with the spirit and power of an Elijah, in the garb and mode of life of a prophet, accompanying his close preaching with the ordinance of baptism; and **all men reasoned in their hearts**—questioned the matter there—**concerning John, whether haply he were the Christ** (Messiah). See John i. 19, ff. True, John did no miracle; but, after all, might not he possibly be the Expected One? Now the people were in such a state as to be led pretty easily by one who had, for his character and preaching, so commanded their attention and respect as John had. The Baptist had means of knowing the popular feeling, and might have ridden on a high wave of popularity into military leadership. But this humble great man was

faithful to his mission, and met the popular feeling with explicit and repeated denial of his being what they thought he might be, while he pointed steadfastly to One at hand who *was* the long-expected, the Messiah.

16. John answered, saying unto them all, I indeed baptize you with water; but there cometh he that is mightier than I, the latchet of whose shoes I an not worthy to unloose: he shall baptize you with the Holy Ghost and *with* fire;

16. John's testimony was open **unto them all.** In it he contrasted the persons and the baptisms of himself and the Coming One. I . . . **he that is mightier than I.** I, said he afterwards, must decrease; but He must increase. The friend of the bridegroom, he seeks not to take His room, but rejoices in His nearness. **The latchet,** thong, **of whose shoes,** sandals, **I am not worthy to unloose,** am not worthy to be His most lowly servant. Considering the popular estimate of John, how exalting to Jesus must his testimony have been in their eyes! **I baptize you with water . . . he shall baptize you with the Holy Ghost and with fire.** The elements of the ordinance differed as much as the administrators thereof. Water was the *symbol* of purification; the Holy Ghost and fire were to be the *agencies* thereof. The former was the sign; the latter the substance. See Acts ii. 1-4, 17-21, 33; xi. 15-17. Some understand the "fire" here to refer to judgment, as in ver. 17; but the better interpretation refers it to the tongues of fire at Pentecost, fire being also a symbol of purifying and of the Holy Ghost. John's baptism was preliminary and preparatory to Christ's. (See Acts xix. 4-6.)

Has Jesus baptized you? (ver. 16). Was it an empty form? Do you let the fire of His Spirit burn within you, purifying your heart and shedding light both within and around you?

17. Whose fan is in his hand, thoroughly to cleanse his threshing-floor and to gather the wheat into his garner; but the chaff he will burn up with unquenchable fire.

17. Here the preacher of repentance testifies of judgment to come, and represents the Messiah as the Great Harvester, **whose fan**, or winnowing-shovel, **is in his hand**, ready **thoroughly to cleanse his threshing-floor.** In those days the floor was a place in the open field looking much like a ring seen on the commons, in these days, after a circus performance. The mangled wheat, chaff, and broken straw, over which the oxen had trodden and perhaps drawn a sledge, was thrown up in the air, and the wind separated the wheat from the chaff. Jesus will discriminate, and will **gather the wheat**, the godly, **into his garner**, into heaven; **but the chaff**, the ungodly (see Ps. i. 4), **he will burn up with unquenchable fire.** Remediless destruction. The figure is taken from setting fire on the windward side to the pile of refuse chaff and straw of the threshing-floor; how irresistible the flame!

18. With many other exhortations therefore preached he good tidings unto the people;

18. **With many other exhortations**, some of which we read in John i. 15–36; iii. 25–36; Mark vi. 17, 18, and allusion to some of which we find in Luke xi. 1, **preached he good tidings unto the people.** The sacred writers give us only an outline of John's preaching.

19, 20. But Herod the tetrarch, being reproved by him for Herodias his brother's wife, and for all the evil things which Herod had done, added yet this above all, that he shut up John in prison.

Herod, Antipas, **the tetrarch** of Galilee (see on ver. 1), son of the Herod that slew the innocents in hope of destroying Jesus, was like his father in bad character, and came in, with the rest of the people, for reproof at the hands of John, who without fear or favor proclaimed truth and righteousness. Like the "prophet of fire," Elijah, in whose spirit and power he came, John rebuked kings for the truth's sake. But Herod preferred **Herodias, his brother Philip's wife,** with whom he, forsaking his lawful wife, the daughter of Aretas, of Arabia, was living adulterously. For this **and for all the evil things** of his life John faithfully reproved the politically distinguished offender. And for this faithfulness the wicked misrepresentative of rightful authority **shut up John in prison,** where the Forerunner at length, his mission ended, ended his life, a martyr to truth. See this matter more fully set forth in Matt. xiv. 1-12; Mark. vi.17-29. Luke merely mentions the fact here while speaking of John's ministry which practically ends with the introduction of Jesus into His public ministry.

21, 22. Now it came to pass, when all the people were baptized, that Jesus also having been baptized, and praying, the heaven was opened, and the Holy Ghost descended in a bodily form, as a dove, upon him, and a voice came out of heaven, Thou art my beloved Son; in thee I am well pleased.

But before John passed off the scene of his preaching, he performed the most important act of his ministry, as narrated in these verses. **When all the people were baptized** by John, should not Jesus be baptized? Was not He one of "the people"? But why should a sinless one be baptized unto repentance? Because He was to be made "in all things like unto his brethren." He represented mankind. Hence He was born, was circumcised the eighth day, and here now was **baptized.** In connection with the ordinance, while Jesus was **praying** (holy example for us) **the heaven was opened,** the vaulted dome above undid its doors, **and the Holy Ghost** descended in the sight of John and we know not of whom else, **in a bodily form,** taking a shape **as a dove,** and rested **upon him,** upon Jesus; and this was not all, for **a voice came out of heaven** too, and said, **Thou art my beloved son; in thee I am well pleased.** Here each person of the adorable Holy Trinity was manifest to the senses of men, and the doctrine of the Trinity is plainly set forth and incontrovertibly established. At the same time Jesus appears as having the fulness of the Godhead dwelling in Him, and from this time entered upon His public ministry as the Lord's Anointed, the Messiah, the Christ. (See on Matt. iii. 13-17; Mark. i. 9-11.) Careful readers and thinkers will distinguish between this assuming of the form of a dove by the Holy Spirit and the incarnation of the Son of God. The spirit did not *become* a dove, but only *assumed* that bodily form; but the Word became flesh, did not merely assume human nature. The Son of God became the Son of man and Christ *is* man as well as God.

23. And Jesus himself, when he began *to teach*, was about thirty years of age, being the son (as was supposed) of Joseph, the *son* of Heli.

23. Having finished all he has to say about John, the Forerunner and his ministry, Luke now comes to the public ministry of **Jesus himself,** and records that, **when he began** (comp. Acts i. 21) His ministry, He was **about thirty years of age.** Learn here that it is the divine way for one to become prepared for his work before entering upon it. QUESNEL says, "How important the lesson of *silence and humility*, if Christ gave thirty years of life and example to this, and but three to all the other gospel truths!" **Being the son (as was supposed,** since no other stood apparently in the relation of father to Him) **of Joseph.** He passed for Joseph's son. (See

CHAPTER III.

ii. 27, 33, 41, 49; iv. 22; John i. 45 vi. 42.) Legally He was Joseph's son; in fact He had no human father, and no earthly genealogy except through His mother, Mary. With this in view, and considering the differences between the genealogical table here following and that of Matt. (i. 1–16), the opinion most commonly adopted is that Luke in his table gives the descent of Mary, and that she, as well as Joseph, was descended from David. (See on i. 32.) **Heli**, then, was Mary's father (and there is a tradition to this effect), and Joseph was his son-in-law. Except in this verse there is no word in the original, throughout the whole list, for "son;" it is, however, naturally and usually, in such lists, supplied; but the descent indicated may be other than this specific natural relation, as we see in ver. 38, where Adam is called "the son of God." The genitives indicate source, origin, whether natural or otherwise. There is nothing inconsistent with the Greek or with usage in the explanation that Jesus was the grandson of Heli through Mary, His mother.

Matthew, it is argued with much reason, writing for the Jews, felt the necessity of showing Jesus to be the son of Abraham and the son of David; Luke, writing for Gentiles, showing the Gospel to be for mankind, traces the genealogy of Jesus "according to the flesh" (Rom. i. 3; Acts xiii. 23), and shows Him to be, through David's line, sprung from Adam, the father of the race, who came into being by the direct creation of God. Matthew's list begins with Abraham and comes down to Jesus, very carefully showing by the language he uses (Matt i. 16) that Joseph was "the husband of Mary," but not the father of Jesus. Luke's list begins with Jesus and runs back to Adam and God.

An old theory holds that the genealogy here given by Luke is, as Matthew's is, Joseph's, and explains Matthew's calling him the son of "Jacob" (Matt. i. 16) and Luke "the son of Heli" by a Levirate marriage (Deut. xxv. 5, 6, 10) and that Jacob was the real and Heli the legal father of Joseph; Matthew's list, then, would be the real, and Luke's the legal, descent of Joseph.

A more recent theory advocates the view that Matthew gives Joseph's legal descent as successor to the throne of David, whilst Luke gives Joseph's real parentage—this theory also resorting to a Levirate marriage of Jacob's widow by Heli.

We must refer any who wish to study this intricate subject exhaustively to the extended literature that has appeared upon it or to cyclopedias which give digests of, and references to, said literature. (See on Matt. i. 1–17.)

Let it be noted that, in the early centuries, the Jews, who were so careful about genealogies, founded no cavil against the gospel history upon anything in either of these lists.

24–31. The *son* of Matthat, the *son* of Levi, the *son* of Melchi, the *son* of Jannai, the *son* of Joseph, the *son* of Mattathias, the *son* of Amos, the *son* of Nahum, the *son* of Esli, the *son* of Naggai, the *son* of Maath, the *son* of Mattathias, the *son* of Semein, the *son* of Josech, the *son* of Joda, the *son* of Joanan, the *son* of Rhesa, the *son* of Zerubbabel, the *son* of Shealtiel, the *son* of Neri, the *son* of Melchi, the *son* of Addi, the *son* of Cosam, the *son* of Elmadam, the *son* of Er, the *son* of Jesus, the *son* of Eliezer, the *son* of Jorim, the *son* of Matthat, the *son* of Levi, the *son* of Symeon, the *son* of Judas, the *son* of Joseph, the *son* of Jonam, the *son* of Eliakim, the *son* of Melea, the *son* of Menna, the *son* of Mattatha, the *son* of Nathan, the *son* of David,

24–31. There are a great many more names between Joseph and David in Luke's list than in Matthew's, and the lists come together only in **Zerubbabel** and **Shealtiel**. (Observe that there are different ways of spelling the same names.) If these are the same persons in the two lists, a Levirate marriage is again resorted to for explanation, by which Shealtiel was the natural **son of Neri**, but legally the son of "Jechoniah" (Matt. i. 12): the lists part again in **the son of Zerubbabel,** Joseph taking his lineage from Abiud, one of his sons, and Heli, the father of Mary, from **Rhesa,** another of his sons. Similarly, whilst Joseph descended from David through Solomon (Matt. i. 6, 7), Heli came through **Nathan,** another of David's sons.

32-34. The *son* of Jesse, the *son* of Obed, the *son* of Boaz, the *son* of Salmon, the *son* of Nahshon, the *son* of Amminadab, the *son* of Arni, the *son* of Hezron, the *son* of Perez, the *son* of Judah, the *son* of Jacob, the *son* of Isaac, the *son* of Abraham, the *son* of Terah, the *son* of Nahor,

32-34. From David to Abraham the lists agree. Matthew runs his genealogy no further back.

35-38. The *son* of Serug, the *son* of Reu, the *son* of Peleg, the *son* of Eber, the *son* of Shelah, the *son* of Cainan, the *son* of Arphaxad, the *son* of Shem, the *son* of Noah, the *son* of Lamech, the *son* of Methuselah, the *son* of Enoch, the *son* of Jared; the *son* of Mahalaleel, the *son* of Cainan, the *son* of Enos, the *son* of Seth, the *son* of Adam, the *son* of God.

35-38. Luke runs back, through names that may be traced in Gen. v.., x., xi., to **Adam,** who was **the son of God,** not as progenitor but as Creator.

CHAPTER IV.

The Temptation. (Comp. Matt. iv. 1-11; Mark i. 12, 13.) Mark merely states the fact of the temptation; Matthew, as well as Luke, gives details.

1, 2. And Jesus, full of the Holy Spirit, returned from the Jordan, and was led by the Spirit in the wilderness during forty days, being tempted of the devil. And he did eat nothing in those days: and when they were completed, he hungered.

1, 2. **Full of the Holy Spirit,** who came upon Him at His baptism and abode upon Him (John i. 33). **From the Jordan,** the scene of his baptism. Whilst the other two evangelists indicate that Jesus was urged into the wilderness by the Spirit for the purpose of enduring temptation, Luke points out that He **was led by** (or, rather, in) **the Spirit** while there, and that He **did eat nothing,** a complete fast, and was tempted during the whole period of the **forty days,** though details are given only of the tempter's last grand assault **when they were completed.** No doubt Jesus' mind was all this while taken up with His mission, "absorbed by spiritual realities; a state which, although never fully attained by any person, yet, even in the modified degree reached by ordinary men, renders them, for a considerable period, independent of the common necessaries of life" (LANGE). Jesus at the well said, "I have meat to eat that ye know not: My meat is to do the will of Him that sent Me and to accomplish His work" (John iv. 32-34). That afterwards **he hungered** was merely natural, as a human weakness.

Characteristically, taking advantage of this His condition Satan made the desperate onslaughts whose recital follows.

The narrative of the temptation is a simple one, yet full of mystery to us owing to our want of knowledge. The events chronicled are, however, as real as any in the sacred history. They are no myth or parable, but a necessary part of the human history of Him who, to become our Saviour, was made in all things like unto us. For His own sake, as the second Adam (1 Cor. xv. 45), and as Mediator to be perfected through suffering (Heb. ii. 10; v. 9), including the common lot of men (Heb. ii. 17, 18), as well as for our sakes, a sublime example of faith and duty, Jesus was tempted.

<small>3, 4. And the devil said unto him, If thou art the Son of God, command this stone that it become bread. And Jesus answered unto him, It is written, Man shall not live by bread alone.</small>

3, 4. Same as in Matthew, except that Luke uses the singular, **this stone,** and makes it the direct object of address, and, further, gives only the first part of the quotation from Deut. viii. 3.

The personality of the devil is clearly indicated in the account of the temptation, and as in Eden he assumed the form of a serpent, so here in the wilderness he may have transformed himself into an angel of light (2 Cor. xi. 14), to approach the holy Saviour. Observe that what Satan bade Jesus do was not wrong in itself.

The time was coming when His power would be seen in the wilderness, multiplying the loaves and fishes, and so providing food for hungry thousands. But "himself he cannot save;" He came to personal humiliation and poverty; He came to obey and suffer; and all the conditions of human nature as it is in the world He must meet with patience. **So he answered, It is written,** a divine word to inspire human trust.

God's typical son, Israel, fell into Satan's snares, and murmured against Moses and against God, and said, Whence shall we get bread in the wilderness? God showed them whence: the manna came, according to His word (Deut. viii. 2-5). God's true Son, in whom He is ever well pleased, will not distrust His Father. Humbled though He be, He will rest in God's word, and wait. Our first parents, listening to Satan, thought they knew better than God, and, to serve their appetite, lost Paradise; but the second Adam, in the wilderness, rejects the tempter and gains it back to us! "Trust in the Lord and do good: so shalt thou dwell in the land, and verily thou shalt be fed." The temptation to distrust failed.

<small>5-8. And he led him up and shewed him all the kingdoms of the world in a moment of time. And the devil said unto him, To thee will I give all this authority, and the glory of them: for it hath been delivered unto me: and to whomsoever I will I give it. If thou therefore wilt worship before me, it shall be thine. And Jesus answered and said unto him, It is written, Thou shalt worship the Lord thy God, and him only shalt thou serve.</small>

5-8. Luke gives second what Matthew puts third in the narrative of the temptation. Such variations as this, and other verbal ones noted, are wont to be found in several truthful witnesses of the same thing, or narrators of the same story. Exact correspondence in order and words would open suspicion of collusion, and mar the record.

He led him up to the rugged top of *Quarantania*, north of Jericho, or wherever it was, from which there was an enchanting view not only over the beautiful land of promise but across the Jordan and north and south far away. From that height **in a moment of time** all was easily taken in—have you never been on such a high place of commanding view? **And showed him all the**

kingdoms of the world. There before His eyes they were in miniature, land and water, hill and dale, fruitful field and barren mountain, a beautiful, enrapturing prospect; a picture representative of the whole world. What further appeal to Jesus' imagination Satan made we are not told. **To thee will I give all this authority, and the glory of them,** said he. Had he them to give? We think that as "the god of this world," "the prince of this world," he in some measure had. He did not claim it as a native right, but **it hath been delivered unto me.** (See Rev. xii. 12; xiii. 2, 7.) The Lord did not charge him with making a lying offer of what he in no way had control of. Yet it appeared a better offer than it was; for Satan's influence is neither absolute nor permanent. His offer was a half-truth or less. The condition was, **If thou wilt worship before me.** Truly Jesus had come to gain back the empire of this world, but not in that way; at dreadful cost indeed, but cost of love and suffering, not of character. Satan asks an exhorbitant price for that for which he could give no good title. Had Jesus turned aside from His perfection, to enter the arena with worldly rulers and ambitions, He would no doubt have pleased the carnal hopes of those who afterwards opposed Him. The chief priests and scribes would then have persuaded the people to cry, "Live, King Jesus! Down with the Romans!" instead of that cry of servitude to Pilate, "Crucify Him! Crucify Him!" Satan, and afterwards the multitudes, proposed to make Jesus a king. But He was already a king, whom they knew not, and had already been worshipped by the representative first-fruits of the nations of the earth! (See Matt. ii. 11.) Still there was in this assault of Satan a real and powerful temptation, to and through vain worldly ambition. It also failed.

84   *THE GOSPEL OF ST. LUKE.*   [IV. 9-11.

9-12. And he led him to Jerusalem, and set him on the pinnacle of the temple, and said unto him, If thou art the Son of God, cast thyself down from hence : For it is written,
   He shall give his angels charge concerning thee to guard thee: And,
       On their hands they shall bear thee up,
       Lest haply thou dash thy foot against a stone.
And Jesus answering said unto him, It is written, Thou shalt not tempt the Lord thy God.

9, 10, 11, 12. Luke says **to Jerusalem,** which was "the holy city" (Matt.), and which was not far off from the wilderness in which they were. Jesus was not yet known in Jerusalem; this was the very beginning of His public ministry. No crowd would gather about Him now. That He suffered Satan to conduct Him thither was part of His humiliation, submission to man's experiences. The evil suggestion was, **Cast thyself down.** Do something extraordinary. Try thy powers, and, at the same time, astonish and attract the multitude—who are always taken by some such wonderful *feat.* **If thou art the Son of God,** do not seem to be just like the sons of men. Use thy prerogatives. Triumph where man fears and draws back. Then the crafty pretender tries to use the weapon with which he had before been vanquished, and *he* too *quotes Scripture.* **For it is written,** quoth he, **He** (thy Father, God) **shall give his angels,** whose office it is to minister to God's chosen ones, **charge concerning thee to guard thee** safe from harm. What particular and constant care is here indicated; and Satan quotes from a Psalm (xci.) acknowledged to have the Messiah for its theme. Seeing the Lord will go by what is written, Satan resorts to that, and brings out a text. But, like some preachers, he wanted to get out of it what was not in it, omitting the phrase, "in all thy ways" (Ps. xci. 11), and quoting it as though the promise could be plead for *all* ways, whether right or wrong ways, whether of presumption or of obedience.

But God's children can claim God's promises only when they are walking in God's ways, "as obedient children." To act otherwise and then come claiming the promises, is to do presumptuously, is *trying*, as we say, to God. And **it is said** in the same Scriptures (Deut. vi. 16), Jesus replies, **Thou shalt not tempt** (test, try, provoke) **the Lord thy God.** This command was given in view of what that other son of God, Israel, had done repeatedly, now testing God's power to provide, saying, "Is the Lord among us or not?" (Ex. xvii. 1–7; Num. xx. 1–13; xxi. 4–6); and now again His power to judge and punish (Ex. xxxii. 1–6; Num. xxv. 1–3). Comp. Ps. lxxviii. 17–24, 56–58; xcv. 8–11; cvi. 14; 1 Cor. x. 6–12. Now Jesus here refuses to tempt God by presumptuously rushing into danger, looking at the same time for divine protection. Safety lies only in the line of duty; dangers there should not deter; but we may not court danger, or needlessly expose ourselves.

13. And when the devil had completed every temptation, he departed from him for a season.

13. **Every temptation** that he then had ready, that then came into his mind. Some think it means every kind of temptation, that Satan had assailed the Saviour in every point of His human nature, and refer to Heb. iv. 15. **For a season.** Rather should this read, *Until an opportunity.* Satan would tempt Jesus again, when he would find a likely occasion for so doing. He found the Jews (John viii. 44) serviceable instruments in such temptation (comp. xix. 47; xx. 40), and afterwards Judas (xxii. 3; John xiii. 2, 27); and in Gethsemane (xxii. 39–46), and on the cross (xxiii. 33–46; Matt. xxvii. 39–50), he found, and used to the utmost, his last opportunity.

Matthew and Mark finish their account of the temptation of Jesus with the coming and ministration to Him of the holy angels. LANGE adds," Without doubt, it is in the spirit of the narration if we conceive to ourselves these as invisible witnesses of the combat and triumph of Jesus."

14, 15. And Jesus returned in the power of the Spirit into Galilee: and a fame went out concerning him through all the region round about. And he taught in their synagogues, being glorified of all.

14, 15. **Returned** from Judæa whither He had gone to be baptized, and where He was tempted, **into Galilee,** whence He had at the first set out. **In the power of the Spirit** given to Him without measure (John iii. 34) at His baptism and abiding on Him. **Fame** lifted up her head and stalked throughout all the region around, speaking **concerning him.** This was altogether natural, considering who He was and what He did; for now He was manifesting Himself to Israel. **He,** for His part, was teaching **in their synagogues.** The synagogue was the Jews' place of religious assembly, corresponding to our "church." After the captivity one might be found in every considerable town where Jews dwelt, and large cities had many synagogues. Here was the proper place for the first preaching of the gospel, the fulfilment of the Jews' religion; here Jesus would find the people, especially on the Sabbath day. The Aramæan Syro-Chaldaic dialect had taken the place of the pure Hebrew in Palestine since the Babylonish captivity, and was the current language of Palestine in our Lord's day. This He likely used in His preaching. Greek was the medium of communication with strangers, foreigners; Jesus' quotations from the Scriptures show a familiarity with them in the original Hebrew as well as with the Greek translation, called the Septuagint.

Glorified of all. His praise was in every one's mouth.

Luke's account by itself would lead us to suppose that, right upon Jesus' baptism and temptation, He began His ministry in Galilee. But a comparison of all the gospel narratives leads to a different conclusion. From Matt. iv. 12 and Mark i. 14 we conclude that Jesus' preaching tours in Galilee did not begin till after John the Baptist's imprisonment ; and John, up to iv. 43, gives an outline of Jesus' movements, covering over a year of time (if the accepted harmonists are right), of which the other evangelists give no account. At John ii. 13 we find it was the time of the Passover, always occurring in springtime, in our March or April, and at John iv. 43 we find another mark of time indicating as late a period as December. (See John xx. 30, 31 ; xxi. 25, for explanation of so bare an outline of the period referred to, as well as of the whole period of Jesus' ministry.) Jesus appears to have begun His ministry in Judæa (John iii. 25-30 ; iv. 1-3) and to have left that country upon the opposition which His success among the common people was arousing among the leaders. Thereupon He went into Galilee and there preached the kingdom of God.

16. And he came to Nazareth, where he had been brought up: and he entered, as his custom was, into the synagogue, on the sabbath day, and stood up to read.

16. In the course of Jesus' preaching tour **he came to Nazareth.** This visit seems to have occurred more than a year after Jesus' entering on His ministry. In Mark vi. 1-6 and Luke xiii. 54-58 we have accounts of a later visit of Jesus to Nazareth, when He received similar treatment. Nazareth was **where he had been brought up,** known among neighbors and acquaintance there for thirty years, a place of peculiar interest for the preacher as well as for the hearers. His movements among the people there during the week-days, and His converse

with them, are not told us. So much we know, that even His brothers did not believe in Him, and there was no disposition in the community there to accord distinction to one of themselves. Jesus' **custom** of attending the synagogue is an example to us. **Stood up** at the proper time, **to read** from the Scriptures. EDERSHEIM takes it that He had previously been invited and appointed by the ruler of the synagogue to take this part in the services, and that He had also conducted the earlier liturgical service, including the prayer. For (see vers. 14, 15 ; John iv. 45–54), "The service of the synagogue," says FARRAR, "was not unlike our own. After the prayers two lessons were always read, one from the Law, and one from the Prophets; and as there were no ordained ministers to conduct the services—for the office of priests and Levites at Jerusalem was wholly different —these lessons might not only be read by any competent person who received permission from the ruler of the synagogue, but he was even at liberty to add his own comment." At the reading all were accustomed to stand. The same custom is observed in most Lutheran churches in Europe. They thus show and teach reverence for and appreciation of God's Word. This also is the purpose of the sentences said or sung by the people after the reading of the Epistle and Gospel in "The Common Service." There was doubtless some flutter of excitement when the young carpenter, who, in his life before, had been but an attentive listener, stepped forward to the place of the reader.

17–19. And there was delivered unto him the book of the prophet Isaiah. And he opened the book, and found the place where it was written,

  The Spirit of the Lord is upon me,
  Because he anointed me to preach good tidings to the poor :

He hath sent me to proclaim release to the captives,
And recovering of sight to the blind,
To set at liberty them that are bruised,
To proclaim the acceptable year of the Lord.

17. The reading of the Law was over when Jesus stood up. The reading from the Prophets came next. The officer in charge of the sacred rolls **delivered unto him the book of the prophet Isaiah,** the "Evangelical Prophet," so full of testimony to Jesus. It was **opened by unrolling. He found the place.** It is doubtful whether the Rabbinical cycle of Sabbath readings or lessons was as yet in use; so that it cannot be proved that the place found was the lesson for the day—yet it may have been. Jesus would scarcely depart from whatever established order there was: yet it may have been allowed to read other Scripture too, and He may have found this place for the special purpose He had in view; found it for what **was written** there. The passage read is found in our Bibles in Is. lxi. 1, 2; lviii. 6, quoted freely by Luke from the Septuagint. It belongs to a portion descriptive of the person, office and work of the Messiah. The prophets represented God, and often spoke for Him in the first person. What is here quoted was not the whole of the passage read, which custom required to be longer, but the part which Jesus took as "the text" upon which He based His following remarks. The stringing together of passages from different parts of the Scriptures, illustrative of each other, was a common custom of Jewish teaching.

18. Anticipating here what is said in ver. 21, let us try to see how this prophecy of Isaiah was fulfilled in Him who that day commented on it in the synagogue at Nazareth. **The Spirit of the Lord is upon me,** having descended visibly at His baptism (Luke iii. 22; John i. 32)

and abode upon Him, in the power of which Spirit (ver. 14) He now was preaching in the cities of Galilee. Note that afterwards Jesus breathed on His disciples and said, "Receive ye the Holy Ghost" (John xx. 22), and on the day of Pentecost, after His ascension, fulfilled His promise of another Comforter by baptizing the infant church with the Holy Ghost and fire. **Because he anointed me.** It was customary to appoint prophets, priests and kings to their respective offices by anointing. "Messiah," in Hebrew, and "Christ," in Greek, mean *anointed:* Jesus here claims to be, by the baptism and abiding of the Spirit upon Him, the Lord's Anointed (Ps. ii. 2; xlv. 7; Acts iv. 27). **To preach good tidings to** (evangelize) **the poor.** Glad tidings to those in need, in sorrow, in want. The full, the rich, have already their consolation. The gospel comes to the hungry and thirsty, the longing, the unsatisfied; it blesses "the poor in spirit" (Matt. v. 3); it calls to "whosoever will" (Rev. xxii. 17). God hath chosen the poor of this world rich in faith (Jas. ii. 5); but not many wise men after the flesh, not many mighty, not many noble (1 Cor. i. 26). Jesus pointed John to the fact that "to the poor the gospel is preached" as evidence that He was the Messiah. Even so Jesus received sinners and ate with them, to the disgust of the proud Pharisees; and publicans and harlots, centurions and heathen "dogs" heard the good tidings and entered into the kingdom of God. (Comp. Ps. xxxiv. 18; li. 17; cxlvii. 3; Is. lvii. 15; 18; lxvi. 2, and Jesus' invitation, "Come unto Me all ye that labor and are heavy-laden, and I will give you rest!") **To proclaim release to the captives.** Not Herod's captives, such as John the Baptist now was, in the prison beyond the Dead Sea, but the worse captives of sin and Satan; and Jesus' healing of the demoniacs and diseased (Satan-bound, Luke xiii.

16), was an object lesson on His work of ransoming the mind and soul also. **Recovering of sight to the blind.** Literally, in many instances, illustrative of His being in a higher, spiritual sense "the light of the world," "the true light that lighteth every man," "the day-spring from on high," "the sun of righteousness," the revealer of the Father, the Way. **To set at liberty,** let go, **them that are bruised,** broken, shattered, oppressed. The Jewish teachers of that day bound burdens, grievous to be borne, upon men's shoulders (Matt. xxiii. 4), but Jesus invited the heavy laden to Him, with the promise of rest (Matt. xi. 28-30 ; comp. Is. lviii. 6).

19. **To proclaim the acceptable year of the Lord,** the Lord's year of acceptance and favor. This sums up the whole, and probably alludes to the Jews' year of the Jubilee, every fiftieth year, when slaves were set free, debts cancelled, lands restored, and joy abounded. So Jesus proclaimed the year of grace to men. This is admirably and constantly proclaimed in the course of the Christian Year, whose central sun and regulating principle is Jesus Christ. Grace and truth came by Jesus Christ. It is noticeable that our Lord ended His quotation at this point, not going on to "the day of vengeance" which immediately followed this clause in Isaiah's prophecy. Jesus' second coming will be for judgment ; His first was for salvation. "Now is the accepted time ; this is the day of salvation." Use it, improve it before it is gone forever!

_{20. And he closed the book, and gave it back to the attendant, and sat down; and the eyes of all in the synagogue were fastened on him.}

20. **Closed the book.** Rolled up the scroll. **Gave it back to the attendant.** This officer was sexton more than anything else. **Sat down.** All sat, commonly, after the Scripture reading. The next clause we can readily

conceive; it is vivid—**and the eyes of all in the synagogue were fastened,** in fixed gaze and expectancy, **on him.** What an interesting moment! Perhaps His mother and brothers and sisters were there; and former playmates and companions; and those for whom He had worked in Joseph's shop. "He came unto His own;" will they receive Him?

<small>21. And he began to say unto them, To-day hath this scripture been fulfilled in your ears.</small>

21. How much we would like to have Jesus' sermon! But Luke simply gives us the theme of it—**He began to say unto them, To-day,** right now, **in your ears,** your hearing, **hath this Scripture been fulfilled.** His reading had already fulfilled it. But what did He go on to say? We are not told, except that His words were words of grace that made the whole congregation wonder. The living Word took a text from *the written word*, and preached its fulfilment. Let none of us try to be wise above what is written, or give heed to any pretended preachers that do. Jesus here clearly claimed to be the Messiah: and presently the people's wonder gave place to anger at what they thought presumption, and they rose up to do Him violence. "His own received Him not!"

<small>22. And all bear him witness, and wondered at the words of grace which proceeded out of his mouth: and they said, Is not this Joseph's son?</small>

22. **They said, Is not this Joseph's son?** Who is His father? Mark says they recognized Him as "the carpenter." His words in the synagogue now did not seem to them to befit Him, and seemed to place Him so above them, His fellow-townsmen, that they were already a good deal excited by jealousy and wrath.

<small>23. 24. And he said unto them, Doubtless ye will say unto me this par-</small>

able, Physician, heal thyself : whatsoever we have heard done at Capernaum, do also here in thine own country. And he said, Verily I say unto you, No prophet is acceptable in his own country.

23. Observing this Jesus anticipated the expression of their feelings with, **Doubtless ye will say,** etc. In the proverb He then quotes, suitably to His works hitherto and to the purpose of His coming into the world, referring back to what He had read from Isaiah (vers. 18 and 19), He calls Himself *Physician.* The application of the proverb to the then present situation is given in the latter part of ver. 23 ; that is, **Do here in thine own country,** Nazareth, and among thine own acquaintances, what **we have heard done** by thee **at Capernaum.** Jesus had been at Capernaum (see vers. 14, 15 and John ii. 12), and its neighborhood, previously to this, and probably had done many works not recorded in our Scriptures. Why go off there and give honor to others? Do something in and for your own town. Accredit yourself here. Jesus saw in them a narrow, self-serving spirit, not such as is open to the gospel.

24. Moreover, well understanding fallen human nature, He further explained, **No prophet is acceptable in his own country.** He came to His own knowing this (John iv. 44). A prophet is one who tells forth the things of God, not merely one who foretells future events. A prophet, representative of God among men, is regarded as against men, because of their sins, and he is an instructor of men in all right ways. Jesus declared, and applied to Himself and them, this fact, that people are not apt to accept one from right among them in this position. This proverb cannot be applied to every position of distinction, but specially to a *prophet.* Jesus had lived among these people about thirty years. In all that time He "emptied himself" (Phil. ii. 6, 7) of the

exercise of the divine attributes that belonged to Him and was " found in fashion as a man " like those about Him. When now He began to manifest His glory as the Son of God, His fellow-townspeople were offended and yielded to their evil nature.

> 25-27. But of a truth, I say unto you, There were many widows in Israel in the days of Elijah, when the heaven was shut up three years and six months, when there came a great famine over all the land; and unto none of them was Elijah sent, but only to Zarephath, in the land of Sidon, unto a woman that was a widow. And there were many lepers in Israel in the time of Elisha the prophet: and none of them was cleansed, but only Naaman the Syrian.

25-27. They were thus in danger of forsaking and cutting off their own mercies. Therefore Jesus warned them by illustrations from their ancestors, Israel of old. He recalled former prophets, **Elijah** and **Elisha**, great prophets like to whom the Messiah was expected to be, prophets who did such things as were spoken of (vers. 18 and 19) in the passage from Isaiah on which Jesus had been commenting. It appears that though there were **widows in Israel** and **lepers in Israel** in those days, it was not these who got the benefit of the saving, healing ministrations of those great prophets, but **a woman of Sidon** and **Naaman the Syrian,** both of them outside of Israel, heathen, who are recorded as the beneficiaries of those prophets' bounty (1 Kings xvii. 8-24; 2 Kings v. 1-19). The warning from these illustrations was, Take heed lest there be also in you an evil heart of unbelief, in consequence of which you will fail to receive the benefit of the presence among you of a greater than Elijah and Elisha! Trust not to your natural birth; rest not in opportunities which you do not embrace! Take care lest the kingdom of God be taken from you and given to others! This result Jesus afterwards declared in so many words. (See Matt.

xxi. 43.) Jesus' warning here is like John the Baptist's, as recorded in Matt. iii. 9, 10.

> 28, 29. And they were all filled with wrath in the synagogue, as they heard these things; and they rose up, and cast him forth out of the city, and led him unto the brow of the hill whereon their city was built, that they might throw him down headlong.

28, 29. Here is proof that Jesus read their hearts aright. They thought much of themselves, though they were from despised Nazareth; they were not willing to be thus warned; their prejudices left little room for judgment. **They were all filled with wrath,** there **in the synagogue.** " His own received Him not," but **cast him forth** not only from the synagogue but **out of the city** (a small thing of a "city" it was), and not content with this, **led him to the brow of the hill** near by, on the slope of which Nazareth stood, proposing to **throw him down headlong,** the only cause for such procedure being their ungoverned anger and pride. What a picture is here set before us!

> 30. But he passing through the midst of them went his way.

30. **But he,** having suffered their rude manners thus far, now assuming that dignity and manner which belonged to Him, but which He mostly laid aside, **passing through the midst of them** in conscious power, now sufficiently manifested in His person as to restrain them (comp. John xviii. 6, and Mark x. 32), **went his way** unmolested further. There is something exceedingly interesting in this restraining and awing power exercised by Jesus, by the simple inherent force of His nature, allowed to manifest itself. How will He impress mankind when " every eye shall see Him " in His glory? (Rev. i. 7).

> 31, 32. And he came down to Capernaum, a city of Galilee. And he

was teaching them on the sabbath day: and they were astonished at his teaching; for his word was with authority.

31, 32. **Capernaum,** where Jesus so far fixed His residence, that it was called " his own city " (Matt. ix. 1), a wider field, a place where, amid plenty of unbelief, there was also enough faith to enable Him to do many mighty works. (Comp. Mark vi. 5, 6.) Moreover every way whether in mighty works or in **his teaching, his word was with authority** unlike anything in the experience of that generation or within the memory of any that were living (Mark i. 22). Capernaum was thus " exalted to heaven ; " but, withal, she has been now so " brought down to hell " (Hades), that the very site of the place is unknown. Even Nazareth more fully survives the ravages of time. There is plenty of warning here for us. " See that ye refuse not him that speaketh."

(See Vol. I., p. 383, EXCURSUS II. on DEMONIACS.)

33, 34. And in the synagogue there was a man, which had a spirit of an unclean devil; and he cried out with a loud voice, Ah! what have we to do with thee, thou Jesus of Nazareth? art thou come to destroy us? I know thee who thou art, the Holy One of God.

33. This shows that **the synagogue,** like our churches, was open to whoever saw fit to attend. All sorts of people are found in the church. But what was **a man which had a spirit of an unclean devil** doing in the house of God? Well, in Job i. 6; ii. 1, we are told that Satan himself came among the sons of God, when they came to present themselves before the Lord. Whether this man came by his own will or by the will of the devil that possessed him, we do not know. Enough that he was there. But another was there whose presence the evil spirit could not brook. So, using the organs of the man whom he possessed, the devil **cried out with a loud voice,** re-

gardless of all propriety and decency, and perhaps frightening many of the people.

34. **Ah! what have we** (speaking for all his kind) **to do with thee, thou Jesus of Nazareth?** What is there in common between us? And, what now? **Art thou come to destroy us?** The devils evidently know their destiny. Jesus took not hold of angels (Heb. ii. 16, Revision), but of the seed of Abraham. There is no redemption for fallen spirits, but for fallen man only. The devils know that. They knew Jesus too, as man did not, as witness this demon's words, **I know thee who thou art!** They knew Him too as more than Jesus of Nazareth, even as **the Holy One of God,** that promised seed of the woman (Gen. iii. 15) that should bruise the serpent's head, becoming the second Adam to restore the ruin wrought by the first and cast out the prince of this world from his ill-gained seat. This demon knew that something good could come, should come, out of Nazareth. Had Satan, after being vanquished in the wilderness of the temptation, reported to his minions, and warned them of this Jesus? Surely this superior knowledge of the possessed man did not come from idiocy or any human infirmity—such causes do not produce such results—but from the indwelling of a spirit superior in knowledge, who speaks sometimes in the singular, from personal consciousness, and sometimes in the plural from a consciousness of the common character and doom that belongs to the fallen angels. (See Matt. xxv. 41.)

35. And Jesus rebuked him, saying, Hold thy peace, and come out of him. And when the devil had thrown him down in the midst, he came out of him, having done him no hurt.

35. Probably all in the synagogue were afraid, as no doubt they had been greatly startled by the man's un-

seemly outcry. But Jesus, with composed dignity yet fervor, spoke to the unseen spirit rebukingly, saying, **Hold thy peace,** what hast thou to do to declare (Ps. l. 16) the truth of God, **and come out of him.** So Jesus, as He had said in the synagogue at Nazareth He was sent to do (ver. 18), proclaimed release to the captive. Unwillingly, and not before he had **thrown him down in the midst** whom he possessed, but of necessity, **the devil came out of him,** and the bruised was set at liberty. It was only consistent with the presence of the stronger than he that, despite his ill-will, the devil came out of the man without having in his going **done him** any **hurt.** Note the observations of the *physician* (Luke) narrator.

36, 37. And amazement came upon all, and they spake together, one with another, saying, What is this word? for with authority and power he commandeth the unclean spirits, and they come out. And there went forth a rumour concerning him into every place in the region round about.

36, 37. We can readily appreciate what these verses say. The **amazement** right there and the **rumour** gone all abroad **into every place** of the surrounding region, were altogether natural and what was to be expected. The people who witnessed this exorcism were right too in inquiring into the **authority and power** of **this word,** so different from anything they had ever heard, to which **the unclean spirits,** under dreadful stress, yielded so completely. Yes, Jesus' word, what a power is it! He speaks and it is done; He commands and it stands fast as He orders! "The words that I speak unto you, they are spirit and they are life."

38, 39. And he rose up from the synagogue, and entered into the house of Simon. And Simon's wife's mother was holden with a great fever; and they besought him for her. And he stood over her, and rebuked the fever; and it left her: and immediately she rose up and ministered unto them.

38. **Into the house of Simon** Jesus went from the

synagogue. Simon and Andrew were originally from Bethsaida, north of the sea of Galilee; but they seem to have removed to the larger city, Capernaum. Whilst we are told that Jesus some considerable time before this had made Capernaum His home to such an extent that it was called " His own city," we are not told with whom there He was accustomed to sojourn. Perhaps it was at Simon's house: and, if so, these brethren are already getting repaid for leaving all and following Him, by having the blessed Lord Jesus as their guest! Ah, this made heaven in that home! But sin with its consequences had been there too, and **Simon's wife's mother** was now sick. **A great fever** ailed her, the physician Luke says. That was a malarial district, and fever was common. Jesus never was sick. His nature was like Adam's before the Fall. It was sin that opened the door for sickness, sorrow and death. Jesus was one of us, " yet without sin " and its natural effects. But Jesus could sympathize with all human sorrows, and now **they besought him for her** that was sick. Could not, and would not, He that had healed the nobleman's son (John iv. 46–54), and cast out the unclean spirit, cure this woman too?

39. Yes, and now, among the household and others who stood about her bed, Jesus **stood over her,** the Great Physician, considering her case. He gave her no medicine, but, with that same wonderful word of authority which He had used awhile before to the unclean spirit in the synagogue, He **rebuked the fever.** And with what result? **It left her,** and it did not leave her weak, as fevers usually do; but **immediately she rose up and ministered unto them,** at once restored to her position of helpful usefulness in that household! Wonderful guest, what a privilege to minister to Him! Gracious presence before which the effects of sin fade away!

40. And when the sun was setting, all they that had any sick with divers diseases, brought them unto him٠ and he laid his hands on every one of them, and healed them.

40. They waited till **the sun was setting** because it was the Sabbath day, when by Jewish law no one was allowed to carry a burden. But, as the day closed with sunset, now there was a great stir in the city where there were **any sick** persons. These, whatever their **diseases**, their friends **brought to** this wonderful Physician. Nor were they disappointed, for **he laid his hands on every one of them**, a gesture or posture He sometimes used, expressive in itself and suited to impress the recipients of His blessings with a sense of their source, **and healed them** in every instance.

41. And devils also came out from many, crying out, and saying, Thou art the Son of God. And rebuking them, he suffered them not to speak, because they knew that he was the Christ.

41. Here again demoniacal possession is clearly distinguished from disease. **Devils also came out of many.** The case in the synagogue, that morning, was a fine advertisement to all such captives to come and be delivered, and to these besieged ones to come and be set at liberty (Luke iv. 18). **Thou art the Son of God**, the devils cried, **for they knew that he was the Christ.** See on vers. 33 and 34, above. It is an interesting question how much angelic spirits, good or bad, know about our earth and the things that are going on upon it. Outspoken as the devils were disposed to be, and though what they said was true, Jesus **suffered them not to speak.** He neither wanted such testimony, nor wanted men to look for or depend on such testimony. There was other and sufficient evidence for faith. STIER says, " The devils malignantly and maliciously, with all fear,

anticipate the plan of His life with a view to perplex Him in regard to it, and to prepare for Him (Mark iii. 11) scandal and suspicion. Therefore, as the Master, He does exactly what (Acts xvi. 16–18) His apostle afterwards did; and what, unfortunately, His disciples nowadays often fail to do when they do not reject, with sufficient decision, any testimony given from hell in their favor."

42, 43. And when it was day, he came out and went into a desert place: and the multitudes sought after him, and came unto him, and would have stayed him, that he should not go from them. But he said unto them, I must preach the good tidings of the kingdom of God to the other cities also: for therefore was I sent.

42. That Sabbath had been a very busy day with Jesus, and His human powers must have been severely taxed. It is the day chosen by Delitzsch as the basis of his interesting book, "A Day in Capernaum." Much as Jesus needed and enjoyed that night's sleep, as soon as **it was day,** Mark (i. 35) says, "While it was yet night," He left His bed **and went into a desert place,** where, undisturbed by the throng (which soon gathered again at Peter's house, next morning), He might pray. Even Jesus found it good to go and be alone in prayer to God! Wondering and wanting, **the multitudes sought after him,** and, when Peter had found Him in the desert place, **came unto him and would have stayed him** from going **from them.** But, as STIER says, "He who commanded the devils to be silent, will by no means suffer Himself to be lauded with turbulence even by men, as a mere worker of miracles; when matters are taking this turn He goes away, as He does everywhere else in similar circumstances."

43. **I must preach,** said He, and **to the other cities also.** "Miracles were wrought only to introduce and confirm the word; never in such numbers as the people desired; but always to such an extent only as was good

for directing them to that work, which He was always commencing afresh as His proper work, the preaching of the word" (STIER). **For therefore was I sent,** and therefore He came, the Messenger of the covenant, the Herald of **good tidings of the kingdom of God.** Is there any grander work among men whether we consider the end or the great Example!

44. And he was preaching in the synagogues of Galilee.

44. "As my Father hath sent Me, even so send I you," is Jesus' word to His disciples: only, whilst Jesus' own ministry was, according to the divine plan, confined to the land of Israel, our ministry, by the Lord's own great commission (Matt. xxviii. 19), is to "all the nations," even "to every creature" (Mark xvi. 15 ; comp. Acts i. 8, etc.). Jesus preaching throughout the synagogues of Galilee, and of Judæa too, is an affecting picture of the divine condescension and love, and a winning example to faithful though poorly appreciated labor on the part of all Christian ministers and teachers. According to the harmonists this verse refers to the first of three preaching tours of Jesus throughout Galilee, this first one centering, probably, more closely than the others, about Capernaum.

CHAPTER V.

1, 2. Now it came to pass, while the multitude pressed upon him and heard the word of God, that he was standing by the lake Gennesaret; and he saw two boats standing by the lake: but the fishermen had gone out of them, and were washing their nets.

1. **Now it came to pass.** This is a frequent way of introducing something new without giving any indication of the time of the occurrence. **The multitude pressed upon him.** He had become famous for both His wondrous teachings and His wondrous works, and people got together then as now, and crowded about this wondrous person. Whatever feelings of envy or jealousy may have begun to possess the leaders among the Jewish people, "the common people heard him gladly." **And heard the word of God.** They came to hear and see. Luke, the narrator, calls His teachings "the word of God," a truth which the people had not yet really perceived or acknowledged. **By the lake of Gennesaret,** and probably but a short distance out of the city, Capernaum, which lay on its northwest shore. This body of water is oval shaped, thirteen miles long and six broad, at its extreme measurements. Its waters were deep and abounding in fish. It is about seven hundred feet below the level of the sea, and its eastern and western banks rise steep, bare and rugged, to the height of two thousand feet. The Jordan enters it at the north point and leaves it at the south. It was called as above and also "The Lake (or Sea) of Tiberias," and "The Sea of

Galilee," these names being taken from the district in which it lies, and from cities on its western bank.

2. **Two boats.** Josephus says there were 230 of these on Gennesaret's waters. At the present time there is scarcely one. In our Lord's day all was life and bustle along the shores of this sea; the cities and villages that thickly studded them resounded with the hum of a busy population, while from hillside and grain-field came the cheerful cry of shepherd and ploughman. To-day a mournful and solitary silence reigns alike over sea and shore.

Gone out of them, and were washing their nets. It was morning, and they were getting ready to go home, putting the tackle in order, after a night's fruitless effort.

3. And he entered into one of the boats, which was Simon's, and asked him to put out a little from the land. And he sat down and taught the multitudes out of the boat.

3. **Which was Simon's.** In John i. 35–42 we have an account of Simon's first acquaintance with Jesus, brought to him by his brother Andrew, and then surnamed by Him Cephas (Aramaic) or Peter (Greek), names signifying the same thing. He was the son of Jonas or John, was a married man, originally from Bethsaida, but probably now living in Capernaum, where he got his wife. Up to this time he had not quit his business as a fisherman. **Asked him,** as owner of the ship, **to put out a little from the land.** So that He could see the people and they Him, and yet He be free from the pressure of the crowd. Here, as in the synagogue, **he sat down,** taking the usual posture of a teacher. **Taught the multitudes out of the boat.** He always was ready to satisfy the longing soul, to do good, and instruct the multitudes.

4. And when he had left speaking, he said unto Simon, Put out into the deep, and let down your nets for a draught.

4. **When he had left speaking.** For, though He had the words of eternal life, there was a time for Him to leave off speaking, and He knew when it was. **He said unto Simon.** Simon figures most conspicuously here, as indeed he always does when present. This arises, probably, both from his earnest, impulsive nature, and from the fact that he was in preparation to become one of the most diligent and effective preachers of Christ. **Put out into the deep** water, further from shore, **and let down your nets,** that you have just been preparing to lay by for some more propitious time, **for a draught,** for a haul of fish.

<small>5. And Simon answered and said, Master, we toiled all night, and took nothing: but at thy word I will let down the nets.</small>

5. **Simon,** answering, called Him **Master.** The original word is not Rabbi, but a Greek word found in the N. T. only in Luke. It signifies one who stands to another as chief, superintendent. It is a term of respect. Simon evidently revered Jesus very highly. He was discouraged over ill-success; **we toiled all night,** the best time for such fishing, **and took nothing.** There was no ordinary or natural prospect, then, that another throw of the net would be successful. All signs were against it; but Peter did not hesitate or grumblingly or slowly go about doing as Jesus bade, but, showing how highly he regarded the Great Teacher, said, as he guided the boat out into the deep, **but at thy word I will let down the nets.** The act was simply in deference to Jesus' bidding. This shows the regard in which Simon held Him.

<small>6, 7. And when they had this done, they had inclosed a great multitude of fishes: and their nets were breaking; and they beckoned unto their partners in the other boat, that they should come and help them. And they came and filled both the boats, so that they began to sink.</small>

6. **They inclosed a great multitude of fishes.** The net

was heavy with them, and they could see them disporting in the water, and by the pressure **their nets were breaking** or began to break (as we may render the word); they could feel the meshes giving way! What excitement they must have been in! A whole night without a fish, and now such a haul! They had never seen anything like it! And now there is danger of losing them, after all; the net proves too weak! Even such of us as, with hook and line, have after long waiting felt a good-sized fish tugging at the bait and got the prize above water far enough to admire its size and beauty, only to see it drop off and escape, can enter somewhat into the feelings and excitement of this boat's crew with their unmanageable catch of fish.

7. But help was near, and **they beckoned to their partners**, those who had been fishing with them, **in the other boat** (ver. 2), near the shore, to **come and help them,** to let down their nets around the breaking ones and save the haul. **They came,** of course, delighted at the unexpected success, and the prize was secured and **filled both the boats,** in its abundance, so full that they even **began to sink,** loaded down to the water's edge. We may toil all the night without Jesus and take nothing; but when obeying His clear word we shall prosper.

8, 9. But Simon Peter, when he saw it, fell down at Jesus' knees, saying, Depart from me; for I am a sinful man, O Lord. For he was amazed, and all that were with him, at the draught of fishes which they had taken.

8. **When Simon Peter saw it,** took in the whole situation, after the first excitement of making and saving the great haul of fish, he was overwhelmed with a sense of his own littleness and Jesus' greatness. (Comp. Is. vi. 5; Dan. x. 16, 17.) "Understanding and heart," says VAN OOSTERZEE, "were constrained to bow themselves before

a present majesty." So he **fell down at Jesus' knees, saying, Depart from me.** Not that he really wanted the Lord to leave him; but in this way, impetuous man that he was in both his feelings and his utterances, "as one in ecstasy or transport, that knew not where he was or what he said" (HENRY), he sought to express his unutterable sense of awe in view of Jesus' work and presence. **For I am a sinful man, O Lord.** Unworthy of such a presence. How can I stand before thee? What am I, that thou art mindful of me! "Lord" is a term of greater reverence than "Master" (ver. 5). Peter associates the power Jesus exhibited with holiness, and his own weakness with sinfulness, and herein he understood the fitness of things. (Comp. his words in Acts iii. 12.)

9. **All that were with him** in his boat, among whom was his brother Andrew (Matt. iv. 18; Mark i. 16)—how many more we are not told—were **amazed at the draught of the fishes.** They were experienced fishermen, and, especially after the previous night's failure, they felt there was something extraordinary and marvellous here. Jesus is set before us in this narrative both as divine in His knowledge and power, and as the ideal man described in Psalm viii. under whose feet "the fish of the sea," as well as other creatures, are put.

10. And so were also James and John, sons of Zebedee, which were partners with Simon. And Jesus said unto Simon, Fear not; from henceforth thou shalt catch men.

10. **James and John** were brothers, **sons of Zebedee,** and Salome, the sister of Jesus' mother. (Comp. Mark xv. 40, and John xix. 25.) They were, therefore, cousins of Jesus. He afterward took them, with Peter and Andrew, into the number of the twelve, and surnamed them Boanerges, or sons of thunder. Along with Peter they be-

came the Lord's inner circle, with whom He was most intimate.

Fear not. How often heaven says that to trembling men, whilst others, self-sufficient, impenitent, careless, are bidden to fear and tremble! Jesus understood Peter's feelings and condition, and sought to reassure him. He knew Peter did not mean that Jesus should desert him. The Lord answered the spirit and true intent of the awed and humbled man's prayer. **From henceforth thou shalt catch men.** In Mark i. 17, 20, we learn that this call and promise was given also to the other three. From fishermen they were to become fishers of men. From this time they were to abandon their previous occupation and follow Jesus' steps as well as His teachings. This was their second call; and the third one was that which chose them to be of the number of the twelve Apostles. "Catch" signifies to *take alive*, and the periphrastic form, "be catching," is used, to signify that this was to be his continuous calling, his business. The letters of the Greek word for fish—'Ιχθύς—form the initials of the Greek word that signify, "Jesus Christ, Son of God, Saviour;" and in the Catacombs and among the early Christians the figure of a fish was a symbol of the Christian faith.

11. And when they had brought their boats to land, they left all, and followed him.

11. **They left all.** It was their *all*, too, however little the boats and nets and fish may have been worth in themselves. They left their business, their tools, their associations, and all. When we "forsake all" for Christ, we get "more than all" in Him. **And followed him.** Going with Him in His preaching tours, continuing in His company. From this time dates their external and constant attendance upon Jesus.

The draught of fishes, here recounted, occurred, apparently, soon after Jesus' rejection at Nazareth and going to Capernaum, and is distinct from a very similar occurrence that took place after His resurrection. The repetition of the miracle after our Lord's resurrection, as recorded by John (xxi. 1-14), seems to have been especially for Peter's reassurance, and occurred in connection with his restoration from his fall. Both miracles are calculated to teach Christian workers their entire dependence on the Lord.

12-16. *And it came to pass, while he was in one of the cities, behold, a man full of leprosy: and when he saw Jesus, he fell on his face, and besought him, saying, Lord, If thou wilt, thou canst make me clean. And he stretched forth his hand, and touched him, saying, I will; be thou made clean. And straightway the leprosy departed from him. And he charged him to tell no man : but go thy way, and shew thyself to the priest, and offer for thy cleansing, according as Moses commanded, for a testimony unto them. But so much the more went abroad the report concerning him : and great multitudes came together to hear, and to be healed of their infirmities. But he withdrew himself in the deserts, and prayed.*

(See on Matt. viii. 2-4; Mark i. 40-45.) Matthew gives this occurrence directly after the Sermon on the Mount. None of them marks exactly the time or place of it.

12. Luke says it was **in one of the cities** and that the man was **full of leprosy** and that he **fell on his face and besought him.**

15. Luke refers to the widespread and abounding **report** that spread abroad, without noting the man's own agency in this, and the **great multitudes** that were gathering **to hear and to be healed.**

16. **But he,** Jesus, by contrast, **withdrew,** was withdrawing, **himself,** so as to be **in the deserts** of the neighborhood, **and prayed.** For this He withdrew. Herein Jesus is an example to all. All men of spiritual power

are men of prayer, and they are the former because they are the latter.

17–26. And it came to pass on one of those days, that he was teaching; and there were Pharisees and doctors of the law sitting by, which were come out of every village of Galilee and Judæa and Jerusalem : and the power of the Lord was with him to heal. And behold, men bring on a bed a man that was palsied: and they sought to bring him in, and to lay him before him. And not finding by what *way* they might bring him in because of the multitude, they went up to the housetop, and let him down through the tiles with his couch into the midst before Jesus. And seeing their faith, he said, Man, thy sins are forgiven thee. And the scribes and the Pharisees began to reason, saying, Who is this that speaketh blasphemies? Who can forgive sins, but God alone? But Jesus perceiving their reasonings, answered and said unto them, What reason ye in your hearts? Whether is easier, to say, Thy sins are forgiven thee; or to say, Arise and walk? But that ye may know that the Son of man hath power on earth to forgive sins (he said unto him that was palsied), I say unto thee, Arise, and take up thy couch, and go unto thy house. And immediately he rose up before them, and took up that whereon he lay, and departed to his house, glorifying God. And amazement took hold on all, and they glorified God; and they were filled with fear, saying, We have seen strange things to-day.

See Matt. ix. 1–8 ; Mark ii. 1–12, the former giving a briefer account, the latter one fully parallel with Luke's. It was at Capernaum. Jesus had but lately returned from a tour with His disciples through Galilee.

17. The time is very generally stated as **one of those days** of Jesus' ministry. **He was teaching.** This was His great vocation until His hour of sacrifice would come. The audience at this time was both distinguished and critical. **There were Pharisees and doctors of the law** (Scribes, the professional lawyers of Judaism,) **sitting by** and taking careful note of everything said or done by this wonderful Jesus, against whom their envy and ill-will had already risen. **Galilee, Judæa, and Jerusalem** were all represented there. **And the power of the Lord** (Jehovah) **was with him to heal.** The idea

seems to be that the Almighty was disposed at that time to manifest His healing power, through His Son Jesus, upon such sick folk as were brought to Him. Jesus' *teaching* was continually getting confirmation from His *works* of power. This was the chief purpose of these works of healing; they were in illustration and type of the greater healing of the soul, and of the ransom, at last, of both body and soul from the evil effects of sin.

19. **Into the midst** of the crowd, **before Jesus.** Best of all places for the needy to be! A place to be persistently sought, whatever may oppose !

True faith and great love break through great obstacles. This man's friends were friends indeed. How precious are such friends! Have you none whom you love that you can and will by all means bring to Jesus?

The paralytic is a type of every sinner. He is helpless before God: he cannot help himself and his friends cannot help him : all they can do is to bring him to Jesus. They can do that. But even here Jesus must first come within reach. God makes the first move to save. These carried their friend to Jesus with their hands. You can, indeed, bring sinners to God's house, and to hear His word, and you can bring them still nearer by your prayers. These men let the paralytic down with the arms of their physical strength: you can lift your friend up to Jesus with the arms of your faith.

25. **And immediately.** As "in the beginning" the Word "spake and it was done," so now " He commanded and it stood fast " (Ps. xxxiii. 9). **He**—who had been carried of four, a helpless paralytic, whose condition was evident to all—**rose up before them**—an open miracle, the fact of which nobody disputed. Not merely strength to walk was given him, but such complete and instantaneous restoration that he **took up that whereon he lay,**

and departed, carrying it, **to his house, glorifying God.** That this man obeyed Jesus' word bidding him to do what naturally he could not, was evidence of his faith. And that he was now able to do what of himself he never could have done, illustrates the important truth that Jesus' word of command is accompanied by power given to obey. We are spiritually all in as bad condition as this paralytic was physically—that is, impotent. But God's word of prevenient grace comes to us, and, bidding us rise from our lost condition and walk with God, enables us so to do. "By grace are ye saved through faith ; and that not of yourselves; it is the gift of God" (Eph. ii. 8).

Amazement (*ecstasy* is the English word derived from the Greek of the original) **took hold on all, and they glorified God, and were filled with fear.** Wonder, gratitude, and fear. These emotions Matthew ascribes to "the multitudes :" suspicion, envy and malignity, we have reason to believe, were mingled with the feelings of the representatives of the hierarchy there. **Strange things to-day.** We can explain them as they could not, having had cumulative evidences, coming down the centuries, that this Jesus was the Christ, the Son of the living God.

27, 28. And after these things he went forth, and beheld a publican, named Levi, sitting at the place of toll, and said unto him, Follow me. And he forsook all, and rose up and followed him.

See Matt. ix. 9; Mark ii. 13, 14.

The man who was here called to follow Jesus was afterwards made one of the Twelve, and became the writer of the gospel history that bears his name.

Having introduced Matthew, it suited the narrator to at once tell about a feast the latter gave Jesus, though it probably occurred later in the history.

29-35. And Levi made him a great feast in his house: and there was a great multitude of publicans and of others that were sitting at meat with them. And the Pharisees and their scribes murmured against his disciples, saying, Why do ye eat and drink with the publicans and sinners? And Jesus answering said unto them, They that are whole have no need of a physician; but they that are sick. I am not come to call the righteous but sinners to repentance. And they said unto him, The disciples of John fast often, and make supplications; likewise also the *disciples* of the Pharisees; but thine eat and drink. And Jesus said unto them, Can ye make the sons of the bride-chamber fast, while the bridegroom is with them? But the days will come; and when the bridegroom shall be taken away from them, then will they fast in those days.

See Matt. ix. 10-15; Mark ii. 15-20.

29. Luke says it was **a great feast** that Levi made for Jesus: and that there was **a great multitude** present, consisting of **others** as well as of publicans. **With them.** With Jesus and His disciples, in whose honor the feast was given.

30. Matthew and Mark make the murmuring Pharisees' and Scribes' question refer to the Master—**He eateth with**, etc. Luke makes them ask them the direct question, **Why do ye eat and drink with,** etc.

32. Luke adds the words **to repentance.**

Jesus' answer takes very high ground with reference to Himself. He did not associate with publicans and sinners as a boon companion, but as their Healer. And though the fault found with Him was in His relation *as a guest,* His answer represents Him as the great *Inviter* of men, while He says, **I came not to call the righteous, but sinners:** and that, not *in* their sins but *from* them, to call them "to repentance." In God's sight "there is none righteous, no, not one" (Ps. xiv. 2, 3; liii.), but "all have sinned and fall short" (Rom. iii. 10, 23). Christ came to seek and to save that which was lost; and all His actions showed it. He had power to forgive publicans and sinners, yea, even Pharisees and Scribes: but the

8

latter did not feel their need, whilst many of the former did; and so publicans and harlots, repenting, believing, entered into the kingdom of God and were redeemed, whilst the self-righteous children of the kingdom were cast out!

Anybody that can be brought to repentance and faith in Jesus can be saved; but nobody, however " righteous," can be saved otherwise.

33, 34. Whilst the other two Evangelists make **the disciples of John** parties to the inquiry, Luke makes the murmurers cite them as well as the disciples **of the Pharisees** as fasting and making prayers over against the festive spirit of Jesus' disciples; and according to Luke, Jesus said strongly, **Ye cannot make . . . fast,** etc., can ye? " I let it content me, that I find in my Lord Jesus Christ a sweet Redeemer and a faithful High-priest. Him will I extol and praise so long as I live. But if any one will not sing to Him and thank Him with me [i. e. wants to fast] what matters that to me? If it likes him, let him howl by himself alone " (LUTHER).

36-39. And he spake also a parable unto them; No man rendeth a piece from a new garment and putteth it upon an old garment; else he will rend the new, and also the piece from the new will not agree with the old. And no man putteth new wine into old wine-skins; else the new wine will burst the skins, and itself will be spilled, and the skins will perish. But new wine must be put into fresh wine-skins. And no man having drunk old *wine* desireth new: for he saith, The old is good.

See Matt. ix. 16, 17; Mark ii. 21, 22.

36. Luke calls this a **parable,** as it is an illustration of the spiritual by the natural. In Matthew and Mark the harm done is by increasing the rent in the old garment; in Luke it is twofold—**he will rend the new** and spoil it, and **the new will not agree with the old,** there will be want of harmony. Christianity is not patchwork;

the new covenant is not something added to the old; whilst it fulfils and completes the old (Matt. v. 17; Heb. viii. 13), it is itself a new spirit, a new life. (Comp. vii. 28.)

37. **The new wine will burst the skins.** They cannot hold it, it exceeds them, its power will break forth and go beyond. Christianity is too lively, free, and working a thing to be restrained by Judaism. Note that all this is in reply to Judaistic objections against Christ and His disciples, preferred by John the Baptist's disciples and the Pharisees (ver. 33).

39. This is peculiar to Luke, and is something of an apology for the hesitancy of many to take up with the new teaching. The habitué of the old saith, **The old is good** enough for me. He says this, however, in ignorance of the real quality of the new. "A wholesome doctrine does this whole passage contain, on the one hand, for those who would weaken the quickening power of the gospel by the imposition of legal fetters, and, on the other hand, for those who wish to lead the weak brother at once to the highest position of faith and freedom, without allowing the leaven time for gradual development. On the whole, we may perhaps say that Rom. xiv. contains the best practical commentary on this word of the Lord. Never were the *suaviter in modo* and the *fortiter in re* more harmoniously united than here" (VAN OOST.).

CHAPTER VI.

1-5. Now it came to pass on a sabbath, that he was going through the cornfields; and his disciples plucked the ears of corn, and did eat, rubbing them in their hands. But certain of the Pharisees said, Why do ye that which it is not lawful to do on the sabbath day? And Jesus answering them said, Have ye not read even this, what David did, when he was an hungred, he, and they that were with him; how he entered into the house of God, and did take and eat the shewbread, and gave also to them that were with him; which it is not lawful to eat save for the priests alone? And he said unto them, The Son of man is lord of the sabbath.

1-5. See on Matt. xii. 1-8; Mark ii. 23-28.

Matthew's account is the fullest, Luke's, the briefest. Luke adds in ver. 1, **rubbing them in their hands,** and in ver. 3 says, **Not even this** have ye read?

Here Jesus declares the purpose of **the sabbath,** and refutes not only all Pharisaism, but also those, on the one hand, who say that the Sabbath was a Jewish institution, and those, on the other hand, who hold that it has been abrogated. He who was in the beginning, by whom God made the worlds, says the Sabbath was made **for man,** and is intended to serve him, and *not for him to serve it;* therefore the necessities of any human being, made in God's image, are more important than any specific regulations about the day. The author of man is the author of the day; both belong to Him, and He prefers the living soul to the lifeless hours!

The observance of the Sabbath had been the great outward mark of distinction while the Jews were in exile; the strict observance of it afterwards became an expression of national Jewish feeling. Here was the stronghold both of Jewish exclusiveness and Pharisaical formalism. Here they make a test for Jesus and His disciples; and just here He antagonizes their ideas. He shows the Sabbath to be a divine institution *for man*, and not a Jewish ceremonial, and declares Himself as **the Son of man**, Messiah and head of the race, to be **Lord even of the Sabbath.** He might abolish it if He chose, but He nowhere did so. He only taught its true nature and observance. The Sabbath is a *means*, not an *end;* and they who use it otherwise, or refuse to use it at all, abuse it or reflect on the wisdom and goodness of God.

> 6-11. And it came to pass on another sabbath, that he entered into the synagogue and taught: and there was a man there, and his right hand was withered. And the scribes and the Pharisees watched him, whether he would heal on the sabbath; that they might find how to accuse him. But he knew their thoughts; and he said to the man that had his hand withered, Rise up, and stand forth in the midst. And he arose and stood forth. And Jesus said unto them, I ask you, Is it lawful on the sabbath to do good, or to do harm? to save a life, or to destroy it? And he looked round about on them all, and said unto him, Stretch forth thy hand. And he did *so:* and his hand was restored. But they were filled with madness; and communed one with another what they might do to Jesus.

6-11. Luke, the accurate narrator and physician, notes that it was the man's **right hand** that was withered, and that it was **the scribes and the Pharisees** who were watching Jesus: also that **he knew their thoughts,** and made the man **stand forth in the midst,** to be himself and his cure a plain, open object lesson to all present. **To save a life, or to destroy it**—which is the thing to do on the Sabbath? **He looked round about on them all,** having made a fair challenge and waiting for an answer, if they had any; and when none came the Lord answered His own question by restoring the man's hand with a word. **But they,** in their false religiousness and zeal for their own opinions,

were filled with madness. The word signifies want of understanding. "And yet," BENGEL says, "at that very time they had reason to have come to their senses." **And communed,** were talking it over, **one with another, what they might do to Jesus,** to destroy Him (Matthew and Mark).

Down with this Jesus! They will join with any person or party to accomplish this! Here again was illustrated the common proverb that religion and politics make strange bedfellows (Mark iii. 6). Moreover the inconsistency of being so zealous for one of God's commandments, concerning the Sabbath, while they were busily violating another, "Thou shalt not kill," and the very spirit of the whole divine law, did not occur to their minds, so blinded were they with bigoted "madness" (Luke vi. 11). It is noticeable that this is the first statement we have of a concerted plan to destroy Jesus.

BROADUS, in his Harmony, notes on John v. 1–47 the hostility of the Jews *at Jerusalem* as having reached the point of a desire to kill Jesus as a blasphemer and a sabbath-breaker as early as a year and probably two years before the crucifixion; and on the passage before us says, "Here at some point near the sea of Galilee, there is already a plot to kill Him, as some had wished to do in Jerusalem."

12, 13. And it came to pass in these days, that he went out into the mountain to pray; and he continued all night in prayer to God. And when it was day, he called his disciples: and he chose from them twelve, whom also he named apostles;

See on Mark iii. 13–19, and comp. Matt. x. 2–4.

12. **In these days** is a loose, general expression of time, sufficiently exact for Luke's purpose. Matt. (xii. 15–21) and Mark (iii. 7–12) report, in this time, great multitudes from all quarters crowding to Jesus, beside the sea of

Galilee, to see and hear Him and be healed of plagues and unclean spirits, whom He suffered not to proclaim Him, as they were disposed to do. From the sea **he went out** (forth) **into the mountain** region. The only considerable elevation on the west side of the sea, about seven miles southwest of Capernaum, and now called the "Horns of Hattin," is supposed to have been the place. Luke alone says that He went there **to pray**—a habit in Jesus which our Evangelist is specially wont to note. (See iii. 21; v. 16; ix. 18, 29, etc.) **And he continued all night in prayer to God.** What a spectacle to angels (then) and to men (now)—the Son of God, the Son of man, engaged all night in prayer! What an example! Did Jesus so often resort to mountain heights because they are further from the world and nearer to God?

13. This night of devotion preceded and had much to do with the choosing of the twelve, which took place **when it was day.** From the whole body of **his disciples,** whom **he called** to the mountain summit, He **chose twelve.** Mark (iii. 14, 15) tells the purpose of their appointment. The number twelve corresponds with the number of the tribes of the chosen people, the typical kingdom of God upon earth. (Comp. xxii. 30; Matt. xix. 28; Rev. xxi. 12, 14.) From Acts i. 21, 22 and 1 Cor. ix. 1 we gather that a necessary prerequisite for this calling and office was to have been an eye-witness of the Lord. **Whom also he named apostles.** The word means persons sent forth, like our word missionary. It occurs only once in Matt. (x. 2), once in Mark (vi. 30), not at all in John except in its original and wide sense of messenger (xiii. 16), six times in Luke's gospel history and thirty times in the Acts. (See 2 Cor. xii. 12 for "the signs of an apostle.") The Seventy (x. 1), afterwards sent forth, He did not name "apostles."

14-16. Simon, whom he also named Peter, and Andrew his brother, and James and John, and Philip and Bartholomew, and Matthew and Thomas, and James *the son* of Alphæus, and Simon which was called the Zealot, and Judas *the son* of James, and Judas Iscariot, which was the traitor;

14. **Simon** was a very common name among the Jews. This man was a son of Jonas, or John, a fisherman of Bethsaida. He was first brought to Jesus by his brother Andrew, more than a year before. At that time Jesus told him, "Thou shalt be called Cephas," which is an Aramaic (Syro-Chaldaic) word meaning a stone or a rock. From a Greek word with the same meaning comes the name **Peter**. This was his apostolic name. Peter had no higher office than the rest of the twelve, but was fitted by nature to take the lead among them, a position he evidently occupied. By his outspoken confession, divinely inspired, of Jesus as "the Christ, the Son of the living God" (Matt. xvi. 16), made in behalf of the twelve, he, in common with them and all true confessors of Christ, became the rock on which the everlasting Church of Christ is built.

Andrew was the first, so far as the record goes, to confess Jesus as the Messiah, and to him as such he brought "his own brother Simon" (John i. 35-42). Aside from the lists of the apostles' names we find him mentioned only in Mark i. 16-18, 29; xiii. 3; John i. 40, 44; vi. 8, 9; xii. 22. **James, the son of Zebedee**, is also sometimes called James the greater, to distinguish him from the other James (ver. 18), either because he was older or taller than he. It is inferred that he was older than **John**, because his name is always put before his, and John is spoken of as "the brother of James." (See Mark iii. 17 for their surname.) The father of these brothers was a man of some means, spoken of as employing "hired servants" (Mark i. 20). John, moreover, had a house of his own (John xix. 27), probably in Jerusalem, and was known to the high priest, Caiaphas (John xviii. 15). James was beheaded by Herod Agrippa I., A.D. 44 (Acts xii. 1, 2), the first martyr from among the twelve, whilst John survived them all, living till the close of the century. Those representations, pictorial or otherwise, which represent John as in any degree effeminate, are *mistaken*. These three, Peter, James, and John, were an inner circle among the twelve, specially near the Lord. (See ch. viii. 51 ; ix. 28 ; Mark xiii. 3 ; xiv. 33.)

Philip was from the same place as the four before mentioned—Bethsaida. The first mention we have of him is in John i. 43, where Jesus found him and took him along to Galilee. This was previous to our Lord's first Passover after His baptism. The last we hear of him in Scripture is in Acts i. 13. Meanwhile he appears in John i. 45; vi. 5-7; xii. 21, 22; xiv. 8, 9; and from these references he appears to have been rather a halting believer. **Bartholomew** means *son of Tholmai*. His distinguishing name, as generally believed, was *Nathanael*. The first we hear of him was when Philip called him to Jesus (John i. 45-51), when, after having first doubted whether any good thing could come out of Nazareth, he afterwards confessed, " Rabbi, thou art the Son of God ; thou art the King of Israel," speaking out of that sincerity of heart which the heart-searcher knew to be so characteristic of the man that, as he was coming toward Him, He said, " Behold an Israelite indeed, in whom is no guile !" He was of Cana in Galilee. This is all the Scriptures tell about him.

15. **Matthew.** Formerly a publican, called also Levi. (See v. 27-29, and on Matt. ix. 9.) He became the writer of the gospel history called by his name. **Thomas,** called also Didymus, both of which mean *Twin*. Whose

twin brother he was, we know not. All we have about him is in John xi. 16; xiv. 5; xx. 24-29; xxi. 1, 2; from which it appears that he was a man that looked at the dark side of things, indisposed to believe without sensible evidence, yet, withal, ardently attached to Jesus. His love surpassed his faith and hope. He is sometimes called the doubting disciple: yet he has given us that magnificent confession, "My Lord and my God."

James, called also (xv. 40) *the less*. (See on ver. 17, above.) **Son of Alphæus**, who in John xix. 25 is called *Clopas*. His mother's name was Mary. Not the same as "the Lord's brother," who was also called James and known as "The Just," and President of the church at Jerusalem and author of the Epistle of James. It was a common name then as well as now. There are other theories of these Jameses. We have given what we consider the most sensible view. We know nothing of this apostle.

Another **Simon, called the Zealot**, a Greek word rendered "Cananæan" (Matt. x. 4; Mark iii. 18) by the Hebrews. The Zealots were a political party extremely violent against Roman rule, and disposed to take all law into their own hands in defence of Mosaism. Nothing is related of him in the Scriptures.

16. **Judas**, distinguished as **of James**, whether son or brother is not certain. Ordinarily it would be **son of James**, as the Rev. Ver. makes it. The Auth. Ver. and others, taking this person to be the same as the writer of the epistle of Jude, where (ver. 1) he is called "brother of James," supply "brother" here instead of "son." This is allowable, but exceptional. In Matthew and Mark he is called **Thaddæus**. The only thing related, in the Scriptures, of Judas the apostle is in John xiv. 22, where he is carefully distinguished from "Iscariot."

Last in the list comes **Judas Iscariot**, i. e. man of Kerioth, a city of Judæa. He was the only Judæan among the twelve, all the others being Galileans. His father's name was Simon (John vi. 71; xiii. 26). The correct reading is not "was the traitor," but **became a traitor**, as the Am. Comm. of the Revisers make it. Judas was a lover of money; while treasurer of the apostolic band he became a defaulter, or "thief," as the Scriptures (John xii. 6) plainly characterize him, and for thirty pieces of silver betrayed Jesus to His enemies. He yielded to the evil propensities of his heart and to the temptations of Satan, and, although he had the same opportunity of becoming good and of doing good that the others of the twelve had, he wilfully became a traitor. He hung himself in remorse (Matt. xxvii. 5). Jesus said of him, "Good were it for that man if he had never been born!" (Matt. xxvi. 24).

Of course Jesus knew beforehand how each of those He chose would turn out; but it was *Judas' own choice*, and that against every argument of his exalted position to a place near the Lord Jesus, to become what he did become.

Such was "the glorious company of the apostles" on earth. There are four lists of them, viz. in Matt. x. 2–4; Mark iii. 16–19; Luke vi. 14–16; Acts i. 13. Although the order of the names varies somewhat in these lists, it is noticeable that *Peter's* always comes *first ; Philip's fifth ;* that of *James* the son of Alphæus, *ninth ;* and *Judas Iscariot's last.* This divides the list of twelve into *three* sets of *four each.*

17–19. And he came down with them, and stood on a level place, and a great multitude of his disciples, and a great number of the people from all Judæa and Jerusalem, and the sea coast of Tyre and Sidon, which came to hear him, and to be healed of their diseases ; and they that were troubled with unclean spirits were healed. And all the multitude sought to touch him : for power came forth from him, and healed *them* all.

17-19. **Down** from the summit He came **with them** the twelve especially, and the other disciples whom He had called to Him, **and stood on a level place,** where there was room for the multitudes. Here Luke mentions the crowds which Matthew and Mark noted earlier. (See on ver. 12.) The region represented was very wide. From every quarter people came **to hear him** and **to be healed.** Luke, the physician, distinguishes between **diseases** and troubles from **unclean spirits.** Man is very prone to some outward sign; hence they **sought to touch him. For power,** might, force, **went forth** continually **from him,** its source, **and healed all** who came under its influence. " I am the Lord that healeth thee " (Exod. xv. 26).

20-23. And he lifted up his eyes on his disciples, and said, Blessed *are* ye poor : for yours is the kingdom of God. Blessed *are* ye that hunger now : for ye shall be filled. Blessed *are* ye that weep now : for ye shall laugh. Blessed are ye, when men shall hate you, and when they shall separate you *from their company,* and reproach you, and cast out your name as evil, for the Son of man's sake. Rejoice in that day, and leap *for joy :* for behold, your reward is great in heaven : for in the same manner did their fathers unto the prophets.

On the identity of the discourse here given by Luke with that given by Matthew, chaps. v. to vii., commonly called the Sermon on the Mount, see " Preliminary Observation," pp. 89, 90, Vol. I., of this commentary, and compare the passages there following and the comments thereon. By some it has been strongly maintained that the two Evangelists report different discourses, spoken either successively on the same occasion —first on the mountain and then on the plain— or on different occasions. But most writers since the

Reformation regard the two passages as two reports of the same discourse, each reporter giving that part of the discourse which suited his purpose as a historian. Matthew gives the longer report, with repetitions, writing for the Jews: Luke gives a shorter report, giving what specially suited his purpose as a writer for the Gentiles, and giving elsewhere some things that Matthew includes in his report of the Sermon on the Mount. There can be no objection to the idea that Jesus often taught the same things, and even in the very same words. Every good teacher does this, and every learner needs it.

20. **And he,** in contrast with the multitudes just spoken of, **lifted up his eyes,** in token of what He was about to do, **on his disciples,** whom He specially, but not exclusively (see vii. 1 and Matt. vii. 28) addressed in what follows.

In Luke the address is more direct, in the second person: **Ye poor, yours is,** where Matthew has "the poor," "theirs is," and so on. Those who are poor as ye are poor, who have left all for the kingdom of God's sake. Poverty, in the sense of want of this world's goods, is not a blessing; it may lead to the blessing here pronounced, if the discipline of it is rightly used; but poverty is often accompanied by pride; "poor and proud" has become an aphorism. Evidently it is a character and not a condition that is here pronounced blessed. It is Matthew's "poor in spirit"—those who in their spirit, within, feel their emptiness and need. Opposite to this are the proud in spirit, who are an abomination to the Lord (Prov. xvi. 5), such, e. g. as the Laodiceans mentioned in Rev. iii. 17. This character is fundamental and accordant with that fundamental law of God's kingdom, "He that exalteth himself shall be abased, and he that humbleth himself shall be exalted" (xiv. 11, xviii. 14). We must be emptied of ourselves and of the world before God can fill us with Himself. This spirit, taking refuge in God, says, "Let me *hide myself* in Thee!" and, "Nothing in my hand I bring." It may exist in him who has much of this world's goods but does not set his heart upon them. Yet the Scriptures and observation warn that worldly riches are apt to exalt the spirit and make it trust in them, whilst poverty tends to produce a sense of dependence, and makes room for faith. Why **blessed?** Because **yours is the kingdom of God.** Matthew says "the kingdom of heaven." (See Excursus I., Appendix, Vol. I. of this Commentary.) The blessings of God's rule in redemption, the privileges of heavenly citizenship (Phil. iii. 20; Eph. ii. 10), are yours. Here is full supply for your felt spiritual need.

21. **Now,** of this present earthly sphere, is contrasted with hereafter, in the kingdom of God. The beatitudes, whilst asserting a present blessing, look chiefly to the future. **Shall be filled.** "I shall be satisfied" (Ps. xvii. 15). **Weep** and **laugh** are short ways of expressing states, conditions. (See ver. 25.)

22. **Separate you**—" from the congregation of the synagogue and the intercourse of common life " (MEYER), carrying out their **hate.** (See John ix. 22; xii. 42; Matt. x. 17, 18; xxiii. 34, 35). **For the Son of man's sake.** Because ye are His disciples. On the title "Son of man," commonly used by the Lord of Himself, here first occurring in Luke, see on Matt. viii. 20. He is *the* Son of man, in distinction from all other sons of men, the second Adam.

23. **Rejoice in that day** of persecution for Christ's sake, even **leap for joy**—not because of the persecution and evil treatment, not in the suffering, but because it

marks you as among those who shall have a **reward in heaven**, one that is **great**. Your treatment, like that which **the prophets** received of old, shows you to be, like them, God's chosen ones, to belong to those over whom He exercises special care and for whom He has prepared a glorious hereafter. The suffering Christian rejoices in hope.

24-26. But woe unto you that are rich! for we have received your consolation. Woe unto you, ye that are full now! for ye shall hunger. Woe *unto you*, ye that laugh now! for ye shall mourn and weep. Woe *unto you*, when all men shall speak well of you! for in the same manner did their fathers to the false prophets.

24-26. **Woe** is the opposite of blessing, and we have in these verses the converse of the beatitudes just given. Jesus not only could, but must, pronounce woes as well as benedictions; for He was honest, was the Truth. Opposite characters must meet opposite treatment from the just and holy God. (See Matt. xi. 21 ; xxiii. 13-15, 23-29 ; xxvi. 24 ; also Rev. vi. 16, which speaks of " the wrath of the Lamb.")

When Jesus here says, **you that are rich,** etc., He extends His vision beyond the circle indicated in ver. 20: "you," whoever and wherever you are. See the parable of the rich man and Lazarus (ch. xvi.). It is not a good sign **when all men shall speak well of you.** So it was of old (1 Kings xxii. 6-27 ; Jer. v. 31 ; xxiii. 16, 17 ; Mic. ii. 11), with **the false prophets,** who uttered "smooth things" (Is. xxx. 10) to please. Men of positive convictions and the courage of them, upright men, who speak out the truth, are sure to meet opposition and to be spoken against. We are not to court or unnecessarily provoke opposition, but it would be strange if we, as faithful disciples of Christ, did not meet it in this present evil world.

27, 28. But I say unto you which hear, Love your enemies, do good to them that hate you, bless them that curse you, pray for them that despitefully use you.

27, 28. You which hear seems to point a contrast with those who set up their own wilful judgment as an interpreter of the law, and refuse to hear its inner spiritual sense, as expounded by the Lord. *The Bible Commentary* says, " Our Lord now turns from the two classes whom He has been apostrophizing, to His actual hearers." **I say unto you.** The true expositor, that living Law, Jesus, the fulfiller, says, **Love your enemies**; and illustrates in three particulars—**do good to**—**bless**—**pray for**; even though the objects of these acts of love **hate you— curse you—despitefully use you.** Return not like for like, but good for evil. This is a retaliation which is divine! The Apostle inculcates it to the Romans (xii. 21),—a new doctrine, doubtless, for them—" Be not overcome of evil, but overcome evil with good."

29. To him that smiteth thee on the *one* cheek offer also the other: and from him that taketh away thy cloke withhold not thy coat also.

29. Here are two illustrations of evil treatment, and the Lord's method of overcoming them. The first is personal affront, as when one **smiteth thee on the cheek,** a something not easy for the natural man to bear. The like has often made a quarrel and even resulted in murder. The second, as when one **taketh away thy cloke,** seems (from Matt. v. 40) to refer to a legal process entered on in a litigious, unkindly spirit. In the first instance the Christian retaliation here urged is, **Offer also the other** cheek to the smiter ; in the second it is **withhold not thy coat also.** This is certainly unusual teaching, very different from both teachings and customs current among men. That we are to regard the spirit of the Lord's teaching here, rather than a formal obedience to the letter, is evident from our Lord's own conduct when smitten on the cheek (John xviii. 22, 23): on the other hand, the wrong and Pharisaic interpretation of our Lord's words is illustrated in that reported case of the Quaker (a mythical case most likely) who, when smitten, having first turned the other cheek, in fulfilment of the law, as he thought, thereupon proceeded to flog the evildoer! The spirit forbidden in these verses is a spirit of revenge and strife; that which is enjoined is a spirit of *forbearance*, patience under injuries, and is illustrated chiefly in the Lord Himself (1 Pet. ii. 23), and notably in the Apostle Paul (1 Cor. iv. 11–13).

30. Give to every one that asketh thee; and of him that taketh away thy goods ask them not again.

30. **Give,** rather than exact. Giving is divine. Every good gift and every perfect gift is from above. God is always giving: be like Him. Yes, this is a much needed grace in the Church, not enough preached or practised either in the pulpit or in the pew! **To every one that asketh thee.** Whether formally or not. All *need*, coming to our knowledge, is an "asking." Therefore it will not do to shut ourselves out from access to those who would ask and then say, "Nobody asked me," or from knowledge of need and then say, "I didn't know it." AUGUSTINE comments thus on this passage: "'To every one that asketh,' says He; not, everything to him that asketh: so that you are to give that which you can honestly and justly give. For, what if he should ask money wherewith he may endeavor to oppress an innocent man? What if, in short, he should ask something unchaste? . . . That certainly is to be given which may hurt neither thyself nor the other party, as far as can be

known or supposed by man; and in the case of him to whom you have justly denied what he asks, justice itself is to be made known, so that you may not send him away empty. Thus you will give to every one that asketh you, although you will not always give what he asks; and you will sometimes give something better, when you have set him right who was making unjust requests."

ALFORD says, "To give everything to every one—the sword to the madman, the alms to the impostor, the criminal request to the temptress—would be to act as the enemy of others and ourselves."

The latter part of the verse teaches us to think more of our own well-kept, sweet-tempered spirit, and of our fellow-man's need, than of our earthly **goods.** 'Tis better to lose our goods than our temper. In all these illustrations of a Christly spirit, the supposition is an extreme one, so as to cover all cases: if such a spirit is to be shown in so unlikely cases, let it by all means appear in the common intercourse of daily life.

31. And as ye would that men should do to you, do ye also to them likewise.

31. Here is a summary of our duty to our fellow-man, which was the subject of our Lord's teaching in the previous verses. Such duty is specifically laid down in the second table of the law, which, morover, cannot be fulfilled without regard to the first table coming before it; as is constantly kept before us in Luther's explanations of the requirements of the Commandments, each one starting with " We should fear and love God and," etc. *Love* to our neighbor springs out of supreme love to God (Matt. xxii. 37-40; Rom. xiii. 8; 1 Tim. i. 5). **As ye would that men should do to you, do ye also to them likewise**—notice that this covers much more than

just those things you might wish in this or that instance; it denotes a habitual *manner* of life and action. Notice, too, the *positive* form of the rule—not "refrain from," but "*do* thus." This is the Saviour's Golden Rule, but the Saviour does not give it as something *new;* for the law and the prophets had given it before (Matt. vii. 12). We find it, indeed, in quite a number of the Pagan writers of Greece, Rome, India and China, echoes of God's fundamental truth. Yet there is a depth here in our Lord's word to which theirs did not reach; for as ADAM CLARKE well says, "None but he whose heart is filled with love to God and all mankind can keep this precept, either in its *spirit* or *letter*." We must, therefore, go to the Fulfiller and be made complete in Him. "In Cicero and Plato, and other such writers," said AUGUSTINE, "I meet with many things acutely said, and things that awaken some fervor and desire; but in none of them do I find the words, Come unto me all ye that labor and are heavy laden, and I will give you rest"— rest even from the heavy laden consciousness of not having kept this perfect law.

32–34. And if ye love them that love you, what thank have ye? for even sinners love those that love them. And if ye do good to them that do good to you, what thank have ye? for even sinners do the same. And if ye lend to them of whom ye hope to receive, what thank have ye? even sinners lend to sinners, to receive again as much.

32–34. **If ye love them that love you,** and in other respects do to others just as they do to you, what is it, after all, but selfishness, and the working of the merely natural heart. **Even sinners,** those who make no profession even of any better character than what they have by nature, **do the same.** "No man," says STIER, "is so wicked and abandoned, no sinner is so essentially devilish, as not to have some objects of his selfish election, of whom he may say—I love them because they love me."

But Jesus is speaking to His disciples, and showing them what *they* are to be. Christians are to have better principles and live on a higher plane than merely natural men. **What thank have ye?** What is your grace, wherein are ye above man's common nature? Not only God, but men too, expect more of Christians than of others. Let them not be disappointed in *you* !

> 35. But love your enemies, and do *them* good, and lend, never despairing; and your reward shall be great, and ye shall be sons of the Most High: for he is kind toward the unthankful and evil.

35. Here the teaching of vers. 27 and 28 is reiterated. **Love—do good—lend.** The first embraces the other two: or the last two are exhibitions of the first. "Love" that does nothing and helps nobody is just as dead as faith without works. Light must shine; and love must lend a helping hand, and not an empty one. See the parable of the Good Samaritan.

Never despairing is the interesting rendering of the Revised Version. God will requite you if man does not. There will be a **reward** for the character and acts here inculcated, and it will be **great**, even as is its giver: **and ye shall be,** herein, **sons of the Most High,** children of God, which is far above being children of Abraham, a fleshly relation of which your teachers are wont to boast! Here the only-begotten Son teaches them what is the spirit of God, and must characterize them that are His. (Compare John i. 12.) **He is kind to the unthankful and evil.** So He witnesses (Acts xiv. 15-17; xvii. 24-28; Rom. i. 19, 20) His loving care for mankind, and would bring them to know, love and serve Him, and thus become happy. "God gives indeed, without our prayer even to the wicked also their daily bread" (*Luther's Catechism*). See Matt. v. 45.

36. Be ye merciful, even as your Father is merciful.

36. **Be** should read *become* (γίνεσθε). We are to *become* by grace what our Heavenly Father is by nature. **Merciful.** In the parallel passage of Matthew (ver. 48) the word is *perfect*. This shows wherein we may imitate God—in being *merciful*. It is in His moral perfections that God is imitable, and that we may reflect His image, showing ourselves to be, indeed, His sons.

37, 38. And judge not, and ye shall not be judged: and condemn not, and ye shall not be condemned: release, and ye shall be released: give, and it shall be given unto you: good measure, pressed down, shaken together, running over, shall they give into your bosom. For with what measure ye meet it shall be measured to you again.

37. **And judge not.** Notice the connection in which this warning is put and compare it with the fifth beatitude and the fifth petition of the Lord's Prayer and our Lord's comments thereon (Matt. vi. 12, 14, 15). The faculty of judging, comparing and deciding is inherent in the human mind as God made it, and this cannot mean to ignore or destroy that faculty. Indeed, on the contrary, it is divinely appealed to, as well as allowed (see Luke xii. 57; John vii. 24); and Is. v. 20 pronounces woe upon those who, failing to discriminate, bring about confusion. Further, it is God's prerogative to judge finally (Ps. xciv. 1, 2, 23; Rom. ii. 16; iii. 9; xii. 19; Heb. xii. 23; James v. 9), and meanwhile "the powers that be are ordained of God" for this purpose (John x. 35; Rom. xiii.; 1 Pet. ii. 13, 14; and Matt. v. 25, 26), and there is a proper and official judgment in the Church (1 Cor. v. 12; vi. 2-5). The prohibition, therefore, cannot be against such judgment; it must therefore be against personal, private, unauthorized, unloving judg-

ment of one another—such, for example, as is spoken of in Rom. xiv. 3, 4, 10, 13; Col. ii. 16; James iv. 11, 12. "*Judge not*—without knowledge, love, necessity. Yet a dog is to be accounted a dog, and a swine a swine; see ver. 5" (BENGEL). "It is a sad abuse to make this passage teach us to be as tolerant of falsehood and wrong as of truth and right. It would then contradict the prophets (Is. v. 20; Ezek. xiii. 10), and condemn Jesus Himself, Matt. xxiii. 14, 33" (THOLUCK). "But he here forbids the evil eye, which ever prefers to apply the inward rule of right to *others* rather than to self. As ye have not been *judged*, but *forgiven*, so deal with others after God's forgiving love" (STIER). "Do not constitute yourselves judges of others' faults" (MEYER). "The way to righteousness lies in finding, not others' sins, but our own" (OLSHAUSEN). **And ye shall not be judged.** For your judgment of others recoils on yourselves, since you are of the same nature with them, sinners, imperfect, exposed to criticism. (See Rom. ii. 1–3.) This reminder of themselves, as like other men, liable to be tempted and to sin, and indeed in many things offending (Jas. iii. 2), this recollection, that we are all dust and children of wrath by nature as Adam's children, seems to be the spirit of the various propositions of these verses. We awake in others the spirit and temper we ourselves show. Love begets love, and hate produces hate in return. The recompenses here promised refer, it seems, both to this world and to the world to come.

38. If it be asked who are referred to in **shall they give,** we answer that the proposition is generic, and refers to all who give in return, whether men or angels (Matt. xxiv. 31). **Into your bosom** is explained by the loose robe then worn, gathered by a belt at the waist and so affording a capacious pocket in the folds on the bosom.

We can afford to be like our Heavenly Father; we will lose nothing thereby; but we cannot afford to be called Christians and live as sinners.

Some persons think they cannot afford to give, cannot be liberal, for fear of future need. But here, and everywhere, the Lord teaches that "the liberal soul shall be made fat." It is, indeed, a very low motive: but it is one set before us in the Scriptures, one that ought to move those who think much of such a motive —that it *pays* to be liberal, merciful, loving!

39. And he spake also a parable unto them, Can the blind guide the blind? shall they not both fall into a pit?

39. Luke omits all that is found in Matt. vi. Among the many things spoken unto them was **a parable** which Matthew relates in another connection (Matt. xv. 14) and Luke sees fit to record here. The natural meaning is plain. So a spiritual **guide** must be one who sees spiritual things and knows the way. The professed spiritual teachers of that day were not such. (See on Matt. xv. 14.)

40. The disciple is not above his master: but every one when he is perfected shall be as his master.

40. Further statement and illustration of the same principle. **The master**—schoolmaster, teacher—is the guide of whoever stands to him in the relation of **disciple**, learner; and the latter is **not above**, over, superior to, the former, else their respective positions will be reversed; the most to be expected, desired, aimed at, is that he be **as his master,** up to him, equal to him. Then, so far as that school is concerned, he is **perfected,** the result aimed at is attained, defects have been removed and what was lacking supplied. Jesus is the Teacher sent

from God (John iii. 2), and it is for us, as His disciples, to become like Him.

See James iii. 1 ; and learn also to answer correctly the oft-asked question whether we shall have unconverted teachers in Sunday School—or anywhere teachers of what they do not know and love and live !

> 41, 42. And why beholdest thou the mote that is in thy brother's eye, but considerest not the beam that is in thine own eye? Or how canst thou say to thy brother, Brother, let me cast out the mote that is in thine eye, when thou thyself beholdest not the beam that is in thine own eye? Thou hypocrite, cast out first the beam out of thine own eye, and then shalt thou see clearly to cast out the mote that is in thy brother's eye.

41, 42. See on Matt. vii. 3–5. "Thou that teachest another, teachest thou not thyself?" (Rom. ii. 21).

> 43, 44. For there is no good tree that bringeth forth corrupt fruit; nor again a corrupt tree that bringeth forth good fruit. For each tree is known by its own fruit. For of thorns men do not gather figs, nor of a bramble bush gather they grapes.

43, 44. See on Matt. vii. 16–20. A good tree may occasionally have on it specimens of poor, imperfect fruit, but this is exceptional, and not characteristic of the tree. The tree bears the fruit, and the fruit marks the tree.

> 45. The good man out of the good treasure of his heart bringeth forth that which is good ; and the evil *man* out of the evil *treasure* bringeth forth that which is evil : for out of the abundance of the heart his mouth speaketh.

45. As the application of the principle enunciated was to teachers (vers. 39, 40, ff.), so here, going away from the figure of a tree, we come to what **his mouth speaketh**, and learn that this proceeds, as much as a tree's fruits from its roots, from **the abundance of the heart.** What his heart is full of, that he, the teacher (and, indeed, every man), **bringeth forth**, uttereth. **The good man,** as well as **the evil man,** is known by what he bringeth forth,

what **his mouth speaketh.** See—but not so much with reference to teachers—Matt. xii. 33–37. The same truth has many applications. (Comp. James i. 26; iii. 1–12; iv. 11, 12; v. 12.)

46. And why call ye me, Lord, Lord, and do not the things which I say?

46. If He is **Lord,** He has a right to command, and it is for us to obey. To say **Lord, Lord,** and at the same time be disobedient, is to prove false, to " say and do not." A profession of the lips without a corresponding confession of the life, marks a hypocrite. (See on Matt. vii. 22, 23.)

47–49. Every one that cometh unto me, and heareth my words, and doeth them, I will shew you to whom he is like : he is like a man building a house, who digged and went deep, and laid a foundation upon the rock : and when a flood arose, the stream brake against that house, and could not shake it: because it had been well builded. But he that heareth, and doeth not, is like a man that built a house upon the earth without a foundation; against which the stream brake, and straightway it fell in; and the ruin of that house was great.

47–49. See on Matt. vii. 24–27. Every one **that cometh unto me.** There is much exhortation to come to Jesus. Whoever does so must not only **hear** His words, but **do them.** (See Jas. i. 22–25.)

The Lord taught much by showing likenesses. All the parables are of this nature. Building a character is very much like **building a house.** He not only **digged** but **went deep,** going on down to **the rock.** And his house, because thus **well builded,** was proof against the storm, so that it **could not shake it.** But his house, and his hopes, who built **upon the earth without a foundation,** when the trial came, **fell in,** collapsed, and proved a **great ruin.** (See the First Epistle of John, especially i. 6, 7; ii. 3–6, 29; iii. 14–24; v. 1–4.)

CHAPTER VII.

See on Matt. viii. 5-13.

<small>1. After he had ended all his sayings in the ears of the people, he entered into Capernaum.</small>

1. Luke brings Jesus directly from the scene of the Sermon on the Mount to Capernaum, having previously (v. 12-16) given the healing of the leper, which Matthew records here. **Entered into Capernaum.** Here is one of the marks that distinguish the healing of the nobleman's son (John iv. 46-54) from this of the centurion's servant. That was done when Jesus was at Cana, and was a much earlier occurrence than this.

<small>2. And a certain centurion's servant, who was dear unto him, was sick and at the point of death.</small>

2. Four centurions have favorable mention in the New Testament; this one, that one at the cross, Cornelius (Acts x.), and Julius, Paul's guard to Rome. It was this man's **servant** that **was sick, and ready** (about) **to die.** Matthew says he was paralyzed and an acute sufferer. Some forms of what was then classed under paralysis were, we are told, attended with great suffering and speedy death. This servant **was dear unto** his master, and, when we consider the rugged character generally characterizing the Roman soldier, we are struck by this tenderness of feeling of the superior to the inferior.

<small>3. And when he heard concerning Jesus, he sent unto him elders of the Jews, asking him that he would come and save his servant.</small>

3. The centurion had **heard of Jesus**, and was not inattentive to the reports of His wonderful teachings and works. He had likely heard of His healing power, and of His demeanor both there in Capernaum, and wherever Jesus went; knew, perhaps, of the healing of the nobleman's son. **He sent unto him the elders of the Jews.** Luke gives more particulars. Matthew merely says, "He went," on the common principle that what one does through another he may be said to do himself. Thus we say Noah built the Ark, and Solomon built the Temple. This mode of speech is very common. Such simple discrepancies between the various narrators of the same thing serve rather to confirm than invalidate the truthfulness of the narrative. The Roman soldier probably thought that as Jesus was a Jewish teacher, his suit would be served by employing a deputation of distinguished men of that people. Self-interest, too, would impel these men to seek to please this captain. But we need not impute unworthy motives to them. **That he would come.** If this was the centurion's request, he recalled it afterwards (ver. 7) as asking too much. Perhaps he personally only asked that Jesus would **save** (heal) **his servant**, whilst those sent added to this that He would come to the house.

4, 5. And they, when they came to Jesus, besought him earnestly, saying, He is worthy that thou shouldest do this for him: for he loveth our nation, and himself built us our synagogue.

4, 5. **Besought him instantly** (urgently). They entered fully into the matter entrusted to them; and they added **that he was worthy** of Jesus' good offices. So they estimated him, judging from their own feelings. **For he loveth our nation.** That would go far with the Jews of that day. There was not much love lost between them and the Romans, whom they looked upon as the subjectors of God's people, and from whose yoke they thought the expected Messiah would deliver them. **Himself built us our synagogue.** Yes, "built it himself," out of his own funds! It is not said or necessarily implied, though it is not unlikely, that he was a proselyte, of that class " whom the providence of God had so wonderfully prepared in all the great cities of the Greek and Roman world as a link of communication between Gentile and Jew, in contact with both, holding to the first by their race, and to the last by their religion; and who must have greatly helped to the ultimate fusion of both into one Christian church " (TRENCH). A man who builds a church in these days is generally well thought of, especially by those for whom he builds it. There are other instances in history of Gentiles doing this for Jews. We gather from the whole narrative that this captain was wealthy, liberal, and religiously inclined.

Here we have a beautiful instance of intercessory prayer. If Jesus could heal from a distance, as evidently the centurion believed, He could also know, without seeing or being told, what was going on at a distance. And so He does. But we are instructed and permitted in everything, by prayer and supplication, with thanksgiving, to make our requests known to God, and taught to pray one for another, and to agree together for what to pray. This faith of the centurion, recorded for our instruction and imitation, was *prayerful*.

<small>6, 7. And Jesus went with them. And when he was now not far from the house, the centurion sent friends to him, saying unto him, Lord, trouble not thyself: for I am not worthy that thou shouldest come under my roof: wherefore neither thought I myself worthy to come unto thee: but say the word, and my servant shall be healed.</small>

6, 7. Jesus went with them. On the contrary, when

the nobleman cried, "Sir, come down, ere my child die," as if the Lord's bodily presence was necessary to His putting forth healing power, Jesus never stirred to go, but simply said, "Go thy way, thy son liveth!" **When he was now not far from the house the centurion,** finding that Jesus was approaching, felt called in courtesy to go and meet Him, yet thought himself unworthy, and therefore **sent friends** to represent him and say, **trouble not thyself,** this is more than I expected; **for I am not worthy that thou shouldest enter under my roof.** What an awe of Jesus' greatness possessed this man! Remember, too, that he was a Roman, an officer, and a man of wealth and influence, whereas Jesus was a Jew and of obscure descent, and had only His character and works to recommend Him. This centurion must have been a man of more than ordinary thoughtfulness and penetration. Further he sends word, **Not even did I think myself worthy to come unto thee.** He felt as Peter did when he cried, "Depart from me; for I am a sinful man, O Lord!" (ver. 8). His estimate of the greatness of Jesus' power and holiness was accompanied with a correspondingly low estimate of himself; there seemed a distance between himself and Jesus, greater than he had ever felt in the contemplation of any other character. This faith of the centurion was *humble;* and he realized a fulfilment of that principle of the divine government, "He that humbleth himself shall be exalted!" Further his faith was confident. **Say in a word.** Give but the command, **and my servant shall be healed.** How confidently he speaks; here is no wavering; no doubt.

8. For I also am a man set under authority, having under myself soldiers: and I say to this one, Go, and he goeth; and to another, Come, and he cometh; and to my servant, Do this, and he doeth it.

8. For I also am a man set under authority, or, supplying the ellipsis involved in this form of construction in the Greek, we might paraphrase it thus: "And I speak thus confidently not without reason; for I understand the nature of authority, and the relation of commander and commanded, being myself under the orders of higher officers." **Having under me soldiers** also, so that it is in my province now to obey and now to command and enforce obedience. **And I say unto one, Go, and he goeth; to another, Come, and he cometh.** Whatever orders I, as captain, give, are sure to be obeyed, according to the strictness of Roman discipline. **And to my servant,** I, as master, say, **Do this, and he doeth it.** Command then the evil disease, which is subject to thy power, and it will as readily, it must as obediently, obey thy mandate. The centurion seems imbued with the spirit of the Psalmist, who declares concerning the word of the Lord, "All are thy servants" (Ps. cxix. 91). He attributes to Jesus here the attributes of Jehovah, who "spake and it was done; he commanded and it stood fast" (Ps. xxxiii. 9). "The word of the Lord abideth forever" (1 Pet. i. 23).

9. And when Jesus heard these things, he marvelled at him, and turned and said unto the multitude that followed him, I say unto you, I have not found so great faith, no, not in Israel.

9. Jesus **marvelled at him**, wondered at such faith, and that in a Gentile. In His own country, and among His own kin, he marvelled because of their *unbelief* (Mark vi. 6). So **great faith** as this of the Roman centurion He had **not found, no, not in Israel,** where their history and their privileges would have led to the expectation of faith, if anywhere. Here is another and later illustration of what Jesus said to His fellow-citizens of Nazareth, that

geographical contiguity and hereditary descent are not necessarily followed by faith and its fruits, yet are worthless without them; that opportunity is not of itself followed by benefit; that outside of Israel sometimes God's most favored ones are found. Faith is the gift of God, and in this centurion God had found a suitable place for that gift. Jesus was so impressed that He **turned him about and said unto the people that followed him** what he thought of the centurion's faith. He held it up to the Jews as an example.

A Roman and a soldier outstrips favored Israel in faith. Perhaps at the judgment Socrates will rise up, to condemn members of our Christian Churches. Not by privileges, but "by grace ye are saved, through faith."

Observe in this account three estimates of the centurion's character: first, his own, *not worthy* because a Gentile and because a sinner; second, the Jewish estimate, *worthy* because he had built a Jewish synagogue, the highest encomium on character which a Jewish elder could pass on a Gentile outcast; third, Jesus' estimate, *worthy because of his faith*, and needing no commendation from Jewish elders, but himself an example and a rebuke to them.

10. And they that were sent, returning to the house, found the servant whole.

10. **Returning to the house,** the elders of the Jews and the friends **found the servant whole that had been sick.** According to his faith it was done unto the centurion. Through another's faith the sick was healed. "The prayer of faith shall save the sick" (James v. 15).

11. And it came to pass soon afterwards, that he went to a city called Nain; and his disciples went with him, and a great multitude.

11. **Soon afterwards,** that is, after the healing of the

centurion's servant at Capernaum, **he went to a city called Nain,** a place in the plain of Esdraelon, near Mt. Tabor, not far from Endor, about twenty-five miles south of Capernaum. Though here called a "city," it was a little place that would never have been heard of but for the events of our lesson, which have made it never to be forgotten. Dr. Thompson says there are no antiquities there now but tombs! It was probably evening, as it was a long day's walk from Capernaum, and as that was the usual time for funerals, the custom being to bury the dead the day of their death, or very soon afterward. **His disciples went with him and a great multitude,** besides, from Capernaum and thereabouts. It would have been strange if crowds had not followed such a man. Why, representatives of earthly governments, who are not specially wonderful in looks, words, or works, but manifestly are men like those about them, are often beset with curious crowds, and can scarcely be alone except as they shut themselves up from such following. How much more then would Jesus, like whom man never spake or wrought, be followed by the multitudes. So there were plenty of witnesses to His deeds and of His teachings. Jesus before Pilate said, "I have spoken openly to the world," "In secret spake I nothing."

12. Now when he drew near to the gate of the city, behold, there was carried out one that was dead, the only son of his mother, and she was a widow; and much people of the city was with her.

12. **Near to the gate of the city.** It was a walled town. **Behold,** there was something to see. The little town had been unusually stirred that day. **There was carried out one that was dead,** towards the burial place, which was always, except in the case of the royal descendants of David, outside of the city limits. So are our cemeteries.

usually. This was a peculiarly sad funeral. It was a young man that had died, and he was **the only son of his mother.** Oh, how her heart's affections had twined around the only son. " Mourning as for an only son" was an expression for the greatest sorrow. And to add to her desolation in that hour **she was a widow.** She had previously followed her husband to the tomb, and probably been looking upon her son as the stay of her increasing years, but now he is gone, snatched away so remorselessly by grim death. Though no family was left to accompany her in this trying hour, **much people of the city was with her,** moved alike by respect and compassion for her. This death was one of those that move the whole community and bring them out to the funeral.

So then here were two large companies about meeting just outside the city, plenty of witnesses on both sides. It was a grand opportunity for the gospel, and, as we shall see, it was well improved.

13. And when the Lord saw her, he had compassion on her, and said unto her, Weep not.

13. **And when the Lord** (a term applied to Jesus most frequently by Luke) **saw her,** the chief mourner, knowing in Himself her history and circumstances and all about this death, **he had compassion on her.** (See Heb. ii. 18; iv. 15.) His was a heart of love and pity; His sensibilities were undimmed by any sin; it was pity brought Him from heaven to earth. So here there needed no intercession for the woman. Jesus was self-moved in this act of pity and power. **And said unto her, Weep not.** For any ordinary person to have done the like of that would have been heartless, rude and insulting. But the way in which it was done, the tones of voice in which the words were uttered, the crowd that was attending

Him who thus spoke, who (it now flashed on their minds) perhaps was the wonderful teacher of whom they had already heard something, everything conspired to make the poor woman and those with her feel that this "Weep not" was a word of gracious power that would be joyfully enforced by what was to follow. Quicker than it takes us to tell it, the greatest sorrow was turning to joy.

"Weep not," is a weak, cold, presumptuous word coming from a fellow-creature and fellow-sufferer: but coming from Jesus it is a word of gracious power, and has dried many an overflowing eye and comforted many a sad heart. When the kingdom for which we pray is fully established and triumphant, "God shall wipe away all tears from their eyes" (Rev. vii. 17). Of this glorious result we now have a foretaste. Christianity is not moping or sorrowful. No; it is "glad tidings of great joy:" it says, and says with power, "Weep not!"

14. And he came nigh and touched the bier: and the bearers stood still. And he said, Young man, I say unto thee, Arise.

14. Look now! **He came and touched the bier** on which the dead body lay, wrapped in cloths, but not encased in a coffin as we bury. They were accustomed to lay away the bodies of their dead in built tombs or sepulchres cut out of the rock; and for this no tight box was used. Jesus' presence itself possessed commanding power, and, when He came and laid His hand on the bier, **the bearers stood still**, awaiting something unusual to follow. Now hear! He addressed not them, but spake directly to the dead; not as an orator in a funeral oration apostrophizing the dead, but as He which calleth things that are not as though they were. He said, **Young man, I say unto thee, Arise.** "Unto thee!"

Why, wasn't he dead? Had not the soul left this body? Yet, here is the word, "I say unto thee, Arise!" Time and space are relative notions. They hedge around this mortal life; but are they anything to spirits or to God?

> 15. And he that was dead sat up, and began to speak. And he gave him to his mother.

15. **And he that was dead** heard the voice of the Son of God (John v. 25-29) and **sat up, and began to speak**, giving abundant evidence that he was no longer dead; and this before crowds of witnesses, many of whom, doubtless, were living when Luke wrote his Gospel, and were able to say, "Yes, I was there and saw and heard it all!"

How mysterious the relation between soul and body! How easily the departed spirit returns to its former house, when bidden by Jesus' word! It has been observed that Jairus' daughter was raised to life from the couch on which she had fallen "asleep;" the widow's son, from the bier on which he was being borne to the grave; and Lazarus, from the tomb in which he had lain four days already, exciting in his sister's breast the fear that putrefaction had already begun; and that one was a child, or youth, another a young man, a third, a mature man. It will be just as easy for the same divine word of power to call back to the bodies of the saints, now gone to the dust, then risen incorruptible, their immortal spirits, for a time separated from them and waiting to be thus glorified with their bodies. Jesus is the victor over death, leaving the monster no permanent triumph over either body or soul. Who, then, will doubt or deny the resurrection of the body?

And he delivered him to his mother. How beautiful in its simplicity! Jesus is the God of the widow. A mark of pure and undefiled religion is to visit the fatherless and widows in their affliction (Jas. i. 27). This lad could serve God, to whom he owed his renewed life, better at home, providing for his own house, than anywhere else.

As the widow knew her son when raised as well as she had before, as Jairus' daughter and Lazarus looked not strange, but familiar, to their kinsfolk and friends, so *we shall know each other there and then*, when we shall either in a moment, the twinkling of an eye, living, be changed into our glorified state, or be raised from our graves incorruptible (1 Thess. iv. 13-18).

It is supposed, and properly enough, that in the case of this young man, new spiritual life also followed, by God's grace, upon his renewed natural life. To quicken the soul from its death of sin, to raise from moral and spiritual death, and make men "new creatures in Christ Jesus," is a greater miracle than this of the raising of the son of the widow of Nain. "Greater works than these shall ye do, because I go unto the Father" (John xiv. 12). Yet it has become so common as not to excite surprise; an everyday miracle ceases to be a "miracle:" how few, too, mark and are impressed by the power of God thus set forth in His church!

To the dead Jesus spake, and said, "Arise." What inability is there greater than death? Yet at Jesus' word "he that was dead sat up and began to speak!" Do not say you are not able to obey the word of the Lord Jesus, bidding you arise from unbelief and sin and walk in newness of life (John v. 25; Eph. ii. 1). Simply believe and obey.

16. And fear took hold on all: and they glorified God, saying, A great prophet is arisen among us: and, God hath visited his people.

16. **And fear took hold on all.** Naturally enough.

Suppose you had been in that crowd of witnesses; how would you have felt? Did funeral ever end thus? The Wonder-worker had cured lepers and paralytics and all kinds of disease; but now first He proves Himself master of death. **They glorified God.** Evidently His almighty hand was in this work. **A great prophet,** like Elijah and Elisha (who were called "great" prophets and also raised the dead), **is risen up among us.** Yet we see a vast difference between Jesus' authoritative word, " I say unto you," with its instant effects, and the comparatively difficult, laborious, and manifestly dependent efforts of those Old Testament prophets who, calling upon God, raised the dead (1 Kings xvii. 17–24; 2 Kings v. 18–37). Jesus speaks as the Prince of Life! **God hath visited his people.** (Comp. i. 54, 55, 68, 78, 79.) This was more true than they thought when they used such words. The Day-spring from on high had visited them—the greater than Solomon, than the great prophets, than the Temple. God Himself had, indeed, visited His people, and they were beholding His glory.

17. And this report went forth concerning him in the whole of Judæa, and all the region round about.

17. **This report** expressed in the preceding verse, and the account of His raising the widow's son from the dead, **went forth concerning him in the whole of Judæa,** away to the south, and **all the region,** of Galilee, **round about.** And Samaria, too, must have heard it.

18. And the disciples of John told him all these things.

18. The news reached John the Baptist, away down in the prison of Machærus east of the Dead Sea. (See iii. 19, 20.) How long John had been in prison we cannot certainly tell; some say a number of months, others a little more than a year—long enough, however, to wear

the spirit of the prophet, who had all his life been used to the freedom of "the deserts" in which he grew up. From a year to a year and a half had passed since Jesus' baptism, in which time Jesus had preached and wrought many miracles, in both Judæa and Galilee, the raising of the widow's son at Nain being among the latest of His wonderful works. **All these things** were reported to John by his disciples. (See on Matt. xi. 2-19.)

19-23. And John calling unto him two of his disciples sent them to the Lord, saying, Art thou he that cometh, or look we for another? And when the men were come unto him, they said, John the Baptist hath sent us unto thee, saying, Art thou he that cometh, or look we for another? In that hour he cured many of diseases and plagues and evil spirits; and on many that were blind he bestowed sight. And he answered and said unto them, Go your way, and tell John what things ye have seen and heard; the blind receive their sight, the lame walk, the lepers are cleansed, and the deaf hear, the dead are raised up, the poor have good tidings preached to them. And blessed is he, whosoever shall find none occasion of stumbling in me.

19-23. See on Matt. xi. 2-19.

19. Thereupon he sent **two**—a "certain two"—**of his disciples** on an embassy to Jesus, inquiring, **Art thou he that should come, or look we for another?** In view of John's mission and the way he fulfilled it, the query arises, How are we to understand this embassy and question of the Baptist? Some say it was meant entirely for the benefit of John's disciples, that they might hear from Jesus Himself what John had often told them of Him, and so be led to faith in Jesus and a following of Him. This view is adopted by Dr. Schæffer in Vol. I. of this Commentary. But against it is the whole tenor of the narrative, with the impression it makes on an ordinary reader, together with the evident fact that the Lord's answer was sent to *John*, as the real propounder of the question.

Another explanation is that John did not think Jesus was conducting the affairs of the kingdom they had both preached as at hand, as vigorously as He should, and that the question was intended to urge Jesus to a more open and pronounced declaration of Himself and to show some of that *judgment* which John had declared (Matt. iii. 12) He would execute; that John undertook, as Peter sometimes afterwards did, to instruct the Lord *how* to do His work. Another explanation, which seems to us the best, though not without difficulties, is that John had fallen into a state of depression and gloom, such as his situation was well suited to produce, and that his question is a despondent outcry, " Lord, I believe; help thou mine unbelief!" Such contrasts, from preëminent boldness and outspoken testimony, to impatient despondency and shadows of doubt, are quite consistent with man's feeble nature, are psychologically quite explicable, and have appeared in some of the greatest characters of both common and Bible history. " What wonder," says CANON FARRAR, after fervidly reciting the situation, "if the eye of the caged eagle began to film?" John, who had gone before Jesus "in the spirit and power of Elijah," was here too in his despondency and impatience like the great Prophet of Fire when, fleeing from Jezebel, he rested under the broom tree (1 Kings xix. 1–8), thoroughly broken in spirit.

21. Luke adds the important statement that **in that hour,** right before John's ambassadors, Jesus **cured many** of various afflictions, giving them fresh evidences to report to their master.

24–28. And when the messengers of John were departed, he began to say unto the multitude concerning John, What went ye out into the wilderness to behold? a reed shaken with the wind? But what went ye out to see? a man clothed in soft raiment? Behold, they which are gorgeously apparelled, and live delicately, are in kings' courts. But what went ye out to see? a prophet? Yea, I say unto you, and much more than a prophet. This is he of whom it is written,

Behold, I send my messenger before thy face,
Who shall prepare thy way before thee.
I say unto you, Among them that are born of women there is none greater than John: yet he that is but little in the kingdom of God is greater than he.

24. Not until **the messengers of John were departed** did Jesus utter the grand testimony to the Baptist that follows. He would have them, who were already devoted to John, neither think more highly of their Master than they ought to think, nor cleave longer to him as their highest teacher (see His call to them in ver. 23), nor would He have these words of eulogy carried to John's ear. John had rightly said to them (John iii. 30) of himself that he "must decrease." But it was becoming and necessary that Jesus should testify to John's mission, whom "all men" had received as a prophet (Mark xi. 32), and who had clearly announced that he was only the forerunner of the Messiah, whom he spoke of as "standing among you" (John i. 26), right at hand. Jesus must own John's testimony and work, nor should this last desponding question of John's operate against his previous testimony.

29, 30. And all the people when they heard, and the publicans, justified God, being baptized with the baptism of John. But the Pharisees and the lawyers rejected for themselves the counsel of God, being not baptized of him.

29, 30. Most older and some later commentators regard these verses as a historical statement by Luke introductory to what follows. MEYER, with others, regards them as a continuation of Jesus' words, noting the different reception John's mission met with and preparing the way for His following words (vers. 31–35). This view is supported by the rejection at ver. 31 of the words, "And the Lord said," which appear in the Auth. Ver., thus leaving the whole as a continuous discourse of the Lord. **All the people,** the masses, **and the publicans,** usually classified with "sinners," **justified God,** acknowledged God's righteousness and method in the affairs of His Kingdom, by **being baptized** of him, by submitting to John's baptism, but **the Pharisees and the lawyers,** the men of the land, the Scribes refused this submission (see Matt. iii. 5-7, ff.; Mark. xi. 27-33), and in their self-will thereby **rejected for themselves,** as far as they were concerned, the **counsel of God,** which in itself cannot be overturned. God's counsel stands, but we may sometimes make it inoperative, in its original purpose, toward us.

31-35. Whereunto then shall I liken the men of this generation, and to what are they like? They are like unto children that sit in the marketplace, and call one to another; which say, We piped unto you, and ye did not dance; we wailed, and ye did not weep. For John the Baptist is come eating no bread nor drinking wine; and ye say, He hath a devil. The Son of man is come eating and drinking; and ye say, Behold, a gluttonous man, and a winebibber, a friend of publicans and sinners? And wisdom is justified of all her children.

35. **And wisdom**—an attribute of God (Job. xii. 13; xxviii. 20; Prov. viii. 14-36; Rom. xi. 33), possible in a limited degree to man, the gift of God to those who seek it from Him (Jas. i. 5), here personified—**is justified,** approved, counted right (see "justified God," ver. 29, above), acknowledged, accredited, **by all her children,** all who are of her, like her, by all who are wise. Whether in John or in Jesus wisdom was shown, she was recognized and approved by the wise. In Matt. xi. 19 the reading is "by her works;" all her works do praise and attest her. So do her children, in every instance. Wisdom's children know when to dance and when to weep—in harmony with their mother's leading.

36. And one of the Pharisees desired him that he would eat with him. And he entered into the Pharisee's house, and sat down to meat.

There is an account by the other three Evangelists

(Matt. xxvi. 6–13; Mark xiv. 3–9; John xii. 1–11) of an occasion in some respects similar to that which here follows; but examination will show that to have occurred at a *later period*, in a *different locality*, and with *circumstances so differing* as to prove it not the same occasion of which Luke here gives account. That the name of the host on both these occasions was Simon, and of the woman Mary, is no proof of their identity, these names being very common. There are at least fifteen distinct persons mentioned in the New Testament by the name Simon. Moreover, the tradition, to which the Romish Church holds, that the woman of our narrative was Mary Magdalene, cannot be sustained. There is no proof that Mary Magdalene had been a woman of loose character; and our searching times are beginning to lift off from her name this reproach. All we can certainly determine about the locality where this scene occurred is that it was in Galilee. That other anointing took place in Bethany, near Jerusalem, and just before the close of our Lord's ministry.

36. **One of the Pharisees.** The Pharisees were prominent among the ruling aristocracy. They felt themselves to be the preservers of Jewish orthodoxy. They became the most violent opposers of the lowly Nazarene, but at this time their opposition had not become so pronounced and violent as it became later in the history. (But see on vi. 11.) This one, Simon, seems not to have had his mind as yet fully made up about Jesus, and **desired him that he would eat with him,** perhaps in order to observe Him more closely. Simon seems to have invited Jesus not from any bad motive; there probably was some feeling and show of patronage on his part towards one who was becoming so illustrious among men. Jesus **went into the Pharisee's house,** according to His custom to go where

He was bidden. (Comp. 1 Cor. x. 27.) No matter whether it was chief of the Pharisees or chief of the publicans, man of social standing or of proscribed class, Jesus was ready to go and eat with him, to do him good. One place on earth was as much home to Him as any other; and He came "eating and drinking" (ver. 34), in contrast with the ascetic John. **Sat down to meat.** This phrase is a single word in the Greek and means *reclined:* the Eastern custom of lying down with the head resting on the left arm, and so partaking of their meals, had been introduced into Palestine, and was common at this time. The reclining tables were disposed around a hollow square, open on one side, from which the servants waited on the guests.

37, 38. And behold, a woman which was in the city, a sinner; and when she knew that he was sitting at meat in the Pharisee's house, she brought an alabaster cruse of ointment, and standing behind at his feet, weeping, she began to wet his feet with her tears, and wiped them with the hair of her head, and kissed his feet, and anointed them with the ointment.

37, 38. Now a notable scene occurred which has been deemed worthy a place in the Sacred Scriptures. **Behold, a woman in the city,** whom, probably, we would call a woman of the town, known to all as a **sinner,** made her way into the house and hall of the feast. A man's house, in those days and places, we are told, was not his castle. He lived with almost open doors, according to the everywhere prevalent laws of hospitality; and this was especially so when an entertainment was going on. The presence, therefore, of uninvited persons, sitting on benches around the room, was not uncommon; and the same thing has been noticed by travellers at a later day. So, **when she knew that he was sitting at meat in the Pharisee's house,** this poor woman, who had evidently not only heard of Him, but had herself heard Him—perhaps heard those gracious words of broad invitation, spoken shortly before this (Matt. xi. 28–30), " Come unto me all ye that labor and are heavy laden, and I will give you rest,"—and, hearing, had believed and found a sense of forgiveness poured into her sad heart, now boldly made her way to the Pharisee's house, and found no difficulty in gaining admittance. True, for a *woman* to come thus was out of place; but, besides having become accustomed to unwomanly boldness, she never thought of that; she made nothing of appearances; her heart was so full of getting near to the Saviour and of hearing from His lips the blessing her poor heart had already so deeply felt, that she thought of nothing else. **She brought an alabaster cruse of ointment** along, such as she had been wont to use; costly, for only such was wont to be kept in those vases of gypsum, called here "alabaster," **and standing behind at his feet,** more in sight of many of the others at table than of the Lord Himself. Before she had time to break the box of ointment on His feet, her full heart broke out in tears, and she **was weeping**, and the falling tears **began to wet his feet,** bare and unsandalled as they lay before her. Seeing this she **wiped them with the hair of her head,** which fell in loose profusion in a way that a woman who had been thinking of her appearance and reputation would not have allowed. STIER says slaves were wont to wipe their master's feet with their tresses. **And kissed his feet** from time to time, and **anointed them with the ointment**, the thing she had come expressly to do. She did all this quietly, and too much occupied to notice any eyes that were gazing at her. Moreover, Jesus seems not to have taken notice of what the woman was doing. He was waiting for the proper time for this.

39. Now when the Pharisee which had bidden him saw it, he spake within himself, saying, This man, if he were a prophet, would have perceived who and what manner of woman this is which toucheth him, that she is a sinner.

39. But His host, **the Pharisee**, whose position at the head of the table gave him opportunity to observe what was passing, was mentally taking notes, and coming to a more decided opinion concerning Jesus. **This man**, said he to himself, **if he were a prophet**, as some say, **would have perceived** (*would perceive*)—for the prophets were supposed to know intuitively everything secret—**who and what manner of** person (her character) the **woman is which toucheth him, that she is a sinner,** well known as such. But before the occasion was over Simon found He knew not only this, but the secret thoughts of the heart. Simon would have felt polluted by her touch as though she were a leper; and he did not know that Jesus was *a Saviour.*

How reputation sticks to people. This woman was known as a "sinner." Society had no room for her: the leaders of the Jewish church gathered up their robes from contact with her. But Jesus came to save, to save sinners. There was her hope and her salvation.

"She is a sinner!" Then let her come to Jesus; for He came to seek and save that which was lost, to call, not the righteous, but sinners to repentance (ch. v. 32).

40. And Jesus answering said unto him, Simon, I have somewhat to say unto thee. And he saith, Master, say on.

40. Though nothing had yet been said, Jesus knew what was passing in Simon's thought—such knowledge being one proof of His being all He professed to be —and **answering** his thought, invited his personal attention by the words, **Simon, I have somewhat to say unto thee,** and then proceeded to utter a parable in which,

kindly yet pointedly, the host and the uninvited guest were compared to the advantage of the latter. Simon's **Master** (Teacher), **say on,** indicates the Pharisee's willingness to hear, and a mind still open to conviction respecting this Jesus.

> 41, 42. A certain lender had two debtors: the one owed five hundred pence, and the other fifty. When they had not *wherewith* to pay, he forgave them both. Which of them therefore will love him most?

41, 42. **A certain lender** and **two debtors** are the persons of this parable. Of these one was ten times as much in debt as the other. The word **pence** seems to have been used by the translators for want of an English word of equivalent value to the Greek *denarion*. The larger amount was about $70 of our money, and the smaller $7. The debtors were both alike in that they **had not wherewith to pay** their debts: they were utterly bankrupt, had no assets. Whereupon the creditor freely **forgave them both,** cancelled their indebtedness. Then Simon was asked to decide the question, **which of them,** these forgiven debtors, **will love** and esteem **him,** the gracious creditor, **most?**

> 43. Simon answered, and said, He, I suppose, to whom he forgave the most. And he said unto him, Thou hast rightly judged.

43. **I suppose,** answered Simon, not seeing as yet the application of the parable, **he to whom he forgave the most**: and the Master pronounced the matter **rightly judged.** Love is here shown to come after and as a consequence of forgiveness. Is not this the reason why in our Order of Worship we first confess our transgressions unto the Lord and receive assurance of His forgiveness, and then our love glows in glorious songs and hallelujahs?

> 44-46. And turning unto the woman, he said unto Simon, Seest thou this woman? I entered into thine house, thou gavest me no water for my

feet: but she hath wetted my feet with her tears, and wiped them with her hair. Thou gavest me no kiss: but she, since the time I came in, hath not ceased to kiss my feet. My head with oil thou didst not anoint: but she hath anointed my feet with ointment.

44-46. Thereupon Jesus **turned to the woman,** still behind Him, bent over His feet in tears : the mere turning of His head would enable Him to see her and point to her. No doubt, when the Master began to speak, she listened eagerly, though with bowed head. But not to her at first were the Lord's words addressed. The parable was for the host : **And he said unto Simon, Seest thou this woman ?** Her of whom Simon was ashamed, her whom Simon disdained, whose bestowals of affection on Jesus' feet and permitted touch Simon thought discredited Jesus' claim as a prophet, her, the sinner, Jesus now makes the observed of all in the room, and is none ashamed of her bearing toward Him. This woman the Master sets before them all as a teacher, even of the Pharisee, Simon. **Seest thou,** then, **this woman ?** Look at her now, and at what she has done ; and compare thyself with her ! **I entered into thine house,** an invited guest ; it was thine to show acts of hospitality, ordinary or extraordinary. But thou wast sparing in friendship's offices. **Thou gavest me no water for my feet: but she hath wetted** (see on ver. 38) **my feet with her tears,** a heartsome flood, **and wiped them with her hair,** laying her glory (1 Cor. xi. 15) at my feet, a willing servant. **Thou gavest me no kiss,** that common mode of salutation and welcome among men—and so easily given—**but she, since the time I came in, hath not ceased to kiss my feet.** Thou gavest me not one kiss upon my face ; but she has been for quite a while repeating her kisses on my feet. **My head with oil thou didst not anoint,** as is the custom to anoint a much esteemed and highly honored guest. **But**

she hath anointed my feet with ointment more precious than oil. Thou hast not gone far in acts of hospitality; thou didst barely invite me, but hast not esteemed me. But see, in contrast, what this woman thou despisest has done.

47. Wherefore I say unto thee, Her sins, which are many, are forgiven; for she loved much: but to whom little is forgiven, *the same* loveth little.

47. Now how is it thou hast been so saving in thy bestowals, and she so lavish? How is it the uninvited guest, a woman, a sinner, has outdone Simon the Pharisee, and that in his own house? **I say unto thee** how it is; the parable just spoken explains it; **her sins, which are many, are forgiven;** therefore **she loved much,** so much that she *must* express it somehow; and here in thy house has been the expression of it! It is the *sense* of *forgiven* sin, of *great* sin, of *much* sin, but now *forgiven*, that has called forth these, to thee unseemly, but to me precious, acts of devotion. **But to whom little is forgiven,** whose sense of benefit is small, he **loveth little;** his love is comparatively cold, and finds little expression. So hast thou judged, Simon; and so it is with respect to thee and this woman. She, a great sinner, has found a great Saviour, and her heart is surcharged with His love; but thou, with perhaps less open acts of sin to be charged against thee, and with still less sense of the true nature of sin and of the depth of thine own depravity, thou feelest little need of a Saviour, thou lovest little! There are sinners and sinners. Blessed be God that there are forgiven sinners! 'Tis better to be a penitent sinner than a proud, self-satisfied Pharisee. There's much hope for the former, very little for the latter.

It is God's forgiving love that brings us to love God. "I, if I be lifted up from the earth, will draw all men unto me" (John xii. 32). "We love him because he first loved us" (1 John iv. 10, 19).

48. And he said unto her, Thy sins are forgiven.

48. All this while nothing had as yet been said to the woman. She stood there a most impressive object-lesson, explained by the Master. But now her turn was come, to hear from the Saviour's own lips that absolution which she had felt in her heart before she entered Simon's house. **Thy sins are forgiven.** She had not been mistaken in thinking so; it is the great fact of her life. What He had just said (ver. 47) of her He now says *to* her, reassuring her faith. The word rendered "are forgiven" is an irregular and peculiar form, which very excellent critics regard as the *perfect* tense, a tense denoting a past action whose effects continue. The "wherefore" at the beginning of ver. 47 does not give a reason why her sins were forgiven, but introduces the reason for her expressions of love.

49, 50. And they that sat at meat with him began to say within themselves, Who is this that even forgiveth sins? And he said unto the woman, Thy faith hath saved thee; go in peace.

49, 50. There were others at the table, and they **began to say within themselves, Who is this that even forgiveth sins?** They were amazed; for it was well understood that none could forgive sins but God. Now He who knew the woman's heart and Simon's thought was not unaware of what was passing in their minds. They were right in thinking none could forgive sins but God; yet Jesus drew not back from such assumption of power, but **said to the woman, Thy faith** (not "thy works," or "thy love") **hath saved thee; go in** (literally, *into*) **peace.** Faith, forgiveness, peace! We enter into peace through

11

forgiveness; we gain forgiveness through faith in Christ Jesus; there is no peace to the impenitent, unforgiven sinner.

In the parable above God is the creditor, and man the debtor; no man can ever pay the debt of his sins; but Jesus of Nazareth undertakes to forgive the debt, thereby clearly enough professing to be God. "Jesus paid it all." And so Paul (2 Cor. v. 19) sums up the Gospel, "To wit, that God was in Christ, reconciling the world unto himself, not imputing their trespasses unto them." As to difference of debt, we may say there are degrees of sinfulness in act, though all men have the same depraved nature. But it is not always the greatest sinner that has the greatest sense of sin; often quite otherwise. The whole tenor of the parable shows that reference is to *acknowledged* debt, sin *known* and *felt*, and *sense of forgiveness*—not so much to abstract guilt and pardon.

"Though your sins be as scarlet, they shall be as white as snow" (Is. i. 18). "If we confess our sins, God is faithful and just to forgive us our sins, and to cleanse us from all unrighteousness" (1 John i. 9). "There is forgiveness with thee that thou mayest be feared" (Ps. cxxx. 4). Hence we may say in the creed, "I believe the forgiveness of sins."

The woman of the above narrative brought an alabaster box of ointment; perhaps you can bring a box of gold, of silver, of clothing to expend upon Christ's church in Missions, Education, Church Extension, the Orphans' Home. "Inasmuch as ye did it unto one of these my brethren, even these least, ye did it unto me," the Lord will say at the last (Matt. xxv. 40).

CHAPTER VIII.

1-3. And it came to pass soon afterwards, that he went about through cities and villages, preaching and bringing the good tidings of the kingdom of God, and with him the twelve, and certain women which had been healed of evil spirits and infirmities, Mary that was called Magdalene, from whom seven devils had gone out, and Joanna the wife of Chuza Herod's steward, and Susanna, and many others, which ministered unto them of their substance.

1. **Soon afterwards.** After the feast in Simon's house where the "sinner" was the object lesson. **He went about** continuously through city and village, from place to place, in a second (see on v. 43, 44) circuit of Galilee, **preaching and bringing good tidings.** "He went about doing good" (Acts x. 38).

2. This time **the twelve,** who had been chosen during the first circuit (iv. 42-44) were with Him, **and certain women** (here first introduced), whose gratitude for **having been healed** led them to this service. Luke, the physician, here, as usually, distinguishes between **evil spirits** and other infirmities, sicknesses. This **Mary** was **called Magdalene** because she was from Magdala or Magdalan (Magadan, Matt. xv. 39) on the west side of the sea of Galilee, and to distinguish her from the many other Marys. **Seven devils** (demons) **had gone out** of her at Jesus' word. (See on Mark i. 23; v. 9; xvi. 9, and Exc. ii. p. 383, Vol. I., and, above, introduction, after ver. 35, to preceding narrative. Comp. the case of the man of Gadara, vers. 36-39 of this chapter.)

3. We know nothing of **Joanna** more than is here given (comp. xxiv. 10) nor of **Susanna**. Some suppose, but without proof, that **Herod** (Antipas) **'s steward** was the " nobleman " of John iv. 46–54. **Many others** there were with them, not here named. These women **ministered** (the original word is the verbal form of that from which we get our word " deacon " and " deaconess ") **to them,** Jesus and the twelve, **of their substance,** of what they had that could be made serviceable to the needs of those they ministered to. BENGEL says, " It was a Jewish custom for women, especially widows, to aid public teachers from their private property, and therefore to accompany them on their journeys." VAN OOST. thinks these women must " for the most part have belonged to the well-circumstanced higher class, since the here-mentioned ministration doubtless consisted principally in support rendered to earthly necessities from their property."

The presence of these and other women at the crucifixion is noted by Matthew (xxvii. 55, 56), Mark (xv. 40, 41), Luke (xxiii. 49), and John (xix. 25). See also Matt. xxvii. 61 ; xxviii. 1–10 ; Mark xv. 47 ; xvi. 1–8 ; Luke xxiii. 55, 56 ; xxiv. 1–11, 22, 23 ; John xx. 1, 2, 11–18. Woman's emancipation and love and service to Christ was beginning. Now, at the close of the nineteenth century her loving service is taking new forms and beautifully abounding.

<small>4-15. And when a great multitude came together, and they of every city resorted unto him, he spake by a parable : The sower went forth to sow his seed: and as he sowed, some fell by the wayside ; and it was trodden under foot, and the birds of the heaven devoured it. And other fell on the rock ; and as soon as it grew, it withered away, because it had no moisture. And other fell amidst the thorns ; and the thorns grew with it, and choked it. And other fell into the good ground, and grew, and brought forth fruit a hundredfold. As he said these things, he cried, He that hath ears to hear,</small>

let him hear. And his disciples asked him what this parable might be. And he said, Unto you it is given to know the mysteries of the kingdom of God: but to the rest in parables; that seeing they may not see, and hearing they may not understand. Now the parable is this: The seed is the word of God. And those by the wayside are they that have heard; then cometh the devil, and taketh away the word from their heart, that they may not believe and be saved. And those on the rock *are* they which, when they have heard, receive the word with joy; and these have no root, which for a while believe, and in time of temptation fall away. And that which fell among the thorns, these are they that have heard, and as they go on their way they are choked with cares and riches and pleasures of *this* life, and bring no fruit to perfection. And that in the good ground, these are such as in an honest and good heart, having heard the word, hold it fast, and bring forth fruit with patience.

See *Prel. Obs.* to Matt. xiii., p. 306, Vol. I. Also for comment on the parable of the Sower see on Matt. xiii. 1-23; Mark iv. 1-25.

4. **A parable.** Luke, whose habit is to be concise, gives here only one parable, whilst Matthew groups seven together in his narrative.

5. **Trodden under foot,** a thing most likely on the pathway through the fields, is an item added by Luke.

6. **The rock** is explained by Matthew and Mark as "rocky places," where the soil was thin; it could hold **no moisture.** The consequence was a ready start and a speedy scorching and withering.

7. Matthew says "upon," Mark "among," Luke **amidst,** the thorns; and Luke notes the thorns as growing **with** the seed sown.

8. Luke allows the maximum yield, **a hundredfold,** to stand for all the yields. **Ears** are meant **to hear,** though they do not always truly serve this purpose.

9. The statements of the different Evangelists about the disciples' questioning vary but agree substantially, especially when taken with their reports of Jesus' answer.

10. **The rest** are explained by Matthew and Mark as

"them" (the people in general) and "them that are without," not in the circle of Jesus' disciples. There are **mysteries of the kingdom of God,** which those in that kingdom may **know** as others may not. (Comp. John vii. 17.) **That seeing,** etc., Matthew says "because seeing," etc. What Matthew represents as a fact and a cause, Mark and Luke represent as a judgment. People are often, in judgment, left to the way they have chosen. Judicial blindness and want of other sense is a sad condition.

11. Even here the substantive verb—**is** and **are**—is not to be weakened into "represents," although a parable is a similitude. **The seed** well sets forth **the word of God,** since each has in it, by the divine Spirit, the germ of life, one in the natural world, the other in the spiritual (John vi. 63, 68; Heb. iv. 12).

12. **The devil,** Matthew says "the evil one," Mark "Satan." His purpose, in accordance with his nature (John viii. 44), is, **that they may not believe and** (so) **be saved.** (See the need of watchfulness!)

13. The **temptation** comes from "tribulation or persecution" (Matt., Mark), and they so "stumble" as to **fall away,** stand aloof, from the gospel.

14. **As they go on their way,** coming under the influence of **cares, riches** and **pleasures** presented by **this life,** by them they are spiritually **choked,** so that they **bring no fruit to perfection**—there is no maturing of fruit from the good seed sown. This is disappointing to both men and God.

15. The **honest and good heart** is that which understands (Matt.) the word and accepts (Luke) it, and there **holds it fast** persistently unto and until fruitfulness. The word abides in the heart and the heart abides by the word—**with patience** (Jas. v. 7).

16-18. And no man, when he hath lighted a lamp, covereth it with a vessel, or putteth it under a bed; but putteth it on a stand, that they which enter in may see the light. For nothing is hid, that shall not be made manifest; nor *anything* secret, that shall not be known and come to light. Take heed therefore how ye hear: for whosoever hath, to him shall be given; and whosoever hath not, from him shall be taken away even that which he thinketh he hath.

See on Mark iv. 21-25.

16. See Matt. v. 15. Light is made to shine. Christians are to be bearers of light. In relation to the preceding parable the application is, that the word is to remain in the heart and shine forth in the life; it is not to fail to hold its ground in time of temptation; and is not to be covered over by riches and cares of life; fruitfulness is the shining forth of the light.

17. See Matt. x. 26, 27. God is light; God makes manifest, and what is **hid**, as, e. g. in parables, shall in due time be **made manifest.** Accordingly we are to inquire into **secret** things, that for us and others they may **come to light.** Dig, delve, enter into the word, that its light may to you, and through you, increasingly break forth.

18. See Matt. xiii. 10; xxv. 29. Mark the **therefore.** For this reason **take heed;** for upon the **how ye hear** depends whether you will get and be able to give anything. Then follows the law by which heedfulness gets, and so is able to give, more and more, whilst heedlessness loses even what one **thinketh he hath.** There is great need of this warning; for there are many heedless hearers, who sit in God's house when His word is read and preached, and get no more than silly birds that sit on the telegraph wires and know nothing of the important messages that are passing under their feet.

19-21. And there came to him his mother and brethren, and they could not come at him for the crowd. And it was told him, Thy mother and thy brethren stand without, desiring to see thee. But he answered and said unto them, My mother and my brethren are these which hear the word of God, and do it.

See on Matt. xii. 46–50 and Mark. iii. 31–35 ; and comp. Matt. xiii. 54–57.

On the relationship sustained to Jesus by those who are here called "brothers," see on Matt. xiii. 55, and on Mark iii. 31, *note*. We prefer the view pronounced in this latter reference the best, and as held by modern exegetical scholars.

19-20. Luke says **brethren**, or brothers (as it would better be rendered in English), and though the Greek ἀδελφός is sometimes used for other relationships, what we understand by "brother" (and in Matt. xiii. 56 we have its cognate, "sisters") is its first and natural meaning, from which there is no sufficient reason here to depart. So good a Greek scholar as Luke knew the proper word for cousin (ἀνεψιός), and would have used it if he meant it.

Here it is distinctly stated that the inability of Jesus' relatives to get near Him was because of **the crowd.**

21. Luke's account particularizes in **these**, viz. the disciples then present. Jesus' own brothers did not believe on Him at this time. Spiritual relationships are the ones that avail in the kingdom of God.

22-25. Now it came to pass on one of those days, that he entered into a boat, himself and his disciples; and he said unto them, Let us go over unto the other side of the lake: and they launched forth. But as they sailed he fell asleep: and there came down a storm of wind on the lake; and they were filling *with water*, and were in jeopardy. And they came to him, and awoke him, saying, Master, master, we perish. And he awoke, and rebuked the wind and the raging of the water: and they ceased, and there was a calm. And he said unto them, Where is your faith ? And being afraid they marvelled, saying one to another, Who then is this, that he commandeth even the winds and the water, and they obey him ?

See on Matt. viii. 18-27; Mark iv. 35-41.

22. On one of those [the] days. The connection is not as close here as in Matthew and Mark. From the two latter also we learn the reason of their embarkation. There were great crowds about them, it was late, and the Lord had need of rest.

23. He fell asleep. For as true man He had the normal weaknesses and necessities of man, though He was without sin. By a common figure that is said of them which refers properly to the boat—**they were filling** with water through the waves that repeatedly broke over them (Matt.). They were really **in jeopardy**, humanly speaking.

24. The variations in the calls upon the Lord, as reported by the different writers, may be ascribed to the different calls made by several disciples in their terror: one said one thing; another, another; and probably several spoke at the same time.

25. Where is your faith? Trying times prove our faith. These disciples had some faith, but it was still feeble. Faith triumphs over fear, that is, when there is real ground for fear. Here was a great epiphany of Jesus as Lord of nature.

26-39. And they arrived at the country of the Gerasenes, which is over against Galilee. And when he was come forth upon the land, there met him a certain man out of the city, who had devils; and for a long time he had worn no clothes, and abode not in *any* house, but in the tombs. And when he saw Jesus, he cried out, and fell down before him, and with a voice said, What have I to do with thee Jesus, thou Son of the Most High God? I beseech thee, torment me not. For he commanded the unclean spirit to come out from the man. For oftentimes it had seized him: and he was kept under guard, and bound with chains and fetters; and breaking the bands asunder, he was driven of the devil into the deserts. And Jesus asked him, What is thy name? And he said, Legion; for many devils were entered into him. And they intreated him that he would not command them to depart into the abyss. Now there was there a herd of many swine feeding on the mountain : and they intreated him that he would give them leave to enter into them. And he gave them leave. And the devils came out from the man, and entered into the swine: and the herd rushed down the steep into the lake, and were choked. And when they that fed them saw what had come to pass, they fled, and told it in the city and in the country. And they went out to see what had come to pass ; and they came to Jesus, and found the man, from whom the devils were gone out, sitting, clothed and in his right mind, at the feet of Jesus: and they were afraid. And they that saw it told them how he that was possessed with devils was made whole. And all the people of the country of the Gerasenes round about asked him to depart from them ; for they were holden with great fear: and he entered into a boat, and returned. But the man from whom the devils were gone out prayed him that he might be with him : but he sent him away, saying, Return to thy house, and declare how great things God hath done for thee. And he went his way, publishing throughout the whole city how great things Jesus had done for him.

See on Matt. viii. 28-34; Mark, v. 1-20.

26. **Gerasenes.** Another reading is *Gergesenes*, and Matthew has *Gadarenes*. " The long famous instance of ' discrepancy ' as to the *place* in this narrative has been cleared up in recent years by the decision of textual critics that the correct text in Luke is Gerasenes, as well as in Mark, and by Dr. Thompson's discovery of a ruin on the lake shore, named Khersa (Gerasa). If this village was included (a very natural supposition) in the district belonging to the city of Gadara, some miles southeastward, then the locality could be described as either in the country of the Gadarenes, or in the country of the Gerasenes " (BROADUS, in his Harmony).

27. **Out of the city.** He belonged to the neighboring city, though his customary abode was **not in any house, but in the tombs,** suitably to his demonized condition, in consequence of which, too, he was without **clothes.**

28. **Fell down,** in awful fear, the man being entirely controlled by the demons in him. (See EXCURSUS II. p. 383, Vol. I., and p. 31, Vol. III., on Demoniacal Possession.)

Luke says **beseech thee** where Mark has "adjure thee by God." Probably both utterances were used.

29. **Oftentimes** MEYER translates "during a long time." **Seized**, etc., shows the entire possession of and power over the man exercised by the demons, superior to all bonds and compelling the human being, making **deserts** more congenial to him than abodes of men.

31. Acknowledging Jesus' authority and power, **they intreated him.** Even devils can make request. **The abyss** evidently means hell, the demons' own place. They were abroad by sufferance.

32. They would rather enter the swine than be dispossessed and sent home(?). "It is torment to demons to have no body either of man or beast to possess, in their desire to quench their own consuming fire" (BENGEL).

33. But they miscalculated this time : for, unable to hold the soul-less swine, their refuge in this case became their ruin, and they were dispossessed after all! Devils' prayers are always selfish prayers, and such prayers answered may work their authors' ruin.

The destruction of property need not trouble us. God is continually allowing Satan, in one way or other, by sickness, calamity, fraud, to take away not only men's property, but their health, their loved ones, desired gain, and even their lives. Even the best Christians are not secure from loss of temporal possessions; and why should these swine-herding Gergesenes be? Moreover, one human soul is worth more than two thousand swine, and, if God allowed it to be tormented by demoniacal possession, we need not wonder that He allowed them to be destroyed in the sea.

35. Everything about the man now showed that **the devils were gone out**, and Luke adds his posture **at the feet of Jesus,** a humble learner.

36. **Made whole**, says our physician author.

37. Luke enlarges the scope of the influence of the tidings of this event to **all . . . the country . . . round about.** This is one of the saddest verses in all the Scriptures. **And he . . . returned.** Jesus does not stay where He is not wanted!

38. The redeemed, cleansed soul desires to **be with** Jesus. Contrast the preceding conduct of the demons and of the people of that neighborhood.

39. **God**: Mark says, "The Lord:" the redeemed man said **Jesus**: they are one. Here was an early and earnest missionary. He is the best preacher who speaks from experience. "That Jesus did not here forbid the diffusion of the matter (see Mark v. 43; Matt. viii. 4), but *enjoined* it, may be explained from the locality (Peræa), where He was less known, and where concourse around His person was not to be apprehended as in Galilee" (MEYER). The history just related gives an epiphany of Jesus as Lord of demons.

40. And as Jesus returned, the multitude welcomed him; for they were all waiting for him.

40. **The multitude** on this side, westward, was differently disposed toward Jesus from that on the farther side. These were better acquainted with Him and **were all waiting for him.** But the multitude is always fickle.

41-56. And behold, there came a man named Jairus, and he was a ruler of the synagogue: and he fell down at Jesus' feet, and besought him to come into his house; for he had an only daughter, about twelve years of age, and she lay a dying. But as he went the multitudes thronged him. And a woman having an issue of blood twelve years, which had spent all her living upon physicians, and could not be healed of any, came behind him, and touched the border of his garment: and immediately the issue of her blood stanched. And Jesus said, Who is it that touched me? And when all denied, Peter said, and they that were with him, Master, the multitudes press thee and crush *thee.* But Jesus said, Some one did touch me : for I perceived that power had gone forth from me. And when the woman saw that she was not hid, she came trembling, and falling down before him declared in the presence of all the people for what cause she touched him, and how she was healed immediately. And he said unto her, Daughter, thy faith hath made thee whole ; go in peace. While he yet spake, there cometh one from the ruler of the synagogue's *house,* saying, Thy daughter is dead; trouble not the Master. But Jesus hearing it, answered him, Fear not : only believe, and she shall be made whole. And when he came to the house, he suffered not any man to enter in with him, save Peter, and John, and James, and the father of the maiden and her mother. And all were weeping, and bewailing her; but he said, Weep not; for she is not dead, but sleepeth. And they laughed him to scorn, knowing that she was dead. But he, taking her by the hand, called, saying, Maiden, arise. And her spirit returned, and she rose up immediately : and he commanded that *something* be given her to eat. And her parents were amazed : but he charged them to tell no man what had been done.

See on Matt. ix. 18–26; Mark v. 22–43 ; Mark's account is the fullest.

41. The Greek form of the name shows it is to be pronounced in three syllables—**Ja-i-rus.**

42. Luke alone says she was **an only daughter** and gives her **age.** That she **lay a dying** naturally called for haste in the physician. But the circumstances following prevented this, and doubtless caused the father's heart great trial.

43. This was a desperate case, that **could not be healed of any** earthly physicians, for she had, in addition to all that she had suffered, **spent all her living** upon them to no curative effect, and our physician author does not hesitate to tell it.

44. There was but one hope left. No case had yet been too hard for Jesus, and His power was exercised " without money " recompense. She had faith and, humbly coming **behind him, touched the border of his garment,** probably the fringe of that part of His outer robe that hung over His shoulder.

45. **All denied,** probably more by look and want of words than by anything uttered. None as yet acknowledged the act. The **press** and **crush** of **the multitudes** was not what Jesus was referring to.

46. It was a voluntary, purposeful **touch** which drew forth that inherent **power** which belonged to Jesus' person (not His clothes), and the going forth of which was not without His knowledge.

47. **Saw she was not hid.** (See viii. 17.) God seeth in secret, and rewardeth openly. Faith must not hide, but shine forth in testimony to Him who produces it. We must *confess* our faith.

48. And see what faith can do, that is, be the means of. **Go in** [into] **peace.** Find and rejoice in a new condition—of peace.

49, 50. Meanwhile Jairus' fears were realized. A messenger from his house brought the sad tidings that his only daughter, whom he had left at the point of death, was **dead** and all was over in her case. **But Jesus,** though He heard the report, was not of that mind, and cheered the father with the encouraging word that she should yet be **made whole,** saved out of death, if he would **only believe.** A greater boon would be secured by his faith than had just been won by the timid woman. Christ's word speaks faith within us. We all come to places where there is no recourse but to *only believe.* Moreover when there is abundant ground for **fear** and when it seems the very thing the circumstances justify (comp. vers. 23–25), right then and there comes the reassuring word calling to faith.

51. Only four, it appears, of the multitude that **came to** the house, entered it; and only the six persons mentioned were allowed to go into the room where the child lay.

52. These all were already in the house when Jesus arrived.

53. Knowing that she was dead. Yes; so far as they had any power or knew any relief, *dead* indeed. Their scornful laugh was the comment of their assurance of the child's death. It serves us a good purpose. Here was no counterfeit of death.

54. But he. In marked contrast with all of them, both in His views of things and in His power. He calleth things that are not as though they were (Rom. iv. 17).

55. Her spirit returned and reanimated her body: **and she rose up**—the first resurrection of the body in the history of Jesus' working.

Something to eat. For the restored life was to be nourished just as other lives are nourished. God does not put forth His extraordinary power to accomplish what He has put within the reach of ordinary means. Moreover that she could eat and needed food was a strong evidence of her complete restoration.

56. To tell no man. An admonition worthy of its source. Jesus was not seeking notoriety. These parents were to *talk* little about it, that they might *think* much. There is a time to be silent, as well as a time to speak.

CHAPTER IX.

1-6. And he called the twelve together, and gave them power and authority over all devils, and to cure diseases. And he sent them forth to preach the kingdom of God, and to heal the sick. And he said unto them, Take nothing for your journey, neither staff, nor wallet, nor bread, nor money; neither have two coats. And into whatsoever house ye enter, there abide, and thence depart. And as many as receive you not, when ye depart from that city, shake off the dust from your feet for a testimony against them. And they departed, and went throughout the villages, preaching the gospel, and healing everywhere.

See on Matt. x. 1-14, ff.; Mark vi. 7-13.

1. Luke mentions **power** along with **authority**: the former is the latter in action, exercising itself. He also says **all devils,** or demons, parallel with " unclean spirits " of Matthew and Mark.

2. **To preach,** as heralds, **the kingdom of God,** which the Baptist declared to be at hand and Jesus proclaimed as come. **And to heal,** as a testimony to their word and a striking proof of the power of the kingdom of God over that of Satan's empire. When there had been enough of that testimony, it ceased.

5. The testimony of shaking off the dust of their feet was not merely " unto them " (Mark), but **against them** " in the day of judgment " (Matt.).

6. **Throughout the villages.** There was no country population. This appears to have been a third circuit of Galilee; the first being that of Matt. iv. 23; Mark. i. 39; Luke iv. 43, 44; and the second, that of Luke viii. 1-3; on this third occasion the twelve were sent forth by

twos, in different directions, and in advance, perhaps, of Himself.

Preaching the gospel. That is the business of those whom Jesus sends forth to preach.

7–9. Now Herod the tetrarch heard of all that was done: and he was much perplexed, because that it was said by some, that John was risen from the dead; and by some, that Elijah had appeared; and by others, that one of the old prophets was risen again. And Herod said, John I beheaded: but who is this, about whom I hear such things? And he sought to see him.

See on Matt. xiv. 1–12 ; Mark. vi. 14–29.

7. **Herod** Antipas ruled in Galilee (and Peræa), the scene of most of **all that was done** so wonderfully by Jesus. Naturally the report reached him and he was **much perplexed** because of the accusations and imaginings of a guilty conscience. Matthew and Mark represent him as saying what is here referred to **some.** No doubt he took it up from them and betimes superstitiously questioned, if he did not believe, it.

8. The suggestions **by others** were scarcely more quieting to this unprincipled man. Hardly as well as Ahab of old could he have faced **Elijah** or **one of the old prophets.** Elijah could have **appeared** without rising from the dead, for he had never died.

9. **John I beheaded** was Herod's guilty recollection, **but who is this** was his startled question concerning Jesus. To satisfy his curiosity and quiet his startled imagination, he **sought to see him**—but was not gratified till the day of Jesus' death. (See ch. xxiii. 6–12.)

10–17. And the apostles, when they were returned, declared unto him what things they had done. And he took them, and withdrew apart to a city called Bethsaida. But the multitudes perceiving it followed him : and he welcomed them, and spake to them of the kingdom of God, and them that had need of healing he healed. And the day began to wear away; and the twelve came, and said unto him, Send the multitude away, that they may go into the villages and country round about, and lodge, and get victuals: for we are here in a desert place. But he said unto them, Give ye them to eat. And they said, We have no more than five loaves and two fishes; except we should go and buy food for all this people. For they were about five thousand men. And he said unto his disciples, Make them sit down in companies, about fifty each. And they did so, and made them all sit down. And he took the five loaves and the two fishes, and looking up to heaven, he blessed them, and brake; and gave to the disciples to set before the multitude. And they did eat, and were all filled: and there was taken up that which remained over to them of broken pieces, twelve baskets.

See on Matt. xiv. 13-21; Mark vi. 30-44; John vi. 1-14. This is the only miracle that is reported by all four of the Evangelists.

10. Their return was to Jesus by whom they had been sent forth. What a satisfaction it must have been to them to go over all the experiences of their mission. Go and tell Jesus—without any need of mediating virgin, priest or saint! The **Bethsaida** to which they withdrew was on the northeast side of the sea of Galilee, known as Bethsaida (Julias). There was another place of same name on the western side (Mark vi. 45).

11. **He welcomed them,** though their coming frustrated the purpose of rest for which they had set out: so loving was He to men, intent on **the kingdom of God** by which all human needs are **healed.**

12. Luke adds **and lodge;** for it was, perhaps, too late for many of them to get back home, and some of them were *en route* for the Feast at Jerusalem.

13. To **go and buy** would have been quite an undertaking, especially at that hour and with their slim purse.

14. In view of Mark's "by hundreds and by fifties" we take it that **about fifty each** refers to the number in front line of each company, though it may have been a hundred lines deep, in which case there would be five

hundred in each company, ten of which would make up the whole number **five thousand.** Nothing is indicated of the disposition of the "women and children" who were present besides.

This miracle of the feeding of the five thousand is one of the most significant and humanly inexplicable of all our Lord's wonderful works. There is no second cause which any rationalizing interpreter can possibly bring in to help account for the increase of the loaves and fishes: moreover, the facts were attested to the multitude and the disciples by at least four of man's five senses, and we have the record, substantially the same, by all four Evangelists, two of them having been eye-witnesses. Moreover the whole is a miniature picture of the kingdom of God. Here is Jesus, the Master, Lord and Provider; here are the disciples, His ministers, the bearers of His bounty; and here are the multitudes, the people of the world. Jesus Himself is the bread of life, the food of our souls, supernaturally given yet in natural channels; His disciples are the ministers, offering this true Bread from Heaven to all people and nations, the multitudes in a desert world where they cannot provide for themselves. "Give ye them to eat."—So says the Master to us Christians, with reference to the multitudes of heathen, famishing for the bread of life.

18-22. And it came to pass, as he was praying alone, the disciples were with him; and he asked them, saying, Who do the multitudes say that I am? And they answering said, John the Baptist; but others *say*, Elijah; and others, that one of the old prophets is risen again. And he said unto them, But who say ye that I am? And Peter answering said, The Christ of God. But he charged them, and commanded *them* to tell this to no man; saying, The son of man must suffer many things, and be rejected of the elders and chief priests and scribes, and be killed, and the third day be raised up.

See on Matt. xvi. 13-23 and Mark viii. 27-33, where

the region of Cæsarea Philippi, northwest of the sea of Galilee, is given as the scene of this passage.

18. Probably He went thither, where He was less known, to be more **alone.** Luke alone, as often, notes that He **was praying.** Blessed, perfect, holy example! And do not *we*, then, need to *pray?*

19. One of the **old** prophets, says Luke here, as in ver. 8, those of olden time, great prophets.

20. Peter's response is given substantially the same by all three Evangelists, but Luke briefly combines Matthew and Mark in his **the Christ of God.**

21, 22. It was not yet the time, in God's wise providence, to declare the Messiah, for His course of *suffering*, from this time on often spoken of to His disciples, must not be hindered, and the disciples must be prepared for it. Much as the Old Testament sets forth a suffering Saviour, that was not the expectation of the Jews.

> 23-27. And he said unto all, If any man would come after me, let him deny himself, and take up his cross daily, and follow me. For whosoever would save his life shall lose it; but whosoever shall lose his life for my sake, the same shall save it. For what is a man profited if he gain the whole world, and lose or forfeit his own self? For whosoever shall be ashamed of me and of my words, of him shall the Son of man be ashamed, when he cometh in his own glory, and *the glory* of the Father, and of the holy angels. But I tell you of a truth, There be some of them that stand here, which shall in no wise taste of death, till they see the kingdom of God.

See on Matt. x. 38, 39; xvi. 24-28; Mark viii. 34—ix. 1.

Jesus' disciples must be partakers of His sufferings. The way to the hills leads through the valleys.

23. Luke adds **daily.** Thus it is even easier.

25. **His own self** here explains "his soul" (Auth. Ver.) or "his life" (Revised Version.) in Matthew and Mark.

26. Luke adds **in his own glory**—which is very important.

27. This verse clearly refers to some powerful manifestation of **the kingdom of God** within the lifetime of some of the twelve. Besides the interpretations given in previous volumes of this Commentary, nearly all the early expositors, the Fathers and the mediæval interpreters regard the succeeding event of the transfiguration as a fulfilment of the prophecy of this verse. There is a very close connection, but, perhaps, the transfiguration was rather of the nature of "a symbol, a pledge, and a partial manifestation of the glory of Messiah's kingdom" (BIBLE COMMENTARY).

28-36. And it came to pass about eight days after these sayings, he took with him Peter and John and James, and went up into the mountain to pray. And as he was praying, the fashion of his countenance was altered, and his raiment *became* white *and* dazzling. And behold, there talked with him two men, which were Moses and Elijah; who appeared in glory, and spake of his decease which he was about to accomplish at Jerusalem. Now Peter and they that were with him were heavy with sleep: but when they were fully awake, they saw his glory, and the two men that stood with him. And it came to pass, as they were parting from him, Peter said unto Jesus, Master, it is good for us to be here: and let us make three tabernacles; one for thee, and one for Moses, and one for Elijah: not knowing what he said. And while he said these things, there came a cloud, and overshadowed them: and they feared as they entered into the cloud. And a voice came out of the cloud, saying, This is my Son, my chosen: hear ye him. And when the voice came, Jesus was found alone. And they held their peace, and told no man in those days any of the things which they had seen.

See on Matt. xvii. 1-13; Mark ix. 2-13.

28, 29. Luke's **eight days** include parts of days before and after the "six days" of Matthew and Mark. The words **after these sayings** show the close connection with the preceding record. As usual it is Luke who notes Jesus' purpose, in now seeking solitude, **to pray,** and that **as he was praying** the transfiguration occurred. **Fashion . . . altered.** His countenance became different. Matthew gives the effect. **White** is the color of glorious purity (Matt. xxv. 31 ; Rev. xx. 11). **Dazzling, like lightning.** The glory of the transfiguration was not poured down upon Jesus, but broke forth from Him. The potency of it was in Him, but ordinarily restrained from manifestation by His voluntary humiliation : for " he emptied himself" (Phil. ii. 7).

30, 31. **Two men,** not angels or spirits ; and they had not gone up the mountain with them and were not there on their arrival : but, all at once, there they were *talking* with Jesus! Their appearance was **in glory,** correspondent with the glory of Jesus' transfiguration. The subject of their conversation was **his decease which he was about to accomplish at Jerusalem.** The word rendered " decease " is *exodus.* **Moses,** who had led the children of Israel out of Egypt, through the Red Sea, was concerned about his great prototype's leading mankind safely through the fiery trials of Satan out of this present evil world into the heavenly Canaan, in whose borders he was waiting for the host that should come : **Elijah,** who had stood for the true God before Ahab and the priests of Baal, and had become discouraged, was anxious that in the great and decisive conflict with Satan and all his forces, the greatest of all the prophets, He whom the rest faintly prefigured and fore-announced, should overcome. Great subject, which Peter and the twelve had not wanted to hear about (Matt. xvi. 21-23), but which absorbed the three on the Mount. Christ's cross is the centre of all history, the focus of interest for earth and heaven, for this world and the world of spirits.

So then the sleepy doctrine of the "soul-sleepers" is not true, but those who have gone before have some knowledge of and are interested in what is yet transpiring on the earth. Moreover Peter, James and John *knew* Moses and Elijah, whom they had never seen ; and " we shall know each other there," as by intuition, with powers greatly enlarged and quickened above what we now possess.

32, 33. Everything about the transfiguration goes to show that it took place at night. The disciples, laboring men before their call and used to full measures of sleep, **were heavy with sleep,** and probably it was while they were in this condition that the transfiguration began and the visitants from the unseen world appeared. The first the disciples knew, they were there and talking with Him. But presently they became **fully awake,** and wonderingly contemplated the scene before them. As the heavenly visitants **were parting from** Jesus, impetuous **Peter** seems to have felt it incumbent on him to *say something*, though he wist not what, so dazzled were they and sore afraid. His general impression was that the occasion was a **good** and excellent one that ought to be prolonged. Therefore he proposed to **make three tabernacles,** tents, places of dwelling, one for each of the great three, putting them seemingly on a par. Peter had much yet to learn ; and his headlong zeal must be properly directed and controlled. The remembrance of this scene was afterwards to him a tower of strength (2 Pet. i. 16–21).

34. Luke's addition is to call attention to their fear **as they entered the cloud.**

35. **Chosen.** Matthew and Mark say *beloved*. The three reports are substantially the same.

36. **When the voice came** they fell on their faces in fear (Matt.), and after it was past and they looked up **Jesus was found alone.**

The disciples **held their peace** about what had transpired on the Mount, not so much because they were not disposed to talk about those wonderful events, but because, as the other narrators tell us, Jesus strictly charged them to this effect. It was a time for silence again. But why? Because neither were the disciples yet prepared for proclaiming the truths involved in the Transfiguration nor were the people prepared to hear them.

This was a revelation that, like prophecy, would have its chief force in after times; it and coming events would mutually explain one another. The disciples were learning, that they might teach others. They will not be able to teach, however, until they have better learned. They had seen glimpses of Jesus' glory: His sufferings were yet to pass before them and become the dark background of their recollections of Him and the interpreter of His glory.

Jesus' ministry in Galilee was now ended. Henceforth there will be more of the *suffering* Saviour.

37–42. And it came to pass, on the next day, when they were come down from the mountain, a great multitude met him. And behold, a man from the multitude cried, saying, Master, I beseech thee to look upon my son; for he is mine only child: and behold, a spirit taketh him, and he suddenly crieth out; and it teareth him that he foameth, and it hardly departeth from him, bruising him sorely. And I besought thy disciples to cast it out; and they could not. And Jesus answered and said, O faithless and perverse generation, how long shall I be with you, and bear with you? bring hither thy son. And as he was yet a coming, the devil dashed him down, and tare him grievously. But Jesus rebuked the unclean spirit, and healed the boy and gave him back to his father.

See on Matt. xvii. 14–20; Mark ix. 14–29; the latter gives the fullest report.

37. They did not come down till **the next day**, having spent the night on the mountain.

38. **Look upon.** Bring under thy compassionate attention. Luke alone says it was an **only child.**

39. **He crieth out,** that is, the boy; for the possessing spirit in this case was "dumb" (Mark). **Hardly.** Scarcely, with difficulty. **Bruising him sorely.** Only hurt comes from the evil spirits.

42. **Dashed ... tare ... grievously,** illustrating his evil nature and hostility to man. **But Jesus ... healed the boy,** illustrating His nature, and mercifully gave him **back to his father.** O what a happy recovery.

43-45. And they were all astonished at the majesty of God. But while all were marvelling at all the things which he did, he said unto his disciples, Let these words sink into your ears: for the Son of man shall be delivered up into the hands of men. But they understood not this saying, and it was concealed from them, that they should not perceive it: and they were afraid to ask him about this saying.

See on Matt. xvii. 22, 23; Mark ix. 30-32.

43, 44. **The majesty of God,** exhibited in Jesus' power over Satan and his kingdom, and in this particular instance in marked contrast with the impotence of the disciples (vers. 40, 41), was a matter of universal astonishment. In direct connection—**while all were marvelling** —and in contrast with this, Luke puts the now repeated admonition concerning coming sufferings. This majestic **Son of man** is destined to fall, seemingly helplessly, **into the hands of men,** a victim. MEYER and others refer **these words** to expressions of praise and wonder that had been uttered; ALFORD, STIER, and others, to Jesus' own utterances, previously and here following again, concerning His sufferings and cruel treatment.

45. **But,** though their ears heard **this saying** about Jesus' coming sufferings, they failed to apprehend or com-

prehend it, and there was divine purpose in this—**it was concealed from them**, for wise reasons, and they feared to *question* Him about it. The subject was dark in every sense.

> 46–50. And there arose a reasoning among them, which of them should be greatest. But when Jesus saw the reasoning of their heart, he took a little child, and set him by his side, and said unto them, Whosoever shall receive this little child in my name receiveth me ; and whosoever shall receive me receiveth him that sent me: for he that is least among you all, the same is great. And John answered and said, Master, we saw one casting out devils in thy name ; and we forbade him, because he followeth not with us. But Jesus said unto him, Forbid *him* not: for he that is not against you is for you.

See on Matt. xviii. 1–14 ; Mark ix. 33–50.
The place was Simon's house in Capernaum.

46, 47. The **reasoning** or dispute among them was not openly before Jesus, but He **saw** and knew what was in **their heart,** and proposed to teach them a needed lesson. The Great Teacher often taught by objects presented to the senses, and now a **little child** of the household served this purpose. Put **by his side**—beautiful sight—he was then "in the midst of them," an effective object-lesson.

48. That Luke says **this little child** and Matthew and Mark " such little child," illustrates the truth that *child* is to be taken literally as well as tropically. Many a little child comes into this world and is not received in Christ's name. This is a fundamental evil. **Least** is comparative in the original and means *less* or *very little ;* " in his own estimation," MEYER thinks and takes **is great** " objectively, in accordance with his real worth." God's estimates are always correct. See in this passage an easy and delightful way of receiving the great God : and how children are here honored !

49, 50. Same text as in Mark, except that there it is "us" and here **you**, a difference of only one letter in the original, and not making a different sense.

51. And it came to pass, when the days were well-nigh come that he should be received up, he stedfastly set his face to go to Jerusalem,

51. **Well-nigh come** is not so good as the margin *were being fulfilled*, but may serve as an interpretation. The days of Jesus' ministry were passing on, and He was now six months from their completion by His being **received up** into heaven. (See similar expression in Acts i. 2; 1 Tim. iii. 16.) The things concerning Him were to have an end (xxii. 37), and though this would be in glory, it would also be by the way of the cross. He was about to set out on His *final* departure from Galilee, the scene of the larger part of His ministry, and was leaving "his own" city and neighborhood for the last time. Conscious of all this and aware of all that awaited Him in the fulfilling of His mission, conscious that He was setting out for ignominy and death, it required firmness and decision to thus set out. Accordingly He **set his face** thus determinedly **to go to Jerusalem**. That was the goal where all was to be accomplished.

52, 53. And sent messengers before his face : and they went, and entered into a village of the Samaritans, to make ready for him. And they did not receive him, because his face was *as though he were* going to Jerusalem.

52, 53. **Messengers . . . to make ready.** The company was quite a considerable one, and not likely to find accommodations ready just anywhere for their lodging and supply. Following, it seems, the direct route, they entered into **a village of the Samaritans,** looking for hospitality. But the Samaritans **did not receive him.** Their reason for this incivility was that **his face was Jerusalem-**

wards. Now, if He had been proclaimed as a Messiah going to their religious centre, Mt. Gerizim, they would no doubt have felt and acted differently; but this was evidently a *Jewish* company, and the Samaritans had no favor to show them. (See John iv. 9.) Before, when Jesus was kindly treated in this district, He was leaving Jerusalem; now He was going towards the hated capital, and bitter envy prevailed in the Samaritans' hearts—a thing not at all unusual with them.

54. And when his disciples James and John saw *this*, they said, Lord, wilt thou that we bid fire to come down from heaven, and consume them?

54. The **disciples,** we must not forget, were men of like passions with us, and grace overcame nature in them gradually, as it does in us. The old nature we see cropping out, now and then, in the best of them. They contradict, doubt, fear, forsake, deny. Peter, from his impulsive nature, appears oftenest in the wrong; but this time **James and John,** Zebedee's sons, came forward in their old, natural character. Jesus had surnamed them "Sons of Thunder" (Mark. iii. 17), and here we have a touch of their vehement spirit. Great was their attachment to their Master; they had recently seen His glory in the Mount of Transfiguration, and now to see Him treated with neglect and despite by Samaritans was more than their natural spirits could brook. So they seriously proposed to **command fire . . . from heaven, and consume them,** and thus vindicate the Lord by summary judgment. Elijah had once done the like, perhaps in this very neighborhood (see 2 Kings i. 5–16), and had won renown for the God of Israel. Why should not they? Their faith seems to have been strong as to their ability to do this; and all they wanted was an affirmative answer to their application, **wilt thou?**

The Revised Version throws out from the text all reference to Elijah, although " many ancient authorities " have the words "even as Elijah did."

55, 56. But he turned, and rebuked them. And they went to another village.

55, 56. In like manner the Revised Version rejects from these verses the words "and said, Ye know not what manner of spirit ye are of. For the Son of man is not come to destroy men's lives, but to save them." These words are wanting in the most important uncial MSS., while they are found wholly or in part in many ancient uncial MSS. and versions, and are recognized by early Fathers of high authority. Certainly Jesus **rebuked** the ardent two who were ready to execute judgment.

There will be a time when Jesus will sit on the throne of judgment, but it was not yet; the dispensation inaugurated by the preaching of the kingdom of heaven is one of *salvation*: in it men are not to be coerced; the religion of Christ is not to be advanced by measures of violence. Jesus many a time relieved human sorrow, healing the sick and raising the dead; only once did He perform a miracle of destruction, and that was on the barren fig-tree. All His acts corresponded with His name, *Saviour*. So then, we are to exercise *patient love* even towards those who do not receive Christ, and leave judgment where it belongs. So will we truly follow Jesus. **To another village.** Some think He retired across the border again, and then pursued His journey around instead of through Samaria. At all events, He meekly went on.

57-60. And as they went in the way, a certain man said unto him, I will follow thee whithersoever thou goest. And Jesus said unto him, The foxes have holes, and the birds of the heaven *have* nests; but the Son of man hath not where to lay his head. And he said unto another, Follow me.

But he said, Lord, suffer me first to go and bury my father. But he said unto him, Leave the dead to bury their own dead; but go thou and publish abroad the kingdom of God.

See on Matt. viii. 19–22.

57, 58. This seems to have been a man of sanguine temperament, impulsive; and he needed to be put on his guard as to the consequences of his eagerness.

We must not have an exaggerated condition of Jesus' poverty; we suppose He always had lodging and shelter, when He needed it, and all His state of humiliation was voluntarily assumed and endured : but he was a pilgrim and stranger on the earth, and His followers must expect no higher state. Jesus did not refuse this proffered close disciple, but only would have him *count the cost*, realize what his profession *meant*. " The disciple is not above his master, nor the servant above his lord : " and let every one who calls Jesus Master and Lord, duly consider the path He trod and marked out for His followers.

59, 60. This seems to have been a man of phlegmatic temperament, sluggish ; and he needed to be stimulated to determined, entire consecration. Whilst in Matthew the proposition to follow Jesus came from the man himself with the condition of waiting till he buried his father, in Luke the Lord bids him follow Him, and he puts forward an objection to immediate compliance ; it is this objection and hindrance that makes the point of the narrative. **First . . . bury my father.** Whether his father was now a corpse, waiting to be buried, or whether the petitioner asked to remain with his (now aged) father until his death, whenever that should be, is a question which divides commentators. We agree with ELLICOTT and others who think the latter supposition " by far the most probable." It was a plea for indefinite postponement, based on the plausible ground of filial duty.

Seeing thoroughly this man's heart, and his disposition to make excuse, Jesus replied, **Leave the dead to bury their own dead.** Burying the dead is something anybody can do, and something that there will always be enough to do. Do not trouble thyself about that; there's a higher call for thee—**Go thou and publish abroad the kingdom of God,** be a herald of life and salvation. This is a higher call than to bury the dead: and "he that loveth father or mother more than me, is not worthy of me" (Matt. x. 37). The spriritual bond is higher than the natural (viii. 19-21), and whenever there is a conflict the former must have preference. "Seek ye first the kingdom of God and his righteousness." Now, let it not escape the Bible student that filial duty is everywhere sustained in the Bible, one of the Ten Commandmants being devoted to its enforcement, and Jesus Himself enforcing it by precept and example. But here was a case where a procrastinator plead a lower duty to escape doing the higher one. The first part of our Lord's answer is somewhat paradoxical, and the common interpretation of the words is, " Let the spiritually dead bury the naturally dead."

61. And another also said, I will follow thee, Lord; but first suffer me to bid farewell to them that are at my house.

61. **Another** and somewhat different character now comes up. He says, **Lord, I will follow thee**—but conditionally. He is only half-hearted in his profession. **Let me first** have a little of my own way yet; let me renew my old associations and have one last good time with them: let me first **go bid them farewell,** take leave of **them that are at my house.** D. BROWN illustrates this request by the experience of missionaries in India with new converts. Their parents, he says, go to the mission-house and plead with tears and threats that

they will not be baptized. Failing thus to shake their resolution, they ask at least for one parting visit— "to bid them farewell which are at home at their house." This seemingly reasonable request once conceded, the convert is lost to Christianity, never, or seldom, returning from the charm and power of the old pagan home control.

> 62. But Jesus said unto him, No man, having put his hand to the plough, and looking back, is fit for the kingdom of God.

62. Jesus' reply to this one was couched in a figure taken from husbandry, and very familiar to all. Every ploughman must look ahead, and be intent upon the plough and team. Particularly was this necessary in Palestine, where the plough was very primitive and rude. No one there **having put his hand to the plough** was in condition to draw a furrow or succeed at his work while **looking back.** So, preëminently, whoever gives himself to **the kingdom of God** must do it with *entire devotion*, not looking back to the things which have been left behind, given up, forsaken. See Paul's example in Phil. iii. 13, 14. Compare Luke xi. 24–26, and Hosea x. 2. A divided heart will not produce a straightforward Christian life. "Thou shalt love the Lord thy God with all thy heart, and with all thy soul, and with all thy mind. This is the first and great commandment."

Having been baptized into Christ and so put on Christ, own Him in your confirmation, and then follow on to know the Lord!

CHAPTER X.

1. Now after these things the Lord appointed seventy others, and sent them two and two before his face into every city and place, whither he himself was about to come.

1. **After these things** is a very general mark of time. The following narrative belongs to the quite considerable portion of the Gospel history narrated by Luke alone. He calls Jesus **the Lord** a number of times, Mark but once (Mark xvi. 19), and Matthew not at all. **Seventy,** as many as the elders chosen by Moses (Num. xi. 16–25) as assistants, a not unusual number. **Others** than those mentioned in ix. 52, and than the Twelve (ix. 1, 2), who were sent out perhaps six months previously and who had a permanent mission as "The Apostles," of whose appointment each of the Synoptists gives an account. That He found so many suited to go before Him as heralds of the kingdom, points perhaps to a larger and better discipleship than we are wont to accord to that period. He sent them **two and two,** as He had done the Twelve. Why? Because two witnesses were enough to establish a matter by Jewish law, and for sympathy and help: for "two are better than one."

The places to which they were sent were those to which **he himself was about to come,** and He was setting out through Samaria and Peræa to Jerusalem.

Many of the directions given the seventy are, naturally, the same as or like those given to the Twelve. (Comp. Matt. x. throughout.)

2. And he said unto them. The harvest is plenteous, but the laborers are few: pray ye therefore the Lord of the harvest, that he send forth labourers into his harvest.

2. **Harvest.** The figure here is plain. (See on Matt. ix. 37, 38.)

3. The object of having them to **pray the Lord** to do what He would naturally be solicitous to do, seems to be to bring them into active fellowship with the divine mind and purpose. When we truly pray for a cause we become interested in it so as to give and labor for it. Surely we do not pray to God to change His mind or to persuade Him to that for which He has no liking. The matter of prayer needs deeper and fuller consideration by Christians.

3. Go your ways: behold, I send you forth as lambs in the midst of wolves.

This was not of itself very encouraging to those sent; but when they remembered that it was the Good Shepherd who said, **Behold, I send you,** they could go bravely, trusting Him for the consequences. Probably the contrast between the sent and those to whom they are sent is not so striking now in Christian lands; but withal, the world is still enmity against God.

4. Carry no purse, no wallet, no shoes : and salute no man on the way.

4. These directions indicate that the mission was to be a hasty one and was to support itself. Eastern salutations took up a great deal of time. "The king's business requireth haste."

5, 6. And into whatsoever house ye shall enter, first say, Peace *be* to this house. And if a son of peace be there, your peace shall rest upon him: but if not, it shall turn to you again.

5. They were to offer **peace** to whoever in the **house** could take it.

6. **A son of peace,** according to Eastern idiom, is one who is of that turn and disposition. **It shall turn to you again.** So it seems a benediction, to be real and complete, must be accepted as well as pronounced. Remember this when the minister speaks God's grace and peace to you in the Benediction. One cannot force peace upon others!

7. And in that same house remain, eating and drinking such things as they give: for the labourer is worthy of his hire. Go not from house to house.

7. **In that same house remain,** not going from house to house. Put up at one place and stay there till your mission in that town or city is over. Be content with **such things as they give,** and do not receive it as "charity;" **for the labourer is worthy of his hire.** You are the Lord's, and "the earth is the Lord's and the fulness thereof." It is taken for granted that they will be courteous.

8, 9. And whatsoever city ye enter, and they receive you, eat such things as are set before you: And heal the sick that are therein, and say unto them, The kingdom of God is come nigh unto you.

8. **City** gives a larger field than "house" of ver. 6. That **they receive you** is necessary to your remaining any time among them. The whole time of operation for them was limited and short.

9. You not only receive but give. **Heal the sick.** What a glorious power to exercise, what a heavenly blessing to receive! They were also to bring the gracious word of spiritual healing at hand, saying, **The kingdom of God is come nigh unto you** for your salvation. Surely

such words and works were worthy of daily bread and shelter, all hospitality.

10, 11. But into whatsoever city ye shall enter, and they receive you not, go out into the streets thereof and say, Even the dust from your city, that cleaveth to our feet, we do wipe off against you: howbeit know this, that the kingdom of God is come nigh.

10, 11. But suppose **they receive you not**, what then? For men have power to reject not only the ambassadors but the grace of Christ. Eastern people abound in external manifestation of feeling. The Lord here instructs the seventy to use a well understood action of laying the responsibility of rejection of offered good upon the rejecters. The preachers would not be responsible if the people would not receive them and their word.

12. I say unto you, it shall be more tolerable in that day for Sodom, than for that city.

12. **In that day.** Ver. 14 and the usual meaning of the term "that day" show that this means the day of judgment: and the term **more tolerable** indicates degrees of condemnation at that time. **Sodom** had not the opportunities of **that city** to which these ambassadors of Christ would come, and, though so wicked, would not be so severely judged, according to the law, "To whom much is given of them much will be required." Moreover here is illustrated that the greatest of all sins is to reject Christ. See John xvi. 9 for the Spirit's great argument to convince the world of sin.

13, 14. Woe unto thee, Chorazin! woe unto thee, Bethsaida! for if the mighty works had been done in Tyre and Sidon, which were done in you, they would have repented long ago, sitting in sackcloth and ashes. Howbeit it shall be more tolerable for Tyre and Sidon in the judgment than for you.

13. The cities here mentioned are supposed to have

been in the neighborhood of Capernaum. They saw many **mighty works** done by the Master and His disciples. They had wonderful opportunities; but they did not appreciate or improve these. The all-knowing Judge says **Tyre and Sidon** with like advantages **would have repented.**

14. But **the judgment** will be qualified by a consideration of the opportunities enjoyed. What are your opportunities and how are you improving them?

15. And thou, Capernaum, shalt thou be exalted unto heaven? thou shalt be brought down unto Hades.

15. **Capernaum** had been especially exalted in privilege from Jesus' making it His point of departure and return in Galilee. **Shalt thou be exalted unto heaven,** by the residence of the Son of God in thee, making it " his own city?" From so great a height, for rejecting the Lord, **thou shalt be brought down unto Hades,** to the state of the dead, brought to nothing, wiped off of the earth. So fully has this been done that the site of Capernaum is not now certainly known. Of the cities mentioned Bethsaida only can be found: they all have gone to ruin!

16. He that heareth you heareth me; and he that rejecteth you rejecteth me; and he that rejecteth me rejecteth him that sent me.

See almost the very same words in Matt. xi. 20–24, and comp. comments thereon. Also John xii. 48; xiii. 20.

16. **Heareth me—despiseth me.** Because the heavenly King is represented by His ambassadors. See 2 Cor. v. 20. Christ speaks not to men directly, but through His ministers, those whom He sends. As we treat them, so we treat Him. (See Matt. xxv. 31–46.) And as we treat them and Him, so we treat **him that sent me,** Jesus says; that is, so we treat God the Father. See, then, that

ye refuse not him that speaketh! Look how you treat God's ministers! "Woe unto him that contends with the priest" (Deut. xvii. 12; Hosea iv. 4).

But **he that heareth you heareth me.** "What unspeakable mercy it is that God speaks with us through His word and speaks so graciously, that by it He announces and offers to us His blessed peace and everlasting kingdom" (LUTHER). Receive, then, O believing heart, the declaration of grace and the benediction, as well as the words of exhortation to confession of sin and newness of life, coming from the minister's lips, as from God Himself!

17. And the seventy returned with joy, saying, Lord, even the devils are subject unto us in thy name.

17. **Returned.** How long after they were sent we do not know. Thirty-five places or cities, at least, in Samaria and Judæa would come within the scope of their visit. It is not said or implied that they returned all at once. They may have kept coming in at different times, in pairs, from places more or less remote, but with the same general exuberance. The scene was probably in or near Jerusalem. **With joy.** They had gone forth bearing precious seed, and were now come again with rejoicing. Nothing is said, either here or elsewhere, of any sheaves brought with them. Their work was probably chiefly as a testimony, and to prepare the way of the Lord. They did what they were sent to do, and, in that consciousness, and having had divine power with them to substantiate their word, they returned jubilant. **Even the devils are subject.** This seems to have impressed them most. This power was not specifically mentioned in their commission, as it had been in that of the Twelve (ix. 1), and their exercise of it nevertheless indicates their strong

faith. Not long before this (ix. 37-42) nine of the Twelve Apostles had failed to cast out an evil spirit. **In thy name.** They wrought by another's power—the power of Jesus' name. This always distinguished miracles of mere men—disciples—from the wonderful works of the Lord and Master Himself.

18. And he said unto them, I beheld Satan fallen as lightning from heaven.

18. I beheld Satan fallen as lightning from heaven. The form of the verb here used in the original is the imperfect and denotes continued action in past time; or action begun but not completed; I *was beholding* or I *began to see.* The question arises, to what time does the Lord refer? As Satan's fall is yet to be consummated at the final judgment, it may be considered as still going on. Jesus came to destroy Satan and his works, and frequently refers to his judgment as going on and to be completed. The certainty of it Jesus never doubted, and the processes of it were before His omniscient mind from the time that Satan led the revolt in heaven and was banished therefrom with his rebellious hosts (2 Peter ii. 4; Jude 6). Perhaps our Lord speaks here of this His knowledge and assurance. Some think He refers to the time when the Seventy set out, and that He here says He was taking note, from the beginning, of their triumphs over the adversary. **From heaven.** For he was once there, a pure spirit; now **fallen,** yet powerful, superhuman. (Comp. Rev. xii. 9; John xii. 31; Isaiah xiv. 12.) **As lightning.** Swiftly, notably; an angel of light fallen! MEYER strongly denies that "from heaven" is to be taken with "lightning," i. e. as lightning from heaven. The prose of the verse is—Satan is fallen, doomed; of this I assure you, and in this rejoice with you.

19. Behold, I have given you authority to tread upon serpents and scorpions, and over all the power of the enemy: and nothing shall in any wise hurt you.

19. **Have given,** when you were sent out, and you have it, **authority to tread on serpents and scorpions,** as representative of "that old serpent, the devil," who assumed the serpent's form in tempting man to his fall. **And over all the power of the enemy.** The enemy is Satan, who is a Prince of evil, and chief ruler of the darkness of this world. (See Eph. ii. 2; vi. 12; Col. i. 13, etc.) His power is exercised to do evil; but the Seventy were so far made superior to it as to have Jesus' assurance that **nothing shall in any wise hurt you.** We see this promise given more generally in Mark xvi. 17, 18, and exemplified in Paul's experience at Melita (Acts xxviii. 3-6). Doubtless such immunity from natural hurt was far more common among believers than the few instances given would indicate. An uninspired book would have excited our wonder and gratified our curiosity here as the Bible does not. In this exemption there was a foretaste and prefigurement of the times of complete redemption, when the groaning and travailing of creation shall cease, the curse be removed, and the new creation, characterized by righteousness and peace, be inaugurated.

20. Howbeit in this rejoice not, that the spirits are subject unto you: but rejoice that your names are written in heaven.

20. **Howbeit in this rejoice not.** That is, as the chief or prominent cause of rejoicing: for He does not absolutely forbid joy at the power they were enabled to exercise through faith. He, however, tempers their joy, and warns them against laying too much stress on those natural (as we may call them) wonders. There was better

cause of joy in this,—**your names are written in heaven,** enrolled in God's book as citizens there. So Paul says (Phil. iii. 20), " Our citizenship is in heaven." This implies that we may know, and should know, our adoption as sons, and our enrolment in the Lamb's book of life. This is a knowledge and joy that belongs to all believers.

21. In that same hour he rejoiced in the Holy Spirit, and said, I thank thee, O Father, Lord of heaven and earth, that thou didst hide these things from the wise and understanding, and didst reveal them unto babes : yea, Father; for so it was well-pleasing in thy sight.

21. **In that hour** is a very specific mark of time. **Rejoiced.** The word here used signifies *rejoiced exceedingly*, rendered in Matt. v. 12, " Be exceeding glad." The Revised Version, following the reading of many of the best MSS. and of some versions, reads **in the Holy Spirit.** So LACHM. and TISCH. We know that Jesus was filled with the Holy Spirit abiding on Him from His baptism, and that He rejoiced in the sphere of and by the Holy Spirit gives a fairly good sense ; but the reading " in the spirit," meaning His own personal spirit, is simple and gives a better sense. MEYER is strongly for the latter. Jesus was indeed "a man of sorrows," but this belonged to His humiliation, and, occasionally, as here, a divine and glorious joy filled His soul and beamed from His countenance, even amid the thickening conflict of His earthly life. When He looked beyond, He exulted ; so may His true disciples. " Weeping may endure for a night, but joy cometh in the morning ! " His joy expressed itself in thanksgiving to God. **Father,** expressing His sense of affectionate nearness ; **Lord of heaven and earth,** indicating God's omnipotence. **These things** are the things of the Kingdom of God. **The wise and understanding** are the sagacious ones of the world. **Babes** does not signify the unwise or imprudent, but simple-hearted,

docile ones, *believing*. **Well-pleasing.** Here is the same noun rendered " good will " in the angels ' song of the nativity. The men of God's "good will" are those who receive the Kingdom of God as a little child (xviii. 17). " Not many wise men after the flesh, not many mighty, not many noble, are called," etc. (1 Cor. i. 26-29). Such is God's plan, and Jesus praises the Father in view of it. In what sense has He **hid these things** from the wise and prudent? In the sense that their wisdom and prudence, natural capacity and attainments cannot reach or fathom the things of redemption. " The natural man understandeth not the things of the Spirit of God, neither can he know them, because they are spiritually discerned ! " Yet these naturally wise men are apt to be so conceited over their abilities that they will not accept anything they cannot understand, and so divine things are hidden from them. What delights the Lord is not that any shall perish through the blindness of their own wisdom, but that God in His infinite wisdom has granted salvation and the knowledge of God to simple faith, humble belief. In Rom. vi. 17 we have a concentrated thanksgiving similar in form to that of this verse. There " that ye were the servants of sin " marks the contrast and thereby heightens the joy, but is not in itself a cause of thanksgiving.

22. All things have been delivered unto me of my Father: and no one knoweth who the Son is, save the Father; and who the Father is, save the Son, and he to whomsoever the Son willeth to reveal *him*.

22. This verse is noted as being so much like those declarations of Jesus which abound in John's gospel but are not recorded by the first three Evangelists. Its purpose seems to be to set forth the oneness of Jesus with God the Father, and the entire harmony of their action.

Jesus is the manifested and operating God. **All things have been delivered unto me of my Father.** It is the dispensation of the Mediator. Jesus is King; yet in perfect harmony with the Father Almighty. It was not a new government, but a new revelation of the old. **And no one knoweth** fully, comprehendeth, **who the Son is, save the Father.** What wonder then if no one can explain the incarnate mystery! VAN OOST. well says this utterance "is one of the most convincing testimonies for the true Godhead of Christ. One who was only a created spirit or an immaculate man could not possibly without blasphemy against God testify this of himself." "Knoweth" is used in this verse in its highest and deepest sense. **And who the Father is, save the Son.** This is the converse of the former statement, "Who by searching can find out God?" This knowledge is not attained by worldly wisdom and prudence, by scientific research or intellectual grasp. Only **he to whomsoever the Son willeth to reveal him** can know God. The only way to the true knowledge of God is by Jesus Christ, who came to reveal Him to humble faith. He who will not sit at Jesus' feet to learn, however great in all manner of attainments he may be, will never attain to the knowledge of the highest object in the universe; however much he may have learned of the creation, he will never know the Creator. The unbelieving savants of the day are illustrating the statements of Jesus here when they call God the Unknown and the Unknowable! The great things of God are *still* " hid from the wise and prudent!" God's plan has not changed. Yet, withal, "this is eternal life, that they should know thee, the only true God, and him whom thou didst send, even Jesus Christ."

23, 24. And turning to the disciples, he said privately, Blessed *are* the eyes which see the things that ye see: for I say unto you, that many prophets and kings desired to see the things which ye see, and saw them not; and to hear the things which ye hear, and heard them not.

23, 24. **His disciples** were those to whom the Son willed to reveal the Father. Often He taught them **privately** what the unreceptive multitudes heard only in parables. Here He congratulated them on the times in which they lived and their posture of faith. **Many prophets** of the olden time (see 1 Peter i. 10–12), who testified of these latter days, **and kings**, such as David and Solomon, Hezekiah and Josiah, **desired** in vain **the things ye see and hear.** All the promises concentrated in the person of Jesus, whose words and example were their daily school, as they followed His blessed steps and called Him Master. Yet have we the Lord's own word of blessing also, where He says (John xx. 29), "Blessed are they that have not seen, and yet have believed." With an open and preached Bible, with the word and the sacraments, committed to the Church as means of grace, and accompanied by the outpoured Spirit of all truth, and with the test of so many centuries approving Jesus and His teachings, we are better off than even those early disciples. Moreover, we should remember the divine rule that "to whom much is given, of him much will be required." Our responsibilities keep pace with our privileges.

25. And behold, a certain lawyer stood up and tempted him, saying, Master, what shall I do to inherit eternal life?

25. The word **lawyer** is one that occurs but seldom in the New Testament, and its precise meaning is not certainly known. Ordinarily it refers to one of that class, often called scribes, whose business it was to transcribe

the books (written) of the law, and who were, in consequence of this service, well versed in a knowledge of the law. Some think it includes any one that is learned in the law. MORISON says that it perhaps denotes a higher grade of scribes, who devoted themselves to giving counsel on matters of law. LIGHTFOOT'S idea is that it refers to persons who interpreted and applied the written law, as over against the elders who did the same in regard to the traditions.

Tempted does not necessarily imply an evil intention in respect to Christ, its primary meaning being that of proving or testing. In what respects this man wished to try the Saviour, we do not know certainly. Perhaps he wanted to find out whether, as a teacher, He was properly acquainted with the law, or whether His views as to the manner of obtaining life were in accord with the teaching of Moses. On **inherit life eternal**, see on Mark x. 17.

Jesus' answer to the question, the lawyer thinks, will prove His knowledge of the Scriptures and the correctness of His views—or the opposite. The question, in itself considered, is the most important that any man can propose, and one that all should ask and answer fully and definitely. See it asked late in the history and with a practical purpose, in ch. xviii. 18–23. (Comp. Matt. xxii. 34-40; Mark. xii. 28–34.)

26. And he said unto him, What is written in the law? how readest thou?

26. The Saviour answers by asking another question, **What is written in the law? how readest thou?** Jesus always honored the past in God's dealings with men. He came not to destroy the law or the prophets, but to fulfil (Matt. v. 17, 18). God is one, and is consistent with

Himself. The Living Law will not invalidate or change the principles of the written law. Moreover here He turns the question of the tempter against him, throws a searchlight into his mind.

How readest thou? As STIER well says, "What is written requires to be read aright." We must correctly understand what we read, otherwise we will be misled. Perhaps this question is intended to suggest also that the Scriptures must be read and studied in the proper spirit; not merely to gain material for controversy, or to find matter to justify ourselves in the wrong course we may have determined to pursue, but to ascertain sincerely and truly what God would have us to do.

27. And he answering said, Thou shalt love the Lord thy God with all thy heart, and with all thy soul, and with all thy strength, and with all thy mind; and thy neighbour as thyself.

27. This answer is found in Deuteronomy vi. 5 and Leviticus xix. 18, and embraces, according to Jesus' own teaching (Matt. xxii. 37-40), the substance of the Old Testament. "On these two commandments hang all the law and the prophets." The first requirement is love to God, which includes a high appreciation of His character, a desire for communion with Him, and a sincere concern to please Him in all things.

Thou shalt love. Notice that this is a thing of *the heart*, the inner and real man, not, primarily, of an act or deed. It is a requirement of *being* rather than of *doing*, the latter, however, being assured where the former exists **The Lord,** the one Jehovah, is **thy God,** to whom thou standest in closest personal relations. He is thy Creator, Preserver, Redeemer, and bountiful Benefactor; thou art His creature, His care, His purchase, His daily dependent, His child. *Love Him.* He is altogether lovely, infinite and perfect. **With all thy heart . . . soul . . . mind . . . strength.** With all thy powers. These terms cover the whole human nature and let nothing slip that can be concerned in loving God. If we love God with all our powers, there will be nothing left with which to love anything else; that is, anything contrary to God. God must be all and in all. He must sit as absolute sovereign on the throne of the heart: and, according to the divine constitution of things, such perfect love and service is man's highest freedom. When this exists man is restored from the fall. Without this heart of love we have not yet begun to keep the law. This view of the truth destroys the moralist's hope. This was what was lacking in the rich young man spoken of later (xviii. 18, etc.)—supreme love to God. If this be wanting, the whole character, however beautiful, falls to the ground condemned. See, from this, the wisdom and beauty of Luther's always beginning his explanations of the Commandments with the foundation principle, "We should fear and love God, and," etc.

And thy neighbour as thyself. We should love God because of His character and perfections and because of the nearness of relation we sustain to Him, our Father in Heaven; we should love mankind because of the family relationship, which makes us all members of the common brotherhood of man. "Whosoever loveth him that begat, loveth him also that is begotten of him."

28. And he said unto him, Thou hast answered right: This do, and thou shalt live.

28. **Answered right.** It appears, then, that it was quite possible to know the substance of the law, the essence of God's requirements.

This do, and . . . live. Adam and Eve failed to do

this, and died. They fell out of fellowship with God. Their heart and will turned aside to the creature. Nor has any one of their descendants done better. No one has kept the law. Indeed no one of us sinners can perfectly keep it. Yet the law is not, therefore, toned down or changed: but by it we are shown our helplessness and led to cry for mercy. The law is our pedagogue to lead us to Christ, who alone has perfectly kept the law as well as atoned for our sins: so that He has become our Redeemer from the condemnation of the unkept law, and He is "of God made unto us wisdom and righteousness and sanctification and redemption" (1 Cor. i. 30), and we are made "complete in him" (Col. ii. 10).

29. But he, desiring to justify himself, said unto Jesus, And who is my neighbour?

29. **Desiring to justify himself.** How natural! Man does not like to own up to his failings and sins, does not like to confess. Since our first parents' time, we, their true children, desire and try to justify ourselves. But we do not usually succeed any better than they did. These lawyers split hairs on interpretation, and the one before us hoped to find some refuge from his sense of having failed to perfectly keep the law in a possible interpretation of "neighbour;" and so he asked with a temper that regarded the letter rather than the spirit of the law, **And who is my neighbour?**

30. Jesus made answer, and said, A certain man was going down from Jerusalem to Jericho; and he fell among robbers, which both stripped him and beat him, and departed, leaving him half dead.

30. **Jesus made answer** in a beautiful parable, which not only showed who is one's neighbor but what neighborly love is, and that one possessed by perfect love would hardly have asked the question this lawyer put.

A certain man. No matter who. Nothing is brought out concerning him in the narrative, except that he was a fellow human being. **Was going down.** Jerusalem was naturally on higher ground than Jericho, and spiritually was at the head, the highest point of Palestine. Hence it was always *up*, and all other places *down*, relatively speaking. The road from **Jerusalem to Jericho** was about twenty miles long. This was the short cut, leading through the desert wilderness, wild and rocky, part of it having once been the ravine through which a stream flowed, and noted for murders and deeds of violence from that time to this. In the fourth century JEROME says it was called "the red or bloody way." HACKETT writes recently of it, " Hardly a season passes in which some luckless wayfarer is not killed or robbed in going down from Jerusalem to Jericho. The place derives its hostile character from its terrible wildness and desolation. If we might conceive of the ocean as being suddenly congealed and petrified when its waves are tossed mountain-high and dashing in wild confusion against each other, we should then have some idea of the aspect of the desert in which the Saviour has placed so truthfully the parable of the good Samaritan."

Jericho, destroyed in Joshua's day, was rebuilt long afterward, and by the time of our Lord it had become again a very considerable city, and Herod the Great had enlarged and improved it. Highway **robbers. Stripped him** of his raiment, in their greed of gain, **beat him,** in their wantonness. **Leaving him half dead.** And no matter to them if he died altogether, only so they might escape detection and punishment. Theirs was active, violent selfishness.

Now there follows another type of this root of sin, so

directly opposite to that crowning virtue, love, which "secketh not her own."

31, 32. And by chance a certain priest was going down that way, and when he saw him, he passed by on the other side. And in like manner a Levite also, when he came to the place, and saw him, passed by on the other side.

31. **By chance.** So we speak; and there is chance to man, but not to God. There was no foresight of man to occasion or foresee such concurrence of events, but God's providence, which lets not a sparrow fall unnoticed, was in it all. **Was going down.** This indicates that he was going from Jerusalem, where, perhaps, he had been in attendance on the sacred duties of the temple. **A certain priest.** Jericho was one of the cities of the priests, convenient to the holy city where they officiated by courses. (See i. 8.) **That way.** There was another, more roundabout but safer, way leading through Bethlehem. **And when he saw him** lying there in such an evil plight, taking counsel, perhaps, of his fears, **he passed by on the other side.** We may suppose this man was full of apprehension from the time he entered that wild defile, and now, more than ever, hastened to get through it. Here was fresh reason for being afraid. The priests' office was to offer sacrifices, conduct the temple service, and instruct the people, and sometimes to act as judges. They were "appointed for men in things pertaining to God" (Heb. v. 1). They were mediators between God and men, a shadow and figure of the office of Christ. One of the great things of that law which they were to honor and exemplify was *mercy* (Matt. xxiii. 23).

32. **In like manner a Levite.** Priests were Levites, but all Levites were not priests. The family of Aaron were priests; the rest of the tribe of Levi were chosen for the service of the tabernacle in place of the first-born

of all Israel, who were consecrated to the Lord. They were aids to the priests, and, giving their time to the offices of religion, were supported by tithes from the rest of the people. This man, in that he **came to the place and saw,** looked on the unfortunate victim by the wayside, seems to have been more deliberate and perhaps kindly disposed than the priest; but, like him, he **passed by on the other side,** without attempting any assistance. Now, in attempting to explain why these two acted so contrary to what might have been expected of them, both as men and as exponents of a religion that forbade such treatment of even the ox or ass of an enemy (Ex. xxiii. 4, 5 ; Deut. xxii. 1-4; Is. lviii. 7), it is not necessary to charge them with an indifferent, cold, cruel inhumanity. It is likely enough that they were so taken up with the sense of their own danger in that place that they turned aside from the law of kindness, which their inmost conscience tied them to, and thought only of themselves. They may have excused themselves by the thought that the man was evidently so ill-used that he would certainly die, or that they did not have any means at hand for succoring him ; and they may have imagined the robbers as near by, with the suffering man as a decoy for other defenceless travellers like themselves, ready to spring out and treat them likewise. Whatever motives influenced them, they both followed that law of selfishness which is a tap-root of sin, and showed none of that love which is the fulfilling of the law.

33, 34. But a certain Samaritan, as he journeyed, came where he was : and when he saw him, he was moved with compassion, and came to him, and bound up his wounds, pouring on *them* oil and wine; and set him on his own beast, and brought him to an inn, and took care of him.

33. **But** here comes another traveller. He is a **Samari-**

tan, one of that mixed people, of heathen and Jewish origin, that came to possess the district between Galilee and Judæa after Israel's captivity, the detestation of the pious (!) Jew. Usually they requited the hatred of the Jews with like feelings. In ix. 51–56 we see something of this spirit, and the Jerusalem Jews gratified their hatred toward Jesus by saying (John viii. 48), "Say we not well that thou art a Samaritan and hast a devil?" **As he journeyed.** On a longer trip than either the priest or the Levite. **When he saw him, he was moved with compassion,** and suffered his sympathies to move him.

34. **He came to** the poor man lying there, got off the beast on which he was riding, instead of whipping him up the faster, **and bound up** the sufferer's **wounds,** likely tearing some of his own garments to do this, and, **pouring on them oil and wine,** whose healing properties made these a usual remedy for wounds, thus did all he could for the distressed man's present relief. Probably the Samaritan had small quantities of oil and wine as wise precautions for one taking the journey he was on. (Comp. Gen. xxviii. 18.) But it would not do to let the man lie there in the hot sun, unattended. So the compassionate Samaritan **set him on his own beast,** and, himself trudging along on foot, **brought him to an inn and took care of him.** All the while, whatever thoughts of his own danger arose in the Samaritan's mind, as he delayed, to dress the man's wounds, and then slowly moved on with his charge, he heeded them not, nor made much of the personal discomfort he was thus put to. Self was kept in abeyance; a fellow-man's need drew out his pity and his help. If the wounded man was a Jew, which he may have been, the instance of kindness becomes still more impressive.

35. And on the morrow he took out two pence, and gave them to the host, and said, Take care of him; and whatsoever thou spendest more, I, when I come back again, will repay thee.

35. When he departed **on the morrow,** he would still provide for the unfortunate. **Two pence** (denaria). Equal to about thirty cents, which was two days' ordinary wages, and would pay for some days' care. **To the host.** This shows that the inn here was not the empty khan often found as a refuge, but a place of entertainment more like our wayside inns, presided over by a host, and where attentions might be secured by paying for them. HACKETT giving account of a visit to this region in 1852 says, "There are the ruins now of such a shelter for the benighted or unfortunate on one of the heights which overlook the infested road." **Whatsoever thou spendest more.** His love goes out to more future contingencies. He is not merely satisfying his conscience, and no more. **When I come again.** This indicates him to have been a known and frequent traveller. **I will repay thee.** The "I" is emphatic.

36, 37. Which of these three, thinkest thou, proved neighbour unto him that fell among the robbers? And he said, He that shewed mercy on him. And Jesus said unto him, Go, and do thou likewise.

36. Here now were specimens of conduct, **these three,** from which the questioning lawyer might judge for himself—**thinkest thou?**—what true neighborly love is. In **him that fell among the robbers** was a needy man, a fellow-mortal. **Which proved neighbour unto him?** Notice the change from the original question (ver. 29).

37. **He that shewed mercy on him.** Some think the lawyer even here avoided saying "The Samaritan," through the hateful spirit alluded to above. But let us give him the benefit of the doubt. His answer was more correct and instructive than if he had used the shorter

and more definite designation. Go, and instead of asking tempting and captious questions, **do thou**—even *thou*, Jewish lawyer—**do thou likewise.** Let your *acts* prove your character. "And what doth the Lord require of thee, but to do justly, and to love mercy, and to walk humbly with thy God?" (Micah vi. 8).

> 38,-42. Now as they went on their way, he entered into a certain village: and a certain woman named Martha received him into her house. And she had a sister called Mary, which also sat at the Lord's feet, and heard his word. But Martha was cumbered about much serving; and she came up to him, and said, Lord, dost thou not care that my sister did leave me to serve alone? bid her therefore that she help me. But the Lord answered and said unto her, Martha, Martha, thou art anxious and troubled about many things: but one thing is needful: for Mary hath chosen the good part, which shall not be taken away from her.

38. **On their way.** In the journey referred to in ix. 51-56. The village was Bethany. Martha seems to have been the housekeeper, the elder of the sisters. See more about this interesting household in John xi. Comp. also John xii. 1-3, which refers to a different entertainment from the one here spoken of.

39. **Mary,** besides what else she did, **also sat at the Lord's feet** as a learner, intent on **his word.** She was of a quiet, contemplative, restful spirit, and listened well and learned.

40. But Martha was **cumbered,** distracted, drawn hither and thither, with **much serving.** She was a bustling busy body, without quiet and repose. She made the house lively in doing "many things" for Jesus. "But in the midst of her work, which she began with good intention, she feels an indistinct presentiment that her sister was enjoying more than herself the presence of Jesus (that she had the better part)" (STIER). Accordingly she **came up to him** who was her guest and ought

not to have been appealed to in such a matter, and plead, **Lord . . . care . . . sister . . . leave me**—it appears that Mary had at first taken hold with Martha, but was so drawn to Jesus as to leave everything and seek His words—**to serve alone?** She would even have Him leave off His edifying converse and **bid her help** in household duties.

41. In reply His repeated **Martha, Martha,** was earnestly startling. **Thou art anxious.** In the Sermon on the Mount He had bidden men avoid this spirit (Matt. vi. 25–34). **Troubled.** In an agitated state of mind. **About many things.** This and that, one thing and another, household cares. Her inner carefulness, or concern, produced outer confusion, tumultuousness. Against her "many things" the Lord declared **one thing** as **needful.** "By these words Jesus, in accordance with the context, can mean nothing else than that from which Martha had withdrawn, while Mary was bestowing pains upon it—*the undivided devotion to His word for the sake of salvation*" (MEYER).

42. He courteously puts aside Martha's "much serving" as not what He desired or she should give her strength to. And in illustration of what He meant, commending her whom Martha asked Him to reprove, He said, **For Mary hath chosen the good part,** the one thing which is above all others in worth, viz. to humbly sit at Jesus' feet and hear His word,—a part **which shall not be taken away from her,** either now, according to Martha's request in ver. 40, or forever!

So the contemplative, quiet-spirited Mary wins the divine commendation, and bustling Martha, with us all, is taught a lesson. Observe that Jesus' word is of more account than things done for Him.

CHAPTER XI.

1. And it came to pass, as he was praying in a certain place, that when he ceased, one of his disciples saith unto him, Lord, teach us to pray, even as John also taught his disciples.

He was praying in a certain place, we know not where. The reference below to John gives color to the view that it was over in Peræa where John at first baptized (John x. 40–42). The Scriptures represent Jesus as a man of prayer. In this, as in all things, He is our great and perfect exemplar. But if Jesus, in whom dwelt all the fulness of the Godhead bodily (Col. ii. 9), and who was filled with the Holy Spirit, given without measure unto Him (John iii. 34), needed to pray, how much more do we, who are full of sin and all unholy and unclean, need to pray! **One of his disciples,** not of the Twelve, but probably one who had not been a disciple, or at least had not been present, when the Sermon on the Mount was spoken, seeing that the Master prayed, this disciple was now moved to ask Him, **Lord, teach us to pray** and refer to the fact **John also taught his disciples** to pray. If any think they do need to be taught to pray, or that prayer is such a spontaneous heart-matter that it ought not and cannot be taught, let them here learn a more humble spirit and sensible view of a most important spiritual act. Children ought to be taught to pray: and all disciples ought to be little children in receiving the kingdom of God. Young men ought to be taught to pray. Theological students ought to be taught to pray.

Indeed everybody needs to be so taught; and how well it would be if every one were willing to learn! To this end a study of the prayers in "The Common Service" and other Liturgies and books of prayer will be found very serviceable. Prayer has been well said to be the highest act of man's mental powers. To make a suitable prayer is often a greater strain upon a man than the preaching of a sermon. It is often, therefore, a help to have at hand a proper form of prayer that may be used.

2–4. And he said unto them, When ye pray, say, Father, Hallowed be thy name. Thy kingdom come. Give us day by day our daily bread. And forgive us our sins; for we ourselves also forgive every one that is indebted to us. And bring us not into temptation.

Jesus had nothing better to offer these inquiring pupils than what He had given them in the Sermon on the Mount (Matt. vi. 9–13) perhaps a year and a half before this.

2. **When ye pray, say.** He gives them a form as well as a model; yet it is not an empty form, but one full of the soul of worship and devotion. A perfect model, taught by Him who is the way to God (in whose name, Phil. ii. 10, every knee shall bow, to be accepted), it is called "The Lord's Prayer." It has in it the sum and substance of all right prayer. Books upon books have been written upon it; it is an inexhaustible mine of instruction and devotion. One of the divisions of Luther's Catechism is devoted to it. Study that, and see comments in detail on Matt. vi. 9–13. The prayer here is substantially the same as there, but more condensed, according to the text adopted by the Revisers of the Authorized Version. It is to be noted, however, that there is about equal authority for retaining as for omitting the passages which make the text here read almost identically as in Matthew. The address of this prayer

is **Father**, not "Most Dread Sovereign," "Almighty Maker," "All-Holy God," but "*Father*," a word of hopeful trust. "Be ye followers of God as dear children" (Eph. v. 1).

Hallowed, counted holy, reverenced, **be thy name**, be thou, however thou be manifested—be thou thus regarded and treated, with fear, love and trust. God is the stay of the universe: "Yea, let God be true, but every man a liar." First, last, and all the time be the only, the holy God *sanctified* by all, by *me!* Man's chief end is fellowship with God. God's "name" is not the letters that spell any of His appellations, but "Himself, as He is made known to us, and conceivable by us, and differenced from all other beings" (LEIGHTON). **Thy kingdom**—proclaimed in the Law and the Prophets, and by Jesus, their Fulfiller; of which the Son is King (Ps. ii. "Crown Him Lord of All"); the fruits of which are "righteousness and peace and joy in the Holy Ghost" (Rom. xiv. 17)—**come**, in all the world, in *me!* First the kingdom of grace, then the kingdom of glory!

3. **Give us.** This marks a sense of dependence. **Day by day.** This shows that our sense of dependence should be a *daily* one, constant, and so our prayer. "Sufficient unto the day is the evil thereof," and the food thereof. **Our daily bread.** So Agur's prayer, Prov. xxx. 8, "Food convenient (proportionable) for me, (or, of my allowance)." *Ours* by thy gift upon our proper industry (2 Thess. iii. 10–12), not earned by the unrecompensed sweat of some other body's face!

4. **And forgive us our sins.** In Matt. (vi. 12) the word is "debts," explained (in vers. 14 and 15) "as trespasses;" which word is oftenest used in the public use of this prayer. It certainly refers to moral delinquencies; and the petition implies a sense of sin and guilt, humble ac-

knowledgment of the same, belief that there is forgiveness with God, and earnest desire for deliverance. **For we ourselves also forgive** those morally delinquent toward us. That "as" in Matthew vi. 12 is equivalent to *inasmuch as, since*, is shown by Luke's "for," indicating a gracious preparedness in the supplicant to receive the divine forgiveness. It is not to be used as a word of measure or of merit. **And bring us not,** in Thy providence which is over all Thy works, and in Thy power which is greater than the devil's, who is only *permitted* to assail character (Job i. 12; ii. 6), **into temptation.** Here is expressed a consciousness of weakness which runs to God for protection. (Comp. Matt. iv. 1; xxvi. 41; 1 Cor. x. 13; Jas. i. 2, 3, 12-18; Rev. iii. 10.)

5, 6. And he said unto them, Which of you shall have a friend, and shall go unto him at midnight, and say unto him, Friend, lend me three loaves; for a friend of mine is come to me from a journey, and I have nothing to set before him.

5, 6. **Shall have a friend.** He illustrates from ordinary relations in life and common experience, and the argument is what is called *à fortiori*, from the less to the greater. **Shall go unto him,** relying on his friendship, according to the proverb, "A friend loveth at all times." A friend in need is a friend indeed. **At midnight.** A very unseasonable hour. A call then would be a severer test of friendship than at other times. It is midday for us who are here encouraged to go to God. The Sun of Righteousness is shining in His power: and "now is the accepted time."

Three loaves. Their loaves were small. "Three" are asked, probably, both for abundance and for hospitable appearance. The appeal was not for his own needs : **a friend . . . come . . . from a journey.** Just arrived, night being the pleasant time for travel in many parts of the East. Our missionaries in India write about their journeyings in the night. This petition, then, was *intercessory*, for another. The friend would naturally need food after travelling. **Nothing to set before him.** The pantry was empty; a poor show for hospitality on the one hand, and for a hungry stomach on the other.

I have nothing. That is our human inability to supply the needs of a perishing sinner. We have nothing to satisfy the hungry soul; and none can save his brother alive. Hence we must go to the source of all supply, to find grace for ourselves and for our fellow-men.

7. And he from within shall answer and say, Trouble me not: the door is now shut, and my children are with me in bed; I cannot rise and give thee?

7. We all know the disagreeableness of being waked up about midnight from the soundness of our first sleep, and can understand the situation of the friend appealed to. **He from within** is represented as calling out, without getting up or opening the door. **Trouble me not.** Selfishness asserted itself against neighborly love. **The door . . . shut,** bolted for the night: **children . . .** all of us **in bed ;** it will disturb the whole house. The house is not to be supposed a capacious one like many of ours. **I cannot rise and give thee.** You are welcome enough to the bread, but I cannot be disturbed now to get it. Such is the situation and prospect.

8. I say unto you, Though he will not rise and give him, because he is his friend, yet because of his importunity he will arise and give him as many as he needeth.

8. He does not prove to be a very good friend, but he has plenty of human nature, and the Lord knows it perfectly and adds, **I say unto you, Though . . . not . . . because . . . his friend, yet because of his importunity,** because he keeps on knocking and asking, worrying the

housekeeper out of patience, **he will arise**, moved by selfishness, to get rid of the man and his disturbance, **and give him as many as he needeth.** The point seems to be that after all the applicant gets what he came for.

9. And I say unto you, Ask, and it shall be given you; seek, and ye shall find; knock, and it shall be opened unto you.

See on Matt. vii. 7–11, where almost the same words are found as here in vers. 9–13.

9. **And I** (emphatic) **say unto you.** Of course in illustrating divine by human things many points of comparison must necessarily fail. Here there is more contrast than comparison, as in the parable of the unjust judge (xviii. 1–7). If a selfish sinner, and an unjust judge, can be moved by persistence to do what his selfishness or injustice at first refused, shall not the holy and righteous God be appealed to with the greater certainty of success? Right principle will go further than wrong. **Ask—seek—knock.** A climax of intensity of desire and effort. We ask for what we need; we seek what we do not have, or what is lost; we knock to gain admittance where this is in another power than our own. The ordinary law, which holds also in our relations to God, is that **it shall be given** to him who asks, he who seeks **shall find,** and **it shall be opened** to him who knocks. Now, "as a Son over his own house," Jesus with authority applies this law to the heavenly kingdom.

10. For every one that asketh receiveth; and he that seeketh findeth; and to him that knocketh it shall be opened.

10. Of course arbitrariness is excluded. This law does not subvert the other laws and general character of God's kingdom and dealings with men. "Ye ask and receive not, because ye ask amiss," says James (iv. 3), "that ye may consume it upon your lusts." Every one that

asketh in faith and according to the will of God, **receiveth**: not always the exact thing asked for, or at that particular time, yet some time. Paul prayed that his " thorn in the flesh " might be removed ; but, instead of doing just that, God said, " My grace is sufficient for thee." Jesus, in the Garden of Gethsemane, prayed so earnestly, " O, my Father, if it be possible, let this cup pass from me!" An angel was sent to strengthen Him, but He drank the bitter cup to the dregs. " Wait on the Lord, and he shall save thee." If God does not give us what we importune Him for, He gives us something better. **And he that seeketh, findeth.** Yet is there a time and order for seeking. " Seek ye the Lord while he may be found; call ye upon him while he is near." " Seek ye first the kingdom of God and his righteousness, and all these things (see Matt. vi. 33) shall be added unto you." The time is coming when " many shall seek to enter in (at the strait gate), and shall not be able" (xiii. 24). **And to him that knocketh it shall be opened.** Yet is there a time coming when the door will be shut, and to those who stand without and knock, and cry, " Lord, open unto us," it will still remain shut. Too late! See xiii. 24–30 ; and Matt. xxv. 1–46. But the Lord in our lesson speaks of this present gracious time when the kingdom of God is come nigh to men and they press into it. " *Now* is the *accepted* time ; *this* is the day of *salvation.*" Therefore ask, seek, knock! There is also another side to this: how often Jesus knocks at people's hearts, and is refused admittance! " Behold, I stand at the door and knock. If any man open the door, I will come in to him." That " *if* " marks man's tremendous power of rejecting his Saviour!

11, 12. And of which of you that is a father shall his son ask a loaf, and he give him a stone? or a fish, and he for a fish give him a serpent? Or *if* he shall ask an egg, will he give him a scorpion?

11, 12. Now the Lord appeals to their consciousness of the tender love existing between a son and a father. He had just taught them to address God as "Father;" He will carry out the relation to its consequences. And first, how is it with any of you? **If a son** of yours **shall ask a loaf, will he give him a stone,** deceiving and vexing him? We are told that their loaves were shaped like a smooth, flat stone. **For a fish.** Bread and fish were common articles of food. **Give him a serpent?** Which might resemble a fish, as an eel or perch, but would be hurtful. **Will he give him a scorpion?** Which, of the white kind and rolled up, might resemble the asked-for egg, but in no way take its place, being utterly unfit for food, and, besides, dangerous to handle.

Now, suppose a son should, in his ignorance or error, ask a scorpion for an egg, or a serpent for a fish, or a stone for bread; would any of you that is a father give it to him, to his hurt? So, if we ask amiss, for things that are not good for us, it is our heavenly Father's kindness and love *not* to grant such requests. And He knows *what* is best, and *how*, and *when*.

13. If ye then, being evil, know how to give good gifts unto your children, how much more shall *your* heavenly Father give the Holy Spirit to them that ask him?

13. Here is a summing up of the argument. **Ye,** earthly fathers, **being evil,** belonging to Adam's fallen race, imperfect, depraved in knowledge, affections and will, nevertheless **know how to give good gifts,** beneficial, helpful, answering the need, **unto your children,** because they are flesh of your flesh and near to your hearts, loving and beloved; **how much more shall your heavenly**

Father, your Father from heaven (for so the original is), not sinful or imperfect, like all earthly things, but unselfish, loving, faithful, **give the Holy Spirit**—in Matthew it is "good things"—**to them that ask him?** The best thing God can give His children is the Holy Spirit, and He, therefore, stands as comprehending all "good things." Nor are we justified from this in referring to spiritual gifts and graces only the great promises here given to importunity in prayer, though we know that such things are according to the divine will and we may always plead for them, if we do so in a proper spirit; but the promises and incitements here refer to "all things" (Matt. xxi. 22) that may be needful for us, including daily bread and temporal good: for *spiritual*, it has been well said, is not opposite to *temporal* but to *carnal*, that which serves and inflames our depraved nature. There is nothing which engages a Christian, in reference to which he may not seek God and ask wisdom and direction. "Whether, therefore, ye eat or drink, or whatsoever ye do, do all to the glory of God." But all our askings, seekings and knockings should be in humble acknowledgment of our Father's greater knowledge and in humble submission to His ever-wise will. We may not ever *demand* anything from our heavenly Father! But why ask Him if He already is fully acquainted with our wants?—For several obvious reasons. First, Asking, seeking, knocking, prepares us to receive God's good gifts. Here is the subjective side of prayer, in which, by the very nature of the exercise, and by communion with God, our souls are lifted into a higher sphere and we receive a spiritual power. Secondly, because God has seen fit to make His gifts in many respects dependent on our asking, seeking, knocking. "Even so, Father, for so it seemed good in Thy sight." **Prayer** is both a privilege and a duty. It is its own reward, at the same time that it secures for the petitioner what he otherwise would not get.

14-23. And he was casting out a devil *which was* dumb. And it came to pass, when the devil was gone out, the dumb man spake ; and the multitudes marvelled. But some of them said, By Beelzebub the prince of the devils casteth he out devils. And others, tempting *him*, sought of him a sign from heaven. But he, knowing their thoughts, said unto them, Every kingdom divided against itself is brought to desolation ; and a house *divided* against a house falleth. And if Satan also is divided against himself, how shall his kingdom stand ? because ye say that I cast out devils by Beelzebub. And if I by Beelzebub cast out devils, by whom do your sons cast them out ? therefore shall they be your judges. But if I by the finger of God cast out devils, then is the kingdom of God come upon you. When the strong *man* fully armed guardeth his own court, his goods are in peace: but when a stronger than he shall come upon him, and overcome him, he taketh from him his whole armour wherein he trusted, and divideth his spoils. He that is not with me is against me ; and he that gathereth not with me scattereth.

See on Matt. xii. 22-30 ; and Mark iii. 22-27. What is here recorded by Luke is almost identical with what Matthew and Mark give in the places referred to, and the exposition there will do for this place also, though Luke's account is probably of an entirely different occasion.[1]

[1] BROADUS, in his Harmony, p. 113, note, says : "It is perfectly natural that the blasphemous accusation made in Galilee (Matt. xii. 22, ff. ; Mark iii. 22, ff.) should be repeated a year or so afterward in Judæa or Peræa, and that Jesus should make substantially the same argument in reply. This sort of thing occurs to every travelling religious teacher. Our Lord does not here give the solemn warning that such an accusation is really blaspheming against the Holy Spirit and is unpardonable. (See Luke xii. 10.) And the subsequent occurrences are quite different in the two cases. In Matthew and Mark He afterward goes out by the lake-side and gives the great group of parables, presently explaining some of them to the disciples in a house, and then crosses the lake to Gerasa, etc. Here, in Luke, He breakfasts with a Pharisee, and utters such solemn woes against the Pharisees as are found only in the closing months of His ministry, and then gives to vast multitudes a series of instructions wholly unlike the great group of parables. So it is quite unsuitable to identify this occurrence with that of Matt. xii. 22, ff. ; Mark iii. 22, ff."

24–26. The unclean spirit when he is gone out of the man, passeth through waterless places, seeking rest; and finding none, he saith, I will turn back unto my house whence I came out. And when he is come, he findeth it swept and garnished. Then goeth he, and taketh *to him* seven other spirits more evil than himself; and they enter in and dwell there: and the last state of that man becometh worse than the first.

See on Matt. xii. 43–45.

27, 28. And it came to pass, as he said these things, a certain woman out of the multitude lifted up her voice, and said unto him, Blessed is the womb that bare thee, and the breasts which thou didst suck. But he said, Yea rather, blessed are they that hear the word of God, and keep it.

27. Thoroughly impressed with Jesus' greatness **as he said these things,** some **woman lifted . . . voice** and right **out of the multitude** cried, **Blessed**—is Thy mother! Whilst some accord to this woman an earnest feeling and deep understanding, STIER, on the contrary, regards her utterance as unenlightened, empty praise, equivalent to " O how must Thy mother rejoice over Thee—would I were she !"

28. It would not to do pass this outcry by unnoticed. What did He say to it? **Yea rather.** This is both confirmatory and corrective of what the woman said : confirmatory, for higher than she had long ago (i. 28, 42) pronounced blessing upon Mary, and she was blessed ; corrective, however, of the merely external and natural basis of the tribute given. " Jesus does not deny His mother's blessedness, but He defines the predicate μακάριος [" blessed "], not as the woman had done, as a special *external* relation, but as a general *moral* relation, which *might* be established in the case of *every one*, and under which even Mary was brought, so that thus the benediction upon the mother, merely considered as *mother*, is corrected " (MEYER). Above this natural relation Jesus puts all who **hear the word of God and keep it.**

"Only *because* Mary had received the word of God with such entire and unhesitating faith, had she received that honor" (STIER)—of being Jesus' mother. (Comp. viii. 19–21; Matt. xii. 46–50; Mark iii. 31–35.)

29–32. And when the multitudes were gathering together unto him, he began to say, This generation is an evil generation: it seeketh after a sign; and there shall no sign be given to it but the sign of Jonah. For even as Jonah became a sign unto the Ninevites, so shall also the Son of man be to this generation. The queen of the south shall rise up in the judgment with the men of this generation, and shall condemn them: for she came from the ends of the earth to hear the wisdom of Solomon; and behold, a greater than Solomon is here. The men of Nineveh shall stand up in the judgment with this generation, and shall condemn it: for they repented at the preaching of Jonah; and behold, a greater than Jonah is here.

See on Matt. xii. 39–42.

33–36. No man, when he hath lighted a lamp, putteth it in a cellar, neither under the bushel, but on the stand, that they which enter in may see the light. The lamp of thy body is thine eye: when thine eye is single, thy whole body also is full of light; but when it is evil, thy body also is full of darkness. Look therefore whether the light that is in thee be not darkness. If therefore thy whole body be full of light, having no part dark, it shall be wholly full of light, as when the lamp with its bright shining doth give thee light.

See on viii. 16; Matt. v. 15; vi. 22, 23; Mark iv. 21.

33–36. God does not do what **no man** would do—make a light and hide it. On the other hand when God sets forth the light, man must see that his **eye is single**, clear, pure, bright, open, that he may see what God sets forth. God has given men something to see and faculties for seeing it. But "an evil generation" (vers. 29–32) may prevent the proper effect of this plan and cause darkness where there should be light. A common proverb says, "There are none so blind as those who will not see."

37. Now as he spake, a Pharisee asketh him to dine with him: and he went in, and sat down to meat.

37. The invitation of **a Pharisee** to Jesus **to dine**—it should be *breakfast*—**with him** was probably not dictated by pure friendship. There was an ulterior reason, as often in similar invitations among us. The further course of the narrative justifies this observation. Jesus was accustomed to accept social invitations. He "came eating and drinking," and was not an ascetic.

38. And when the Pharisee saw it, he marvelled that he had not first washed before dinner.

38. **Washed.** The Greek is ἐβαπτίσθη, and even an English reader can see that this is the word usually translated "baptized." Those who insist that this word must mean immerse must be in a quandary here! MEYER suggests "a bath!" We are quite satisfied with the translation we have. See on Matt. xv. 2 and Mark vii. 2-5.

39-41. And the Lord said unto him, Now do ye Pharisees cleanse the outside of the cup and of the platter; but your inward part is full of extortion and wickedness. Ye foolish ones, did not he that made the outside make the inside also? Howbeit give for alms those things which are within; and behold, all things are clean unto you.

See on Matt. xxiii. 25, 26.

39. **Now** appears to refer to something the Pharisee had said, or to Jesus' knowledge of his thoughts. **Your inward part** at once transfers the thought from the cup and platter to their persons, and makes immediate application of the principle involved. **Extortion and wickedness** are moral characteristics that can belong only to persons. The Pharisees were externally punctilious but internally corrupt. Jesus forcibly rebukes them. He always seasoned social gatherings and repasts with the better fare of divine instruction.

40. **Foolish ones** expresses it better than our abrupt "fools." The Pharisees' course of externalism would

not bear the judgment of reason or wisdom. **The inside of anything is as important as the outside,** but this is especially so, and infinitely more so, in the case of a human being, the chief work on earth of the great Creator. How irrational to act as if man were all or chiefly *outside*, and could realize his destiny by externalism!

41. Instead, therefore, of being filled with extortion, covetousness, rapacity and other wickedness, **give for alms,** make a charitable use of, by loving activity, **those things which are within,** the inside, the contents, and, cleansed within, **all things are clean.** Work from within out, as the true order. Be more concerned for your hearts than for your hands. Be washed with the washing of regeneration and the renewing of the Holy Ghost (Tit. iii. 5) rather than washed with mere water. "Create in me a clean heart, O God, and renew a right spirit within me" (Ps. li. 10), and then "to the pure all things are pure" (Tit. i. 15).

42-44. But woe unto you Pharisees! for ye tithe mint and rue and every herb, and pass over judgment and the love of God: but these ought ye to have done, and not to leave the other undone. Woe unto you Pharisees! for ye love the chief seats in the synagogues, and the salutations in the marketplaces. Woe unto you! for ye are as the tombs which appear not, and the men that walk over *them* know it not.

42. See on Matt. xxiii. 23. Where Matthew has "mercy and faith" Luke has **the love of God**—another way of saying the same thing, going to the source.

43. See on Matt. xxiii. 6, ff.

44. See on Matt. xxiii. 27, 28. Often things and persons, especially the latter, are not what they seem. "All is not gold that glitters."

45, 46. And one of the lawyers answering saith unto him, Master, in saying this thou reproachest us also. And he said, Woe unto you lawyers also! for ye laid men with burdens grievous to be borne, and ye yourselves touch not the burdens with one of your fingers.

45. On **the lawyers** see on x. 25. Most of these were Pharisees. When he says **us also** he distinguishes his class as, perhaps, more learned than others.

46. Jesus did not shrink from the implication, but proceeded to a more direct **woe** on that very class. (See on Matt. xxiii. 4.) Such men could not be in fellowship with Him who "daily beareth our burdens" (Ps. lxviii. 19), or with His Son, the bearer of the sins of the world, the impersonation of the loving direction, "Cast thy burden on the Lord and he will sustain thee" (Ps. lv. 22).

47, 48. Woe unto you! for ye build the tombs of the prophets, and your fathers killed them. So ye are witnesses and consent unto the works of your fathers: for they killed them, and ye build *their tombs*.

See on Matt. xxiii. 29–32.

47. Certainly the building of the tombs of the prophets was not itself a ground of the woe pronounced; for they did this in honor of the prophets. Rather did it confirm the relation in which they stood to the prophet-killing fathers.

48. **They killed . . . you build**—but in character you are not different from them. They disregarded and dishonored the prophets of their day, and whilst you by building tombs profess to honor those prophets, you in like manner dishonor the prophets of your day. "Ask in Moses' times, who are the good people? They will be Abraham, Isaac and Jacob; but not Moses—he should be stoned. Ask in Samuel's times, who are the good people? They will be Moses and Joshua; but not Samuel. Ask in the times of Christ, and they will be all the former prophets with Samuel; but not Christ and His apostles" (BERLENB. BIBEL).

49-51. Therefore also said the wisdom of God, I will send unto them prophets and apostles; and *some* of them they shall kill and persecute; that the blood of all the prophets, which was shed from the foundation of the world, may be required of this generation; from the blood of Abel unto the blood of Zachariah, who perished between the altar and the sanctuary: yea, I say unto you, it shall be required of this generation.

See on Matt. xxiii. 34-36.

49. **The wisdom of God.** In Matthew it is "I." Christ is the wisdom of God. Here in the Pharisee's house it seemed more appropriate to use the impersonal expression. MEYER suggests that the Lord here quotes Himself, reaffirming what He had **said** on a former occasion.

50, 51. **The blood of all ... required from this generation.** An accumulated evil inheritance. A judgment that waited long for repentance and had at last to be poured out. "Woe," sure enough. The destruction of Jerusalem and overthrow of Judaism occurred thirty-eight years after this.

52. Woe unto you lawyers! for ye took away the key of knowledge: ye entered not in yourselves, and them that were entering in ye hindered.

52. **Lawyers** should have used the Law as a pedagogue leading to Christ. But these did not. They **took away the key of knowledge** and did not use it for its legitimate purpose of opening the way. They **entered not** themselves, and perversely **hindered them that were entering**. How dreadful when those who are in the position of teachers and guides either fail to lead or mislead. Well had these earned the **woe** here pronounced.

53, 54. And when he was come out from thence, the scribes and the Pharisees began to press upon *him* venemently, and to provoke him to speak of many things; laying wait for him, to catch something out of his mouth.

53, 54. **Thence.** From the Pharisee's house where He

had taken breakfast. **To press upon . . . vehemently.** They set upon Him intently, with urgent hostile purpose. **Laying wait,** like hunters for prey, **to catch . . . his mouth.** Here they illustrate the character He ascribed to them above (ver. 47, ff.).

CHAPTER XII.

1. In the mean time, when the many thousands of the multitude were gathered together, insomuch that they trode one upon another, he began to say unto his disciples first of all, Beware ye of the leaven of the Pharisees, which is hypocrisy.

1. **In the mean time,** while Jesus was at breakfast in the Pharisee's house, a multitude consisting of **many thousands** had gathered together, and were so intent on getting near Him and seeing and hearing Him that they fairly **trode one upon another,** just as a crowd does now. Jesus met this crowd when He came out of the house of His entertainer. The words **began to say** indicate a prolonged address or addresses, only a report of which is given by Luke. And whilst He addressed **his disciples first,** it was in the hearing of the multitude, and for their instruction too, and afterward (ver. 54) He addressed them directly. **Beware** introduces words of warning. The condemnatory tone begun in the house (see above) is continued. **The leaven of the Pharisees.** Their doctrine and spirit. This, or these, He declares to be characterized by **hypocrisy.** Hypocrisy is etymologically the acting of a part, the putting on of appearances which are unreal. This is its inherent sense. The Pharisees were adepts at this, and their kind has not run out to this day. Such people abound, unreal, insincere, professing without possessing, resting in externals, formalists. Jesus warns His disciples against such a character.

2, 3. But there is nothing covered up, that shall not be revealed: and hid, that shall not be known. Wherefore whatsoever ye have said in the darkness shall be heard in the light; and what ye have spoken in the ear in the inner chambers shall be proclaimed upon the housetop.

See on viii. 17 and on Matt. x. 26, 27.

2. Hypocrisy shall not succeed. It will be exposed. That which is supposed to be **covered up** will, in God's faithful providence, **be revealed**, and what is supposed by hypocritical spirits to be **hid** will certainly come to be **known**. Every sincere, upright, honorable person rejoices at this. There is no hiding from God, who seeth in secret and knows the hidden thoughts and spirit, and He will uncover hypocrisy, to its shame and overthrow. Pretence finds no favor with God.

3. Pre-eminently is it a feature of the gospel to make known, to proclaim, to preach. Secrecy does not belong to it. There is no place in it for a leaven of hypocrisy. It is itself a revelation, and is a revealer of the thoughts and intents of the heart. (Comp. Heb. iv. 12, 13.) There is no room in it for the Pharisaic spirit. It is sincerely outspoken and makes its disciples so.

4–8. And I say unto you my friends, Be not afraid of them which kill the body, and after that have no more that they can do. But I will warn you whom ye shall fear: Fear him, which after he hath killed hath power to cast into hell; yea, I say unto you, Fear him. Are not five sparrows sold for two farthings? and not one of them is forgotten in the sight of God. But the very hairs of your head are all numbered. Fear not: ye are of more value than many sparrows.

See on Matt. x. 28–31.

4. These words are addressed to Jesus' **friends**. They open and close with **fear not** but have in their midst an emphatic **fear**. Jesus' disciples are not to fear those whose power is only over **the body**, is external and temporal, e. g. the persecuting world, or even the persecuting church, gone aside from the spirit and word of her Lord

and Head. See in the Acts of the Apostles illustrations of this power and of the disciples' obedience to this assuring word of Jesus. Like instances are occurring, even while this commentary is in writing, over in Armenia, to say nothing of our own midst. Persecuting powers can do **no more** than hurt that which is external and perishable.

5. **Power,** or authority, **to cast into hell** ($\gamma\acute{\epsilon}\epsilon\nu\nu\alpha\nu$), is another thing, and He who has it, God alone, is to be feared. The word of God appeals, in admirable proportion, to all man's sensibilities, and one of these is fear. We are to fear to sin.

6, 7. At the same time, remembering God's care of every creature, exercised with infinite ease and reaching, in His particular providence, to the veriest *minutiæ*, His friends, abiding in fellowship with Him, are urged to **fear not.** "Perfect love casteth out fear" (1 John iv. 18). "What time I am afraid I will trust in Thee" (Ps. lvi. 3).

8, 9. And I say unto you, Every one who shall confess me before men, him shall the Son of man also confess before the angels of God; but he that denieth me in the presence of men shall be denied in the presence of the angels of God.

See on Matt. x. 32, 33, and comp. on Luke ix. 26 and Mark viii. 38. See also on Rom. x. 10.

10. And every one who shall speak a word against the Son of man, it shall be forgiven him: but unto him that blasphemeth against the Holy Spirit it shall not be forgiven.

See on Matt. xii. 31, 32, and on Mark iii. 28-30.

10. That this is a sin "unto death" (1 John v. 16), never to be **forgiven,** is not because the **Holy Spirit** is greater than the Father or the Son, but because it is through the Holy Spirit, proceeding from the Father and the Son (John xiv. 26; xvi. 7), that the Holy Trinity renews

(John iii. 5, 6; Mark i. 8) and sanctifies (John xvii. 17) the heart of man, leading him to and applying to him the salvation that is in Christ Jesus (John xvi. 13-15). The Holy Spirit's work, we may say, is God's last and utmost effort to save men; and whoever calumniates and abuses the Holy Spirit has gone beyond all hope and help. Nothing is left for him but to go on in his "eternal sin" (Mark *in loc.*). Not that God could not forgive; but such a man *cannot be forgiven!* He is out of the sphere of forgiveness.

The question arises whether this sin is an *act* or a *state*. Let it be remembered that our acts proceed from our state. "Either make the tree good and its fruit good; or else make the tree corrupt and its fruit corrupt; for the tree is known by its fruit" (Matt. xii. 33-37, and see connection preceding); and "out of the abundance of the heart the mouth speaketh." The sin here referred to is evidently deliberate and wilful, not a sin of error, forgetfulness or hasty passion.

One may "grieve" (Eph. iv. 30; comp. 1 Thess. v. 19) the Holy Spirit and yet be brought to repentance; but whoever has gone so far as to "blaspheme" against Him, has exceeded the limits of repentance and salvation.

No one who is sensitive about sin and who honors God's word need be afraid of having committed this sin. No one who will *listen* to the Spirit and seeks His guidance is a blasphemer against the Holy Ghost.

11, 12. And when they bring you before the synagogues, and the rulers, and the authorities, be not anxious how or what ye shall answer, or what ye shall say: for the Holy Spirit shall teach you in that very hour what ye ought to say.

See on Matt. x. 17-20 and Mark xiii. 11.

13. And one out of the multitude said unto him, Master, bid my brother divide the inheritance with me.

13. **One of** this **multitude** showed what was uppermost in his mind, by calling out to Jesus for His interposition to secure him his rights. He seems to have been impressed with the authority manifest in Jesus' words and whole bearing, and probably thought He had come, as the Messiah, to set all things right. He seems to have been dissatisfied, and, likely, with reason, at the manner in which his brother executed their father's estate, and, respectfully calling Jesus **Master**—teacher—made his earnest request. **Bid my brother divide the inheritance with me.** Quarrels over inheritances, then, are not a new thing; they are, however, very common, and often separate chief friends. Jesus had, as usual, been talking to His hearers about the things of the kingdom of God; but, as in our churches and meetings for spiritual improvement, people's thoughts go wandering oft after other things, so here this man's earthly inheritance was his chief thought, and he brings it out even before the Lord. He was very outspoken and candid. It does not appear that our Lord was often appealed to thus to redress private wrongs. Instances are not wanting, however, in which His enemies tried to bring Him into conflict with the civil institutions of the land, and thus involve Him in trouble with the Roman government. In all these He, with infinite wisdom, kept on the high ground of spiritual principles, laying down the higher law, which should govern man in all things, and leaving the particular application for the hearers themselves to make. But in this instance He declines to have anything to do with the matter.

14. But he said unto him, Man, who made me a judge or a divider over you?

14. **Man, who made me a judge or a divider over you**

brothers? Jesus was not an arbiter of such things. He was not an officer of the law, to see that it was in any case complied with. The question of right is not involved. It is taken for granted. Make him give me the money due me! No; Jesus had nothing to do with that, and never meddled with the laws of the land. The inheritance He came to secure to man was a heavenly inheritance, to make men joint heirs with Him of the kingdom of the Father in heaven. In reference to this, it did not matter whether heirs were justly dealt with in earthly settlements or not.

15. And he said unto them, Take heed, and keep yourselves from all covetousness: for a man's life consisteth not in the abundance of the things which he possesseth.

15. **Take heed.** Look out. Be on the watch. See to it. **Keep yourselves from.** The form of expression indicates a very needful and earnest warning. All **covetousness.** Covetousness is a greedy, grasping, selfish desire to have more. Like the horse-leech, its continual cry is, Give, give; more, more. It is repeatedly (Eph. v. 5; Col. iii. 5) represented as idolatry; it is classed with grossest sins of the flesh (Rom. i. 29; 1 Cor. v. 10, 11; vi. 10; Eph. iv. 19; v. 3, 5; 2 Pet. ii. 3, 14). As it is an affection of the heart, it may exist in very poor people as well as among the rich, and quite as likely, to say the least. It may manifest itself among the honest and conscientious, as well as among the dishonest and unscrupulous; it may show itself in the manner in which we hold and reclaim our own, as truly as in the undue snatching for what belongs to others. Putting "money" for all worldly gain, it is the love of money, and this is infallibly (1 Tim. vi. 10) pronounced a "root of all evil." There is scarcely a crime in the whole catalogue to which covetousness has not given, and may not naturally give,

rise. The daily records of abuse of trust, defalcations, murders, robberies, frauds, have their origin chiefly in this root of evil. Insidious in its nature as well as overbearing, deceiving ofttimes by the appearance of thrift, prudence, long-headedness, sharpness in business, and not necessarily conflicting with honesty and strict justice, it is a sin that especially needs to be guarded against, that calls for most earnest and repeated warnings. It is the more dangerous as being tolerated by individuals and churches, a respectable sin, notwithstanding the Bible puts it in the grossest and most disreputable company. (See references above.) We may safely say that no sin is more reproved in Scripture than this one, and none seems more common. **For a man's life consisteth not in the abundance of the things which he possesseth.** Covetousness absorbs a man. Such is its tendency. It belittles a man; it trenches on the best part of our nature and keeps out God's image. But should a human being, an immortal soul, one for whom Christ died, take so low a view of life as to give it over thus? This fails to realize what life in its full and true sense is. Possessions are lifeless, and cannot give what does not belong to them. Possessors of abundance are, other things being equal, as liable to sorrow, disease, accident, death, as those who have merely a supply of their needs. Possessions do not give education, culture, refinement, fitness for society either here or in heaven. "To the question, What is a man worth? the world replies by enumerating what he has; the Son of man, by estimating what he is" (ROBERTSON). In looking over mankind and seeing the almost everywhere prevailing spirit of desire of gain, one would think very few *believe* what our Lord here says; they act so much as if He had said just the opposite.

16, 17. And he spake a parable unto them, saying, The ground of a certain rich man brought forth plentifully: and he reasoned within himself, saying, What shall I do, because I have not where to bestow my fruits?

16. **He spake a parable,** to illustrate and enforce His warning, and to fix it more abidingly in their memories. His parables were taken from the sphere of ordinary affairs, and are so true to life as that there is no stretch in supposing that the circumstances composing them may have actually occurred. **The ground.** The place—his farm. He was **a rich man,** and his farm was a good one.

17. **And he reasoned within himself.** And this was a key to his character; for "as a man thinketh in his heart, so is he." It is a distinguishing characteristic of man that he is able to reflect. **What shall I do?** Note his perplexity, caused by his abundance. **I have not where to bestow my fruits.** If he had reflected a little further, he might have thought of those not blessed as he was, who had plenty of room for some of the fruits the great Provider had entrusted to him as a steward. But, whilst the clouds above said, Give, and the little streams through his fields said, Give, and the goodness of God said, Give, and the needs of the poor said, Give, he heard not, or, at least, heeded not these voices, and sought only for room on his own place for these gifts of a good Providence. "Willing to distribute" was no one of his characteristics; likely he never thought of such a thing.

18, 19. And he said, This will I do: I will pull down my barns and build greater; and there will I bestow all my corn and my goods. And I will say to my soul, Soul, thou hast much goods laid up for many years; take thine ease, eat, drink, be merry.

18. The **barns** over there were vaults—underground depositories. To **pull down, and build greater** accom-

modations—enlargement—was the rich man's device to get out of his dilemma. **There, in my own granaries, I will bestow all my corn and my goods.** The frequency with which he says "I" and "my," leaving God and men alike out of his count and plans, is the thing to be noted here. There was no wrong in his enlarging his farm facilities.

19. **And I will say to my soul,** as the sequel to all this, and demonstrating the spirit in which it was all done. The word rendered "soul" in these verses is the one that represents not the immortal nature but the animal life—the personal existence in this world. **Soul,** life, self, **thou hast** (note the sense of possession—property) **much goods,** many good things, **laid up for many years.** Christ had taught men to say, "*Give us this day our daily bread*," and to keep sensible of their dependence on a higher power. But, on the contrary, this man's bank was his confidence. He needn't pray for his daily bread, having enough on hand for many years. **Take thine ease.** He proposes to retire, and take life easy. **Eat, drink, be merry.** Enjoy thyself; have a good time. He took up the motto of the Epicureans. He looked only to the animal life and its physical gratification. Sensualism is the key-note here. "Modern materialism can offer the soul nothing better than this."

20. But God said unto him, Thou foolish one, this night is thy soul required of thee; and the things which thou hast prepared, whose shall they be?

20. **But God,** overlooked by the rich man, had something to say. All are His messengers, and in various ways He might speak to the man. **Thou foolish one.** Ah! to be called so by infinite wisdom—fool! Acting as though without understanding; giving thy mind, thy sense, no

16

chance to act or determine; governed only by the lower nature; regardless of the fitness of things. **This night, before thy plans are well begun! Thy soul is required of thee.** " They demand of thee thy life," is a more exact rendering. "They" may be a general designation for God's messengers, in whatever form; some propose to refer it to robbers, who readily turn murderers to accomplish their purposes, and suppose the rich man to be about to be the victim. This night thy life will be gone. **And the things which thou hast prepared, whose shall they be?** " Riches take to themselves wings and fly away;" and, if they do not fly from us, we soon fly from them. They must be *used* or *left!*

21. So is he that layeth up treasure for himself, and is not rich toward God.

21. **So.** So foolish, so truly destitute. **Is he . . . treasure for himself, . . . not rich toward God.** " Layeth up treasure," treasuring up, as embracing a man's activities, is set over against " is not rich," a being something, a character, which, indeed, is not do-less, but is moved by a higher spring than self: " for himself" is contrasted with " toward God." Selfishness is opposed to godliness. A man treasures up what is outside of himself; but he is *rich* in what he *is*.

We are all stewards of God's gifts; not owners by natural or purchased right. We cannot, in the absolute sense, say, " my" or " mine," of anything. For even of ourselves the Apostle says, " Ye are not your own, for ye are bought with a price; therefore glorify God."

" Many owners of millions are paupers, before God " (RYLE). And so they will appear before men at the great gathering of all mankind, at the settling up of the world.

The episode with the man who wanted the Lord to

secure him his inheritance led directly to what follows, in which we find the same teaching in almost the same words as in the Sermon on the Mount. See on Matt. vi. 25-34.

22, 23. *And he said unto his disciples, Therefore I say unto you, Be not anxious for your life, what ye shall eat: nor yet for your body, what ye shall put on. For the life is more than the food, and the body than the raiment.*

22. **Therefore,** in view of the tendency of the natural heart to set its affections on worldly good, **I say unto you** — here comes again that forceful authoritative word of the Great Teacher—**Be not anxious for your life,** here in the sense of *livelihood*, your sustenance, daily bread, **nor yet for your body, what ye shall put on.** Now in the sweat of his face and laborious providence man is divinely enjoined to seek, while he prays for, his "daily bread," and for his household; therefore that labor and toil cannot be forbidden. But that indicates only *means*, not the *end* and *purpose* of life.

23. **For** (and this gives the reason) **the life is more than meat,** or than its *nourishment;* and **the body than the raiment** that is put upon it, *its clothing.* The life of a human being is more than the life of a plant or of a mere animal.

24. *Consider the ravens, that they sow not, neither reap; which have no store-chamber nor barn; and God feedeth them: of how much more value are ye than the birds!*

24. **Consider the ravens.** In Matt. vi. 26 it is "the fowls of the air," free as the air in their flights hither and thither, chirping and carolling cheerfully, or soaring grandly in the high ether, *untroubled!* Here it is "the ravens," with a name kindred to our word "ravenous," for they are voracious birds. The argument is *à fortiori*. "We never knew an earthly father take care of his *fowls*

and neglect his *children;* and shall we fear this from our heavenly Father?" (A. CLARKE.)

Pointing to the irrational animals the Great Teacher says: "Are ye not much better than they?" To which the *knowing* (!) ones reply, "Not much; only a further development!"

<small>25, 26. And which of you by being anxious can add a cubit unto his stature? If then ye are not able to do even that which is least, why are ye anxious concerning the rest?</small>

25, 26. **Which of you** by such a process, **by being anxious, can add a cubit unto his stature?** The word rendered stature means also age. A cubit is about eighteen inches. This added to one's "stature" could hardly be called **that which is least;** but it would be very little to add to one's time of life, his life's journey. (See Ps. xxxix. 5.) As you cannot create life, so you cannot add to it—at all events by anxiety! Why then fret and be disquieted?

<small>27. Consider the lilies, how they grow: they toil not, neither do they spin: yet I say unto you, Even Solomon in all his glory was not arrayed like one of these.</small>

27. Having gone to school to the birds, concerning food, now for raiment **consider the lilies** that cover the fields and meadows all around. See them : **they toil not, neither spin,** to clothe themselves withal. Yet they **grow;** and look at them, they are not ashamed, for nakedness, to hold up their heads! The grandeur of Solomon and his times is to you Jews the ideal of all earthly splendor; **yet I say unto you, Even Solomon in all his glory was not arrayed like one**—even a single flower—**of these.** What exquisite delicacy of texture, and perfect beauty of form and color! And the more minutely, as with a miscroscope, you examine, the more beautiful will it appear.

28. But if God doth so clothe the grass in the field, which to-day is, and to-morrow is cast into the oven ; how much more *shall he clothe* you, O ye of little faith?

28. Incomparably beautiful as these lilies are, they are yet counted as only **the grass in the field,** mid which they grow, and with which they are soon cut down and wither. It **to-day is,** in all its exquisite apparel, **and to-morrow is cast into the oven,** the earthen pot in which they baked their cakes, and which might easily be heated by burning therein dried grass and stubble. The argument is, **if God so clothe** what is so short lived, **much more** will He clothe with needed raiment the bodies of immortal souls! **Ye of little faith** He calls those who can doubt this, who by their continued troubled care about such things show they *do* doubt it.

29-32. And seek ye not what ye shall eat, and what ye shall drink, neither be ye of doubtful mind. For all these things do the nations of the world seek after: but your Father knoweth that ye have need of these things. Howbeit seek ye his kingdom, and these things shall be added unto you. Fear not, little flock; for it is your Father's good pleasure to give you the kingdom.

30. **These things the nations of the world,** the nations that know not God, **seek after,** knowing neither the source nor the end of their life; they do it in their blindness. But you know God; He has been revealed to you as **your father,** and you are His children, graciously received into His family, and He **knoweth ye have need of these things.** Do not be anxious, then as if you were orphans in the world, as if your Father would forget to provide for you, or not be able!

31, 32. **Howbeit seek ye,** as your life's seeking, your end and aim, **his kingdom,** even as already you have been taught to pray, " Thy kingdom come," before any mention of " our daily bread "—that kingdom which it is

your Father's good pleasure to give you. Jesus calls them **little flock,** but comforts and encourages them with great and abiding promises and prospects. The Good Shepherd bids them **Fear not,** but hope on and ever. Even **these things** of the natural life **shall be added unto you** who are devoted to God. Live to God, and He will see that you are provided for.

"At one time I was sorely vexed and tried by my own sinfulness, by the wickedness of the world, and by the dangers that beset the Church. One morning I saw my wife dressed in mourning. Surprised, I asked her who had died! 'Do you not know?' she replied; 'God in heaven is dead.' 'How can you talk such nonsense, Katie?' I said; 'how can God die? Why, He is immortal, and will live through all eternity!' 'Is that really true?' she asked. 'Of course!' I said, still not perceiving what she was aiming at; 'how can you doubt it? As surely as there is a God in heaven, so sure is it that He can never die!' 'And yet,' she said, 'though you do not doubt that, yet you are so hopeless and discouraged!' Then I observed what a wise woman my wife was, and mastered my sadness" (LUTHER).

33. Sell that ye have, and give alms; make for yourselves purses which wax not old, a treasure in the heavens that fadeth not, where no thief draweth near, neither moth destroyeth.

33. Even **sell that ye have.** Lay it not up with anxious thought for the future. Here is a good piece of advice to those who are always buying and getting and are "land-poor" and "property-poor," so that they cannot give to the cause of God's kingdom. **Give alms.** For "there is that scattereth and increaseth yet more; and there is that withholdeth more than is meet, but it tendeth only to want."

Purses which wax not old. Evidently this kind is not to be found in earthly stores. **Make** them **for yourselves,** God says. They are made by giving, by benevolence, by your *offerings*. These become a **treasure in the heavens** —a safe investment ; it **faileth not.** (See on xvi. 9.)

34. For where your treasure is, there will your heart be also.

34. Our affections follow our treasures. There are many kinds of treasures. Lay up, but in heaven ; " set your affection on things above." " How hardly shall they that trust in riches enter into the kingdom of heaven ! "

35-38. Let your loins be girded about, and your lamps burning ; and be ye yourselves like unto men looking for their lord, when he shall return from the marriage feast ; that, when he cometh and knocketh, they may straightway open unto him. Blessed are those servants, whom the lord when he cometh shall find watching : verily I say unto you, that he shall gird himself, and make them sit down to meat, and shall come and serve them. And if he shall come in the second watch, and if in the third, and find *them* so, blessed are those *servants*.

Comp. Matt. xxiv. 42-44.

The teaching of trustful heavenly-mindedness is fittingly followed by one on watchfulness.

35, 36. **Loins girded,** as was necessary for those wearing Oriental long robes, both for readiness, work and haste, and **lamps burning,** indicative of wakeful waiting in the night, are both externals, followed by the **ye yourselves** of internal, personal preparation and expectancy, **looking for their lord,** as becomes faithful, devoted servants. " Patience makes longing mighty, gives a strength, and saves it from being overstrained ; longing makes patience watchful, and saves it from growing torpid. Without this longing, patience would enervate the servant ; without the patience, his longing would fret and corrode him " (BRAUNE).

Here the lord is represented as coming **from**, and in other places *to*, **the marriage feast.** In the application marriage feast may stand for any joyous occasion, and perhaps does not here need particular reference. **Cometh and knocketh.** See ver. 40. Is at the door. **Straightway,** as expectant of and prepared for his coming: in full sympathy with their lord.

37. **Blessed** they who shall be found doing and having done their part, fulfilled their mission, come up to their Lord's expectation of them, found **watching,** awake, on the *qui vive*, always ready for their lord. They will be treated as if their relations were reversed. **He**—the lord—**shall serve them,** the servants! This Jesus did later when He washed the disciples' feet (John xiii.). What honor and glory are here promised to those who have proved faithful servants!

38. There is uncertainty, purposely, as to the time of his coming; he is not likely to come in the first watch, for that was the time of the wedding, nor to put off his coming till the last or morning watch. Therefore neither of these is mentioned in the supposition, but only **the second watch,** from nine o'clock to midnight, and **the third,** from midnight to three o'clock.

<small>39, 40. But know this, that if the master of the house had known in what hour the thief was coming, he would have watched, and not have left his house to be broken through. Be ye also ready: for in an hour that ye think not the Son of man cometh.</small>

See on Matt. xxiv. 43, 44.

39. A familiar and frequent method of illustration of watchfulness, good house-keeping.

40. And **ye,** servants of the Lord of heaven and earth, be not behind faithful servants of earthly lords, but **be** [rather, *become*, γίνεσθε,] **ready.** For, thus uncertain is the time of your Lord's coming, and only a spirit of watch-

fulness, of life, will prevent a great and sad surprise. **The Son of man** is the Lord of those to whom He is speaking, and the application of the preceding illustrations is to them as His servants. He **cometh,** no one knows when. Whilst this illustration and argument may be used with reference to death, holding true there also, we believe this interpretation to be only an accommodation and somewhat objectionable. The coming of the Son of man is a glorious something, very different from death. But the teaching of the passage is watchful faithfulness.

41–46. And Peter said, Lord, speakest thou this parable unto us, or even unto all? And the Lord said, Who then is the faithful and wise steward, whom his lord shall set over his household, to give them their portion of food in due season? Blessed is that servant, whom his lord when he cometh shall find so doing. Of a truth I say unto you, that he will set him over all that he hath. But if that servant shall say in his heart, My lord delayeth his coming; and shall begin to beat the menservants and the maidservants, and to eat and drink, and to be drunken; the lord of that servant shall come in a day when he expecteth not, and in an hour when he knoweth not, and shall cut him asunder, and appoint his portion with the unfaithful.

See on Matt. xxiv. 45–51.

41. Peter by his question seeks to find the aim of **this parable** or similitude, whether it be **us,** the disciples, **or even all.**

42–44. The indirect answer applies the teaching to any **steward set over** his lord's **household,** and so eminently to Peter and the other apostles. **The faithful and wise** steward devoted to **doing** what was appointed him, is the **blessed** one, in their case and in every case.

45. **But if that servant,** instead of so doing, shall relax his sense of responsibility and possibly quick accountability, and **shall begin** an unworthy, autocratic, selfish course, he will be surprised some day by his lord's coming and will, too late for change, find his **portion with**

the unfaithful. Matthew says "with the hypocrites": an unfaithful man is a hypocrite, in that he acts a part which he really is not; he pretends. Their portion is Gehenna (ver. 5).

> 47, 48. And that servant, which knew his lord's will, and made not ready, nor did according to his will, shall be beaten with many *stripes;* but he that knew not, and did things worthy of stripes, shall be beaten with few *stripes.* And to whomsoever much is given, of him shall much be required: and to whom they commit much, of him will they ask the more.

47, 48. He that **knew** is contrasted with him that **knew not.** They are alike in having done **things worthy of stripes.** (Comp. Rom. ii. 12 ff.) Of course the one was not punished for guilt in matters he did not know, but for unworthy deeds which nature itself taught him were unworthy. Of course he who knew and **made not ready** but neglected his lord's known **will,** as the guiltier one, shall receive the heavier punishment, **many stripes,** whilst the other, less guilty, shall receive comparatively **few.** (Comp. Rom. i. and ii.)

Knowledge, opportunity, and many other things of nature and circumstance, go to make up the **much given** from which, in fair stewardship, there is **much required.** This is the spiritual law of supply and demand. **The more,** proportionately. Expectation according to gifts, ability and opportunity.

> 49, 50. I came to cast fire upon the earth; and what will I, if it is already kindled? But I have a baptism to be baptized with; and how am I straitened till it be accomplished!

49. What is this **fire?** The Fathers generally explain it of the Holy Spirit (comp. Matt. iii. 11): but the expression **to cast upon the earth** and the connection do not favor this. MEYER understands by it "the vehement *spiritual excitement,* forcing its way through all

earthly relations, and loosing their closest ties, which Christ was destined to kindle." LUTHER says, "discord through the Gospel." *Fire* is the emphatic word in the sentence. **And what will I, if it be already kindled?** We cannot agree with the many able interpreters who make this a wish, equivalent to "How I wish that it were already kindled!" Rather does the Lord here indicate that this fire has been already kindled, and in a manner soliloquizes thus, "What more do I desire, if it burns? The aim of my operation upon earth is so far attained!" So NEANDER.

50. **But** there is yet a great completing event to be enacted. **A baptism to be baptized with** is His coming passion, for which He had set His face steadfastly toward Jerusalem (ix. 51). **How am I straitened,** in what straits, how constrained, oppressed, **till it be accomplished!** The fire which was already kindled was to burn first against Him in its devouring opposition. The Lord would Himself lead the way into and through the fire, opening a passage through which all His followers might subsequently pass safely. The evil of every day was not sufficient (Matt. vi. 34) for Jesus, but He saw full before Him coming sorrows, to endure which He had come, and so His plastic soul was fashioned. He bare our burdens before He hung upon the cross.

51-53. Think ye that I am come to give peace in the earth? I tell you, Nay; but rather division: for there shall be from henceforth five in one house divided, three against two, and two against three. They shall be divided, father against son, and son against father; mother against daughter, and daughter against her mother; mother in law against her daughter in law, and daughter in law against her mother in law.

See on Matt. x. 34-36.

51-53. All this was especially so when the Gospel was first preached in and to an ungodly world. It is now particularly observed in India and other heathen countries, where the household stripes here spoken of, in consequence of the Gospel, are common occurrences. Family opposition to the claims of Christ on any of its members is one of the greatest hindrances missionaries have to meet. See in Matt. x. 37–39 the course to be pursued by disciples of Jesus.

> 54–56. And he said to the multitudes also, When ye see a cloud rising in the west, straightway ye say, There cometh a shower; and so it cometh to pass. And when ye see a south wind blowing, ye say, There will be a scorching heat; and it cometh to pass. Ye hypocrites, ye know how to interpret the face of the earth and the heaven; but how is it that ye know not how to interpret this time?

See on Matt. xvi. 2, 3.

54, 55. In ver. 1 of this chapter we read that this discourse began to be addressed "to his disciples first of all." At ver. 13 Jesus was interrupted by "one out of the multitude." At ver. 22 the discourse again recurred "to his disciples." Now at its close He addresses Himself **to the multitudes also,** and gives them the benefit of the application of the whole discourse. The weather conditions here spoken of were such as occurred in Judæa and thereabout, where He now was.

56. Among this multitude, not unlikely, were Pharisees, whose spirit was a false one, whose leaven too much permeated the masses, so that the term Jesus specially applied (ver. 1) to Pharisees He here uses of them all and says, **Ye hypocrites.** The Lord was very outspoken. He did not study to please. He was free from the fear of man which bringeth a snare. And He spake with an authority that was penetrative. They were hypocrites because they saw only what they wanted to see, and clear enough in their discernment of weather signs they failed **to interpret this time,** this occasion of the Messiah's

manifestation. (See i. 68; vii. 16.) They might have known it if they had wanted to; but they were not sincere. A common proverb says there are none so blind as those who will not see: such were these people, and yet they professed to see (John ix. 41); hence they were suitably called hypocrites.

57. And why even of yourselves judge ye not what is right?

57. "Can, then, the natural understanding, for the sufficiency of which this text has strangely enough been cited, test these things and discern what is right? Assuredly— but, first of all, only when a revelation of God in its signs lies obviously before it (for that is the question here); and, secondly, alas! it *might* and it *should*, indeed; but it *cannot* and it *will not*, for the most part, because of other reasons which the Lord here bewails, discloses, and rebukes; it does not draw the simple and necessary deduction from the plainest and most indubitable premises, *because* the sinner does not conscientiously use his reason, and will not of and in *himself* judge that which is right!" (STIER.)

58. For as thou art going with thy adversary before the magistrate, on the way give diligence to be quit of him, lest haply he hale thee unto the judge, and the judge shall deliver thee to the officer, and the officer shall cast thee into prison. I say unto thee, Thou shalt by no means come out thence, till thou have paid the very last mite.

See on Matt. v. 25, 26.

58. While still **on the way** and not yet before the officers for trial and judgment there is opportunity to **be quit of,** released from, **thine adversary,** the one who has a case against thee, to whom thou art a debtor; you may come to an agreement with him and so avoid court proceedings and judgment. And to do so is the part of wisdom. Whilst there is no occasion for giving any special

interpretation to the various officers of the law here mentioned, since they are but the *imagery* of the illustration, it is clear that man's relation to God as a debtor is here set forth, and the wisdom of making terms with Him while there is opportunity. In human relations (as illustrated in the interruption at ver. 13) they were quick enough to demand what was right; why not in their relations to God? By repentance and faith we come to an agreement with God; and while we are " on the way," in life, is the time for this.

59. Otherwise it will be too late, and eternity itself will be too short for sinners to pay in it their dues to God. And after the judgment there will be no recourse to the unreconciled sinner.

CHAPTER XIII.

1-3. Now there were some present at that very season which told him of the Galilæans, whose blood Pilate had mingled with their sacrifices. And he answered and said unto them, Think ye that these Galilæans were sinners above all the Galilæans, because they have suffered these things? I tell you, Nay: but, except ye repent, ye shall all in like manner perish.

1. **At that very season,** or occasion, marks close connection with the address of the previous chapter. The historical occasion referred to in the story here told is not known. That they now **told him** seems to indicate that it was comparatively late news, and that the article is used—of **the** Galileans—indicates that the story was known, i. e. current. The expression **blood . . . mingled . . . sacrifices** is a vivid way of saying that Pilate had come upon them and slaughtered them while at their religious rites, sacrificing, disregarding even the sanctity of the temple. The disposition of the Galileans to revolt against Roman domination is noted by Josephus. Though they were really Herod's subjects, Pilate seems to have ruthlessly set upon them in Jerusalem. Why they now **told** Jesus this, does not appear. Perhaps the story was brought out by the references to legal measures and judgment in vers. 58, 59 of preceding chapter.

2, 3. Whatever their thought or purpose, Jesus turned their story at once to practical account. **Think ye**—as is so common to think that great, sudden and unusual calamity marks the sufferers of it as unusual sinners—**these Galileans sinners above all** their countrymen, and by this calamity so made known? **Nay;** such is a false opinion and judgment. **I tell you,** over against common notions. "The Lord utters this in the fulness of His divine knowledge" (BENGEL). To **perish** is the destiny of all men by nature, sinful nature, to be overwhelmed by death and so separated forever from God, who is life. But there is a saving clause, and the loving Saviour urges it—**except ye repent!** They who hear the divine call and face about from their course that leads to ruin and go the other way, need not and shall not perish. The **likewise** of this passage does not refer to the manner but to the fact of perishing.

4, 5. Or those eighteen, upon whom the tower in Siloam fell, and killed them, think ye that they were offenders above all the men that dwell in Jerusalem? I tell you, Nay: but, except ye repent, ye shall all likewise perish.

4, 5. The case reported to Jesus was about Galileans; now He refers them to a similar sudden calamity that fell upon **men that dwell in Jerusalem,** so as to broaden the teaching. **Those** well-known **eighteen** who were killed by the fall of **the tower in Siloam,** a place in Jerusalem, did this prove them **offenders,** *debtors,* **above all?** The historical fact here as before is otherwise unknown to us. But the teaching is emphasized. If it is not a cruel ruler, nor a sudden accident, yet whatever it is that cuts you off from this life, if you go unrepentant, unreconciled to God, you **shall perish** in the fullest, deepest sense of those words. No wonder John and Jesus both came preaching repentance; and so should their successors preach.

6–9. And he spake this parable; A certain man had a fig tree planted in his vineyard; and he came seeking fruit thereon, and found none. And he said unto the vinedresser, Behold, these three years I come seeking fruit on this fig tree, and find none: cut it down; why doth it also cumber the ground? And he answering saith unto him, Lord, let it alone this year also, till I shall dig about it, and dung it; and if it bear fruit thenceforth, *well;* but if not, thou shalt cut it down.

6. **This parable** seems intended to illustrate and confirm what had just been said about man's responsibility to God and the certainty of punishment if he fails to recognize and meet it, whilst, therefore, some interpret the **fig tree** as referring to the people of Israel, we think better to give it the most general interpretation, and applicable rather to every person **in his vineyard,** that is, the church. **Seeking fruit.** The fig tree is naturally very fruitful. It very appropriately represents any one or all of God's people. He looks for fruit from them. In Is. lxi. 3, they are called " trees of righteousness, the planting of the Lord," and they are to " bear much fruit " (John xv. 8), if He is to be glorified in them. See in Mic. vi. 8 ; Matt. xxv. 35, 36 ; Gal. v. 22, 23, some description of the kind of fruit God looks for.

7. **Three years** has had many fanciful interpretations— such as the times of the law, the prophets, and Jesus ; the three politics of the judges, the kings, and the high priests; the three years since John began to preach repentance, followed by Jesus—but we think it merely denotes a period of time abundantly sufficient to prove the tree. The disappointing, deficient response thus often fully justified the order, **cut it down ; why doth it also,** besides being fruitless, **cumber,** *make useless,* **the ground** on which it stands, preventing other things from growing. A fruitless tree is not merely a negative, but also a positive evil. So in the application to mankind.

8, 9. The intercessor begs to have the probation period extended to **this year also,** once more. " Now is the acceptable time ; now is the day of salvation." To **dig about and dung** it were the means for natural growth and fruitfulness; the word of God and the sacraments, offered and used, are the means (of grace) for spiritual growth and fruitfulness. "As the Holy Ghost saith, To-day if ye shall hear his voice," etc. **If.** There is a condition; fulfilled, the tree shall remain; unfulfilled, the decree again goes forth, **cut it down.** So the Lord waits to be gracious; but He will not always wait. Judgment of destruction shall issue against the unfaithful, the unfruitful, just as surely as Pilate overwhelmed and cut off the Galileans, and the tower of Siloam crushed those eighteen of Jerusalem.

10. And he was teaching in one of the synagogues on the sabbath day.

10. Jesus frequented **the synagogues.** There He taught, as well as joined in the worship. This is a principal way of keeping the Sabbath day holy. Hence Luther explains the meaning of the third Commandment that "We should fear and love God and not despise his word and the preaching of the gospel, but deem it holy, and willingly hear and learn it." The word of God is the great means of grace, and this heard rather than read. Hence the services of God's house are the prime way of spending a good Sabbath, of setting it apart from the other and common days. Whatever tends to foster an undevout frame of mind, and takes time and thought from the sacred privileges and duties of the day, is to be avoided as a profanation.

Where the synagogue was where Jesus worshipped that day we do not know.

11. And behold, a woman which had a spirit of infirmity eighteen years and she was bowed together, and could in no wise lift herself up.

11. **And behold** a sight calculated to stir kindly human sympathy: **a woman bowed together** instead of erect,

not able at all to **lift herself up.** That distinguishing characteristic of mankind, that he is erect and can look backward and forward and up to the stars and heaven of God, this poor woman lacked. She **had a spirit of infirmity,** which is an expression rather hard to understand. Some, coupling it with what is said in ver. 16, refer her affliction to a mild form of Satanic possession. Along with STIER, we scarcely can think this. But her body and spirit, in their close relation, were afflicted with this infirmity. Perhaps she did not, in her constrained position, see Jesus. 'But she came to the synagogue, and sets an example to people now not to be kept from church even by severe bodily affliction. For **eighteen years** she had been thus afflicted. Ah, poor woman, how much thou hadst to bear! Yet thou didst seek God's house and didst find healing there!

12, 13. And when Jesus saw her, he called her, and said to her, Woman, thou art loosed from thine infirmity. And he laid his hands upon her: and immediately she was made straight, and glorified God.

12. Be sure **Jesus saw her,** and did not turn away, selfishly, from so sad a sight. **No; he called her,** and what wonderful words He spake to her! **Woman, thou art loosed from thine infirmity.** His word was enough, for it is law; but, to help her faith and impress His word, **he laid his hands upon her.**

13. All were looking on in wonderful amazement. **And immediately she was made straight** as any of them. Her chronic infirmity was gone. And she did first that which was most befitting: she **glorified God,** from whom all blessings flow. It is not said that she said anything to Jesus. The situation very soon changed from her praise to the ruler's loud and angry remonstrance to the people.

14. And the ruler of the synagogue, being moved with indignation because Jesus had healed on the sabbath, answered and said to the multitude, There are six days in which men ought to work: in them therefore come and be healed, and not on the day of the sabbath.

14. What shall we think of such a **ruler of the synagogue!** Ah, in church and in state the wrong men often get into office. This man, who, if of a heavenly spirit, if in harmony with the rest and peace of God, if a lover of his fellow, would have been moved with great joy at the woman's deliverance, this miracle of mercy, was **moved with indignation** only, indignation at **Jesus** because He had healed **on the sabbath!** He cared (or pretended to) more for the sabbath than for mankind. He preferred sacrifice to mercy. His spirit was the opposite of the divine spirit—yet he was a ruler of the synagogue. He hadn't the courage to address Jesus directly, but put forth his opinion **to the multitude,** and, in his words to them, showed he had lost his head. He spoke like an angry man, as he was; and his words do not show very much sense or consistency. **Work!** Who had been doing any work? **Come and be healed.** What does this mean from the ruler's mouth? He couldn't heal any! Come where? Be healed by whom? The ruler talks wildly.

15, 16. But the Lord answered him, and said, Ye hypocrites, doth not each one of you on the sabbath loose his ox or his ass from the stall, and lead him away to watering? And ought not this woman, being a daughter of Abraham, whom Satan had bound, lo, *these* eighteen years, to have been loosed from this bond on the day of the sabbath?

15. **But the Lord** (Luke's frequent designation of Jesus), though not directly addressed, **answered him.** He took up the people's cause. He rebuked the proud, the false, the erring teachers. He saw in him a sample of his class, and addressed them all through him. **Ye hypocrites,**

teaching one thing and practising another, ye actors of a part, ye insincere! **Each one of you,** is it not the common practice? will **loose his ox or his ass and lead him away to watering,** a comparatively long and troublesome process, all **on the sabbath** and without any compunction of conscience. And this is all right. But how about **this woman,** a human being, yea, more, **a daughter of Abraham,** both by natural descent and by her faith which brought her, crippled as she was, to God's house? **Satan,** the enemy of God and man, the head and front of all evil, the Prince of darkness, **had bound** her, think of it, **these eighteen years!**

16. And **ought not . . . loosed . . . on the day of the sabbath?** For shame, ye that care for your cattle more than for your kind! You may take care for oxen, and look out for your flocks and herds, your wealth; Christ will care for mankind in Satan's bondage held and loose them from his galling chains. It is lawful to do well on the sabbath day; and to refrain from doing well is to do ill!

17. And as he said these things, all his adversaries were put to shame: and all the multitude rejoiced for all the glorious things that were done by him.

17. Well might **his adversaries** be **put to shame** by such an exhibition of their heartlessness and of His love. **The multitude,** as usual, **rejoiced,** and counted the **things done by him** to be **glorious.** So, indeed, they were. As "everything in his temple [of nature] saith, Glory" (Ps. xxix. 9), so everything that Jesus ever said or did set forth in beauty the glory of God.

18-21. He said therefore, Unto what is the kingdom of God like? and whereunto shall I liken it? It is like unto a grain of mustard seed, which a man took, and cast into his own garden; and it grew, and became a tree; and the birds of the heaven lodged in the branches thereof. And again he said, Whereunto shall I liken the kingdom of God? It is like unto leaven, which a woman took and hid in three measures of meal, till it was all leavened.

See on Matt. xiii. 31-33; Mark iv. 31, 32.

Whilst STIER can find no connection of these parables with what precedes, MEYER shows connection thus: "After the conclusion of the preceding incident (ver. 17), Jesus, in consequence (οὖν) of the joy manifested by the people, sees Himself justified in conceiving the fairest hopes on behalf of the Messianic kingdom, and these He gives utterance to in these parables." Their exposition may be found in the references above.

22. *And he went on his way through cities and villages, teaching, and journeying on unto Jerusalem.*

22. "The mention of the journey holds the historical thread" (MEYER). (See ix. 51, 57; x. 38.) Between Jesus' final leaving of Galilee and His final going to Jerusalem, He visited Jerusalem twice, viz.: at the Feast of Tabernacles (John viii. 11-52) in the fall (October), and at the Feast of Dedication in the winter (December). Meanwhile He went about **teaching** the things of the kingdom of God. We cannot trace certainly all His steps in this time. The **cities and villages** here mentioned were in Judæa and Peræa.

23. *And one said unto him, Lord, are they few that be saved?*

23. Somewhere in this journey, **one,** of whom we know nothing further, but who seems to have been a Jew, put the question, **Are there few that be saved?** *Are the saved few* in number? Why such a question? The Jews thought, *of course, they* would be saved. Perhaps Jewish pride dictated it. Perhaps curiosity dictated it. At all events it was an idle question, in the sense of useless, unimportant. Instead of questioning thus, this

man's duty was to see to it that *he* was *one of* the saved first, and then to seek to save as many others as possible. Jesus did not directly reply to this man, yet gave a serious answer for him and all to consider. **He said unto them all,** using the plural number in the following verses, and directing them all to a personal and practical consideration of salvation.

24, 25. And he said unto them, Strive to enter in by the narrow door: for many, I say unto you, shall seek to enter in, and shall not be able.

24. **Strive.** The word indicates that earnestness of purpose and action that characterized a contest for the prize in the public games. **To enter in by the narrow door.** (See on Matt. vii. 13, 14.) To get to heaven, to be saved. Christian character involves a constant struggle against opposing influences, and entrance to heaven is a triumph over all the powers of evil in earth and hell, in human nature and surrounding it. Hence we need to *strive.* "Eternal life is the gift of God," indeed; but we must strive to keep our spiritual foes from preventing us from taking this gift in the way in which it is offered. **Many,** alas (and He says it who is the way and will at last be the judge), will **seek to enter in, and shall not be able.** Whether the saved be few or not, here we are assured that many will be lost. (See on Matt. vii. 21-23.)

26, 27. When once the master of the house is risen up, and hath shut to the door, and ye begin to stand without, and to knock at the door, saying, Lord, open to us; and he shall answer and say to you, I know you not whence ye are; then shall ye begin to say, We did eat and drink in thy presence, and thou didst teach in our streets; and he shall say, I tell you, I know not whence ye are; depart from me, all ye workers of iniquity.

25. **When once.** Better rendered, *From the time that.* To this the "then" of next verse refers. **The master of the house** has the decision of such matters. Some think

the illustration here is taken from a wedding, or a feast of some kind; others that it is from a family whose head has waited as long as possible for the return of its members. **Is risen up and hath shut to the door.** This marks a crisis. The door is shut authoritatively. **And ye begin to stand without and to knock.** " Ye " is very personal, and, indeed, Jesus' Jewish hearers well represented this class, resting as they did on their ancient heritage as God's people, and so not striving, but taking salvation for granted. They stand, knock, call and argue, but all in vain. The answer comes from within, **I know not whence ye are.** That is, *ye are strangers to me*. He knows their character, as is clear from ver. 27. But He knows them not in the sense of acknowledging them as entitled to enter there.

26. **Begin to say.** The following gives only a specimen of their plea. **We did eat and drink in thy presence.** So might they say who had been at the miracles of the feeding of the multitudes, as also those who had sat with Jesus at tables where He was a guest. **And thou didst teach in our streets.** This again marks those very hearers, together with all His rejectors in the lands His steps traversed on earth, as the particular ones to whom He referred. At the same time they represent all who trust to some external connection or acquaintance with the Lord.

27. **Workers of iniquity.** What if He had taught in their streets, since they were only hearers of the word and not doers thereof! Their guilt was thereby only aggravated, and they testify against themselves that they had highest privileges which they failed to improve. " Actions speak louder than words."

28–30. There shall be the weeping and gnashing of teeth, when ye shall see Abraham, and Isaac, and Jacob, and all the prophets, in the kingdom of

God, and yourselves cast forth without. And they shall come from the east and west, and from the north and south, and shall sit down in the kingdom of God. And behold, there are last which shall be first, and there are first which shall be last.

28. **There. In that place. Shall be. Future state. Weeping and gnashing of teeth.** In the original these nouns have the article, *the* weeping and *the* gnashing of teeth. There are similar evidences of despair and rage here, sometimes; but nothing equal to what will be there. **When ye shall see.** The parable of the rich man and Lazarus justifies us in interpreting this of literal, real sight. **Abraham, and Isaac, and Jacob,** the patriarchs, from whom those addressed boasted their descent, **and all the prophets,** whose books they had and whose teachings they and their fathers had neglected, **in the kingdom of God,** in heaven, saved, and **yourselves.** the very ones who thought yourselves "the children of the kingdom," **cast forth without.** Abraham saw Christ's day (John viii. 56) better than his descendants among whom Jesus walked and talked; for he saw it by faith, whilst theirs was only the seeing of the eye. "*Old Testament saints* are in the kingdom of God. . . . *New Testament sinners* will be thrust out" (HENRY).

29. **And they shall come.** Yes, *many* of them, as we read in Matt. viii. 11, and this "many" is a set-off to the one in ver. 24. Here too is an answer, a gladsome one, to the question which started this train of thought. From all quarters of the globe—East—West—North—South—people shall come **and shall sit down in the kingdom of God;** first on earth, and at last in heaven; first in the church militant, and then in the church triumphant. Here is a glorious assurance of redemption reaching to all quarters: and the prophecies (e. g. Is. xlix.) of the coming in of the Gentiles are here confirmed

by the Lord's own lips. Blessed are our eyes to have seen already in our day so many thus reclaimed from sin and Satan's power. The good word from the missionaries in all quarters now is that they are thus coming in; and we should more than ever give and pray and work to bring about so glorious a consummation.

30. This proverbial expression occurs several times in the Scriptures (Matt. xix. 30; xx. 16; Mark x. 31).

The Jews were first in God's choice of them as a people, but have not yet accepted the great salvation. Only when the fulness of the Gentiles is brought in will they turn to the Lord. The East was first, but now is receiving missionaries from the West. The principle is applicable to individuals, churches and nations, and exemplified throughout history.

31–33. In that very hour there came certain Pharisees, saying to him, Get thee out, and go hence: for Herod would fain kill thee. And he said unto them, Go and say to that fox, Behold, I cast out devils and perform cures to-day and to-morrow, and the third *day* I am perfected. Howbeit I must go on my way to-day and to-morrow and the day following: for it cannot be that a prophet perish out of Jerusalem.

31. The word **hour** ($\mathring{\omega}\rho\alpha$) may mean the limited time we assign to the word, or, more inclusively, the season or time marked out by the circumstances of the narrative. The **Pharisees** were hostile to Jesus and certainly did not want to bring Him a friendly message of warning; rather was this word of theirs an unkindly banter. STIER thinks, and well maintains his view, that they either invented the whole story or took up "some groundless report and brought it to the Lord—in order that they might put an end to His too long wandering about and evasion, and thus hypocritically hasten Him to Jerusalem with the design, further, of testing whether He would be accessible to fear." So also BRAUNE, EBRARD, OLSHAU-

SEN, *et al*. **Go hence ; for Herod would fain,** intends to, **kill thee !** Peræa, where we suppose Jesus now was, as well as Galilee, belonged to Herod's domain. We have notes of Herod's desiring to see Jesus (ix. 9, xxiii. 8), but nothing of any desire on his part to kill Him, though he was none too good for this.

32. Perceiving their designing, cunning scheme, Jesus answered them accordingly, **Go tell**—but, as they had not come from Herod, so He had no idea they would go to him—**that** (it should read *this*, ταύτῃ) **fox,** this fox of yours, as you make him out by your report, this cunning one of your designing story, made to frighten and hasten me. So that what He tells them to carry to Herod is intended as an answer to themselves. **Behold.** Make a note of it. **I cast out,** or, am casting out, **devils and perform,** or, am performing (the present tense of action going on continuously), **cures** (it was His wonderful works not His teachings that had excited Herod's curiosity) right along, **to-day and to-morrow,** that is, as we take it, indefinitely for some time to come, yet not long ; **and the third day,** the climactic day in my going, finally and not till then, **I am perfected,** finish my course, complete my work. MEYER makes this mean merely, " I come to a conclusion, I have done : " but most interpreters refer it to His death, even as the following verses indicate : but this idea is purposely veiled from those to whom He spake.

33. **I must go on my way,** proceed, continue my journey. **To-day and to-morrow and the day following** must mean the same thing as the like words in ver. 32, and we have taken them in an indefinite, proverbial rather than in a definite, literal sense. Jesus certainly was not now within three literal days of His taking off at Jerusalem. **For it cannot be,** He says with the same incisive irony as this whole reply indicates, **that a prophet perish out of**

Jerusalem. That city, called and meant to be "the holy city," had, through the hierarchy represented by these Pharisees, won the evil distinction of being the slaughter house of the prophets. See xi. 49-51 and on Matt. xxiii. 34-39. Thither Jesus had for some time stedfastly set His face, knowing perfectly what awaited Him there. Not Herod but the Jews of Jerusalem would kill Him.

34, 35. O Jerusalem, Jerusalem, which killeth the prophets, and stoneth them that are sent unto her! how often would I have gathered thy children together, even as a hen *gathereth* her own brood unto her wings, and ye would not! Behold, your house is left unto you *desolate:* and I say unto you, Ye shall not see me, until ye shall say, Blessed *is* he that cometh in the name of the Lord.

34, 35. Then from irony the Lord melts into sad pity, and makes this apostrophe to Jerusalem. It is nearly the same as what He uttered later, as recorded in Matt. xxiii. 37-39, where see detailed comments. **Jerusalem** was a representative city, and as such it is here lamented over though at a distance from its locality. The Pharisees to whom He had just replied were Jerusalemites. The "henceforth" and "desolate" of Matthew are not found here. Those additions suited best our Lord's last visit to the city and His final departure from the temple.

CHAPTER XIV.

1. And it came to pass, when he went into the house of one of the rulers of the Pharisees on a sabbath to eat bread, that they were watching him.

1. **One of the rulers of the Pharisees.** As the Pharisees did not have any officials called rulers, this must mean a ruler who belonged to the party of the Pharisees. GROTIUS and KUINOEL take him to have been a member of the Sanhedrin, and DE WETTE, a president of the synagogue; whilst MEYER, as also the Auth. Ver., makes him nothing more than one of the chiefs of the Pharisees. Jesus **went** not without having been invited (ver. 12), though it is more than doubtful whether the invitation was given from friendliness. **On a sabbath.** The Jews were accustomed to make visits and give entertainments on the Sabbath, for which, however, the preparations had all been made beforehand. **To eat bread.** "It belongs to the peculiarities of Luke, that he loves to represent to us the Saviour as sitting at a social table, where He most beautifully reveals His pure humanity" (VAN OOST.). **And they,** the Pharisees, true to their spirit of opposition to Jesus, **were watching him,** to see if He would not say or do something or somehow come short, to His discredit, on which they were ready eagerly to seize.

2–4. And behold, there was before him a certain man which had the dropsy. And Jesus answering spake unto the lawyers and Pharisees, saying, Is it lawful to heal on the sabbath, or not? But they held their peace. And he took him, and healed him, and let him go.

2. **And behold,** probably in the court of the house, just by the entrance, confronting Jesus as He went in, **a man with the dropsy.** Some think, and not unreasonably, that this man's presence there had been contrived by the Pharisees—that there was a plot against Jesus, yet all unknown to the sick man.

3. This view suits the word **answering** here; for Jesus knew their thoughts and that they were watching Him. MEYER makes this a response merely to the appeal which the invalid's presence made to Jesus. **The lawyers and Pharisees** were the guests. The question Jesus put to them was a puzzler. By their traditions they could not say, Yes; and by common humanity they could not say, No. So they prudently **held their peace,** insincere men (hypocrites) that they were!

4. Jesus' act now answered His question, and showed Him to have no sympathy with their false externalism as to the keeping of the Sabbath. **He took him.** Took hold of him. **Healed him** by His word, supernaturally. **Let him go** again, a well man. This was, we may say, a proceeding short, sharp, and decisive.

<small>5, 6. And he said unto them, Which of you shall have an ass or an ox fallen into a well, and will not straightway draw him up on a sabbath day? And they could not answer again unto these things.</small>

5. Not till the cured man had gone did He thus pungently apply the subject to His host and fellow-guests. See xiii. 15 and notes there, and on Matt. xii. 11, 12.

There is a reading of considerable authority which has **son** instead of **ass.** The two Greek words υἱός, son, and ὄνος, ass, look a little alike. MEYER, adopting the former, explains " from the ethical principle that the helpful compassion which we show in reference to that which is *our own* (be it son or beast) on the sabbath, we are also bound to show *to others* (love thy neighbor *as thyself*)."

6. Much as the Pharisees would have liked to gainsay the Lord's teachings and act, **they could not.** Jesus was too much for them: for He was the Truth, and they were hypocrites!

> 7-11. And he spake a parable unto those which were bidden, when he marked how they chose out the chief seats; saying unto them, When thou art bidden of any man to a marriage feast, sit not down in the chief seat; lest haply a more honourable man than thou be bidden of him, and he that bade thee and him shall come and say to thee, Give this man place; and then thou shalt begin with shame to take the lowest place. But when thou art bidden, go and sit down in the lowest place; that when he that hath bidden thee cometh, he may say to thee, Friend, go up higher: then shalt thou have glory in the presence of all that sit at meat with thee. For every one that exalteth himself shall be humbled; and he that humbleth himself shall be exalted.

7. **Spake a parable.** As usual in His table-talk, giving spiritual food. This was addressed to the guests in general. **When he marked,** etc. Jesus was always observant, and often found in passing circumstances occasion for instruction. Having healed the dropsical man before the supper, " one might almost say that the Saviour now essays to heal that far worse than bodily dropsy, the inflation of pride, the dropsy of the heart, in these miserable men" (STIER). " The dignity of these words appears in this, that without any appearance of profoundness or severity, they lay bare the secret disposition lying at the foundation of the external behavior which they condemn " (SCHLEIERMACHER).

8, 9. The **thou** is general in its reference. **A marriage feast.** BENGEL thinks the Lord, out of courtesy, illustrated by a different occasion from that which had brought them then together: MEYER says, "the typical representations of the future establishment of the kingdom as a wedding celebration obviously suggested the expression (Matt. xxii.)." **Chief seat, more honourable man than thou, and give this man place,** show that people were customarily placed at table according to their rank or precedence in the eyes of the host. Why **the lowest place?** Because he had assumed the highest place without having it assigned him, and now all the other places but the lowest were filled. **Begin to take** denotes a **shame** that was not momentary but continued. The Lord would save us from shame, and so here gives a proper course for honor.

10. **But** take the opposite course. Begin with **the lowest place** and wait till you are assigned to position by the host, **when he cometh.** This looks to the heavenly Bridegroom. **Glory,** honor, reputation.

11. The emphatic word here is **himself,** and only when it is so read is the full sense of the passage brought out. Self-exaltation is met by humiliation from a higher source, and self-abasement with exaltation. (See Prov. xxv. 6, 7.) See this sentiment in same words in xviii. 14; Matt. xxiii. 14, and comp. Jas. iv. 6; Pet. v. 5; Ps. xviii. 27; Job xxii. 29; Dan. iv. 37.

12-14. And he said to him also that had bidden him, When thou makest a dinner or a supper, call not thy friends, nor thy brethren, nor thy kinsmen, nor rich neighbours; lest haply they also bid thee again, and a recompense be made thee. But when thou makest a feast, bid the poor, the maimed, the lame, the blind: and thou shall be blessed; because they have not *wherewith* to recompense thee: for thou shalt be recompensed in the resurrection of the just.

12. The preceding words had been addressed to the guests; now He had a word of admonition to **him also that had bidden him,** the host. **Call** here is a word of more dignity than " bid " in the next verse. Here the invitation seems to be one in person. **Friends . . . brethren,** brothers, closer than other **kinsmen . . . rich**

neighbours; all these are the ones usually invited to friendly social entertainments. It is generally expected that they will **bid thee again.** All this is well enough from a temporal and worldly standpoint. Jesus does not condemn such social civilities. But since in their very nature and course they bring **a recompense,** they have no reward besides, they count nothing spiritually and for the hereafter. As in Matt. vi. 2, 5, such things have their record in full in this life. Claim no credit for them ; the account is squared.

13, 14. **But** the Saviour shows a more excellent way (1 Cor. xii. 31, xiii.) of charity, love. **The poor,** etc., have not wherewith to recompense thee ; therefore **bid** them, show them kindness, do them service, and not only will it be clear to men that your deed springs from unselfish love, but thou **shalt be recompensed** by the Lord of men and angels—and so be **blessed—in the resurrection of the just,** when the just are raised. Comp. Matt. vi. 1 ; xxv. 34–40; John v. 29 ; Acts xxiv. 15.

The resurrection is not the subject under discussion, and we do not see here any reference to the apocalyptic (Rev. xx. 4–6) idea of two resurrections. That deeds of unselfishness, love and mercy will be rewarded hereafter, as well as their opposites, is clear from many passages of Scripture. (See Ps. lxii. 12 ; Prov. xxiv. 12, 29 ; Matt. xvi. 27; Rom. ii. 6 ; 2 Tim. iv. 14 ; Rev. ii. 23, and, particularly here, see Luke xvi. 9 and comments.)

15. And when one of them that sat at meat with him heard these things, he said unto them, Blessed is he that shall eat bread in the kingdom of God.

15. Now the resurrection of the just was associated in the Jewish mind with the open setting up of the kingdom of God, which they thought would be inaugurated with a great feast, at which the Jews certainly would be guests.
18

One of those at meat with Him, kindling with enthusiasm at thoughts of all this, called up by Jesus' words, exclaimed, **Blessed is he that shall eat bread in the kingdom of God.** This gave Jesus occasion to utter the parable of the Great Supper.

16. But he said unto him, A certain man made a great supper; and he bade many.

16. **A certain man** here represents God. **Made a great supper.** The word rendered "supper" is the one used for the principal meal of the day, no matter when eaten. The figure of eating and drinking is a very frequent one to set forth participation in the blessings of salvation. Isaiah (xxv. 6) speaks of gospel blessings as "a feast of fat things." (Comp. Is. lv. 1, 2; Matt. v. 6.)

The Lord's Supper is a visible gospel under the form of eating and drinking; and the final happiness of the saved is represented as "the marriage supper of the Lamb" (Rev. xix. 9). The blessings of salvation are *provided*, provisions of grace; yet must they be *partaken of*, if any benefit is to be received. God gives, man takes: God sets the table, man comes to it and eats. This provision is **great** in both quality and quantity. "Whosoever will, let him take," is written over it. **And bade many.** The many to whom this points are the first bidden, the Jews, and particularly, as after verses show, the hierarchy, the most religious among them, priests, scribes, Pharisees.

17. And he sent forth his servant at supper time, to say to them that were bidden, Come, for *all* things are now ready.

17. **Sent his servant at supper time.** This was the second sending, according to eastern custom. It was to tell **them that were bidden** before, and had accepted the invitation, that **all things are now ready.** It was **supper time,** and they were expected to **come** right off. "Supper

time" in the application must refer to "the fullness of the time" (Gal. iv. 4; Eph. i. 10), when God was manifest in flesh, the beginning of this dispensation. The "servant" sent to call the invited guests, then, must refer not to the prophets and Old Testament preachers, but to the preachers of righteousness from the time of John the Baptist, especially all since Pentecost. The seed of the woman has come and bruised the serpent's head; the Redeemer of men has cried, "It is finished;" the Holy Ghost has come, power from on high, to abide with the church forever; the Lord's Supper has been instituted to strengthen and refresh His people and show forth His death till He come again: and though there are many servants, they all are gone forth in the same spirit, with the same message, "Come; for all things are now ready."

18-20. And they all with one *consent* began to make excuse. The first said unto him, I have bought a field, and I must needs go out and see it: I pray thee have me excused. And another said, I have bought five yoke of oxen, and I go to prove them: I pray thee have me excused. And another said, I have married a wife, and therefore I cannot come.

18. **And they all.** The first invited. The Jews as a whole, especially those of influence and in position, rejected the gospel call. **With one consent.** With one spirit, mind, disposition. **Began to make excuse.** To beg off from going to the feast. **The first** to whom the servant came was a property holder, well-off, and must look after his field. The shallowness of this excuse is evident; for the land would not run away; he could go and see it at some other time. There was not the *need* that he pretended.

19. Another's plea was, **I have bought five yoke of oxen**—he too must have been well-off—**and I go to prove them**, to test them. But the oxen were already bought, and at any time he might prove them; indeed a sensible man would have done that *before* he bought them.

20. **I have married a wife,** another said, **and therefore I cannot come.** Marrying a wife would, according to the law, excuse him for a year from going to war (Deut. xxiv. 5), but naturally would rather bind him to social duties. But he positively refuses to come. **Excused** is the emphatic word in the request of each of the other two. TRENCH sees in the first excuse the pride of the world, elated through acquired possessions, and desiring to feast the eye upon them; in the second, the care and anxiety of business, filling the soul; and in the last, the pleasure of the world, which does not even beg off, but contumaciously refuses. Possessions, business, pleasure—how operative still in keeping men from falling in with the overtures of mercy! Observe that there is no sin in possessing lands, or in being diligent in business, or in marriage: but to let any or all of these keep us from Christ, to put any or all of them above the call of the gospel, to make them our chief love—this is the sin.

21. And the servant came, and told his lord these things. Then the master of the house being angry said to his servant, Go out quickly into the streets and lanes of the city, and bring in hither the poor and maimed and blind and lame.

21. **Angry.** And justly so. The treatment received was most insulting, and without a shadow of justification. Jesus is represented (Mark iii. 5) as looking around with anger on the hypocritical Jews about him; and God is said to be "angry with the wicked every day."

Then. This result was known by God, however, from all eternity, and then His purpose was determined to open the provisions of grace to all. **Go out quickly into the streets and lanes of the city.** To people of the same neighborhood, and such as could be reached " quickly "—meaning still the Jews, but **the poor, and the maimed, and the blind,** who will have no such excuses to offer; to the publicans and sinners, whom those first called despise and call accursed (John vii. 49); to the weary and heavy laden. "To the poor the gospel is preached!"

22. And the servant said, Lord, what thou didst command is done, and yet there is room.

22. This done, the servant reports, **And yet there is room.** There is much room at the gospel feast. See above on ver. 16. "And yet there is room" today. Therefore should we as God's servants be diligent to give the gospel call to as many as possible. Missions! Missions!! Missions!!!

23. And the lord said unto the servant, Go out into the highways and hedges, and constrain *them* to come in, that my house may be filled.

23. **Go out into the highways and hedges,** outside the city, into the roads and fields, outside of Jewry into the world that lieth in wickedness, to the Gentiles—all abroad, **and constrain them to come in.** Of course this compulsion could only be moral. It might be hard to persuade these classes that *they* were invited, that they, in their poverty, rags, and wretched condition, would be *welcome* at the "great supper." But overcome their objections; *urge* them to come in. **That my house may be filled.** Grace, as well as nature, BENGEL remarks, abhors a vacuum. To fill God's house will take a great many people. Here is another answer to the question, "Are there few that be saved?"

24. For I say unto you, that none of those men which were bidden shall taste of my supper.

24. **I say unto you.** These are the words of the giver of the supper, the "master of the house." We have seen that in the application of the parable he represents God. **None of those men which were bidden** and refused to come, **shall taste of my supper.** If they come after

this, it will be too late; the door will be shut. Such is the doom of all who refuse the invitations of grace and despise the riches of God's goodness. Those Jews, as individuals and as a people, were cut off; the time is coming when their descendants shall be called and will obey. Now is the time of the Gentiles' call. (See Rom. ix.–xi.)

25, 26. *Now there went with him great multitudes: and he turned, and said unto them, If any man cometh unto me, and hateth not his own father, and mother, and wife, and children, and brethren, and sisters, yea, and his own life also, he cannot be my disciple.*

25. **Great multitudes** were going with Jesus. He did not feel flattered by this. He saw deeper than appearances. He knew the difference between following Him with their feet and following Him with their hearts. Great multitudes may come to church and crowd the building: but this does not prove that many are becoming Jesus' disciples. **He turned** to them with a warning and a statement of what is involved in following Christ that seems severe and repellent. But Jesus never kept back the truth because it was hard and would not be acceptable. He wanted disciples but not mere followers. He kept back the crowd with the plain and forcible truth.

26. What is said here is doubtless very repulsive to men now: and many, without seeking to know His meaning, turn away disdainfully from such a statement. It is only another way of saying, "Thou shalt love the Lord thy God with all thy heart, and with all thy soul, and with all thy mind, and with all thy strength." And one who does this, or even tries to do it, may and will love his fellowmen, to say nothing of his near kin, who are dear to him by natural and proper affection. The *first* table of the law teaches supreme love to God: and this teaches and enables us to love our fellowmen, as

taught in the *second* table. We are not to *hate* anybody. What is this, then, about *hating* **father, mother, wife, children,** and so on? This is only a strong way of putting it that *nothing* may stand between us and God, *nothing* may claim our love before and greater than love to Him. God is nearer to us, more to us, and should be *dearer* than any earthly kin. Only as we understand and fulfil our relationship to God do these other relationships, which He Himself has established, appear in their true light. Everywhere in God's word we are taught love to all those mentioned in this verse, but "only in the Lord." "Thou shalt have no other gods before me:" thou shalt have no other love before love of me. God must be supreme in our affections. This is what Jesus means. **And his own life also.** Comp. Eph. v. 29. The love of life is natural and proper, and to hate it is next thing to impossible. But it was the father of lies that said (Job ii. 4), "All that a man hath will he give for his life." Many men reëcho this sentiment approvingly. There is a half-truth in it. But every one knows that many a one has given his life for his country, for his kin, for his cause, his honor, even his fame. Many a one has given his life for his God, in the home and in the foreign mission-field. There are many things more precious than this natural life.

27. Whosoever doth not bear his own cross, and come after me, cannot be my disciple.

27. **Whosoever.** The same requirement of every one. **His own cross.** So then every one has a cross: he does not and should not make it: circumstances will make it, under the divine providence: but he must *bear* it (Gal. vi. 5 and 2). In bearing his cross, one has only to **come after** the Master. He asks us only to follow Him.

28-30. For which of you desiring to build a tower, doth not first sit down and count the cost, whether he hath *wherewith* to complete it? Lest haply, when he hath laid a foundation, and is not able to finish, all that behold begin to mock him, saying, This man began to build, and was not able to finish.

28. The point is that it is desirable and necessary, in our Christian life and character, to go on to a **finish**, to completion. A **foundation** is of prime importance, but to stop with it is to fail and even become a laughing stock. Is this teaching then against making a beginning? Oh, no; for there's no completion without a beginning, no house or **tower** without a foundation. But Jesus will have us all, and every one, enter on discipleship considerately—**count the cost.** Easy, light, unthinking profession, such as is often seen and urged by "evangelists" and in what are called "revival meetings," those votings, holding up of hands and "committing themselves," seem here to be disapproved: on the contrary, our Lutheran method of counting the cost in a study of ourselves and God's word in the light of the catechism, leads to that considerate profession which is likely to go on to a finish.

29, 30. How many mere foundations, mere professions, without any superstructure of godly and growing character, are to be seen, leading the enemies of religion to **mock** not only the person but the cause! Life must follow learning, result of catechization.

31-33. Or what king, as he goeth to encounter another king in war, will not sit down first and take counsel whether he is able with ten thousand to meet him that cometh against him with twenty thousand? Or else, while the other is yet a great way off, he sendeth an ambassage, and asketh conditions of peace. So therefore whosoever he be of you that renounceth not all that he hath, he cannot be my disciple.

31. An illustration from **war.** The one has only **ten thousand** of an army: the other, **twenty thousand.** Will the former enter rashly and blindly into such a con-

test or **sit down first and take counsel?** The question is **whether he is able.** No man is able for this warfare. "Not by might nor by power, but by my Spirit, saith the Lord." Who is sufficient for these things? No one!

32. But there is another alternative—**conditions of peace.** The considerate, self-knowing person will desire these, and **sendeth an ambassage** to this end.

33. **So, whosoever renounceth not all that he hath,** whoever does not surrender, even to giving up all, **he cannot be my disciple,** Jesus says. This is the supreme demand of the Lord. He wants the whole—entire consecration.

34, 35. Salt therefore is good: but if even the salt have lost its savour, wherewith shall it be seasoned? It is fit neither for the land nor for the dunghill: *men* cast it out. He that hath ears to hear, let him hear.

34. **Salt therefore is good.** Notice the connection. Suppose we read it more exactly, "Good (or excellent), therefore, is the salt." A profession of Christ is excellent, is desirable, is the thing. "Ye are the salt of the earth," said Jesus to His disciples. **But if even the salt have lost its savour,** if it is saltless salt, called salt but without the properties of salt, a profession without possession, a mere name, **wherewith shall it** (the saltless salt) **be seasoned?** What can you do with it, or what can it do? What is it good for?

35. **Men cast it out** as worthless: and so does God. An empty profession, a mere name to live (Rev. iii. 1), discipleship that is fruitless of love, life and sacrifice, a Christianity that costs nothing—*is worth nothing.* (See on Matt. v. 13; Mark ix. 50.) **He that hath ears to hear, let him** use them for their proper purpose, not as mere opposite ends of a passage through the head! A frequent admonition of our Lord.

CHAPTER XV.

1, 2. Now all the publicans and sinners were drawing **near** unto him for to hear him. And both the Pharisees and the scribes murmured, saying, This man receiveth sinners and eateth with them.

1. Here were those who were wont to gather about Jesus, **drawing near** at this time in marked and increasing numbers. They found in Him sympathy, not for their sins, but for their undone, pitiful, helpless condition. **The publicans** were doubtless exacting, self-seeking, rude: they were, moreover, considered traitors, since they collected the revenue which showed Israel to be subject to another power, the detested Romans. But our Lord found one of the twelve and many a disciple from among their number. **Sinners** were those who were open and known transgressors; doubtless they were often not so bad as those who despised them, but they neither cared nor tried to cover up their tracks; they were willing to seem what they were. **The Pharisees** were the orthodox party among the Jews, legalists, self-righteous, formal, technical religionists, but without the Spirit. The **scribes** were officially the transcribers and keepers of the books of the law, and also the interpreters of the same, in a day when books were not printed and were not plenty as now. The Pharisees and scribes were the very respectable among the Jews, the aristocracy. They felt toward the publicans and sinners as the Brahmans of India feel toward the Sudras. Caste feeling was conspicuous in Palestine as in India, though not based so much on the circumstances of birth.

2. The despised, the common classes continually **were drawing near unto** the Son of man, the second Head of the race. The other classes **murmured** at the kind reception they received, and deprecatingly spoke of Jesus as **this man** and laid it to His charge as a thing unworthy and condemning that He **receiveth sinners, and eateth with them.** They did not do so, would not do so. They said to such, " Stand off, for I am holier than thou."

What they charged upon Jesus here was eminently true. He did receive and eat with publicans and sinners. And herein is our hope and our example. For none of us can claim by nature or life any higher place than that of *sinner*. The implication of these murmurers that Jesus was like the company He kept was false. While among sinners, to save them from their lost condition, He Himself was "holy, harmless, undefiled and separate from sinners" in character. Not because He loved their ways, but because He loved them and desired to lift them up out of their evil ways, was Jesus personally among them. So the physician goes among the insane, the sick, the leprous: so the lover of mankind goes among the wounded, the prisoners, the fallen—to the rescue. The way to win men is not to despise them, not to come to them as if you were letting yourself very far down, as if you were better than they. Men want sympathy, kindness, love. Jesus has showed us how to win men : and "he that winneth souls is wise."

3, 4. And he spake unto them this parable, saying, What man of you, having a hundred sheep, and having lost one of them, doth not leave the ninety and nine in the wilderness, and go after that which is lost, until he find it ?

3, 4. Here in the parable of the lost sheep Jesus explains Himself and shows the murmurers the reason of His fellowship with outcasts. He appeals to each of them, to their own nature—**what man of you** doth not do likewise in the case of a lost sheep? Though **having a hundred,** the **lost one** will draw out your desire, your sympathy, your search, so as to **leave the ninety and nine** in their pasturage, **the wilderness, and go after the lost.** This belongs to the true and better instincts of our nature, to go out in our affections and endeavors after that of ours which is unfortunate and in trouble more than after that which is safe and sound, not in manifest peril. So a mother looks after a crippled or sickly child more than after the hearty ones, though loving them none the less. Even some of the finer irrational animals have been known to do the same thing. And shall the Lord Jesus be less merciful, less sympathetic, less loving? Oh no; He is "above all" in this too. **Until he find it.** He will not be satisfied till then. The object is not merely to know where it is or how it is, but to find it, to rescue it, to restore it to its place and condition before it was lost. Jesus *finds* and saves the lost. None such can find or save himself. It is God's grace that goes before and finds, woos and wins the sinner.

> 5-7. And when he hath found it, he layeth it on his shoulders, rejoicing. And when he cometh home, he calleth together his friends and his neighbours, saying unto them, Rejoice with me, for I have found my sheep which was lost. I say unto you, that even so there shall be joy in heaven over one sinner that repenteth, *more* than over ninety and nine righteous persons, which need no repentance.

5. See how kindly he treats it **when he hath found it.** He does not kick and cuff it and upbraid it for having got lost. No; **he layeth it on his shoulders,** carries it home, **rejoicing.** Oh, how the tender love of Jesus, the Shepherd true, is here portrayed!

6. One doesn't like to rejoice alone: **friends and neigh-**

bours increase the joy by sharing in it. **Rejoice with me,** says the joyous man. How natural this is: every true heart beats responsive to this representation.

7. We often want to know about heaven and the unseen. Here is an **I say unto you** from the Lord of heaven: and He says **one sinner that repenteth** shall cause **joy in heaven.** The angels will rejoice with the Saviour. (Comp. ver. 10.) Who are the **ninety and nine righteous persons, which need no repentance?** There are none absolutely such, except the holy angels. The Pharisees and Scribes counted themselves such, but it was in ignorance both of themselves and of the depth and spirituality of the divine law. But this expression may refer to those who have not been open and wanton sinners, who have grown up in the fear and love of God from their infant baptism, who neither can expect nor be expected to have a sudden and marked "conversion," a distinct line between the opposite states of "lost" and "found." It is merely natural, and properly so, that the joy over the recovered is more pronounced and felt than that over the safely folded, the abiding, the constantly true.

<small>8, 9. Or what woman, having ten pieces of silver, if she lose one piece, doth not light a lamp, and sweep the house, and seek diligently until she find it? And when she hath found it, she calleth together her friends and neighbours, saying, Rejoice with me, for I have found the piece which I had lost.</small>

8, 9. Here is a second illustration of the propriety of the Saviour's course, in the parable of the lost coin. In the former it was a living creature that could and was likely to go astray of itself. Here it is a piece of money lost by a **woman.** That was lost in the wilderness, this, in **the house.** The piece of silver had on it the stamp of its worth. There is an ordinary and plain interpretation of this parable which needs no exposition. But there is a beautiful, mystical interpretation which the church fathers delighted in, which sees in the woman the church, and in the lost coin a baptized, sealed person lost through want of constant care, not looked after until, when sought for, he is not to be found. **The piece which I had lost,** the woman says, charging herself with the losing of it. Then the lighting of the candle and sweeping the house marks the church's effort and stir to reclaim the back-slidden, such as the preaching of the Gospel, the searching of themselves by the members of the church and their renewed application to Christian love and duty. On this TRENCH remarks, "What a deranging of the house for a time! How does the dust which had been allowed to settle down and accumulate begin to rise and fly about in every direction; how unwelcome that which is going forward to any that may be in the house and have no interest in the finding of that which has been lost. Thus it is with the word of God. Evermore the charge against it is, that it turns the world upside down, even as indeed it does. For only let that word be proclaimed, and how much of open aversion to the truth becomes now open enmity; how much of torpid alienation against God is changed into active hostility; what an outcry is there against the troublers of Israel, against the witnesses that torment the dwellers upon the earth, the men that will not let the world alone. But amid all this, while others are making outcry about the dust and inconvenience, she that bears the candle of the Lord is diligently looking meanwhile for her lost, not ceasing her labor, her care, her diligence, till she has recovered her own again." And then comes the joy, shared by **friends and neighbours.**

10. Even so, I say unto you, there is joy in the presence of the **angels of God** over one sinner that repenteth.

10. The shepherd—one of you—rejoiceth over his lost sheep found; the woman over her lost coin recovered. Even so in the greater matter of **one sinner that repenteth**, a lost soul found and saved, **there is joy in the presence of the angels of God.** The church above rejoices with the church beneath. And what makes angels glad ought not to make right-minded men murmur.

11. And he said, A certain man had two sons.

This is the third parable in succession on the lost found. First it was a sheep that was lost, perhaps in heedlessness; then it was a piece of money, the keeping of which was in other hands; now it is a son, in his wilfulness. This last comes nearer home to us all. We all either are sons (this including daughters) or have sons. The two former lost objects were sought and brought; the last, as he wilfully became lost, so he willingly returned from his lost estate. There's a progress in these parables, and this one is the climax and reaches and teaches all human hearts. LANGE calls this parable "a gospel within the Gospel," and NITZSCH says, "We all must find ourselves reproduced in this parable in some sense, either as we have become, or as we have ever been, or as we are hoping and endeavoring to be." STIER considers it "the crown and the pearl of all our Lord's parables," and exclaims, "How *divinely human* is this parable of the God-man!"

11. Two **sons** are necessary to make up the representation. The occasion of the parable is seen in verses 1–3. It was spoken to the murmuring Pharisees and Scribes, the Jewish leaders, in the presence of the publicans and sinners, the common people. The two sons represent these two classes: herein, too, they represent all men—all found at last unlike their Father, of a different spirit,

fallen from the divine image—but the one showing this in a wanton, prodigal manner, the other, in a quiet and sedate manner. So it includes, and some think is typically representative of, Jews and Gentiles.

12. *And the younger of them said to his father, Father, give me the portion of thy substance that falleth to me. And he divided unto them his living.*

12. It was eminently fitting that **the younger of them** should be represented as the thoughtless, the unfilial, the prodigal. According to Hebrew law the elder received the large portion of the inheritance, and would naturally remain in the homestead (Deut. xxi. 17). He would naturally be the more grave and dignified. The younger son *said*, **Father,** but his words and the way he acted did not show a filial spirit. "And why call ye me Lord, Lord, and do not the things which I say?" **Give me the portion of thy** (the) **substance** (of the property) **that falleth to me,** my share. In the form of petition, it bears the air of demand. A father's property is usually not divided until after his death; it certainly is presumptuous in a young man to ask what this one did. This shows already the spirit of the younger son, before his following acts showed it to the world. So our first parents, before they took the forbidden fruit, alienated their hearts, or suffered them to be alienated from God, and the following outward act of disobedience but manifested that turning from God. In them and in this young man we see *self-will* as the basis of unfilial character. Self-will, over against the divine will, is the essence of sin.

And he divided unto them his living. As he found the son's affections centred on himself, he thought best to not restrain or compel them, but to give him his desire, to let him learn by that hard teacher, experience. So God gave Israel the flesh he demanded for his body, but sent leanness into his soul (Ps. cvi. 15), and again gave him a king despite His anger at the unwise and wicked but importunate demand (Hos. xiii. 11). God does not force character; for then the result would not be character. He respects the free will He has given man, and grants him his way, intending by His providence to bring him to chastisement, repentance, and reformation by it.

13. And not many days after the younger son gathered all together, and took his journey into a far country; and there he wasted his substance with riotous living.

13. **Not many days after** the younger son's feet followed his affections away from his father's house. He **gathered all together,** in his selfishness, **and took his journey.** Whether he went west or east or north or south, we know not. But he went **into a far country,** far from home and all its oversight, restraint and affections. He wanted to be independent. How beautifully this far country sets forth the sinner's place, so far as his affections and ways are concerned, in respect to God! **And there,** in the independence and self-will which delighted him, **he wasted,** scattered, made away with, **his substance,** the portion that had fallen to him, **with riotous living.** The Greek beautifully renders it, *living unsavingly.* He spared nothing, neither money nor self, but was heedless, reckless, prodigal. Even all this was better than to be mean, hoarding, and self-seeking in that way. He was probably generous to a fault, hail fellow well met.

14. And when he hath spent all, there arose a mighty famine in that country; and he began to be in want.

14. But there came a change upon the spirit of his

dreams. Riches do not endure forever. And, presently, the young man found **he had spent all** his patrimony; he had lived so unsavingly and unsavedly that all was gone. And at the same time **there arose a mighty famine in that land.** God's providence joined with his improvidence to bring him into straits. **He began to be in want,** for the first time in his life. He was compelled now to take a sober view of things. It is kindness in God to send sorrow upon us in our sins, that we may not go on in sin till all life and hope are gone. God by His providence chastens men, to bring them to repentance. Moreover it is the very nature of sin, as departure from God, to bring sorrow and death. "Whatsoever a man soweth, that also shall he reap."

15, 16. And he went and joined himself to one of the citizens of that country; and he sent him into his fields to feed swine. And he would fain have been filled with the husks that the swine did eat: and no man gave unto him.

15. The prodigal now sought some recourse from the evils that stared him in the face. First **he went and joined himself to a citizen of that country,** that far country, that land of sinful pleasure and worldly delight. Sinners first try to better themselves away from God, one this way, another that way. Well, this citizen **sent him into his fields to feed swine.** That was about the lowest estate to which a Jew could be brought.

16. The young man was ready to pounce upon **the husks** (pods of the carob tree, sometimes eaten by people in greatest poverty) **that the swine did eat,** and **no man gave unto him** in that selfish land, afar from God, where each sought his own and none cared for another.

17-20. But when he came to himself he said, How many hired servants of my father's have bread enough and to spare, and I perish here with hunger! I will arise and go to my father, and will say unto him, Father, I have sinned against heaven, and in thy sight : I am no more worthy to be called thy son : make me as one of thy hired servants. And he arose, and came to his father. But while he was yet afar off, his father saw him, and was moved with compassion, and ran, and fell on his neck, and kissed him.

17. **He came to himself** at length, was sobered, took time to think, realized the situation. The sinner is deranged, yet wilfully he remains estranged from God, until, in God's providence and grace, he is brought to a true self-consciousness and begins to know himself. The young man *remembered* what he had left, the situation at his **father's** house, where even the hired servants had **bread enough and to spare,** and yet here he was, a son in a hired servant's place, in the far country, and ready to **perish with hunger.** What a contrast between *there* and **here!** The young man is finding out what it is to leave a good home and go off in self-will. His independence has gone into thin air. He is utterly dependent now, and cannot even earn his daily bread.

18. **I will arise**—a good resolution. Start up from the far land and the evil situation. **And go** not further off but back **to my father.** For he is "father" still, though I have forfeited the place of son. **And will say unto him** the truth, will own up, will make humble confession. **I have sinned.** "If we say we have no sin we deceive ourselves." "If we say we have not sinned we make God a liar." But the prodigal said, and David said, and we say (see "Common Service"), "I will confess my transgressions unto the Lord."

19. He does this humbly, as **no more worthy to be called son,** as ready to take a place among the **hired servants.** So the Lord Jesus washed the disciples' feet, and bade us act in like manner. In all this we see the first parts of repentance,—sorrow, resolution to return, a mental turning from self and sin to God and home. But

this in itself is not repentance. There remains the doing of the thing resolved, the actual return.

20. **And he arose and came to his father.** He completed in act what he had begun in thought. His repentance was not a wavering wish or longing hope merely. He actually returned. So the sinner faces about and comes back to God from whom he had gone far away. **But while . . . yet afar off**—mark that: " yet afar off! "—**father saw him**—God's eye is on the sinner; He desires to win back the wanderer, to recover the fallen, to save the lost; He watches over him even in his sins and prodigality, hoping and moving providentially and graciously upon him for his repentance and return—**and was moved with compassion**—" God is love ; " " like as a father pitieth his children, so the Lord pitieth them that fear him," and even those that do not, if only they will come to loving fear of Him—**and ran**—yes, God meets the sinner more than half way ; He sent the trouble upon him, chiefly to bring him back—**and fell on his neck and kissed him ;** the father was not deterred by the prodigal's ragged, filthy and mean condition ; he embraced him ; for the father heart yearned for his son, though clothed in rags. He can wash and clothe him and make him yet appear as he should in the father's house. Here was already proof that the father forgave the prodigal.

21–24. And the son said unto him, Father, I have sinned against heaven, and in thy sight: I am no more worthy to be called thy son. But the father said to his servants, Bring forth quickly the best robe, and put it on him ; and put a ring on his hand, and shoes on his feet : and bring the fatted calf, *and* kill it, and let us eat, and make merry : for this my son was dead, and is alive again ; he was lost, and is found. And they began to be merry.

21–24. But still he makes his confession, as he had purposed. But before he finished it, **the father** interrupted him with orders to the servants, **Bring forth quickly** (God delays not to clothe the unclothed sinner) **the best robe** (the Saviour's righteousness, "fine linen, white and clean") **and put it on him** (on the repentant sinner returned); **and put a ring on his hand, and shoes on his feet,** making him appear as a son, not a hired servant. Restore him, re-instal him in his father's house. **And bring the fatted calf**—kept in store against a great occasion—**and kill it, and let us eat and make merry.** Let the whole house rejoice; for the **lost** that **is found** now is **this my son.** He was dead—"dead in trespasses and in sins" (Eph. ii. 1)—**and is alive again**—"passed from death unto life" (John v. 24), "quickened together with him" (Col. ii. 13).

Suppose this prodigal had said he did not believe all that was going on, that, because he did not deserve all this love and forgiveness, it was only words and a form! You say this is not supposable. But when, after confessing our sins unto the Lord, His ambassador says, "Almighty God, our heavenly Father, hath had mercy upon us, and hath given His only Son to die for us, and for His sake forgiveth us all our sins," some call it "formalism" and will not suffer this Declaration of Grace to be spoken or received as true! "But there is forgiveness with thee, that thou mayest be feared" (Ps. cxxx. 4).

25–28. Now his elder son was in the field: and as he came and drew nigh to the house, he heard music and dancing. And he called to him one of the servants, and inquired what these things might be. And he said unto him, Thy brother is come; and thy father hath killed the fatted calf, because he hath received him safe and sound. But he was angry, and would not go in: and his father came out, and intreated him.

25. The parable began with "two sons." Having traced the course of the younger, it now recurs to the **elder son.** He was **in the field,** industriously engaged

upon the farm. (See on ver. 29.) Coming back **to the house** toward the close of the day, his ear was attracted by the festivities of an entertainment going on there. Nor was he drawn to them; he seemed to himself an outsider and at once felt piqued at the situation.

26, 27. Feeling so he did not go right in but called **one of the servants, and inquired** what was going on, who in his way reported the facts, observing chiefly the salient external points—**brother come**—**safe and sound**, in good health, well—**fatted calf killed**, centralizing the festive joy. The effect of this information was to inflame the glowering spirit already taking hold of him.

28. **He was angry.** Thoughts of self were uppermost, wounded pride, envy, jealousy, recollections of what that brother had done and was supposed to have done. He **would not go in.** Outside in all the arrangements and exercises so far held, unconsulted, disapproving what had been done and was doing, he would remain an outsider. With loving heart his father then came out and **entreated him**, exhorted, urged him to come in and be one among the rejoicing family.

29–30. But he answered and said to his father, Lo, these many years do I serve thee, and I never transgressed a commandment of thine: and *yet* thou never gavest me a kid, that I might make merry with my friends: but when this thy son came, which hath devoured thy living with harlots, thou killedst for him the fatted calf.

29. He plead **many years** of faithful service. Like the young ruler who claimed of the law, "All these things have I observed from my youth up" (xviii. 21), this elder son said, **I never transgressed a commandment of thine.** And now, especially by contrast with his brother's course, he values his services, thinks of reward for his proper, obedient life. His spirit was very different from that inculcated by the Lord (Luke xvii. 10), "Even so ye also

when ye shall have done all the things that are commanded you, say, We are unprofitable servants ; we have done that which it was our duty to do." **To me.** " The ἐμοί placed first [not shown in the translation] has the emphasis of wounded selfish feeling" (MEYER). **Thou never gavest a kid,** the smallest thing, for a merry-making **with my friends.** " The servile tone pervades the elder brother's words throughout, and in this he was a faithful picture of the Pharisees, whose religion was essentially legal and servile in spirit " (BRUCE). " He is looking for certain definite rewards for his obedience, to the getting something *from* God, instead of possessing all things *in* God " (TRENCH).

30. **But**—the contrast—**when this thy son,** etc. He is too angry to call him brother: he says hard things about him, putting the worst phase upon the case. " For thinking of these [moral deliquencies of his brother] he was not to be blamed; his fault lay here, that he was readier to think of the sin than of the repentance, which in the judgment of charity might be presumed to have been the motive impelling the prodigal to return. This was the fault of the Pharisees, of whom he is the type. They thought only of the vices of the class whom Jesus loved, never of their repentance, and hence their inability to comprehend the motives, and to sympathize with the feelings, of Jesus. It was a fault due immediately to the want of a *hopeful spirit* in reference to the moral reformation of the degraded members of society " (BRUCE).

31, 32. And he said unto him, Son, thou art ever with me, and all that is mine is thine. But it was meet to make merry and be glad: for this thy brother was dead, and is alive *again ;* and *was* lost, and is found.

31. **Son.** The original is a very kindly word. The same love speaks here that before greeted the returning

prodigal. **Thou** is emphatic. **Ever with me,** a constant source of joy and comfort, a perennial blessing like an ever flowing river. Such are obedient loving children all their days in the home—however the Pharisees did not measure up to this standard. **And all that is mine**—kid, fatted calf, everything—**is thine.** It was his patrimony which he was enjoying with his father, and not separated from him—and why should he now separate himself, and even exhibit a similar spirit to that which took the younger son away? **But it was meet**—the father takes not back what he had done, nor makes apology, but defends its entire propriety—to **make merry and be glad** when the **lost** was **found**; this time not a lost sheep, or a lost coin, but a lost son! (See on ver. 24.)

CHAPTER XVI.

1, 2. And he said also unto the disciples, There was a certain rich man, which had a steward; and the same was accused unto him that he was wasting his goods. And he called him, and said unto him, What is this that I hear of thee? render the account of thy stewardship; for thou canst be no longer steward.

1. The preceding chapter was spoken to the murmuring Pharisees and Scribes, in the presence of the publicans and sinners. Now in the same presence He spake also **unto the disciples**, not merely the Twelve, among whom, no doubt, were "publicans and sinners." His teaching was by a parable that centred about **a steward** who had charge of the affairs of **a certain rich man.** Many and very diverse have been the interpretations put upon this rich man. As he is only incidental to the teaching, we need not identify him any further than the record does. The charge was made to him against his steward that he **was wasting his goods.** The same word is used here that was used in xv. 13 of the younger son's wasting his substance. Evidently there was a plenty that passed through the steward's hands and came under his oversight; for he was a rich man's steward. (See also vers. 5-7.)

2. The man believed the report that came to him: the evidence, not given here, seems to have been convincing. Summoning the accused he said, **What is this that I hear of thee?** Nor does he ask or give opportunity for explanation and defence. His mind is made up, and he abruptly bids the other to **render the account** of his

stewardship, settle up. **For thou canst be no longer steward.** The man has lost his credit and his office at once. He is brought up at a short turn. Sudden and decisive is the call. So death comes and calls us to account and closes our stewardship. (Comp. ver. 9.)

> 3, 4. And the steward said within himself, What shall I do, seeing that my lord taketh away the stewardship from me? I have not strength to dig; to beg I am ashamed. I am resolved what to do, that, when I am put out of the stewardship, they may receive me into their houses.

3. The steward, thus put to, held a colloquy with himself. **What shall I do?** That he did not think to deny the charge and attempt to prove fidelity to his trust seems to show that he was self-condemned, as guilty in his own consciousness as his employer took him to be. It was an assured thing that he was going to lose the stewardship. What was he to do? **I have not strength to dig** and live by my own exertions; **to beg**—the other alternative—**I am ashamed.** And here we have a man in great straits, pushed to the wall.

4. But he was a man of resources, and bethought him of some other way out of his embarrassment than the alternatives just given. At last he hit upon a plan, and shrewdly **resolved what to do.** The motive was self-interest: the end that they, with whom I have hitherto stood in the relation of steward of a vast property, **may receive me** as a welcome inmate **into their houses.** He proposed to ingratiate himself with his hitherto clients and make them his fast friends. He will do them such a turn that they will not let him suffer when he is **put out of the stewardship.** He will play a sharp game, a wily politician seeking his own ends. Accused of wasting his lord's goods, and conscious that he has done so, why should he not go on further in the same direction?

5-7. And calling to him each one of his lord's debtors, he said to the first, How much owest thou unto my lord? And he said, A hundred measures of oil. And he said unto him, Take thy bond, and sit down quickly and write fifty. Then said he to another, And how much owest thou? And he said, A hundred measures of wheat. He saith unto him, Take thy bond, and write fourscore.

5. So the steward summoned **his lord's debtors**, and had an interview with, and made a proposition to, **each one.** " It must be borne in mind that he is still steward, and, as such, has full power of disposing of his master's affairs. When, therefore, he sends for one after another of his master's debtors, and tells each one to alter the sum in the bond, he does not suggest to them forgery or fraud, but, in remitting part of the debt—whether it had been incurred as rent in kind, or as the price of produce purchased—he acts, although unrighteously, yet strictly within his rights. Thus, neither the steward nor the debtors could be charged with criminality, and the master must have been struck with the cleverness of a man who had thus secured a future provision by making friends, so long as he had the means of so doing (ere his Mammon of unrighteousness failed)" (EDERSHEIM). **How much owest thou?** Each one naturally would have a deep impression of his indebtedness. The colloquy was probably intended to impress each one also with the steward's personal kindness in his case.

6. **A hundred measures** [baths] **of oil.** Payment was to be made in produce. A "bath" amounted, by Galilean measurement, to about 39 *litres* or 41 quarts. The value of one hundred of these was probably about 50 dollars. **Take thy bond**—it was probably inscribed on wax or possibly on parchment, signed by the debtor, and in the steward's keeping—**and quickly** (there was no time to be lost, as the steward's power would soon be gone,) **write fifty**, change the amount by one-half.

7. **Another** reported his indebtedness at **a hundred measures** [cors] **of wheat.** A "cor" was, by measure, ten times the amount of a "bath"; and the amount of the debt would probably be from 500 to 600 dollars. The reduction to **fourscore** would relieve this debtor of about 100 to 125 dollars. These two instances are only illustrations of the steward's method with the whole number, treating each as he thought best.

<small>8. And his lord commended the unrighteous steward because he had done wisely: for the sons of this world are for their own generation wiser than the sons of the light.</small>

8. **And his lord,** that is, the lord of the steward who was the central figure of the parable, **commended** him, despite his **unrighteous** character and acts, **because he had done wisely,** had been smart in looking after his own interests. That is the way with **the sons of this world,** this world's people, the worldly, whose portion is in this life (Ps. xvii. 14); they look out each for himself, take care of their individual interests, and applaud themselves and one another for so doing. They are **for their own generation,** their kind, in their own way and for their own ends, which are selfish and often dishonest, **wiser,** more prudent, sharper, smarter, **than the sons of light,** children of the kingdom of God, Christians, who do not and dare not act like the unjust steward because they are people of character, of righteousness, actuated by principle, fearing and loving God above all and loving their neighbors as themselves, and consequently not given to taking smart advantage of their fellows or seeking their own however they can, be it honestly or dishonestly. "The children of light can pursue only holy purposes with moral means, and consequently (as sons of *wisdom*) must necessarily fall behind in the worldly *prudence,* in which *morality* is of no account" (MEYER). "We see

it daily with our eyes, alas, more than is good, how the world is so very careful how to obtain a profit, and grudges no pains or labor, while, on the other hand, we see the children of light, i. e. Christians, lazy, unwilling, inadvertent and negligent in God's affairs, although they know that God has pleasure therein and that they will enjoy them in eternity" (LUTHER).

9. And I say unto you, Make to yourselves friends by means of the mammon of unrighteousness; that, when it shall fail, they may receive you into the eternal tabernacles.

9. **And I,** your Lord, **say unto you,** in application of the parable just spoken. There is evident contrast here between what the steward's lord said of him and his smartness, and what the Lord Jesus says to His disciples: there is also likeness, from the parable, in commending to Christians an equal, yea greater, and yet righteous, quickness, shrewdness, wisdom. The Lord here teaches the true use of worldly riches, which He calls **the mammon of unrighteousness.** "Mammon" is derived from a Syriac and Rabbinic word and is a term applied to riches, and is sometimes personified, as in ver. 13, as the god of this world. Called the mammon of unrighteousness because it is the god whom the unrighteous worship (ROBERTSON). "As at ver. 8 this predicate [of unrighteousness, comp. the unrighteous mammon, ver. 11 below] is attached to the *steward* because he had *acted* unrighteously towards his lord, so here it is attached to *wealth,* because it, as in the case of that steward, serves, according to usual experience (comp. xviii. 24 f.), *as an instrument of unrighteous dealing.* The moral characteristic of the *use* of it is represented as *adhering to itself"* (MEYER). Jesus bids His disciples make a right use of it. With it, by means of it, from the power and influence it gives you, **make to yourselves friends.** How ?

By doing good and communicating (1 Tim. vi. 18; Heb. xiii. 16), ministering in love to the needy. " He hath dispersed, he hath given to the needy; his righteousness endureth forever: his horn shall be exalted with honor" (Ps. cxii. 9; comp. 2 Cor. ix. 6–15). "He that hath pity upon the poor lendeth unto the Lord, and his good deed will he pay him again" (Prov. xix. 17). Put out your money where it will make you friends—not merely temporary and temporal ones, but such as will **receive you into the eternal tabernacles** when for you the earthly house of this tabernacle shall be dissolved. This receiving is not an act of authority, as though "friends" had a right to admit into the eternal mansions, but a welcoming act. The authority is vested in the Son of man, who, in the judgment scene in Matt. xxv. 31–46, is represented as recounting the deeds done in making friends with worldly goods and saying, "Inasmuch as ye did it unto one of these my brethren, even these least, ye did it unto me." And neither in this place nor in that are these deeds represented as a meritorious ground of heavenly inheritance, but as illustrations of character marked by faith and love. What a simple and effective recipe here for finding many friends in the eternal world! Moreover we are not restricted to a personal distribution of earthly riches, but may reach many through the Church's operations in Missions, Church Extension, Education, Homes for Orphans and the Aged, Deaconess' Homes and the like. The avenues whereby "the unrighteous mammon" may reach those who are to be made "friends" are many. Use them well, and what a reception will be yours in the eternal world!

10–12. He that is faithful in a very little is faithful also in much: and he that is unrighteous in a very little is unrighteous also in much. If therefore ye have not been faithful in the unrighteous mammon, who will commit to your trust the true *riches?* And if ye have not been faithful in that which is another's, who will give you that which is your own?

10. Clearly the Lord does not approve of anything like unfaithfulness, even though He used an unfaithful steward's thoughtfulness for himself as a stimulus to a sensible, provident use of temporal riches on the part of His disciples. Ver. 10 is of the nature of a proverb. One who is **faithful** is so in all things, it is an all-around characteristic : and its existence in any one with reference to what is **very little** argues that it will be found in that one where **much** is concerned. This statement stands as a major premise to a syllogism which is concluded in the next two verses.

11, 12. The connection is **therefore,** and the case is supposed. **The unrighteous mammon** (on which see ver. 9, above, and comments) is contrasted with **the true** riches, the durable riches and righteousness (Prov. viii. 18), the heavenly inheritance : the former is called **another's**—worldly riches, contrary to common opinion, does not properly belong to those who hold it here, they are only *stewards* of it—the latter is called **your own,** for it is an everlasting inheritance, a *possession* forever : the former every one must part with, it is but temporary, a loan to be administered and accounted for (comp. the parable of the pounds, ch. xix.); the latter is the gift of God (Rom. v. 15-18 ; vi. 23 ; Eph. iv. 18), which no one taketh away (John xvi. 22), and from which nothing can separate us (Rom. viii. 35-39). And the argument is from the less to the greater ; if you fail to administer faithfully and righteously, as set forth above, the common, the earthly, the temporal, worldly wealth, be it much or little, this proves you unfitted for the heavenly, which, in that case, must not be expected! This bore hard on the covetous, mammon-worshipping Pharisees who were listening, and it was a very practical lesson, easily understood by them, for the publicans in and out of the circle of disciples: and it is equally instructive and warning to those now who count the riches they have as their own and forget and neglect their stewardship.

13. No servant can serve two masters: for either he will hate the one, and love the other; or else he will hold to one, and despise the other. Ye cannot serve God and mammon.

13. See on Matt. vi. 24, where the same words are found. The only variation here is the addition of the word **servant.** Though many try to do what is here set forth, the Lord Himself has thus twice declared it to be impossible. To the questioning scribe (Mark xii. 28, 29) Jesus laid down as the fundamental principle of the religion of Israel, the true religion, " Hear, O Israel; the Lord our God, the Lord is one: and thou shalt love the Lord thy God with all thy heart," etc., and hence "none other gods before me " is the first requirement of the law. " One is your Master, even the Christ " (Matt. xxiii. 10). Hence He is to be " all and in all " (Col. iii. 11). Administer your worldly goods in His name and to His praise.

14. And the Pharisees, who were lovers of money, heard all these things; and they scoffed at him.

14. Though the preceding verses of this chapter were spoken directly to the disciples (ver. 1), **the Pharisees, and others** (xv. 1, 2), were present, **and heard all,** and found Jesus' words applicable to themselves. They were **lovers of money,** genuine specimens of mammon-worshippers, who, therefore, according to the Lord's teaching, were not and could not be, without a change, true servants of God. Before (xv. 2) they murmured, but now

they scoffed at him. The word signifies to turn up the nose in derision. Catch them taking His instructions about the use of riches! They counted their money their own (see on ver. 12) and did not propose to mix business and religion!

> 15. And he said unto them, Ye are they that justify yourselves in the sight of men; but God knoweth your hearts: for that which is exalted among men is an abomination in the sight of God.

15. Now Jesus spake **unto them** directly again, and on through the parable of the rich man and Lazarus. Their scoffs and sneers invited this address. **Ye** (emphatic) . . . **justify yourselves** (comp. x. 29; xviii. 11), a natural predilection of the natural man, **in the sight of men,** who can see only the outside, the apparent. There you may succeed: **but God knoweth your hearts,** your real selves; and it is something different to be justified in His sight. (See Ps. vii. 10; 1 Kings viii. 39.) The searcher of hearts is not taken up with the appearance, but gets at the inner essence, the true and real character, and so His judgment is apt to, and does, differ from man's. **For that which is exalted,** counted high and great, **among men,** is differently estimated in the sight **of God,** and is even counted **an abomination,** a detestable thing. (Comp. Prov. vi. 16–19; xxix. 23.) "And thus appears the loftiest *human* virtue and 'righteousness' to be no more than a wicked pride of heart" (STIER). God is the unerring judge. Before Him Pharisees have a poor prospect.

> 16–18. The law and the prophets *were* until John: from that time the gospel of the kingdom of God is preached, and every man entereth violently into it. But it is easier for heaven and earth to pass away, than for one tittle of the law to fall. Every one that putteth away his wife, and marrieth another, committeth adultery: and he that marrieth one that is put away from a husband committeth adultery.

16. Comp. Matt. xi. 12, 13, and comments.

God's successive dispensations towards men, represented in His people Israel, are here cited historically. **The law, the prophets,** both of which the Pharisees professed to reverence, but both of which they practically so abused and disregarded—these the preparation for **John,** and John for the preaching of **the gospel of the kingdom of God:** but the Pharisees did not receive John, they refused to come to repentance (Matt. iii. 7-9; Luke xx. 4-6), and now with respect to the kingdom of God, preached as at hand by both John and Jesus, **every man** of them **entereth violently into it,** that is, acteth violently towards it, opposes it. This is one way of understanding the original εἰς αὐτὴν βιάζεται. The last word may have a friendly sense, as our English translators of both 1611 and 1881 seem to have taken it, or an unfriendly sense, as we have explained it above. Those who follow the plain tenor of the English version understand by the expression the urgent pressing into the kingdom of God: but we have to ask where in those days this was exhibited.

17. **But,** though the Pharisees had practically done away with the law, while with their lips they magnified it and even charged the Lord with not regarding it, the gospel did not and does not annul the law: the law is more stable than **heaven and earth.** These may and will **pass away,** having accomplished their purpose: and this grand catastrophe is **easier** to think of and to be accomplished than for **one tittle,** the minutest part, **of the law to fall** to the ground void. The law is a transcript of the divine perfections, and is for ever. Christ came not to destroy but to fulfil. (Comp. Matt. v. 17-20; Rom. iii. 19-31.)

18. Then the Lord illustrated the abiding nature of the

law in a point where the Pharisees notoriously transgressed it. Jesus taught them who readily put away the marriage tie that they could not thus put away the binding force of the law. (See on Matt. v. 31, 32; xix. 9.)

19. Now there was a certain rich man, and he was clothed in purple and fine linen, faring sumptuously every day:

This narrative we take to be a representative, without being a historical, setting forth of what substantially has occurred and will occur again and again. The form of it makes its teachings none the less real, but rather sets them forth as belonging to the abiding nature of things. The parable—as we may call it, for want of a better name—was part of the same general discourse found in this chapter. It is addressed to the covetous, deriding Pharisees, who justified themselves before men (vers. 14, 15), handling the word of God deceitfully, occupying the first positions among the Jews while they were unsound in doctrine and life, and in their self-complacency despised the poor. As "that which is exalted among men is an abomination in the sight of God," who knows the heart, so the hereafter may prove quite a reversal of the estimation and position accorded men here: and this the narrative shows.

19. **There was a certain rich man.** His riches gave him respectability among men, and much ability to do good. Every man has his talent or talents, and this man's talent was his riches. In ver. 9 of this chapter they were taught the right use of riches, and in ver. 13 were warned that it is impossible to serve God and mammon. There is danger, in being rich, that we learn to love and serve wealth, and it become a snare to our souls. Hence it is with difficulty that a rich man shall enter into the king-

dom of God. This man **was clothed in purple and fine linen,** an evidence of his opulence. Purple was a regal color and very costly, made from a rare shell-fish found near Tyre. Linen was made from the flax that grew along the Nile, and Pliny tells of qualities of it, especially white and fine, that were sold for their weight in gold. **Faring sumptuously.** Living deliciously. He had everything he thought would minister to his delight. Nothing was too much for him to spend upon himself. His table groaned with plenty and of the best quality, delicacies of every description; his whole place was magnificent. And he fared thus **every day.**

20, 21. And a certain beggar named Lazarus was laid at his gate, full of sores, and desiring to be fed with the *crumbs* that fell from the rich man's table; yea, even the dogs came and licked his sores.

20, 21. In contrast is put **a certain beggar,** a man in utter poverty. His name, Lazarus, is used now for the whole class of beggars, called "lazars" and "lazaroni" in Europe. This name is by some considered an abbreviation of Eleazar, meaning "God is help;" others make it a symbolical name, meaning "helpless," "forsaken." This man was **laid at his** (the rich man's) **gate,** put there by others who did not want the care of him, or because they thought he would draw forth helpful sympathy from within. Lying there, **full of sores,** the consequence of his poverty-stricken state, he must have been a pitiable object, seen by the rich man every time he went in and out of the door of his house. He would have been glad to get **the crumbs** (bits) **that fell from the rich man's table.** There were other candidates for these, too, in **the dogs** that, as in all Eastern towns, run loose, without masters, as city scavengers. These **came and licked his sores,** probably with pleasant and healing effect on the poor man ; yet this is a further touch to add to the wretchedness of the scene.

Here were the extremes of life ; and we are reminded of Agur's prayer to be delivered from them both (Prov. xxx. 8, 9). Nothing is said of the moral character of these two persons. We are left to infer this from what follows. It is very certain, as all the Bible testifies, that external circumstances, whether of wealth or poverty, do not constitute character. It is no sin to be rich ; it is no virtue to be poor. A rich man may be godly, and a poor man ungodly. In this narrative, however, it is implied that the rich man lived only for himself. God, the Giver of his possessions, and his obligations to Him, to be manifested in proper conduct toward His creatures, was not in all his thoughts. Like the rich fool, he called his wealth his own, and used it only for himself. If the poor beggar got some of the dog's portion of offal, he got no more. The rich man did not act the good Samaritan toward him, and was without neighborly love. The beggar's character he did not inquire into, and knew no more of it than we would do if it were not for the after-part of this narrative. He did not know that Christ was lying hungry at his door (Matt. xxv. 35, 37, 40).

22, 23. And it came to pass, that the beggar died, and that he was carried away by the angels into Abraham's bosom : and the rich man also died, and was buried. And in Hades he lifted up his eyes, being in torments, and seeth Abraham afar off, and Lazarus in his bosom.

22, 23. One experience came alike to both the rich man and the beggar ; they both **died.** Death is the great leveller ; death is no respecter of persons or places. The rich man, we are told, was **buried,** and it is implied that his funeral was as magnificent as his life had been. The beggar's mortal remains were probably hustled out of sight most unceremoniously. " Rattle his bones over the stones, 'tis only a pauper whom nobody owns!" Thus the curtain fell on the scene of this mortal life. Our Lord causes it to rise upon the hereafter.

Does death end all? Our lesson says not. It declares that the beggar was **carried away by the angels into Abraham's bosom.** Abraham was the father of the faithful, the friend of God; and "Abraham's bosom" was a term used by the Jews for future happiness; it meant the same thing to them that *Paradise* does to us. This was in the spirit world, and the agents of his transfer were the angels, of whom it is said, Heb. i. 14, "Are they not all ministering spirits, sent forth to do service for the sake of them that shall inherit salvation?" So then we learn that Lazarus was a child of faith, and an heir of salvation, though so poorly off in this world's goods. The rich man was carried by the pall-bearers to the grave, magnificently attended, **and in Hades he lifted up his eyes being in torments.** The word "hades" means the unseen spirit world. It is as old as the Greek language, and corresponds to the Hebrew *Sheol.* It occurs eleven times in the New Testament, and is rendered "hell" ten times, and "grave" once (1 Cor. xv. 55), in the "Authorized Version." That it does not mean *hell* in the ordinary and circumscribed meaning of that word, is evident from the history of the word, and especially from Rev. xx. 14, which says, "And death and hell (hades) were cast into a lake of fire. This is the second death!" We have no one word wherewith to express its meaning, and, perhaps, therefore, it would be as well to incorporate it into our language, as we have done with other words, and let it stand—"hades"—wherever it occurs, as the Revised Version does. But that this word does not mean "hell" in no way goes to prove that there is no hell. There are other words to express that idea; and right here we have it that the rich man in hades was **in torments**. He says himself, " I am *tormented in this flame,*" and calls it "this place of torment." The words here rendered torment strongly represent all that is conveyed by that word. TRENCH says, "As 'Abraham's bosom' is not heaven, so neither is hades 'hell,' though to issue in it when death and hades shall be cast into the lake of fire, which is the proper hell (Rev. xx. 14). It is the place of painful restraint, where the souls of the wicked are reserved to the judgment of the great day; it is the 'deep,' whither the devils prayed that they might not be sent to be tormented before their time (Luke viii. 31)— for, as that other blessed place has a foretaste of heaven, so has this place a foretaste of hell." **And seeth Abraham.** In all this description the spirits are spoken of as persons, and as if in the body; for how else could we talk intelligibly about them? The eye, moreover, does not see; it is only the instrument of sight. What the disembodied spirits' powers are, and how they act, we do not know. **Afar off.** Their characters had been far apart in this world, and now themselves are at a great remove in the world of spirits. But Lazarus was in Abraham's bosom, and recognized there. We cannot measure the times and spaces of the unseen world.

24. And he cried and said, Father Abraham, have mercy on me, and send Lazarus, that he may dip the tip of his finger in water, and cool my tongue; for I am in anguish in this flame.

24. **And he cried.** JACOBUS remarks that "this is the only instance in Scripture of praying to saints." Looking at all the circumstances of it, it is not very encouraging to that idea. **Father Abraham.** He still hopes something from his earthly descent as an Israelite. **Have mercy on me.** A cry that would have suited his condition, and found answers of peace, if made in time? **Send**

Lazarus. " It is noticeable that he still imagines himself able to direct Lazarus, whom he had all his life lightly esteemed. Even so does he afterwards despise Moses also (ver. 30). Only his external condition, what surrounds him, is altered, but not his individuality " (VAN OOST.). **That he may dip the tip of his finger in water.** How small a request! Lazarus had once wanted *crumbs* from him. **Cool my tongue.** The tongue that has tasted so many delights now craves a drop of water. " This hints," one says, "at the close connection between sin and its punishment." **In anguish in this flame.** A garment of fire instead of the purple and fine linen! " Not subjective (that is, confined to his own feeling) only," says ALFORD, "though perhaps mainly. But where lies the limit between inner and outer, to the disembodied. Hardened sinners have died crying, ' Fire!' Did the fire leave them when they left their bodies?" But it is to no profit to discuss whether or not there is material fire in the world to come; enough that there is unmitigated anguish.

25. But Abraham said, Son, remember that thou in thy lifetime receivedst thy good things, and Lazarus in like manner evil things: but now here he is comforted, and thou art in anguish.

25. **Son.** Abraham speaks kindly and acknowledges the external relationship. That relationship, however, was really an aggravation of the rich man's guilt. **Remember.** Memory survives death, and may live to torment us. Now the word is, " Remember thy Creator in the days of thy youth;" " Remember the Sabbath day to keep it holy;" " Remember the words of the Lord Jesus:"—then it will be the unsaved one's lot to remember an irreparable past. **Thou in thy lifetime receivedst thy good things.** The things thou didst choose, as indicated by " thy." The rich man made his

portion in this life, and had it, got what he craved. "Verily I say unto you, they *have their reward*," said Jesus of the Pharisees. **And Lazarus in like manner evil things.** Not "his" evil things, as though a choice or specific merit of his. **But now** how changed! What a complete reversal! **Here . . . comforted.** Here he has found rest, and is a beggar no more. **And thou art in anguish.** The poor man has become rich, and the rich man poor; and that in infinite degree, and never to be changed.

26. And beside all this, between us and you there is a great gulf fixed, that they which would pass from hence to you may not be able, and that none may cross over from thence to us.

26. **Between us and you,** making a separation, . . . **a great gulf,** chasm, across which, however, the dwellers in hades could see and hear. **Fixed,** established. **So that,** to the end that, for the purpose that, **they which would pass . . . may not be able.** There are limits in the other world. And inasmuch as the inability to cross affects those on each side alike, what becomes of Romish notions of *purgatory*, and of the theory of the Restorationists? This speaks of the status in hades as "fixed."

27, 28. And he said, I pray thee therefore, father, that thou wouldest send him to my father's house; for I have five brethren; that he may testify unto them, lest they also come into this place of torment.

27, 28. **Send him,** this Lazarus, **to my father's house— for I have five brethren—lest they also come** here. As if *he* had not been *sufficiently* warned, but he will have them well informed! Is there here a self-justifying spirit still, and an accusing of God? Is he really concerned for his brethren, or does he fear their coming will only aggravate his own misery? ALFORD says on this, "That a *lost spirit* should feel and express such sympathy, is not to be wondered at; the misery of such will be very much heightened by the awakened and active state of those higher faculties and feelings which selfishness and the body kept down here."

<small>29. But Abraham saith, They have Moses and the prophets; let them hear them.</small>

29. **They have Moses and the prophets,** the Old Testament Scriptures; **let them hear them.** This shows the teachings of the Old Testament to be sufficient to warn men of the wrath to come, and keep them out of it. But while boasting of Moses and the prophets, the Jews did not truly listen to their teachings.

<small>30, 31. And he said, Nay, father Abraham : but if one go to them from the dead, they will repent. And he said unto him, If they hear not Moses and the prophets, neither will they be persuaded, if one rise from the dead.</small>

30. **Nay.** He knows better than Abraham or God. A sinner's presumption goes with him to the other world. **But if one go to them from the dead, they will repent.** The Jews were ever seeking "a sign." People now want something *more* than what they have, something marvellous, portentous. Some of them, as in the olden time, seek to "familiar spirits" that peep and mutter; and though they are easily deceived, defrauded, made game of, they do not *repent* of their sins.

31. **If they hear not Moses and the prophets, neither will they be persuaded,** believe, not to say repent, **if one rise from the dead.** How was it when Lazarus rose and testified? They sought to put him as well as Jesus to death. How was it when Jesus rose? They paid the soldier guards to lie about it, and circulated a report that His disciples had stolen the body.

CHAPTER XVII.

1-4. And he said unto his disciples, It is impossible but that occasions of stumbling should come: but woe unto him, through whom they come! It were well for him if a millstone were hanged about his neck, and he were thrown into the sea, rather than that he should cause one of these little ones to stumble. Take heed to yourselves: if thy brother sin, rebuke him; and if he repent, forgive him. And if he sin against thee seven times in the day, and seven times turn again to thee, saying, I repent, thou shalt forgive him.

1. The discourse turns now again to **his disciples,** not merely the Twelve. Something in the circumstances of the occasion led to these words about **occasions of stumbling.** Perhaps it was the spirit, words and acts of the Pharisees, as revealed in xv. 2, xvi. 14-18. Similar words are found elsewhere, spoken on other occasions. (See on Matt. x. 38-50; xviii. 6-9 ff.; Mark. ix. 38-50.) The Greek word rendered "occasions of stumbling" is σκάνδαλα, from which comes our word "scandals." These must come in the nature of things as they now are in a fallen world; it is not to be expected otherwise, it is not conceivable. This is the meaning of **impossible** here. They are, however, blameworthy, and every one is responsible for affording them: hence the **woe** here denounced on him.

2. He would better be dead—the original words indicate completed action (as to the method see on passages referred to above)—than that he should become an occasion of falling into sin on the part of **one of these little ones,** weak disciples, beginners in grace, referring, perhaps, directly to converted "publicans and

sinners" (xv. 2) among them. MEYER says, "To explain the expression from Matt. xviii. 6 or x. 42 is not allowable," the expression there, at least in the first passage, pointing directly to the little child whom Jesus set in their midst.

3. In view, then, of the certainty of occasions of stumbling, scandals, and of the woe denounced against every author of them, **take heed to yourselves.** Avoid them and the woe attaching to them. Now comes the particular application : **if thy brother,** one of these little ones, least disciples, **sin,** err, come short, commit a fault—though "against thee" is thrown out by textual criticism, the context shows that to be the sense—**rebuke him.** Do this in the interest of truth ; do not become an occasion of his falling by failing to notice and rebuke his error. "Merely to be patient and keep silence, submitting to it resignedly because he is a brother—that would itself be an offence" (STIER). And **if he repent, forgive him.** Forgiveness is not to be pronounced, or completed, until there has been *repentance*, or, at least, a profession of repentance (ver. 4). Here man's forgiveness patterns after the divine.

4. The process **seven times** repeated " finds its justification in its [the representation's] *purpose*, to wit, to lay stress upon forgiveness as *incapable of being wearied out* " (MEYER). As truth required rebuke, so love requires forgiveness. "The lack of *truth* in rebuking and confessing, and still more the lack of rebuking and yet forgiving *love*, is the secret reason of all offences *in the church*, as in the world itself " (STIER).

5, 6. And the apostles said unto the Lord, Increase our faith. And the Lord said, If ye have faith as a grain of mustard seed, ye would say unto this sycamine tree, Be thou rooted up, and be thou planted in the sea ; and it would have obeyed you.

5. **The apostles** were deeply impressed with this discourse to the disciples, and, perhaps from their important position in the church, feeling their especial need, made reply to this discourse on occasions of falling, **Increase our faith,** or, rather, Give us more faith. Only faith could thus pray, but, like him in Mark. ix. 24, they feel how feeble is their faith for the end to be attained—faithfulness in rebuke and persistency in love. If apostles, in the presence of the Lord, needed to put up this prayer, how much more does it become us!

6. The Lord joins them in the highest appreciation of faith. **If you have faith** ye could and should have confidence to overcome all the difficulties that will meet you. Even though that faith be small, **as a grain of mustard seed,** yet there is power in it, even as the grain of mustard seed has in it the force of life, **and ye would** (might, could) **say unto this sycamine tree,** large and deeply rooted in the ground, seemingly so secure, and thus representative of a great difficulty, **Be rooted up,** nor that only, but also **planted in the sea,** a seeming impossibility —and it would have **obeyed you.** ·You are right in your desire for more, greater faith; for it is the disciple's power, for it is the hand that takes hold of almighty strength. With it even in a world where offences must needs come, you may be confident. " All things are possible to him that believeth " (Mark ix. 23).

See on Matt. xvii. 19-21, xxi. 21 ; Mark ix. 23, 24, 29, xi. 22-25.

7-10. But who is there of you, having a servant plowing or keeping sheep, that will say unto him, when he is come in from the field, Come straightway and sit down to meat; and will not rather say unto him, Make ready wherewith I may sup, and gird thyself, and serve me, till I have eaten and drunken ; and afterward thou shalt eat and drink? Doth he thank the servant because he did the things that were commanded? Even so ye also, when ye shall have done all the things that are commanded you, say,

We are unprofitable servants; we have done that which it was our duty to do.

The argument is from the nature of things. From man's way of doing, and human relations, the Lord illustrates God's way and our relation to Him. The purpose is to nurture faith by humility and to keep down in the disciples any sense of merit, any pride and self-exaltation that might follow the possession and exercise of such power as is here ascribed to faith.

7. It is not the custom for any one who has **a servant** —the word signifies a bond-servant, a slave, one who belonged to his master, not a hired servant (and there is no comment here passed on the propriety of such a relation; it was a very common one in those days and in Eastern countries)—whether it be a plowman or a herdsman, no matter what the kind or difficulty of the work he may be doing, **when he is come in** from that work at evening, to bid him **come straightway and sit down to meat.** He does not eat first, but the master.

8. Rather is there something for him yet to do, and he hears the word, **Make ready ... gird thyself** as a waiter, **and serve me .... afterward thou shalt eat and drink.** His place is afterward. So the Lord would teach His apostles to be forward indeed in the interests of His kingdom, in His service, but *afterward* in serving themselves and seeking their own. This is their place, and this marks true devotion, faith in their Lord: the Master and His work first, ourselves afterward. Would there were more of this spirit of true service!

9, 10. Further it is not customary to **thank the servant** at the close of the day for his obedient faithfulness. He did what was commanded him; that was his business, what was expected of him: if he had not done it he would have deserved and received censure. The master is kind to him, treats him well, supplies his needs, but does not *thank* him as though he had done him a favor.

Applying the illustration to the Twelve, Jesus says: **Even so ye,** God's servants, who certainly owe more to Him than any earthly servants to their masters, **when ye have done all**—but who has? The supposition is strained to its furthest limit: however faithful servants ye have been—acknowledge, **We are unprofitable,** we have done nothing more than **it was our duty to do,** we have not exceeded our obligation, we cannot claim *thanks* or *reward.* Men are of no use to God in the sense of being *profitable.* We receive from and do not give to God. With this sense and spirit we will be able to overcome the world with its many occasions of stumbling and will not likely be offending ones against the brethren.

11. And it came to pass, as they were on the way to Jerusalem, that he was passing through the midst of Samaria and Galilee.

11. **It came to pass** marks a very general connection and marks neither time nor place. Luke recurs here again to their being **on the way to Jerusalem.** (Comp. ix. 51; xiii. 22, 33, and comments there.) This begins the concluding period of that great journey. But how comes it that here He is spoken of as **passing through the midst of Samaria and Galilee,** when we supposed Him to have finally left Galilee at ix. 51? The words may mean that their course lay through those countries or through the strip of country bordering on each of them. And why is Samaria mentioned first, if their journey was southward *toward* Samaria? But we have supposed them to have been long ago in Judæa and Peræa, and even to have been in Jerusalem. EDERSHEIM suggests " that, on leaving Ephraim (John xi. 54), Christ made a very brief detour along the northern frontier to some place at the

southern border of Galilee—perhaps to meet at a certain point those who were to accompany Him on His final journey to Jerusalem." He explains that some of Jesus' followers may have naturally wished to pay a brief visit to Galilee again, and refers especially to Mark's statement that many women came up with Him to Jerusalem, noting that a lengthened journeying of these latter with Him and for an indefinite purpose would have been quite contrary to Jewish manners. He thinks all difficulties met "if we suppose that Christ had passed from Ephraim along the border of Samaria to a place in Galilee, there to meet such of His disciples as would go up with Him to Jerusalem. The whole company would then form one of those festive bands which travelled to the Paschal Feast, nor would there be anything strange or unusual in the appearance of such a band, in this instance under the leadership of Jesus." Among many explanations of the chronology and topology of this verse, the one given is sufficient, and we leave further discussion thereof to the harmonists.

12, 13. And as he entered into a certain village, there met him ten men that were lepers, which stood afar off. And they lifted up their voices, saying, Jesus, Master, have mercy on us.

12. Jesus, in His course, was about to enter **a certain village.** But before doing so **there met him,** that is, attracted His attention and stayed for a time His going, **ten men** who dare not follow Him into the village, for they **were lepers.** (See Lev. xiii. 46; 2 Kings xv. 5.) Leprosy has its name from a Greek word which signifies *a scale,* because in this disease the body was often covered with thin white *scales,* giving the appearance of snow. (See Ex. iv. 6; Numb. xii. 10; 2 Kings v. 27.) On leprosy, see Comments on Matt. viii. 2-4; Mark i. 40-45.

Here was a company of unfortunates. In their common misery the hatred between Jew and Samaritan seems to have been lost sight of.

13. They **stood afar off**, according to the law, but **lifted up their voices**, cracked, feeble, indistinct, as they were, with hope. For Jesus had already healed lepers (Matt. viii. 1–4; Luke v. 12–15) and had given the twelve the same power (Matt. x. 8). **Jesus, Master, have mercy on us**, pity us! It was a pitiful sight and a pitiful cry, and it touched the Lord's pitiful heart.

14. And when he saw them, he said unto them, Go and shew yourselves unto the priests. And it came to pass, as they went, they were cleansed.

14. But His way of answering men's cries is not always the same. Before, He *touched* the leper and healed him first, and then sent him to the priest. Now He said, **Go, and show yourselves unto the priests**. What for? There was no doubt in their minds or anybody's else that they were lepers. What were the priests to test or determine concerning them? See in Lev. xiii. 2; xiv. 2, 3, etc., the law on this subject. Though leprosy was incurable by known means, yet sometimes the afflicted recovered. Every such cure had to be attested by the priest, whose certification thereto restored the person to society and relieved him of the strictures put by the law upon the leprous. Jesus' command, therefore, was equivalent to an assurance of their healing, but it tested their faith and required obedience to His word. STIER, noticing Jesus' "systematic principles of propriety," says, " And it should be observed here as well as there (Matt. viii. 4), with what persistency He deferred to the existing ordinances of God even in their deep degradation and perversion, as witnessing against the spirit of separation which would falsely vindicate itself by His example."

As they went, in this faithful obedience, **they were cleansed**, and were conscious of their healing. So, as we obey Jesus' word, in childlike trust, we are cleansed from sin by His word of grace.

<small>15, 16. And one of them, when he saw that he was healed, turned back, with a loud voice glorifying God. And he fell upon his face at his feet, giving him thanks: and he was a Samaritan.</small>

15. **One of them** now acted differently from the others. Conscious of his healing, he **turned back** in the fulness of a thankful heart, and, **with a loud voice,** which itself, so changed from what he had lifted up before (ver. 13), testified the change that had been wrought in his body, **glorifying God,** the giver of every good and perfect gift, who "healeth all our diseases."

16. And not only so, but he **fell upon his face** humbly, in **giving him thanks** as the minister of God's great mercy to him. Did he therein also worship Jesus, pay Him divine homage? Ver. 19 leads us to think it probable he did. **And he was a Samaritan,** as all his features showed. So was it a Samaritan that excelled priest and Levite in neighborly love to him that fell among robbers.

<small>17, 18. And Jesus answering said, Were not the ten cleansed? but where are the nine? Were there none found that returned to give glory to God, save this stranger?</small>

17. **Were not the ten cleansed,** all of them alike made whole? **But where are the nine?** "We might, indeed, find some sort of apology for them in this (ver. 14) commandment of the Lord which they so punctually obeyed; but the Lord looks deeper, and values *this* obedience but lightly. He also regards the occurrence as having a *typical* significance. He beholds in these nine, contrasted with the one, the thanklessness of men as a whole. He sees in them the ingratitude of heart which many whom He had before healed had manifested, having never yet

learned to glorify God; and regards this incident but as a prophetic type of what will also ever take place. Gratitude is the 'beginning, middle, and end of all true human morals,' or rather devotion (see Heb. xii. 28, rightly translated); ingratitude is the origin of all heathenism according to Rom. i. 21, and the root of all apostasy in Israel according to Deut. xxxii. 6" (STIER).

18. Note the interrogative form given in the Revised Version to this verse, and its force. **None found to give glory to God, save this stranger,** this one of another nation? Ah, Israel, as of old, thankless! How many like them, God's favored people, take His constant and His particular benefits *as a matter of course,* as their prerogative! "The ox knoweth his owner, and the ass his master's crib; but Israel doth not know, my people doth not consider!"

What if it be said the nine were thankful in their hearts as they went on to the priests? Well, where was the evidence of this thankfulness? Moreover it is not enough to feel thankful. The Scriptures everywhere exhort us to *expression,* to *give thanks.* "In every thing give thanks." "Through him then let us offer up a sacrifice of praise to God continually, that is, the fruit of lips which make confession to his name. But to do good and to communicate forget not: for with such sacrifices God is well pleased" (Heb. xiii. 15, 16). And this is beautifully set forth in our worship, not only by the frequent occurrence of the *Glorias* and the use of the Doxology, but also by the "Offertory," where, in connection with the singing of parts of Psalm li. or other suitable Scriptures, we give also our offerings of money to the causes of Missions, Church Extension, Education, Orphans' Homes and other good objects—ourselves and our substance laid upon God's altar.

19. And he said unto him, Arise, and go thy way: thy faith hath made thee whole.

19. **Arise.** We must not be always in the posture of worship, on our face before the Lord. **Go thy way,** serve Him on thy feet and in thy course through life. Go to the priest now. **Thy faith hath made thee whole.** Does not this mean more than that his leprosy had been healed? The ten were all healed of that. Yes, we believe it declares him to be now healed of his soul-sickness, worse than leprosy, healed of sin. Here He spake to him, we think, the peace of God. So far as we see the *ten* were *healed*, the *one* was *saved*.

20, 21. And being asked by the Pharisees, when the kingdom of God cometh, he answered them and said, The kingdom of God cometh not with observation: neither shall they say, Lo, here! or, There! for lo, the kingdom of God is within you.

20, 21. **The Pharisees,** last heard from at xvi. 14, where they scoffed at Him, appear again, and, in the same spirit, ask **when the kingdom of God,** which Jesus preached, and to which He referred at that interview (xvi. 16), **cometh.** They ask not *where?* taking it for granted it would be among themselves, the people of God! Their views of the kingdom of God, as their spirit and writings show, were carnal, sensual, political, worldly. Jesus tells them there would be no such coming as they expected, **with observation,** with external show and pageantry, not with espial and like kingdoms of the world. It is not an outside thing, for the senses, "it cannot be marked out on the map" (ROOS); and its coming is accordant with its nature. And so, it will not be heralded with a **Lo, here!** or **There!** as though it were local, earthly, one among others, visible. **For lo**—another and different "lo," and something to be carefully noted—**the kingdom of God.**

(notice this thrice repeated subject in so short a space as these two verses) **is within you,** is already here among you, on the one hand, and, further, is a thing of the inner world of spirit and life, a spiritual thing.

Chrysostom, Luther, Olshausen, Calvin, and others understand by "within you" *in animis vestris.* Meyer and most modern interpreters render it "among you," i. e. already in the midst of you. With Stier we combine both interpretations, giving the expression its fullest meaning. "For the kingdom of God is internal among *you*—but because it is not, O Pharisee, in *thee*, thou wilt never see it" (DRASEKE).

As if He had said to the Pharisees, "*Your* kingdom of God, that which ye expect, cometh never" (STIER), and having shown its differing nature and methods from kingdoms of this world, He presently turned to others (next verse) and proceeded to speak of things to come, connected with the kingdom of God, which should have manifestation and call for "observation."

22-24. And he said unto the disciples, The days will come, when ye shall desire to see one of the days of the Son of man, and ye shall not see it. And they shall say to you, Lo, there! Lo, here! go not away, nor follow after *them :* for as the lightning, when it lighteneth out of the one part under the heaven, shineth unto the other part under heaven; so shall the Son of man be in his day.

22. **Unto the disciples** now, in contrast with "the Pharisees" of ver. 20. **Days will come.** He speaks of the future, and of a strong **desire** that would come to them for **one of the days of the Son of man,** of the Bridegroom's visible presence—would He were with us again as in the days of His appearance on the earth!—a natural longing, yet **ye shall not see it.** That is not God's plan. It will be as useless to be looking for such a day as it was for the sons of the prophets to be hunting for Elijah,

after he had been taken up into heaven (2 Kings ii. 15-18).

23. **They shall say,** giving heed to rumors, pretences, lying wonders, deceitful signs, false prophets, **Lo, there** He is, and **Lo, here!** There will be such cries, but they will be misleading; **go not away** from patient faith and trustful confidence, to **follow after them.** "A warning to all so-called expositors and followers of expositors of prophecy, who cry ἰδοὺ ὧδε and ἰδοὺ ἐκεῖ, every time that war breaks out or revolutions occur" (ALFORD).

24. **The Son of man** indeed cometh with observation, **in his day,** whenever it shall be, as promised throughout the Scriptures (John xiv. 3 ; Acts i. 11 ; 1 Thess. iv. 16). It will be in glory, patent to every eye (Rev. i. 7) like **the lightning** that illumines everything **under heaven.**

25. But first must he suffer many things and be rejected of this generation.

25. A number of things **must,** in the divine order, come **first,** before the *Parousia ;* among them His sufferings and rejection **by this generation,** the Jews of that day. Jesus knew this full well, but it was wholly foreign to the Jews' notion of the Messiah and was also not comprehended by the disciples till after its fulfilment.

26-30. And as it came to pass in the days of Noah, even so shall it be also in the days of the Son of man. They ate, they drank, they married, they were given in marriage, until the day that Noah entered into the ark, and the flood came, and destroyed them all. Likewise even as it came to pass in the days of Lot ; they ate, they drank, they bought, they sold, they planted, they builded ; but in the day that Lot went out from Sodom it rained fire and brimstone from heaven, and destroyed them all: after the same manner shall it be in the day that the Son of man is revealed.

26-30. **The days of Noah** and **of Lot** were days of judgment and salvation and most suitable historical illustrations of like things to come **in the days of the Son of man,** the coming *Parousia.* In those early days the masses of the people went on in the usual tenor of their way, regardless of the preaching of righteousness by God's servants, careless of judgment to come, and when **the flood came,** in the one case, and the **fire and brimstone from heaven,** in the other case, these judgments found them unprepared and **destroyed them all.** Notice that the things mentioned in vers. 27, 28 were not wicked things, but merely secular, worldly things, which so engrossed them that they neglected things spiritual and divine. Certainly they were wicked, and went on as if there was no danger, no judgment to come, and hence no need to seek salvation. **So shall it be also** in the last days yet to come upon the earth. Observe that our Lord takes the flood and the ruin of Sodom as historical.

31–33. In that day, he which shall be on the housetop, and his goods in the house, let him not go down to take them away: and let him that is in the field likewise not return back. Remember Lot's wife. Whosoever shall seek to gain his life shall lose it: but whosoever shall lose *his life* shall preserve it.

See on Matt. xxiv. 17, 18; Mark xiii. 15, 16. Whilst in the places just referred to, the destruction of Jerusalem is spoken of, paralleled in Luke's chap. xxi., there is great diversity among commentators as to whether the passage here has any such reference. Meyer, Van Oosterzee and others deny any such reference. Stier admits "a hint at the destruction of Jerusalem."

31. **That day** is the same that is mentioned in vers. 24, 30. Whether **on the housetop,** at home, resting, or **in the field,** busy, earthly **goods** and that which is **back,** left behind, are not to engage his thoughts or efforts. Worldly ties are not then to bind. Herein are we not taught to be looking off from earthly, temporal things, unto Jesus and spiritual, eternal verities; and we should cultivate this mind now, that when "that day" comes it may be

customary to us and not a new thing, impossible to be taken up at the moment!

32. **Lot's wife** is a perpetual, solemn reminder of the fate of those who look back and so perish.

33. Everything for Christ and the kingdom of God. Venture all, and save all that is worth saving. " Seek ye first the kingdom of God," etc. See on ix. 24 and Matt. x. 39, Mark viii. 35 : but the application here is to the day of the revelation of Jesus Christ.

34, 35. I say unto you, in that night there shall be two men on one bed; the one shall be taken, and the other shall be left. There shall be two women grinding together; the one shall be taken, and the other shall be left.

34, 35. Now the occasion is spoken of as **that night** (the Greek has it "*this* night "), perhaps with allusion to the Lord's coming " as a thief in the night " : but presently daytime is again referred to in the occupation of **grinding** at the mill. " Ye know not the day nor the hour." But then there will be separations of those as intimately associated as **two men on one bed** or **two women grinding** at one mill: joined in like situations and occupations, perhaps to mortal eyes alike, but not so to God ; for **one shall be taken** from the evil to come, **the other left**, overwhelmed by it ; one saved, the other lost !

Ver. 36 of the Auth. Ver. is thrown out by the best criticism.

37. And they answering say unto him, Where, Lord? And he said unto them, Where the body *is*, thither will the eagles also be gathered together.

37. The Pharisees had asked, " When ? " (ver. 20): the disciples now ask, **Where, Lord ?** This cannot be answered definitely : therefore the Lord replies proverbially. See this proverb amply explained in Vol. II. on Matt. xxiv. 28. Reference to the Roman ensigns, however taking, is not admissible. Given the occasion, and there follows the consequence, everywhere.

CHAPTER XVIII.

1. And he spake a parable unto them to the end that they ought always to pray, and not to faint;

1. Many a time, by precept and by example and by formula, Jesus taught His disciples to pray. The point of this parable is **that they ought always to pray, and not to faint**—persistence, importunity. So Paul repeatedly (Rom. xii. 12; Eph. vi. 18; Col. iv. 2; 1 Thess. v. 17) urges Christians to be "praying always," to " pray without ceasing." Keep at it, not formally only, but really, whether in the closet (of the house or of the heart) or in public. Men are apt to faint, to become discouraged and cease from prayer.

2, 3. Saying, There was in a city a judge, which feared not God, and regarded not man: and there was a widow in that city; and she came oft unto him, saying, Avenge me of mine adversary.

2, 3. The two characters of this parable are **a judge** and **a widow.** The judge was by his character utterly unfit for his place. Sitting in the place of God (Ps. lxxxii. 6; John x. 34), he was utterly unlike God. He **feared not God**, and so was without religion; he **regarded not man,** and so was without humanity. The heathen thus, proverbially, characterized an abandoned, wanton, outrageous person. When such men come to be judges, the land mourns. **A widow,** in the East, was a synonym for helplessness. She was a prey to many sorts of oppressors, and this many Scripture passages attest. Here then was a hard man in the place of power, and a helpless woman, begging him, as was his prerogative, to **avenge** her of her **adversary,** to do her simple justice over against her pursuer. **She came oft unto him** who ought to have at the first taken up her case and decided her cause; she kept coming with the same petition. She knew her cause to be just and kept insisting that it be decided.

> 4, 5. And he would not for a while; but afterward he said within himself, Though I fear not God, nor regard man; yet because this widow troubleth me, I will avenge her, lest she wear me out by her continual coming.

4, 5. **And he would not,** was not willing, **for a while.** What did he care? She had no power to compel him and no means to bribe him. He was purely selfish; not right or truth, but merely his own perverse will, governed him. The inhuman villain not only was such, but he acknowledged it to himself and boasted of it inwardly. **I will avenge her,** he concluded, not because it is right, godly or humane, but only because she **troubleth me,** just to get rid of her. **Lest she wear me out by her continual coming.** "Lest, coming, she strike me," Dr. Bruce renders it, supported by Bengel, Meyer and Godet, and the use of the original word in 1 Cor. ix. 27. "The judge humorously affects to fear the exasperated widow's fists." She had gone so far with her tongue and was becoming more and more vehement with a sense of wrong, that, lest he couldn't stand it further, this specimen of a judge says at last, **I will.**

> 6–8. And the Lord said, Hear what the unrighteous judge saith. And shall not God avenge his elect, which cry to him day and night, and he is longsuffering over them? I say unto you, that he will avenge them speedily. Howbeit when the Son of man cometh, shall he find faith on the earth?

6. The argument is by contrast and *à fortiori.* **The**

unrighteous judge can be brought to do the right thing, to execute his office, by touching the only place in him that is tender—his regard for his own feelings.

7. **And shall not God,** the righteous judge of all the earth, **avenge,** defend, come to the succor of, **his elect,** His chosen and loved ones, who are near and dear to His heart, and who **cry to him day and night** in unceasing prayerfulness? Shall such a wanton wretch be moved by selfishness, and shall not the good God be moved by love? The reading, **and he is long suffering over them,** does not seem good: that of the Authorized Version is better: but, better still, we may read it "And he delays (to interpose) in their cause," or "And he deferreth his anger on their behalf."

8. That He does so may seem to indicate indifference or rejection: but it does not, for the Lord says, **I say unto you,** or "I tell you"—and this is the best authority—**he will avenge them** and it will be **speedily,** that is suddenly and without recourse; as the Psalmist says of the wicked, "How are they become a desolation in a moment!" God waits long, but He will make in His time a quick, a speedy end, as at the destruction of Sodom and Gomorrah! **Howbeit** His delay to avenge His church, represented by the widow of the parable, will be so trying to His saints and an occasion of such indifference and boastful opposition on the part of the wicked (see Matt. xxiv. 36–39, 48–51; 2 Pet. iii. 3–10), that the Lord asks, **When the Son of man cometh,** to judge the earth and to avenge His elect, **shall he find faith on the earth?** God's providence is often dark, "clouds and darkness are round about him;" will His people be found looking through all these clouds, certainly expecting the "righteousness and judgment" that are "the stability of his throne?"

9. And he spake also this parable unto certain which trusted in themselves that they were righteous, and set all others at nought:

9. There were two sides to the views of those to whom this parable was spoken. **They trusted in themselves that they were righteous,** they were self-righteous, and they **set all others at nought.** These two dispositions fitted together very well and made a very false and proud character. "Poor and proud" is a proverbial combination: but these were pious (!) and proud.

10. Two men went up into the temple to pray; the one a Pharisee, and the other a publican.

10. Two characters again. **The one a Pharisee.** He belonged to the exclusives among the Jews, the orthodox aristocracy. **The other a publican.** One of the despised class, coupled with "sinners" in the Pharisees' estimation. They were sinners that made no pretence. (See on xv. 1, 2.) Both these men **went up into the temple to pray.** "My house shall be called a house of prayer for all people" (Is. lvi. 7; Mark xi. 17). Some in our day would make it a house of *preaching!* Our lesson emphasizes *prayer*, and gives some specimens.

11, 12. The Pharisee stood and prayed thus with himself, God, I thank thee, that I am not as the rest of men, extortioners, unjust, adulterers, or even as this publican. I fast twice in the week; I give tithes of all that I get.

11, 12. **The Pharisee stood,** having taken up his position, very consciously, **and prayed thus with himself.** He spoke within himself, and, as a prayer, it seems not to have gone farther than himself. It was altogether *self.* True, he said, **God, I thank thee,** but clearly he praised himself more than he praised God. His prayer was "I." He put himself on one side and **the rest of men** on the other. He exalted himself (ver. 14) for what

XVIII. 12, 13.] *CHAPTER XVIII.* 333

he was **not** (negative virtues) and for what he *did* in the small matters of *fasting* and *tithing*. He said nothing of "judgment, mercy and faith." The prophet asked, "And what doth the Lord thy God require of thee but to do justly, love mercy, and walk humbly with thy God?" This Pharisee had not got further than to "do justly," according to his own testimony. Yet he set himself above the rest of men, especially **this publican** in another part of the temple, of whom his proud eye had caught a glance. It is assumed that what he said of himself was true. How many, like him, think themselves good, or better than others, for what they are not and do not do—"I am not so bad," "I haven't done anything very wicked," "I am honest and harm nobody," "Nobody can say anything against me," etc.—and for external observances—"I go to church every Sunday," "I attend two meetings a week," "I give regularly," etc. But this Pharisee did not believe in the *Confitcor ;* he had nothing to *confess.* And those like him are not sensible of sin. Contrast David's thanksgiving in 1 Chron. xxix. 13, 14, 16.

13. But the publican, standing afar off, would not lift up so much as his eyes unto heaven, but smote his breast, saying, God, be merciful to me a sinner.

13. **But the publican,** with contrasting feelings, acts and words, as sincere as the Pharisee, **standing afar off** in the seclusion of humility and a sense of sin, **would not lift up so much as his eyes unto heaven,** so down was he in heart for his character before God, **but smote his breast,** expressing in outward gesture the grief and self-condemnation he felt, and said, **God, be merciful to me a sinner.** The original has the definite article, "*the* sinner," as if there were no other: and so his view of himself and representations of himself before God is just

the opposite of that of the Pharisee, above. "To the Pharisee all are sinners and he only is righteous; to the publican all are righteous and he only *the sinner*" (WESTERMEIER).

14. I say unto you, This man went down to his house justified rather than the other: for every one that exalteth himself shall be humbled; but he that humbleth himself shall be exalted.

14. **This man,** the publican, **went down . . . justified rather than the other,** the Pharisee. Not justified by his character or by his prayer, but by God's grace. For "God resisteth the proud, and giveth grace to the humble." Justification is an act of God's free grace, and He does not justify those who justify themselves, but those who confess their sins and out of their helplessness cry to Him for mercy. "Whoso covereth his sins shall not prosper, but whoso confesseth them shall find mercy." Hence in our morning service of prayer we have first the "Confession of sin," and in the evening we begin with the humble cry, "Make haste, O God, to deliver me: Make haste to help me, O Lord." The Pharisee and self-righteous man's justification is in himself; the sinner's hope is in God's mercy: his help, in the righteousness of Christ. Luke loves to offer hope to the Gentiles, for whom his Gospel history was written.

Then the Lord gave the law of the kingdom for **every one,** showing that self-exaltation, pride, shall be brought down, while self-abnegation, humiliation, is the character and posture of hope from God. "The Lord is nigh unto them that are of a contrite heart, and saveth such as are of a broken spirit:" but "the proud he knoweth afar off!" The Old Testament and the New alike testify to this. So then, prevailing prayer is humble as well as importunate. In converse with God we must know our place. It is "from the dust" that He "lifteth up the poor," "to set him with princes and make him inhabit the throne of his glory."

15. And they brought unto him also their babes, that he should touch them: but when the disciples saw it, they rebuked them.

Matthew (xix. 13-30) and Mark (x. 13-22) give this and the following narrative; this threefold record indicating their importance in the Gospel system. The former part is peculiarly interesting as showing Christ's relation and feeling toward children, a family teaching for the home, and as showing the nature of the kingdom of God by Him who is the King.

15. **Even the babes,** as it may well be read, **they brought** unto Jesus. Yes; why not? Are not babes but little men and women? Is it likely that Jesus was so concerned for mankind as to come and lay down His life for them, and yet have no concern or salvation for children? Shall earthly fathers and mothers care so much and do so much for their little ones, and will He who is the revealer of the Father care nothing and do nothing for them? Evidently the mothers did not have such thoughts or misgivings, and so **they brought unto him also their babes, that he should touch them.** And if the timid woman by touching Him received the Great Physician's healing power, would not His touch of the children, His laying His hands upon them with prayer (Matt.), communicate to them a blessing? **The disciples,** who often showed little faith, seem not to have thought so. They seem to have made the little ones of little account. At all events they **rebuked them** in the persons of "those that brought them" (Mk.). So now, when we bring our babes to Jesus for baptism, the sacrament of initiation into His church, which is His body, that they may be united to Him in this bond of

covenant grace, some *rebuke* us, and say this is not for children. But, hear the Lord.

> 16. But Jesus called them unto him, saying, Suffer the little children to come unto me, and forbid them not: for of such is the kingdom of God.

16. **He called them unto him** whom the disciples would have driven away, and kindly reproved them, saying, **Suffer the little children to come unto me**—shall the lambs not come to the Good Shepherd?—**and forbid them not.** How the sadness and disappointment that had come on the mothers' faces, if not on the babes', now gave way to sweet, peaceful, expectant smiles, as they now went close to the Saviour, and He "took them up in his arms and blessed them," laying His holy hands upon their heads (Mk.)! Hear, moreover, Jesus' reason in that comforting word to all parents, **for of such is the kingdom of God.** To such it belongs; for such are its blessings. It is theirs not by nature, but by grace, by the appointment and will of Him who founded it. Children are by nature what their parents are by nature, the children of Adam, fallen, sinners. But "as in Adam all die, so in Christ shall all be made alive," if they do not reject the counsel of God against themselves, if they they do not refuse and trample upon His life-giving grace; and this the babes do not do. In the first Adam without their act or fault, they are in the second Adam by His sovereign grace who became the second head of the race. Not because of their innocence, but because of His redemption and love that more abounded where sin first abounded, are they of the kingdom of God. But at the same time Jesus teaches (John iii. 5) that "except one be born of water and the Spirit, he cannot enter into the kingdom of God," and this was given to Nicodemas as a universal rule. Hence our church teaches that

baptism is *necessary* to salvation, simply because Christ has made it so in the working plan given His church; but distinguishes this from its being *essential*. Hence the language of Articles II. and IX., Augsburg Confession. We know no such thing as elect and non-elect infants; but, believing redemption to be as universal as the fall, we baptize children into Christ, and believe it dangerous and sinful to neglect or despise this sacrament. After that we leave unbaptized children, in Christian or heathen lands, to the mercy of God in Christ, believing He saves them by His abounding grace, despite their want of baptism, this want occurring not by their own fault or contempt.

17. Verily I say unto you, Whosoever shall not receive the kingdom of God as a little child, he shall in no wise enter therein.

17. Here is a universal law, introduced by **whosoever**. Now how does a little child receive the kingdom of God, so little a thing receive so great a thing? Why, in short, it *does not resist God*, it *lets Him save it;* it puts its hand in God's; it looks up and smiles to have Him put His hand upon its head; it quiets itself upon the Saviour's breast (Ps. cxxxi.). See Mk. ix. 33-42. Any one otherwise disposed **shall not enter therein**.

18, 19. And a certain ruler asked him, saying, Good Master, what shall I do to inherit eternal life? And Jesus said unto him, Why callest thou me good? none is good, save one, *even* God.

18. Here we get another illustration about entering the kingdom of heaven and finding eternal life. There it was babes and their relation to the kingdom; here it is a young man (Matt.), one whose character had so commended him to men that he was already **a ruler** in the synagogue. The other evangelists give some details as to the manner of his coming and of his appeal,

showing his great earnestness. Luke merely reports his words. **Good Master.** Thus he might have addressed any of the Rabbis. His question was one of the utmost importance—**What shall I do to inherit eternal life?** Once in the Old Testament (Dan. xii. 2) and here first in the New, we find these words, "eternal life." The whole Bible is full of the idea they convey, and it is plain enough what the young ruler meant by them. Although there is some contradiction in *doing* in order to *inherit*, not taken account of by the ardent youth, it is evident from the whole account that the man was a *legalist*, bound by the covenant of *works*. He wanted to *do something* to earn eternal life.

19. Now let it be remembered that Jesus knew this man thoroughly, his good qualities and his faults. He saw that the youth came sincerely, not temptingly, and Jesus began to lead him gradually into higher views of truth than he had yet known. How lightly the young ruler used the word "good"—"Good Master" and (according to Matt.) "What good thing shall I do?" That is the word to emphasize in reading the question of ver. 19, "Why callest thou me *good?*" Think more soberly of that word; what does it involve? **None is good save one, even God!** He might have learned that from the Scriptures. David had represented Jehovah as looking down from heaven to see if there were any that did understand and seek God, and concluding, "There is none that doeth good, no, not one!" (Ps. xiv. 1, 3, and Rom. iii. 12). Solomon had said, "There is not a just man upon earth that doeth good and sinneth not" (Eccles. vii. 20), and all experience and observation fully confirm this verdict. Am I good? said Christ. Then am I God —more than thou takest me to be! No mere man is good. Jesus by no means said He was a mere man, but

merely put His questioner to thinking more deeply and correctly concerning *the good*.

20, 21. Thou knowest the commandments, Do not commit adultery, Do not kill, Do not steal, Do not bear false witness, Honour thy father and mother. And he said, All these things have I observed from my youth up.

20. **The commandments.** They are the rule of a rounded, complete, godlike life. (See Levit. xviii. 5 ; Rom. x. 5.) Jesus specifies the precepts of the second table probably because it is easier for us to judge ourselves in our relations to our fellow-men than in our relations directly to God.

21. With a proud consciousness of an externally correct life, the young man replied, **All these things have I observed from my youth up.** Like Saul of Tarsus, touching the righteousness which was of the law he was blameless by the low standard of human judgment. No one could say any evil thing against him. He was a thoroughly moral young man. He was evidently sincerely in earnest, aiming at legal perfection. But he, as evidently, was ignorant both of himself and of the spirituality of God's law ; and now he had addressed himself to one who perfectly knew both these. The Great Teacher will teach him that knowledge too.

22, 23. And when Jesus heard it, he said unto him, One thing thou lackest yet : sell all that thou hast, and distribute unto the poor, and thou shalt have treasure in heaven : and come, follow me. But when he heard these things, he became exceeding sorrowful ; for he was very rich.

22. Jesus' heart went out to this young man (Mark). There was something lovable in his uprightness, openness and earnestness. This drawing towards him, however, did not deter Jesus from a faithfulness which He knew would grieve the young man's inmost soul. Natural gifts and graces are lovely and beautiful, but not saving. Loveliness is not life ; morality is not religion.

One thing thou lackest yet of that perfection at which thou aimest. Eagerly, no doubt, the ruler listened to know what it was. The Master had said, "One thing;" how near, then, he must be to the goal; how intently, in his readiness to *do something* more if necessary, did he regard the word that followed! **Sell all that thou hast** —but, oh, **he was very rich—and distribute unto the poor** with that genuine love that sacrifices itself for others' good, that love that costs something, that "seeketh not her own," that gives expecting not again; **and come follow me.** The Lord had Himself made such sacrifice, and set the example. Though He was rich, for our sakes He became poor (2 Cor. viii. 9), and, from being Creator and Upholder of all things, took so low a place that He had not where to lay His head (Matt. viii. 20); He emptied Himself (Phil. ii. 7) that we might be filled (John i. 16; Eph. iii. 19). The young man was called only to *follow* Jesus' example and steps, not to do the impossible or what had never yet been done. Yes, even *follow me*, says Christ, if you would find the *good;* I am the Shepherd true, the good Shepherd (John x. 1-18). And was it all sacrifice to which he was called? Was there nothing offered in return? Yes: **thou shalt have treasure in heaven,** where moth and rust do not corrupt, nor thieves break through and steal, durable riches and righteousness.

23. The Lord offered this rich man a good investment —beyond any contingency. But, instead of jumping at it, **he became exceeding sorrowful** and showed that his heart was not right toward God.

"How is the gold become dim! How is the most fine gold changed!" Jesus' requirement sounded the depths of the young ruler's character, and tested him just where the Lord knew he was wanting. His possessions were his god: he had not yet kept the first commandment, and how could he then properly keep any of the others? And here is the difference between morality and religion: the former consists in acts or restraints, the latter has its home in the spirit and consists in *love*, first and supremely toward God, and then towards man, made in the image of God.

There is no entering the kingdom without coming to Christ : He is the Door. There is no walking in the way of life without following Christ: He is the Way. Eternal life is not in us or our doing. "This is the promise [mark that word *promise* (Gal. iii. 18)] that he hath promised us, even eternal life" (1 John ii. 25). " He that hath the Son hath the life ; he that hath not the Son of God hath not the life" (1 John v. 12), whether he be very rich or very poor, or neither.

24, 25. And Jesus seeing him said, How hardly shall they that have riches enter into the kingdom of God ! For it is easier for a camel to enter in through a needle's eye, than for a rich man to enter into the kingdom of God.

24, 25. Here is the moral. **How hardly,** with what difficulty, **shall they that have riches enter into the kingdom of God.** The reason seems to have been evident enough, yet the disciples were amazed at His words. Temporal blessings were looked upon under the Old Testament as a mark of God's favor, and were expected to abound in the kingdom of God. Moreover money, or other possessions, we are told, is the all in all with the Orientals. And is it not equally so with the Occidentals? The people of the East cannot understand why people should travel, study, work, or do anything, unless with the hope of gain. Such, no doubt, is the prevailing spirit East and West, modified by the teachings of Christianity. But 'tis universally true that those who have riches are apt to trust in them. And even those who do not have them, hope to have them, try to have them; and their trust comes to be in this hope and attempt. "They that *will be* rich," who have their minds set on that, are in the same danger with the rich. In ver. 25 Jesus used an ordinary proverbial expression to denote the extreme difficulty that hedges about a rich man's entering into the kingdom of heaven. The literalness of the terms **camel** and **a needle's eye** is not to be explained away. MORISON calls this, "A fine, bold way of speaking, that need impose upon no one who has a spark of poetry in his soul. The key to its import is hung at the girdle of common sense."

26, 27. And they that heard it said, Then who can be saved? But he said, The things which are impossible with men are possible with God.

26, 27. **Then who can be saved?** is the quick reply of the amazed disciples. "Do not the poor also cleave to their scrap of possession and strive after more; has not every man at bottom something which as his possession he will not let go? If the entrance into the kingdom of heaven is so narrow, *who* then is small and unencumbered enough to enter? What thou sayest is truly the case of all—we understand thee; then the being saved must be in general a thing of *impossibility!*" (STIER). But, **the things which are impossible with men are possible with God.** His power and grace are equal to the salvation of men. No man, by morality or any other means, can save himself or his brother. Salvation is of God, who is as willing as He is able. Blessed be God for His gracious power and powerful grace!

But what a solemn warning is here, not only to every one, but specially to the rich not to trust in their wealth or set their love upon it or what it may bring; and to all young people, to seek first, in time and in zeal, the kingdom of God and His righteousness and not earthly gains and position ; and to all parents to be earnestly solicitous that their children be Christians, be saved, rather than become rich or distinguished among men ! The danger of riches as well as of seeking them is that you may thus make a *failure of life*, and be in the end bankrupt, with nothing saved.

28–30. And Peter said, Lo, we have left our own, and followed thee. And he said unto them, Verily I say unto you, There is no man that hath left house, or wife, or brethren, or parents, or children, for the kingdom of God's sake, who shall not receive manifold more in this time, and in the world to come eternal life.

28. **Peter** must have something to say. His ideas, moreover, as we have seen on several occasions, were rather crude and false. **Lo, we have left our own, and followed thee:** *we* are surely right and candidates for heaven's rewards. They had indeed left all—their business, their associations, families and friends—at Jesus' word. Imperfect and in error as they in many respects were, they were withal devoted disciples. Jesus had held out to the young ruler the possession of treasure in heaven. It was not improper in them to have respect to the recompense of the reward, if governed by a right spirit therein. Moses had such respect (Heb. xi. 26), and Jesus Himself " for the joy that was set before him endured the cross " (Heb. xii. 2). The Bible appeals very strongly to man's hope of attaining better things.

29. Jesus, therefore, did not chide Peter, but, with a **Verily I say unto you,** proceeded to affirm that in the kingdom of God there are abundant compensations for all sacrifices, even of the dearest things, made in the interests of that kingdom. **For the kingdom of God's sake..** Not for *sake* of the reward, not to purchase it,

but in loving, obedient consecration, the living sacrifice (Rom. xii. 1). **Manifold more in this time.** Godliness hath the promise of the life that now is. God's service makes for man's welfare in all his true needs, as Paul says to the Philippians, who had contributed to his necessities at Rome, "My God shall fulfil every need of yours according to his riches in glory in Christ Jesus." All these things shall be added unto those who seek first God's kingdom and righteousness. But this does not mean that they shall be without sore trials and persecutions in "this present evil world." But the end, the grand result, shall be **eternal life.** This we have now, in hope (Rom. viii. 24); then in full fruition, with nothing to mar or hinder—**in the world to come.**

> " Brief life is here our portion,
> Brief sorrow, short-lived care :
> The life that knows no ending,
> The tearless Life, is *there.*
> O happy retribution !
> Short toil, eternal rest !
> For mortals and for sinners
> A mansion with the blest ! "
> (*Bernard.*)

31–34. *And he took unto him the twelve, and said unto them, Behold, we go up to Jerusalem, and all the things that are written by the prophets shall be accomplished unto the Son of man. For he shall be delivered up unto the Gentiles, and shall be mocked, and shamefully entreated, and spit upon : and they shall scourge and kill him : and the third day he shall rise again. And they understood none of these things; and this saying was hid from them, and they perceived not the things that were said.*

See on Matt. xx. 17-19; Mark x. 32-34.

31. Luke adds Jesus' note of the fulfilment of **all the things that are written by the prophets** for the portion of His cup. See on Chap. xxiv. 25-27.

33. Matthew puts in the passive, "shall be raised up," what Mark and Luke put in the active, **shall rise again.**

Both forms of speech are used of Him throughout the New Testament; which is easily explained from the mystery of His Person, involving both the divine and the human nature.

34. A threefold statement of the disciples' ignorance and want of comprehension of the Saviour's sufferings, involving also the divine purpose that these matters should for the present be **hid from them.** See on ix. 45, x. 21, and comp. xix. 42.

35-43. *And it came to pass as he drew nigh unto Jericho, a certain blind man sat by the way side begging: and hearing a multitude going by, he inquired what this meant. And they told him, that Jesus of Nazareth passeth by. And he cried, saying, Jesus thou son of David, have mercy on me. And they that went before rebuked him, that he should hold his peace: but he cried out the more a great deal, Thou son of David, have mercy on me. And Jesus stood, and commanded him to be brought unto him: and when he was come near, he asked him, What wilt thou that I should do unto thee? And he said, Lord, that I may receive my sight. And Jesus said unto him, Receive thy sight: thy faith hath made thee whole. And immediately he received his sight, and followed him, glorifying God: and all the people, when they saw it, gave praise unto God.*

See on Matt. xx. 29-34; Mark x. 46-52.

43. Luke adds to the common narrative that the sight-restored man, while following his healer, was **glorifying God** from whom all blessings flow, and that **all the people,** in view of the occurrence as described, **gave praise unto God.** This was well done and is a good example for us.

CHAPTER XIX.

We are fast approaching the close of that last journey of our Lord to Jerusalem, which, prolonged and roundabout as it was, has occupied, with incidents that occurred in its course, our attention since the first note of it in ix. 51.

1. And he entered and was passing through Jericho.

1. **Entered and was passing through.** This corresponds with the statement, xviii. 35, that He healed a blind-man "as he drew nigh unto" the city. Some writers think Jesus spent some time in this neighborhood, resting at night in the country, and going into the city by day; and that now He had entered and was passing through, not to return. **Jericho** has become well known to us; overthrown in Joshua's day, a curse pronounced on him who should rebuild it, it at length became a city again, and was wealthy and flourishing at this time, a city of the priests. (See on x. 30–32.) It lay 3600 feet lower than Jerusalem, twenty miles off. It was near the ford of the Jordan, over which the crowds beyond came to Jerusalem.

2. And behold, a man called by name Zacchæus; and he was a chief publican, and he was rich.

2. **A man called Zacchæus** (pronounced with the penult long and accented). This is a Hebrew name and marks its bearer as a Jew; and here we see that some publicans

were Jews. **A chief publican.** There were different grades of publicans, those who were officers over large districts being generally Romans of some rank. Zacchæus was probably such a one's deputy in this rich district, where there was considerable trade in balsam, produced there, and customs duties between Perea and Judæa were collected. **And he was rich.** This enters as an interesting factor into the history.

<blockquote>3, 4. And he sought to see Jesus who he was; and could not for the crowd, because he was little of stature. And he ran on before, and climbed up into a sycamore tree to see him : for he was to pass that way.</blockquote>

3. **And he sought to see Jesus who he was.** Moved by curiosity, but, also, as the context shows, not uninfluenced by higher feelings. **Could not for the crowd.** 'Tis easy to imagine the street of Jericho crowded, as we have often seen crowds pressing to see some object of interest. Many of this crowd, probably, were also *en route* to the coming passover. Zacchæus was **little of stature,** and therefore was at vast disadvantage for seeing. Everybody stood above him and in his way.

4. So earnestly intent, however, was he on gaining his purpose that he **ran on before,** like a little boy, and may be among the boys, **and climbed up into a sycamore tree to see him.** It was an Egyptian fig tree, whose branches come out low down on the trunk, making it easy to climb. It attains a very considerable height and breadth, and is adapted for shade. His riches, his dignity, all were forgotten in the earnest desire to see Jesus. **For he was to pass that way.** And that, not riding or in any circumstances of state, but walking along the dusty street, like one of us, easily lost in the crowd.

<blockquote>5. And when Jesus came to the place, he looked up, and said unto him, Zacchæus, make haste, and come down; for to-day I must abide at thy house.</blockquote>

5. Now see the little, well-known, rich revenue-collector perched up in the tree, waiting the coming of the crowd! **And when Jesus came to the place,** He gave the little seeker a good opportunity not only to see Him, but to look Him in the face, for **he looked up,** answering the seeker's earnest desire which He saw through before, just as He had seen Nathanael under the fig tree (John i. 48). So the seeking was followed by finding. Jesus found Zacchæus, and Zacchæus found Jesus. He who ran and climbed to get a sight of the great Prophet of Israel, now has the unspeakable satisfaction not only of looking into His up-turned, benignant countenance, but of hearing those wonderful lips say to him, **Zacchæus, make haste, and come down.** Why so? **For to day I must abide at thy house.** Ah, those who truly want to see Jesus will find Him ready to come in and sup with them! (Rev. iii. 20.) God's condescending grace exceeds our expectations. The little man was afraid he would not even get to see Jesus; but, behold, now he will entertain Him! Some think his house was out of the city, along the road.

6, 7. And he made haste, and came down, and received him joyfully. And when they saw it, they all murmured, saying, He is gone in to lodge with a man that is a sinner.

6, 7. The little man was now the observed of all as he **made haste and came down** from his tree perch. **Joyfully** did he accept the position of host, in which the Lord put him; but on the other hand **all** the crowd around **murmured.** There were none of them, it seems, that loved Zacchæus. Even his riches did not make way for him in the Jews' estimation. He was an agent of the hated Roman governor, and was, besides, **a sinner,** and with such an one the great Master had **gone in to lodge.** This was not the first time there had been an outcry against the company Jesus kept.

8. And Zacchæus stood, and said unto the Lord, Behold, Lord, the half of my goods I give to the poor: and if I have wrongfully exacted aught of any man, I restore fourfold.

8. And Zacchæus stood, took a prominent position before the Lord, observed by all present. The narrative does not indicate whether this was done immediately or after going to Zacchæus's house.

He said unto the Lord, not making much account of what the crowd thought or said, **Behold, Lord, the half of my goods I give to the poor.** That is, he now determines, vows to do so; not that such had been his custom. And why does he now do this? Not for display. He cared little for popular opinion. No; his heart had been opened by Jesus' treatment of him, and this determination is a result of and proves the change wrought in him. When Jesus came into his heart, as well as his house, the love of money went out. Here was the proof of it. Remember that *he was rich;* and now this "sinner" was ready to do what the good (?) young ruler refused to do (xviii. 22, 23). **And if I have wrongfully exacted aught from any man**—a very probable supposition; see the publicans' character hinted at in John the Baptist's requirement of them, Luke iii. 12, 13. **I restore** (I now resolve to restore him) **fourfold.** The Roman law required this: the Jewish law, only the principal and a fifth more (Num. v. 7). There was no *demand* made for either; but, as if to revenge himself on his hitherto reigning sin (see John xx. 28), and to testify the change he had experienced, besides surrendering the half of his *fair* gains to the poor, he voluntarily determines to give up all that was ill-gotten, quadrupled. He gratefully addressed this to the "Lord," to whom he owed this wonderful change. The first and best proof of his conversion was that he became liberal. The genuineness of that conversion which does not reach the pocket and produce a sense of stewardship, is, to say the least, to be doubted. We are not told the process by which this great change in Zacchæus was wrought, his state of mind before he saw Jesus, the emotions produced by the Master's calling him by name and *finding* him, how the publican reasoned; only the blessed *result*, that he certainly found Jesus, as the next verses plainly state. It was a divine work, greater even than the healing of the physically blind man.

9. And Jesus said unto him, To-day is salvation come to this house, forasmuch as he also is a son of Abraham.

9. **And Jesus,** who knew the man's heart and that his vow was sincere, arising from a changed nature, **said unto him**—and cheering words they were, spoken to him whom man despised—**To-day** (how soon!) **is salvation come** (for Jesus, "Saviour," had come and been welcomed) **to this house,** represented by its head, from whom it was according to the divine constitution of the house to go to all the members. **Forasmuch as he also** (even he) **is a son of Abraham;** and that both by descent, and by having also the faith of Abraham. He, too, is a "friend of God." His natural descent put him in the way of salvation, since Jesus was sent specially (Matt. xv. 24) to the lost sheep of the house of Israel, but, of course, could avail nothing for salvation; there were plenty, aye the most, of the descendants of Abraham of that day, who rejected God's counsel of salvation, to their own ruin.

10. For the Son of man came to seek and to save that which was lost.

10. **The Son of man.** The distinctive title our Lord used of Himself. **Came to seek and to save that which was lost,** whether they were Jews or Gentiles. Any who

were not lost, or did not feel themselves lost, He could not save. The most of the Jews were too proud to be saved; but here one whom they abhorred entered into the kingdom of God before them. Our Lord's work is epitomized in His name Jesus—" Saviour."

In the parables of the rich fool, and of the rich man and Lazarus, we had illustrations of " how hardly shall they that have riches enter into the kingdom of God." Here we learn that even such " impossible " things are " possible with God; " and here we rejoice in a rich man saved.

11. *And as they heard these things, he added and spake a parable, because he was nigh to Jerusalem, and because they supposed that the kingdom of God was immediately to appear.*

11. It was **as they heard** Jesus' words to and of Zacchæus and of the purpose of His own coming into the world (ver. 10), that **he added** to what had been said **and spoke a parable.** This marks the place as Jericho. The parable of the talents recorded by Matthew (xxv. 14-30, comp. comments there) was spoken later, the third day of Passion Week and at Jerusalem. At this time they were only **nigh to Jerusalem.** But the spirit of His many disciples was high-wrought, in expectation of His public inaugural as King in a few days. **They supposed that the kingdom of God was immediately to appear.** See this illustrated in what follows this parable. It was spoken, then, chiefly to disciples, and to correct a false impression of the nature and time of the kingdom of God.

12. *He said therefore, A certain nobleman went into a far country, to receive for himself a kingdom, and to return.*

12. Mark the **therefore. A certain nobleman,** or, *a man well born.* As such he had opportunities which do

not at once belong to every one. Jesus was well born, having been "conceived by the Holy Ghost and born of the virgin Mary." **Went into a far country.** This took time. He would be long gone. **To receive for himself a kingdom.** So Herod the Great, originally a subordinate officer in Judæa, went to Rome, afar off in those days, to be declared by the senate king of the Jews; and afterwards Archelaus his son went on a similar errand, making suit to Augustus in Rome. Though John and Jesus both preached the kingdom of God as at hand, yet it was only then beginning, only then set up (Dan. ii. 44): its coming Jesus taught His disciples to pray (Lord's Prayer) and work for, as a something prolonged. It was not immediately to appear in splendor and all-prevailing power, but Jesus was to go away for long, yet really to receive for Himself a kingdom (1 Cor. xv. 25) **and to return.** So then there would needs be waiting for Him and working for the kingdom.

13. And he called ten servants of his, and gave them ten pounds, and said unto them, Trade ye *herewith* till I come.

13. **Ten servants** here represent the whole number, just as the ten virgins do. These were **servants of his**, standing in a special and near relation. They were *his*. He gave them **ten pounds** (the Greek word is μνᾶ, Latin *mina*, amounting to about $15 of our money). This was a small amount—but he that is faithful in that which is least is faithful also in much. An equal amount was given to each. In the other parable none got less than "a talent," worth sixty times as much; and one got ten of these and another five, "according to their several ability."

The orders given were, **trade ye herewith.** The Lord will have His servants *busy*. There is something for them to do. There is no place for *idle* "Christians." This occupation is for their sakes and for the Lord's. Saul, smitten to the ground, cries, " Lord, what wilt thou have me to do?" And in the judgment, as described in Matt. xxv. 31–46, the rule of the award is, " Inasmuch as ye did it" and " Inasmuch as ye did it not." So the Lord says (Rev. xxii. 12), "Behold, I come quickly; and my reward is with me, to give every man according as his work shall be." Yes, do business, trade ye for your Lord, looking for Him as well as to Him! This is the business of life. They who are in any other may well inquire, " Is life worth living?" **Till I come.** More exactly, *while I am coming.* (See 2 Pet. iii. 12.) The pound represents the person's abilities and opportunities for the Lord's service.

14. But his citizens hated him, and sent an ambassage after him, saying, We will not that this man reign over us.

14. Here, and in ver. 27, there is an element that is not introduced into the parable of the talents at all. **His citizens** are a different class from " his servants." These represent, primarily, those of Jesus' own nation—" He came unto his own and they that were his own received him not "—and, secondarily, all who are not and will not be his servants. They **hated him.** This represents all who hate Him, all who prefer some other rule to Christ's rule. **We will not** have it **that this man** (so they speak of Him contemptuously) **reign over us**—such **an ambassage,** formal message, **they sent after him.** This is the response unbelievers make to Jesus' claims.

15. And it came to pass, when he was come back again, having received the kingdom, that he commanded these servants, unto whom he had given the money, to be called to him, that he might know what they had gained by trading.

15. There is another side to the situation **when he was**

come back again with all His professions verified, **having received the kingdom.** He comes back to rule. He will set right His kingdom. He will "gather out of it all things that cause stumbling, and them that do iniquity" (Matt. xiii. 41). See ver. 27. But first He will reckon with **the servants** who had been entrusted with the pounds, to **know what they had gained by trading,** how they had carried on their business. "Each one of us shall give account of himself to God" (Rom. xiv. 12), an account of his *activities.* Such activities will tell of the character, will indicate the reality, sincerity and devotion of the service.

16, 17. And the first came before him, saying, Lord, thy pound hath made ten pounds more. And he said unto him, Well done, thou good servant: because thou wast found faithful in a very little, have thou authority over ten cities.

16. **The first** servant that answered the call was first also in results. **Ten pounds** more he joyfully reported, acknowledging that the principal had been **thy pound.** He calls him **Lord,** and owns his right. This was a fine increase—a thousand per cent., as the traders to-day would reckon.

17. The pleased lord said, **Well done,** and pronounced him a **good servant.** The man had proved his character and faithfulness: and his reward did not end with commendation. **Faithful in a very little**—" a pound," fifteen dollars—**have thou authority,** said the returned king, making him now also a lord, **over ten cities.** The reward was proportionate to the fidelity to trust committed, but was out of all proportion to the service rendered, being vastly more than principal and interest. So God's rewards, though *according to* our deeds, are infinitely above them in their gracious abundance. The coloring of the parable is from trade and political economy: the ruling

over cities was a great advance over trading with an entrusted pound.

18, 19. And the second came, saying, Thy pound, Lord, hath made five pounds. And he said unto him also, Be thou also over five cities.

18, 19. **The second came** with a good report of **five pounds** gained. The lord does not address this one with the same words of commendation as he did the first one: perhaps this servant might have done better; perhaps he was not as zealous and active a trader as the first. But his reward was proportionate, **be thou also over five cities.**

20, 21. And another came, saying, Lord, Behold, *here is* thy pound, which I kept laid up in a napkin: for I feared thee, because thou art an austere man: thou takest up that thou layedst not down, and reapest that thou didst not sow.

20. Now **another came,** a different sort of person from the other two. All he had to offer was **thy pound,** the original trust. He says he **kept** it **laid up in a napkin.** The original of "napkin" means *sweat-cloth.* This lazy fellow had no sweat to wipe off, and so misapplied his handkerchief to tie up and hide away what he had been told to trade with.

21. He is not only lazy, but impudently slanderous. He charges his lord with being **an austere man** who acted arbitrarily and made unjust demands, in short with being an exactor, as bad as a publican. Thus many men think and some speak of God. They think of Him as a taskmaster rather than as a father, as severe, hard, self-willed in a bad sense, a tyrant. This their view comes from their cultivated evil nature, which is averse from God, out of fellowship with Him through sin.

22, 23. He saith unto him Out of thine own mouth will I judge thee, thou wicked servant, Thou knewest that I am an austere man, taking up that I laid not down, and reaping that I did not sow; then wherefore gavest thou not my money into the bank, and I at my coming should have required it with interest?

22, 23. His lord calls him a **wicked servant**, and proposes to judge him on his own terms: **out of thine own mouth,** from what thou hast just said, will **I judge thee. Thou knewest** (so thou sayest) me to be an **austere,** hard man, exacting and unmerciful, **then wherefore** not act accordingly, why didst thou not trade actively with **my money, and I, at my coming, should have required it with interest?** That would have been the politic way of doing, were the lord such a man as this servant now said he was. But the fact is this servant's excuse was all a vain pretence the outcome of a dissatisfied, rebellious heart. Such a servant must have been a stumbling block among the rest, as is such a "Christian" in the Church. You lazy grumbler, that do nothing but complain, your empty words will be shown up at the last day and your slanders will recoil on your own head! The excuses men make up for not serving God will not bear the light. They are as unreasonable as false in their logic.

24-26. And he said unto them that stood by, Take away from him the pound, and give it unto him that hath the ten pounds. And they said unto him, Lord, he hath ten pounds. I say unto you, that unto every one that hath shall be given; but from him that hath not, even that which he hath shall be taken away from him.

24. The lord made **them that stood by,** who did not belong to the ten servants, but belonged elsewhere in the kingdom —perhaps they were angels—the executioners of the sentence, which was, **Take away from him the pound,** the ability, the opportunity which by God's grace he had, but had not prized and used, **and give it unto him that hath the ten pounds,** to the one who has proved himself most faithful.

25, 26. And when those bystanders objected that **he hath ten pounds** already, the law of the kingdom was plainly laid down as increase **to every one that hath,** and a taking away of **even that which he hath** from the improvident, lazy, do-less one **that hath not** anything to show for what has been entrusted to him, no *fruit.* " Every branch in me that beareth not fruit, he taketh it away" (John xv. 2). There is a balance sheet of gain and loss in spiritual trading as in natural dealings; if there is no gain there will be loss; if there is diligence, there will be gain; if there is slothfulness and neglect, there will be loss until all is gone.

27. Howbeit these mine enemies, which would not that I should reign over them, bring hither, and slay them before me.

27. After dealing with the servants, the lord turned his attention to the citizens of ver. 14, **these mine enemies, bring hither.** The executors were the same as before. The returned lord has power. **Slay them before me.** Those who will not be ruled in the kingdom, will be ruined. " Upon whomsoever this stone shall fall, it will scatter him as dust " (Luke xx. 18). This refers, as before said, primarily to the rebellious Jews. In the next generation Jerusalem was drenched with their blood and their power was utterly destroyed. " The day of vengeance of our God " (Is. lxi. 2), belongs also to the coming kingdom.

28. And when he had thus spoken, he went on before, going up to Jerusalem.

28. After the utterance of this parable Jesus proceeded on His journey **to Jerusalem** (ix. 51), going **on before** His disciples, as their Master and leader. Without recounting His stay at Bethany of a day and a half, including the Sabbath day, of which we learn from the other Evangel-

ists, Luke goes on at once with Jesus' triumphal entry into Jerusalem.

29-38. And it came to pass, when he drew nigh unto Bethphage and Bethany, at the mount that is called *the mount* of Olives, he sent two of the disciples, saying, Go your way into the village over against *you;* in the which as ye enter ye shall find a colt tied, whereon no man ever yet sat: loose him, and bring him. And if any one ask you, Why do ye loose him? thus shall ye say, The Lord hath need of him. And they that were sent went away, and found even as he had said unto them. And as they were loosing the colt, the owners thereof said unto them, Why loose ye the colt? And they said, The Lord hath need of him. And they brought him to Jesus: and they threw their garments upon the colt, and set Jesus thereon. And as he went, they spread their garments in the way. And as he was now drawing nigh, *even* at the descent of the mount of Olives, the whole multitude of the disciples began to rejoice and praise God with a loud voice for all the mighty works which they had seen; saying, Blessed *is* the King that cometh in the name of the Lord: peace in heaven, and glory in the highest.

See on Matt. xxi. 1-9; Mark xi. 1-10; John xii. 12-19.

33. Luke alone says it was **the owners** of the animal that put the question to them who were loosing it.

37, 38. They had now **come nigh** enough to see the city stretched in a beautiful panorama before them. They were **at the descent of the mount of Olives.** The whole scene was enrapturing: the attendant circumstances were such as to excite enthusiasm; the hearts of the believers in Jesus were full of high hopes that He would now be made king. It was these, **the whole multitude of the disciples,** that now **began to rejoice and praise God with a loud voice,** putting forth all their pent-up enthusiasm, recalling **all the mighty works which they had seen,** which, along with His teachings, distinguished Jesus above any person of their time or age. And they shouted in glad acclaim, now from the crowd ahead of Him and then responsively from that which followed, **Blessed is the King that cometh in the name of the Lord,** a shout taken from

Ps. cxviii. 26, and generally acknowledged among the Jews as referring to the Messiah, the Hope of Israel. And as the angels at Jesus' birth sang "peace on earth," this multitude of hoping, excited men, celebrating the same glorious personage, cried **peace in heaven.** Altogether it was a peaceful celebration of the King of Peace. And angels and men united in the doxology, **glory in the highest.** It is meet and right that heaven and earth rejoice together over Him who united in Himself the human and the divine, restoring man from his fall to fellowship with God again. Whilst these rejoicing disciples said things of deepest meaning and things most appropriate, in their jubilation, yet doubtless they were mistaken in their views of the kind of king Jesus would be and of the methods whereby He would establish His kingdom. These disciples were likely among those who thought the kingdom of God would immediately appear, and who had not yet settled down to the teachings Jesus gave them in the parable of the pounds.

39, 40. And some of the Pharisees from the multitude said unto him, Master, rebuke thy disciples. And he answered and said, I tell you that, if these shall hold their peace, the stones will cry out.

39. **Some of the Pharisees** there were all taken aback at this new situation of Jesus. Surely He is now on the tidal wave of popular regard and is going triumphantly into Jerusalem! He whom the rulers are plotting against, ready even now to take Him and put Him to death, see, He seems to have the best of the situation! He is having success right under the eyes and in the teeth of the rulers who hate Him! **Master,** that is, *Teacher*, said they, suggesting propriety to Him; **rebuke thy disciples.** Stop this jubilation; it is unseemly.

40. Jesus' reply is a very telling one. There is much instruction in it. **I tell you,** He says to them, with con-

scious authority, **if these shall hold their peace,** if they praise me not, **the stones will cry out.** For here I must be praised. Jesus' words were somewhat of a proverbial nature, yet they may have had a reference to the coming time, looked to in the following verses, when the ruined heaps of Jerusalem would testify to His word and against the Jews' rejection of Him. Perhaps just then the walls of the city and temple were re-echoing the disciples' jubilant shouts. Stop these, and those walls will in another way cry out in witness to Jesus.

<small>41, 42. And when he drew nigh, he saw the city and wept over it, Saying, If thou hadst known in this day, even thou, the things which belong unto peace! but now they are hid from thine eyes.</small>

41. Amid this great throng the many were rejoicing, a few were angry and indignant, only one was sorrowful. This was Jesus. The sight of the city drew tears from His eyes. **He wept over it** with great emotion. The word here used in the original is different from the one in that shortest verse of the Bible, "Jesus wept," in the account of Lazarus' resurrection. It denotes a breaking forth in weeping. O what a sight, the blessed Jesus thus! But it was not for Himself or because of what He was soon to suffer.

42. **If thou hadst known**—or, O that thou hadst known—said He, addressing Jerusalem, **in this day** when the Sun of Righteousness is shining on thee, around thee, within thee, this day of privilege and opportunity, day of thy merciful visitation (ver. 44), **even thou,** the capital city, the temple city, standing representative of Judaism and Israel, **the things which belong unto peace!** Peace He was going to leave to His disciples, but not to Jerusalem. Her peace, henceforth, was all in her name. Called a "habitation of peace" (Jerusalem), she shall not know peace, since she knew not the Prince of Peace.

For **now they are hid from thine eyes.** Jerusalem's day of grace was ended. Jesus wept because it was inevitably so. When people persistently close their eyes to opportunity set before them, they will one day look in vain for that opportunity.

43, 44. For the days shall come upon thee, when thine enemies shall cast up a bank about thee, and compass thee round, and keep thee in on every side. And shall dash thee to the ground, and thy children within thee; and they shall not leave in thee one stone upon another; because thou knewest not the time of thy visitation.

43, 44. **The days shall come upon thee.** History says they came in the year 70 A. D., about forty years from the time when Jesus spoke these words. **Thine enemies,** the Romans, under Titus, **shall cast up a bank . . . compass thee round, . . . keep thee in on every side.** A very vivid detailed account of the siege of the city, which was made most effectual by the determined and exasperated Romans. **Dash thee to the ground, and thy children within thee.** Josephus, a distinguished Jew and a high military officer among them, was taken prisoner and kept in the Roman camp, often acting as a negotiator between the belligerent parties. An eyewitness of the whole siege, he wrote a history of the "Jewish War," and though he is properly classed as against Christ, yet his history verifies Jesus' prophecy to the letter and shows with what particular exactness Jesus spoke here and in the longer discourse in chap. xxi. (Matt. xxiv.). **Thy children,** though understood by some literally, probably means thy inhabitants—people as well as things shall be dashed to the ground in fearful destruction. **And they shall not leave in thee one stone upon another.** This is in the nature of a proverbial expression, yet it was, in the course of time, almost literally fulfilled. Jerusalem was destroyed utterly and its ruins plowed over. "There is a divinity that shapes our ends," Shakespeare says. "The Lord reigneth," the Bible says. "Things come to pass according to the invariable laws of nature," the deist and atheist say. "Things cannot occur differently from what does occur," the fatalist says. **Because thou knewest not the time of thy visitation,** Jesus says to Jerusalem, giving a reason for the things He prophesied and referring all to the providential government of God. (See ver. 42.) God *visited* the world, and particularly Jerusalem and Israel, with redemption: but He did not force His grace upon them. The Romans, however, forced them to destitution, destruction and nothingness, and God was with the Roman eagles in judgment.

45, 46. And he entered into the temple, and began to cast out them that sold, saying unto them, It is written, And my house shall be a house of prayer: but ye have made it a den of robbers. .

45, 46. **Into the temple.** The religious centre of the nation and of the city of God's true worship, thus far in the history. God Himself had chosen the site of the temple and appointed its services. **A house of prayer** it was to be, of communion with God. The little Jesus was found there, and the great Master always resorted thither when in Jerusalem. **But** money-loving men had made it **a den of robbers,** making secular what was sacred and establishing shops in the temple's courts. It matters not that what was sold pertained to the temple and the needs of worshippers; the sellers sold for money, sought for gain, and robbed God of His own. At the very beginning of His ministry (John ii. 13-17) Jesus had similarly cleansed the temple, but three years had sufficed to restore the bartering again and the sacrilege. So at its close, Luke says, without going into details as Matt. (xxi. 12-16) and Mark (xi. 15-18) have done, He **began**

to cast out them that sold. See what regard Jesus had for God's house and worship, and for what **is written.** Yet there are some in these times who consider the Jewish temple worship, though divinely ordained, as "ritualism!" And are there none now who, though maybe in less manifest ways, turn a house of prayer into a den of robbers?

>   47, 48. And he was teaching daily in the temple. But the chief priests and the scribes and the principal men of the people sought to destroy him: and they could not find what they might do; for the people all hung upon him, listening.

47, 48. **Teaching daily in the temple** indicates Jesus' habit and sets us a worthy example. Ought it not to bring more teachers into the Sunday-school?

Notice that whilst **the chief priests and the scribes** held together in fast and increasing opposition and hatred to Jesus, it was only **the principal men of the people** who sided with them, whereas **the people** themselves **all hung upon him, listening.** The expression here is very strong, and sufficiently familiar. We speak of rapt attention as a hanging upon the speaker's lips. Jesus was popular, but not with the bosses. His very popularity was their incitement to His ruin, which they were determined to accomplish at all hazards. And there have since been disciples that have fared no better than their Master, at the hands of unscrupulous, jealous, envious men who have happened to be temporarily in places of power. But it makes no matter who are with us or against us, or with whom we are, if only we are on the side of Jesus. Where do you stand?

CHAPTER XX.

1-19. And it came to pass, on one of the days, as he was teaching the people in the temple, and preaching the gospel, there came upon him the chief priests and the scribes with the elders; and they spake, saying unto him, Tell us: By what authority doest thou these things? or who is he that gave thee this authority? And he answered and said unto them, I also will ask you a question; and tell me: The baptism of John, was it from heaven, or from men? And they reasoned with themselves, saying, If we shall say, From heaven; he will say, Why did ye not believe him? But if we shall say, From men; all the people will stone us: for they be persuaded that John was a prophet. And they answered, that they knew not whence *it was*. And Jesus said unto them, Neither tell I you by what authority I do these things.

And he began to speak unto the people this parable: A man planted a vineyard, and let it out to husbandmen, and went into another country for a long time. And at the season he sent unto the husbandmen a servant, that they should give him of the fruit of the vineyard: but the husbandmen beat him, and sent him away empty. And he sent yet another servant: and him also they beat, and handled him shamefully, and sent him away empty. And he sent yet a third: and him also they wounded, and cast him forth. And the lord of the vineyard said, What shall I do? I will send my beloved son: it may be they will reverence him. But when the husbandmen saw him, they reasoned one with another, saying, This is the heir: let us kill him, that the inheritance may be ours. And they cast him forth out of the vineyard and killed him. What therefore will the lord of the vineyard do unto them? He will come and destroy the husbandmen, and will give the vineyard unto others. And when they heard it, they said, God forbid. But he looked upon them, and said, What then is this that is written,

 The stone which the builders rejected,
 The same was made the head of the corner?

Every one that falleth on that stone shall be broken to pieces; but on whomsoever it shall fall, it will scatter him as dust.

And the scribes and the chief priests sought to lay hands on him in that very hour; and they feared the people: for they perceived that he spake this parable against them.

See on Matt. xxi. 33 to xxii. 14; Mark xi. 27 to xii. 12.

1. Luke says, very generically, **on one of the days,** i. e. of this last visit of Jesus to Jerusalem, so long an account of His journey to make which Luke has given. The Harmonists make it Tuesday before the crucifixion, to which day they assign a larger mass of our Lord's teaching than to any other single day of His ministry. As usual He was **teaching the people, and preaching the gospel.** Jealous of His influence, the officials tried to interfere, questioning the Lord's authority, but were skilfully silenced by Him. The Son is again in His Father's house (comp. ii. 46-49).

6. **All the people will stone us.** A clear confession that they and the people were not agreed; the people were more open to truth than they; the people, in their way, stood by John as a divine messenger.

9. **Unto the people,** Luke says, though the parable was directed against the false leaders of the people, as these readily perceived (ver. 19) and were still further inflamed against Him. **For a long time.** "Between the people's entrance into Canaan and the destruction of Jerusalem by the Romans more than 1500 years intervened" (BENGEL).

16. Luke alone gives their objecting prayer, **God forbid,** which is more exactly translated, *Let it not come to pass.*

17. **But he looked upon them** with a significant, searching, grave look, and said, **What then**—if there is anything in your objecting prayer—**is this that is written?** and then He proceeded to quote the Scriptures against them, confirmatory of His words. Jesus stuck to the Scriptures.

19. **In that very hour,** says Luke, marking the time more definitely than the other writers here.

20-26. And they watched him, and sent forth spies, which feigned themselves to be righteous, that they might take hold of his speech, so as to deliver him up to the rule and to the authority of the governor. And they asked him, saying, Master, we know that thou sayest and teachest rightly, and acceptest not the person *of any*, but of a truth teachest the way of God: Is it lawful for us to give tribute unto Cæsar, or not? But he perceived their craftiness, and said unto them, Shew me a penny. Whose image and superscription hath it? And they said, Cæsar's. And he said unto them, Then render unto Cæsar the things that are Cæsar's, and unto God the things that are God's. And they were not able to take hold of the saying before the people: and they marvelled at his answer, and held their peace.

See on Matt. xxii. 15-22 : Mark xii. 13-17.

20. Though unable "in that very hour" (ver. 19) to accomplish their hostile purpose, they did not give it up, but **watched** for an opportunity, and, to make one, **sent forth spies,** persons instigated to a certain course, put up to it, **which feigned themselves to be righteous,** just men who sincerely wanted to know and do the right, not instigated to a course by others. They were sent to **take hold of his speech,** to get some expression from His lips, "catch him in talk" (Mark), **so as**—the ultimate design —**to deliver him up to** the secular power **and to the authority of the** Roman **governor.** Anything to destroy Jesus! Matthew notes that, in this attempt, the Pharisees associated with themselves their political opponents, the Herodians, who favored the Romans: and here we have an illustration of the common proverb that politics and religion make strange bed-fellows.

22. **Tribute.** Luke uses the proper Greek word for that tax which was exacted of foreign, subject people. Matthew and Mark use a Roman word.

23. **Craftiness.** Readiness to do any thing to accomplish their ends. Matthew calls it "wickedness," and Mark, "hypocrisy."

26. Luke notes **the people** as still in the way, and strongly puts their complete discomfiture.

27-40. And there came to him certain of the Sadducees, they which say that there is no resurrection; and they asked him, saying, Master, Moses wrote unto us, that if a man's brother die, having a wife, and he be childless, his brother should take the wife, and raise up seed unto his brother. There were therefore seven brethren: and the first took a wife, and died childless; and the second; and the third took her; and likewise the seven also left no children, and died. Afterward the woman also died. In the resurrection therefore whose wife of them shall she be? for the seven had her to wife. And Jesus said unto them, The sons of this world marry, and are given in marriage: but they that are accounted worthy to attain to that world, and the resurrection from the dead, neither marry, nor are given in marriage: for neither can they die any more: for they are equal unto the angels; and are sons of God, being sons of the resurrection. But that the dead are raised, even Moses shewed, in *the place concerning* the Bush, when he calleth the Lord the God of Abraham, and the God of Isaac, and the God of Jacob. Now he is not the God of the dead, but of the living: for all live unto him. And certain of the scribes answering said, Master, thou hast well said. For they durst not any more ask him any question.

See on Matt. xxii. 23–33; Mark xii. 18–27.

34, 36. **This world,** or age, period of existence, order of things, is here contrasted, in respect to the question of the Sadducees, with **that world,** that age, period of existence, order of things, which is beyond, the eternal world. Here and now people **marry and are given in marriage,** according to the purpose and ordinance of God (Gen. i. 27, 28; ii. 20–24; Mark x. 6–9), which is to be "had in honor among all" (Heb. xiii. 4). But this relation belongs to this world or age, and ends with it. **They that are accounted worthy,** etc., clearly refers to the justified, the saved, without any mention of others. Whilst there will be a resurrection both of the just and the unjust, only the former is here referred to. The participants in it **neither marry nor are given in marriage,** whatever peculiarities of sex they may have, of which nothing is here said. **For,** giving a reason, **neither,** or not even, **can they die any more,** they are no longer mortal and need not, therefore, reproduce the species. For, whilst not angels, they are **equal unto the angels,** like them, who came into being in their full powers, among whom there never were parents and children. Doubtless there will be parents and children in that world, but having become so before their entrance there. They all are **sons of God,** immortal, **being sons of the resurrection,** those who have received the adoption for which they waited, even the resurrection of their bodies (Rom. viii. 23; comp. 1 John iii. 1, 2).

37. **But,** aside from the relations sustained to one another in the world to come, the fact **that the dead are raised** is proved by what **Moses showed,** uttered as a divine oracle (ἐμήνυσεν), **in the place concerning the Bush.** Exod. iii. 2-6. The Lord refers them to the authority whom they had just quoted (ver. 28). Divine names are never empty but declare those to whom they are given to possess the qualities they ascribe. In the place quoted, as recorded by Moses, God called Himself **the God of Abraham,** etc. That is His covenant name, by which He was always to be known. But Abraham, Isaac and Jacob, with whom God had made "a covenant well ordered and sure," had died "not having received the promises," yet "in faith" (Heb. xi. 13), in Him who gave them. Their dying, however, did not end their existence or take them away from the scope of those promises. God, speaking at the Bush was still their God, and is still their God to-day. But where are they? Waiting, in the other world, God's time, waiting for the adoption, the redemption of their bodies (Rom. viii. 23). Abraham, Isaac and Jacob were *men*, representatives of mankind, not merely *souls*. It takes body and soul to compose a man. These, originally united in a perfect and immortal state by God, have been separated by sin. But God's promise in redemption refers to the whole

man, and embraces body as well as soul; and not until the bodies of their humiliation, long since returned to dust because of sin, are changed into the likeness of Christ's glorified body (Phil. iii. 21) and bear the image of the heavenly as before they did that of the earthly (1 Cor. xv. 49), of the second Adam as before it did that of the first Adam (1 Cor. xv. 22, 45-49), will God's covenant be perfectly fulfilled, and His name be eternally sustained in honor and glory—a thing that must certainly be, as sure as God is God. His name is above every name, He *is* all that it implies, and His sons shall be all that their name and relation to Him implies. The resurrection of the body is, therefore, here proved, as well as the continued existence of men in the world to come. This point seems to have been too much overlooked by commentators.

38. **All,** whether in this world or the next, whether we call them living or dead, **live unto him,** and necessarily He will recover their bodies to them by the resurrection.

39, 40. So completely answered were they who had been urging Jesus with questions, so signally they all failed to gain a point against Him from His talk, that some owned up, **Master, thou hast well said,** whilst all were silenced from that time on. It does not report the lawyer's query about the great commandment of the law. But Jesus, in turn, now put to them a crucial question, which they left unanswered.

41-44. And he said unto them, How say they that the Christ is David's son? For David himself saith in the book of Psalms,
> The Lord said unto my Lord,
> Sit thou on my right hand,
> Till I make thine enemies the footstool of thy feet.

David therefore calleth him Lord, and how is he his son?

See on Matt. xxii. 41–46, Mark xii. 35–37.

Then He gave a fearful denunciation of the Scribes and Pharisees, characterizing them as hypocrites, and, tearing away their mask, exposed them before all.

<small>45–47. And in the hearing of all the people he said unto his disciples, Beware of the scribes, which desire to walk in long robes, and love salutations in the marketplaces, and chief seats in the synagogues, and chief places at feasts; which devour widows' houses, and for a pretence make long prayers: these shall receive greater condemnation.</small>

See on Matt. xxiii. 1–39, Mark xii. 38–40.

Matthew, who wrote for Jews, gives this tremendous address in full. Mark and Luke, who writes for the Gentiles, merely announce its subject in brief epitome.

What a dreadful state of things when people must beware of those who occupy seats of authoritative teaching, because of their self-seeking, vain-glorious, piously-pretentious, hypocritical character! **Long prayers** are still used to cover up dastardly doings, but still secure from God **greater condemnation.** There is nothing more hateful before God and men than pious frauds. Nor can "conscience" be quoted against truth: God's word is the only infallible rule of faith and life.

CHAPTER XXI.

1-4. And he looked up, and saw the rich men that were casting their gifts into the treasury. And he saw a certain poor widow casting in thither two mites. And he said, Of a truth I say unto you, This poor widow cast in more than they all: for all these did of their superfluity cast in unto the gifts: but she of her want did cast in all the living that she had.

See on Mark xii. 41-44.

1, 2. He who then **saw** now sees, and makes similar distinctions.

3, 4. How did He know this? By His divine knowledge, searcher of hearts that He was and is. Among so many—**all these**—she stood alone as truly making sacrifice and with whole-souled consecration—**all the living that she had,** and it was a free-will offering!

She had heard God say (Jer. xlix. 11), "Let your widows trust in me." Poor in earthly goods, she was rich in faith, and so became rich in good works. She was an heir of God, and so, though "having nothing, yet possessing all things!" It must have been a pleasant thing to Jesus, even as it is pleasant to us to read it, that, amid the ruling hypocrisy which He had so fearfully to denounce, something commendable met His eye and called forth His praise.

Many a widow and poor person is *magnificent* in giving, beyond the reach of anything ever done by millionaires, Peabodys and well-to-do members of churches, whose gifts make the trumpets resound with the praise of men. The true measure of a gift of benevolence is the amount of self-denial and sacrifice that is in it, its *cost* to us. Cultivate in yourself, and encourage in others, *the grace of giving*, and remember that Jesus is still sitting over against the treasury, noting all about you and your gifts.

5-11. And as some spake of the temple, how it was adorned with goodly stones and offerings, he said. As for these things which ye behold, the days will come, in which there shall not be left here one stone upon another, that shall not be thrown down. And they asked him, saying, Master, when therefore shall these things be? and what *shall be* the sign when these things are about to come to pass? And he said, Take heed that ye be not led astray: for many shall come in my name, saying, I am *he*; and, The time is at hand: go ye not after them. And when ye shall hear of wars and tumults, be not terrified: for these things must needs come to pass first; but the end is not immediately.

Then said he unto them, Nation shall rise against nation, and kingdom against kingdom: and there shall be great earthquakes, and in divers places famines and pestilences; and there shall be terrors and great signs from heaven.

See on Matt. xxiv. 1-7; Mark xiii. 1-8.

5. Luke alone speaks of the **offerings**, things laid up there, votive offerings, put there chiefly by heathens, VAN OOST. thinks, and suggests among them the holy vessels presented by the Emperor Augustus and other vessels by the Egyptian Philadelphus, and the golden vine by Herod the Great.

8. **The time**, the Messianic time or occasion, the opportune time.

9. **These things first** is, indeed, the divine order, **but the end is not immediately** after them. The time is not so soon, or so definitely marked.

11. Luke adds **pestilences** to the things here foretold, and **terrors**, things that frighten, and **great signs from heaven.**

12-19. But before all these things, they shall lay their hands on you, and shall persecute you, delivering you up to the synagogues and prisons, bringing you before kings and governors for my name's sake. It shall turn unto you for a testimony. Settle it therefore in your hearts, not to meditate beforehand how to answer: for I will give you a mouth and wisdom, which all your adversaries shall not be able to withstand or to gainsay. But ye shall be delivered up even by parents, and brethren, and kinsfolk, and friends; and *some* of you shall they cause to be put to death. And ye shall be hated of all men for my name's sake. And not a hair of your head shall perish. In your patience ye shall win your souls.

See on Matt. xxiv. 8–10; Mark xiii. 9–13.

12. **Before all these things** seems, from the parallel passages and whole context, to indicate before all these things are accomplished, and to include the persecutions predicted as a part of them.

13. **It shall turn . . . testimony.** The result of your persecutions will be a testimony to Christ and the truth.

14, 15. **Settle it . . . not to meditate beforehand.** Very decided and comforting words for "be not anxious beforehand" (Mark) about this witness you are to give amid persecutions: and with a strong reason—**for I**, in the person of the Holy Spirit (Mark), over against your natural anxiety and **all your adversaries,** God, will be your helper then with **mouth** to speak, utterance, **and wisdom** to know what to say and when. (Comp. Matt. x. 19–20.) "If God be for us, who can be against us?"

18, 19. These verses are peculiar to Luke. The proverbial expression (comp. xii. 7), **not a hair,** etc., giving assurance of entire safety, cannot refer here to corporeal and external safety, seeing ver. 16 prophesied death to some, but, rather, to their safety as Christians, their salvation. Though they lose their heads, they shall be entirely safe and saved. Similarly, **in your patience,** endurance, bearing trustfully and heroically the afflictions predicted, right in that line and sphere **ye shall win,** and not lose, **your souls,** your true lives, yourselves. "A paradox. The worldly seek their soul's safety by repelling force with force. Not so the saints. Rev. xiii. 10" (BENGEL).

20-24. But when ye see Jerusalem compassed with armies, then know that her desolation is at hand. Then let them that are in Judæa flee unto the mountains; and let them that are in the midst of her depart out; and let not them that are in the country enter therein. For these are days of vengeance, that all things which are written may be fulfilled. Woe unto them that are with child and to them that give suck in those days! for there shall be great distress upon the land, and wrath unto this people. And they shall fall by the edge of the sword, and shall be led captive into all the nations. and Jerusalem shall be trodden down of the Gentiles, until the times of the Gentiles be fulfilled.

See on Matt. xxiv. 15-22; Mark xiii. 14-20.

20. **But when** takes the reader back to the close of ver. 11, and comes to more definite things. Whilst Matthew and Mark speak of "the abomination of desolation," the former referring to "Daniel the prophet," our author, writing specially for the Gentiles, does not use this expresion, but, with great plainness, makes the sight of **Jerusalem compassed with armies** the sure sign of her speedy **desolation**, in response to what we read in vers. 5-7. This sign appeared A. D. 70, when the Roman general Titus invested the city.

21. Flight, departure, avoidance of the walled city, would **then** be the course of safety.

22. Explanation of the cause of Jerusalem's desolation and Judaism's overthrow. It was God's **vengeance,** threatened long, away back in Deut. xxviii. and thence on till it came in fury. Long delayed by a most longsuffering God, it was soon to come in such measure and kind as would accomplish **all things written.** See Jesus' tearful lament over this certainty in xix. 41-44.

23, 24. **Upon the land** or, better, as the margin gives it, *earth* in general, whilst **wrath unto this people,** Israel, is the particular designation. See in preceding vols., referred to above, some details of numbers slain and taken captive as given by Josephus in his Jewish War. **Into all the nations.** Where they still are. It is said that Frederick the Great once asked a chaplain of his for a short proof of the truth of Christianity; and he replied, " Your Majesty, *the Jews!* " Ever since A. D. 70 Jerusalem has been **trodden down** under foot **of the Gentiles,** Romans, Persians, Arabs, Crusaders, Islamites, who still have on her the heel of despotism. Until **the times of the Gentiles,** their period of occupation in fulfilment of the divine vengeance, **be fulfilled.** For of this, too, there shall be an end, close on to the end of the world or age.

26, 27. And there shall be signs in sun and moon and stars; and upon the earth distress of nations, in perplexity for the roaring of the sea and the billows; men fainting for fear, and for expectation of the things which are coming on the world : for the powers of the heavens shall be shaken. And then shall they see the Son of man coming in a cloud with power and great glory.

See on Matt. xxiv. 29-31 ; Mark xiii. 24-27.

25, 26. Here there is again a turn in the discourse from the destruction of Jerusalem to the *Parousia* or coming again of the Son of man. Physical **signs** are predicted of that event. Prophecy is understood by the event, and cannot be *interpreted* like history or doctrine. These signs we take to be literal as well as tropical, the seen foreboding the unseen. Luke notes the signs in the heavens in common with Matthew and Mark, and adds those **upon the earth. Nations** comprehensively and **men** individually will be in **distress** and **fear.** The **perplexity** of the former will arise from the **roaring of the sea and the billows.** The allegorical expositors interpret this of tumults of the people. (Comp. Ps. lxv. 7.) The fear of individuals that will produce **fainting** even to " expiring " (*margin*), even unto death, will arise from

expectation of coming things. Tremendous emotion is easily fatal! **The world** is the whole inhabited earth.

27. **And then,** after these signs, **shall they see** the greatest sight of all, **the Son of man,** Jesus, **coming,** etc. This is the *Parousia.* The manner of it, **in a cloud,** as the angels afterwards at the Ascension (Acts i. 9) signified, **with power and great glory,** in marked contrast with His coming into the world at the incarnation, as a feeble little child (Luke i. and ii.).

28. But when these things begin to come to pass, look up, and lift up your heads; because your redemption draweth nigh.

28. **These things,** properly interpreted, instead of causing fear and consternation to Christ's disciples, will be the token of a nearer **redemption,** birth-throes of perfected salvation (comp. Rom. viii. 18–25), the occasion for them to **look up** in joyful hope and **lift up** their heads in hopeful expectation. Judgments, death, the crack of doom, need not frighten Christians; rather do they, and, dear reader, so let them, betoken our Redeemer near!

29–33. And he spake to them a parable: Behold the fig tree, and all the trees: when they now shoot forth, ye see it and know of your own selves that the summer is now nigh. Even so ye also, when ye see these things coming to pass, know ye that the kingdom of God is nigh. Verily I say unto you, This generation shall not pass away, till all things be accomplished. Heaven and earth shall pass away: but my words shall not pass away.

See on Matt. xxiv. 32–36; Mark xiii. 28–32.

29, 30. " Our God wrote the last day not only into books, but also into the trees, that, as often as we see the trees shoot forth in the spring, we remember this parable and the day of the Lord. This is, indeed, a strange explanation, that, when I see the sun and moon darkened, waves and sea roaring, I shall say, Praised be

God, the summer cometh, because the leaves and blossoms shoot forth! But, as we are to become new men, He wills that we also have other and new thoughts, reason and senses, and regard nothing according to reason as the world takes it, but as it is before His eyes, and govern ourselves according to the future, invisible, new being, for which we hope. For this miserable life here upon earth is like the abominable, unfruitful winter. Heaven, earth, sea, stars, air and all creatures are tired of the world's malice which they must see and hear, and regret that they are so awfully abused, and wish for new heavens and a new earth, wherein dwelleth righteousness, 2 Pet. iii. 13 ; Is. lxv. 17 " (LUTHER).

31. Luke gives as the subject—wanting in Matthew and Mark—of is nigh **the kingdom of God,** which LUTHER explains here as " nothing but our redemption. We ourselves are the kingdom of God (xvii. 21), therefore it draweth nigh when we are to be entirely redeemed from sins and evil." Whilst this is true, it is not the whole truth: "the kingdom of God" is to be interpreted here in the light of the disciples' questions and this whole discourse drawn out by them.

32. This passage is a *crux interpretum.* Therefore, though treated in the preceding volumes of this Commentary, we will also offer an explanation of the manifest difficulty. We believe that **this generation** has its usual signification and refers to people then living. But instead of rendering the verb, γένηται, **be accomplished,** by a translation closer to the radical meaning of the verb, we suggest *come to pass* in the sense of finding place on the stage of history, entering upon their accomplishment, the completion of which might require a long time thereafter: so that the meaning would be, all these things will enter upon the stage of their fulfilment, will come on in the

course of history, find place in current events and begin their round, before this present living generation passes away. The coming of the Son of man in the destruction of Jerusalem and the Jewish state took place about forty years after this was spoken. The *era* of the coming of the Son of man in His kingdom began during that then present generation and is now going on to its final scenes. Comp. the contingent aorist and the translation " come to pass " in Luke i. 20 ; John xiii. 19 ; xiv. 29, and the indicative aorist, "it came to pass," times innumerable. See also the Revised Version of John xiii. 2 "during supper " instead of " supper being ended," though here it is the present participle. Comp., as side-lights to the whole passage, Phil. iv. 5 ; Heb. x. 25, 37 ; James v. 8, 9 ; 1 Pet. iv. 7 ; 2 Pet. iii. 8, 9.

34–36. But take heed to yourselves, lest haply your hearts be overcharged with surfeiting, and drunkenness, and cares of this life, and that day come on you suddenly as a snare : for *so* shall it come upon all them that dwell on the face of all the earth. But watch ye at every season, making supplication, that ye may prevail to escape all these things that shall come to pass, and to stand before the Son of man.

See on Matt. xxiv. 42–51 ; Mark xiii. 33–37, passages not exactly parallel, but similar.

34, 35. Here is a present practical admonition. Events are above and beyond you, **but take heed to yourselves.** Unite the certainty of what is coming with the uncertainty of the time of it, and give heed to character and life. **Overcharged**, weighted, burdened. **Surfeiting** is debauch from previous drinking. **Drunkenness** is too familiar to need remark, an old-time and aboundingly present sin, though not among Christians. **Cares of this life**, so common, concern, anxiety about getting along in this world, so beautifully reproved in Matt. vi. 24–34 by a setting forth of our Heavenly Father's care, see in what bad company the Lord puts them, just as covetousness is commonly classified with licentiousness, and learn to "be careful for nothing" (Phil. iv. 6). What is "this life" compared with the life to come which **that day** of the Lord's appearing will gloriously usher in! **Suddenly,** unexpected, when they think not, **as a snare** that springs upon and takes the unwary, shall that day **come in upon all them that dwell,** sit in security ($\varkappa\alpha\theta\eta\mu\acute{\epsilon}\nu\sigma\upsilon\varsigma$), **on the face of all the earth,** mankind in general: but let it not be so with you, Christians.

36. **Watch.** This is the wakefulness of Christian life. **At every season,** in every occasion, joined here to the preceding verb, is by others used to qualify the following **making supplication.** Comp. xviii. 1, 7, and "Pray without ceasing" of 1 Thess. v. 17, and "Watch unto prayer" of 1 Pet. iv. 7. The Christian life depends continually on God and communes with Him. The purpose and context of this supplication is, **that ye may prevail** over all adverse influences, and have the power **to escape** out of and be by no means ensnared by coming perils, **and to stand,** not run to cover of rocks and hills (Rev. vi. 15, 16), or be placed (for the word is passive) by the ministering angels (Matt. xxiv. 31; Mark xiii. 27), **before the Son of man** as the redeemed of the Lord (Is. li. 11; lxii. 12; lxiii. 4; Luke i. 68; ver. 28 above; Rev. v. 9). That day, whose coming is by so many either overlooked, never thought of, or dreadfully feared, should be a day desired, expected, even longed for (2 Pet. iii. 12) by Christians.

37-38. And every day he was teaching in the temple; and every night he went out, and lodged in the mount that is called *the mount* of Olives. And all the people came early in the morning to him in the temple, to hear him.

37, 38. The verbs here are in the imperfect tense, showing customary action. This last week of His ministry Jesus spent the days **teaching in the temple,** but, knowing the Jews' purpose now taking shape more definitely than ever (comp. Mark xiv. 10, 11) to arrest Him, **every night he went out and lodged** among His friends at Bethany (Matt. xxi. 17; Mark xi. 11), in the **mount of Olives.** The eagerness of the people to hear Him is shown in their rising **early in the morning** and resorting to the temple **to hear him.** Nor did He disappoint them by coming late; for the statement of Matt. xxi. 18 seems to indicate that on that day He visited the city before breakfast.

CHAPTER XXII.

1-6. Now the feast of unleavened bread drew nigh, which is called the Passover. And the chief priests and the scribes sought how they might put him to death; for they feared the people.

And Satan entered into Judas who was called Iscariot, being of the number of the twelve. And he went away, and communed with the chief priests and captains, how he might deliver him unto them. And they were glad, and covenanted to give him money. And he consented, and sought opportunity to deliver him unto them in the absence of the multitude.

See on Matt. xxvi. 1-5, 14-16; Mark xiv. 1, 2, 10, 11.

2. That these **chief priests and scribes** sat in Moses' seat (Matt. xxiii. 2), were doctors of the law and chief men in the Jewish church, does not make their purpose and effort to **put him to death** any the less a deed of darkness, inspired from the pit of iniquity. Prompted by envy, jealousy, self-seeking, they feared not God, but only **the people,** who, let alone, sided with Jesus. Nor can any now, who, being in place and outward honor in the church, "turn aside unto their crooked ways," plead their position or external honors to prevent them from being counted in and led forth with the "workers of iniquity" (Ps. cxxv. 5).

Luke gave account (vii. 36-50) of the anointing of Jesus in a Pharisee's house, probably at Capernaum, by a woman that was a sinner, and makes no mention of His anointing at Bethany by Mary, the sister of Lazarus, recorded at this point by Matthew and Mark and John.

3. **Satan,** who operates through men, **entered into Judas,** who gave him room and sway, though Judas had

the position and honor of belonging to **the twelve.** See on vi. 16.

4. He knew where to find kindred spirits and **went away** from the hallowed influences of Jesus' presence, **and communed with them** as to plans for consummating the iniquity they purposed. **Captains** probably refers to the Levitical temple guards.

6. **Money,** of which Judas was a lover (John xii. 6, comp. 1 Tim. vi. 10), and a bargain to which Judas **consented,** and then the watch for **an opportunity,** an occasion suitable to the deed of darkness that was to be done. Men still do such things for money; they betray the innocent blood. **In the absence of the multitude** (see on ver. 2, above), as much as possible secretly.

7. And the day of unleavened bread came, on which the passover must be sacrificed.

See on Matt. xxvi. 17–20; Mark. xiv. 12–17, and Appendix to Vol. III. on "When did Christ eat the Last Supper?"

7. The law was very explicit that the lamb should be killed "between the two evenings" of the specified day.

8, 9. And he sent Peter and John, saying, Go and make ready for us the passover, that we may eat. And they said unto him, Where wilt thou that we make ready?

8, 9. Matthew and Mark report only the disciples' question, **Where wilt thou that we make ready?** But Luke gives first Jesus' command, **Go and make ready for us the passover.** Naturally, as the time was at hand, the Lord and His disciples alike would have this sacred feast and divine appointment upon their minds. They were all accustomed to keep the feasts. These had to be observed in Jerusalem. They were now in Bethany. The question is, **where** shall they keep the feast? Jesus **sent**

Peter and John to make the preparations. They were, likely, the most fit two, of the twelve, for this occasion, being vehement in love as well as in action, and John, especially, being acquainted in Jerusalem, with possibly a home there (see John xix. 27).

> 10-13. And he said unto them, Behold, when ye are entered into the city, there shall meet you a man bearing a pitcher of water; follow him into the house whereinto he goeth. And ye shall say unto the goodman of the house, The Master saith unto thee, Where is the guest-chamber, where I shall eat the passover with my disciples? And he will shew you a large upper room furnished; there make ready. And they went, and found as he had said unto them: and they made ready the passover.

10. Notice that no designation by which the place would be known, is given; so that Judas gets no clue to the place, but must stay and go in with the remainder of the company.

A man bearing a pitcher of water. "A very unusual sight in the East, where the water is drawn by women. He must probably have been the slave of one who was an open or secret disciple; unless we have here a reference to the Jewish custom of the master of a house himself drawing the water with which the unleavened bread was kneaded on Nisan 13. If so, the 'man bearing a pitcher of water' may have been the evangelist St. Mark, in the house of whose mother, and probably in the very upper room where the last supper was held, the disciples used at first to meet (Acts xii. 12). The mysteriousness of the sign was perhaps intended to baffle, as long as was needful, the machinations of Judas" (CAMBRIDGE BIBLE).

11. Peter and John were only to **follow** the pitcher-bearer, and bear the message with which they were charged only to **the goodman of the house.** This goes to show that these were not the same, but different persons. The word rendered "goodman" simply means the

master of the house. Notwithstanding the fact that upon these great festival occasions Eastern hospitality found abundant scope for its exercise and was not found wanting—a general giving up of unoccupied rooms and of furniture, without hire, to strangers—the words Jesus bade them address this man imply that he was a friend or disciple of His: and 'tis pleasant to think, as there was an enemy among His most intimate friends, so there were secret friends of His among His bitter enemies in Jerusalem.

12. **He will show you a large upper room furnished** with tables, couches, basin (John xiii. 5, etc.). Observe the minuteness of Jesus' directions, and an illustration therein of His more than human foreknowledge.

13. Their immediate, unquestioning obedience showed their faith. **They went,** upon orders, **and found as he had said unto them.** So it had always been; so will it always be when the Lord's word is concerned.

14–16. And when the hour was come, he sat down, and the apostles with him. And he said unto them, With desire I have desired to eat this passover with you before I suffer; for I say unto you, I will not eat it, until it be fulfilled in the kingdom of God.

14. **And when the hour,** time, for the eating of the passover, after sunset, **was come,** having meanwhile come into the city from Bethany, **he sat down,** or, rather, *reclined,* as the Greek word signifies and as the custom was, **and the apostles with him,** including Judas, who had to stay with them to know the place whither they were going. Jesus' sayings in these verses are given only by Luke.

15. **With desire I have desired,** that is, greatly have I desired, **to eat this passover with you.** We inquire why, and are answered partly in the words **before I suffer,** and in what follows. This was Jesus' last passover, and the

last one of that dispensation. There was a sorrow and a joy connected with it more than usual. It was to be His farewell meal with His disciples. Great changes were to come to pass right upon it.

16. Soon all that it signified will **be fulfilled in the kingdom of God,** which is not limited to Jews but embraces mankind. Soon the Lamb whose blood cleanses from all sin will be slain and the sin of the world passed over, whosoever in it shall apply that blood to his own heart and house. See latter part of ver. 18.

17, 18. *And he received a cup, and when he had given thanks, he said, Take this, and divide it among yourselves: for I say unto you, I will not drink from henceforth of the fruit of the vine, until the kingdom of God shall come.*

17. The **cup** which Jesus here **received** at the hand of some one of the twelve, was the cup of the passover and has no reference to the cup in the Lord's Supper. **When he had given thanks.** This occurred more than once during the passover meal. Thanksgiving was prominent in all its parts.

18. **I will not drink henceforth,** after this, **of the fruit of the vine,** commonly called wine, a common drink of the country and of the passover, **until the kingdom of God shall come.** (See above on ver. 16.) Evidently the kingdom of God, which both John and Jesus had preached as at hand and come nigh unto them, was now about to *come* in a fuller sense than ever before. The fulness of the time had come. That day, the next day as we reckon, Jesus would be lifted up on the cross and so draw all men unto Him, having established a kingdom, unlike the kingdoms of the world, based on love. Vers. 16 and 18 do not affirm or deny that Jesus Himself ate and drank at this passover; but ver. 15 makes the im-

pression that He did : but now for the last time **until** prophecy would become history.

<small>19. And he took bread, and when he had given thanks, he brake it, and gave to them, saying, This is my body which is given for you: this do in remembrance of me.</small>

See on Matt. xxvi. 26-29 ; Mark xiv. 22-25 ; 1 Cor. xi. 23-25.

19. Here begins the institution of the Lord's Supper, which may be considered as the *proper continuance* and *realization* of the paschal supper. The Lord did not wait till that supper was *done* as if He would establish something *new* in the sense of *unconnected with* the great truths set forth by the passover. On the contrary, the passover was here merged into the Lord's Supper. **He took bread**, one of the unleavened cakes that were there. There was manifest in His actions, in thus *taking* the bread and doing what followed, that He was going beyond the usual appointments of the passover in the exercise of an authority of His own. He did not take any part of the *lamb* in this action, but the *bread*. There was to be *no more shedding of blood* for sins after His all-sufficient sacrifice of Himself, and nothing that might cast a doubt on the prevailing efficacy of *that*. Jesus had, moreover, before declared "I am the bread of life!" Here "is fulfilled the prognostication of the Jews—that when the Messiah should come as a priest after the order of Melchisedek, all (typical animal) sacrifices should cease, and only the (thank) offering of *bread and wine* should remain" (STIER). The giving of **thanks** again indicated a new idea, a fresh beginning. It was only after such a *blessing* that **he brake it, and gave to them.** This is the distribution. He gives, they receive. Every act of His in this connection is significant, as well as what He said. But mark particularly His words.

This is my body. He does not say, This *bread* is my body: the word for bread is masculine whereas the *this* is neuter and is not to be taken with the word *bread*. But, This that I give to thee, **this** is my body. As though He had said, You have eaten the paschal lamb, and for the last time. That lamb represented me. I am "the Lamb of God that takes away the sin of the world," as John preached concerning me. "Lo, I come to do thy will, O God, and a body hast thou prepared for me;" and **this is my body.** Take, eat, and so become *incorporate* with me; for "he that eateth me, even he shall live by me" (John vi. 57). As of old, so now, doubtless, there will be many to say, "How can this man give us his flesh to eat?" But Jesus does not modify His strong and strange words for such, but repeats them with emphasis, the four accounts of the Lord's Supper unvaryingly giving the Lord's declaration, "*This is my body.*" The Lord *knew* how much controversy would arise out of these words, yet adhered to them as the plainest that could express the great fact. You may say with Nicodemus, "How can these things be?" The Lord does not choose to tell you *how* (if you *could understand* that), but simply says, *It is so*—This is my body! Luke adds to Matthew's and Mark's accounts the words **which is given for you,** which some ancient authorities omit, but they are confirmed by Paul's account (1 Cor. xi. 24), which reads, "This is my body which is for you."

To say that our Lord meant, This *represents* my body, is a shallow, unsatisfying and untenable explanation; and to compare His words with Joseph's interpretation of Pharaoh's dreams, "The seven good kine *are* seven years," etc., or with the words of the voice explaining to St. John, "The seven candlesticks *are* the seven churches," is to confound evident prophecy and tropical representation with the sober words of the institution of an ordinance which was to hold together the Church of Christ till the end of time, spoken by the Saviour of mankind on the eve of His separation from His disciples by death. It is to make this new institution of the Lord's Supper more *empty* than the old Passover, which it was to supplant by setting forth the reality of its fulfilment. On the other hand, compare these words with other sayings of Christ concerning Himself, such as, "I am the door," "I am the vine," "I am the way," "I am the true bread that cometh down from heaven." Christ *really is* all these things, and does not *represent* them! Here in Luke there is added to the words "This is my body" the further explanation *which is given for you*, as in Paul's account (1 Cor. xi. 24, Revision). And Paul, far from weakening in any sense the plain words of the institution, argues (1 Cor. x. 16), "The bread which we break, is it not the communion (that is, participation in) the body of Christ?" in this interrogative form strongly affirming the fact of a real participation in the real body of Christ, and he repeatedly sets forth the idea that we Christians "are members of his (Christ's) body"—of course he does not mean that we *represent* members of His body!

If rationalism, in the vein of the Capernaites in John vi., goes on to object that Christ's body was there visible before them, and in it He reached to them the bread, and therefore what He gave them could not be His body, we reply that this objection is based on the false notion that the *bread* was His body, and also on the false notion that there is no other way of partaking of Christ's body than the *natural* eating and drinking, in the same way that we eat and drink common food; and we refer such objectors to such passages as John iii. 13, where Jesus right *in Nicodemus' sight* spoke of Himself as "the Son of man which *is in heaven.*"

"It is a mystery; the touch of the Infinite for a moment through the material nerve of the finite; the presence of God allied to us, but infinitely above us. It is this very element of mystery against which the excessively rationalizing element in Protestantism revolts, which we need to have brought home to us" (DR. C. A. STORK).

This do in remembrance of me. These words, not found at all in the accounts of Matthew and Mark, but given by Paul in several forms, introduce the *memorial* idea of the supper. Those who make this supper *only* memorial, look at but one side of its nature and purpose, making naught of its life-giving power. They rest on what *they* do subjectively in remembering Christ's death; whereas evidently Christ in this sacrament sets before us and gives to us what He has done for us. "Christ our passover is sacrificed for us:" we are made partakers of Him in the holy supper, and our sins are passed over.

20. And the cup in like manner after supper, saying, This cup is the new covenant in my blood, *even* that which is poured out for you.

20. **And the cup in like manner** He took and after giving thanks gave it to them with words similar to those used with the bread. Matthew and Mark here repeat the details which Luke sums up in the expression "in like manner." This cup contained the customary red wine of the country, used during the passover festival. Luke says this was **after supper;** so does Paul (1 Cor. xi. 25, Revision), using exactly the same words as Luke, but our common version renders it by the misleading expression "when he had supped."

Jesus Himself did not partake of this cup. It may be that there was some considerable interval between the former and latter parts of the Lord's Supper.

This cup, said He, as He now handed it to the disciples, **is the new covenant in my blood.** So Paul gives it. Matthew and Mark have it, "This is my blood of the covenant." The several accounts are to be taken together as mutually explanatory. On this new covenant or testament, see Exod. xxiv. 8, with Heb. ix., and Jer. xxxi. 31–34, with Heb. viii. 6–13; also Zech. ix. 9–11. A "covenant" is an agreement or compact between two parties: a "testament" is a *will* or disposition of things in view of one's death, and is effective in consequence of that death. We are made partakers of the new covenant by becoming parties to it by faith.

This verse is to be explained in like manner as ver. 19, on which see comments. See Luther's Catechism on the nature and benefits of the Lord's Supper. "We use the terms true and real, to exclude the idea of a figurative or imaginary presence: and, substantial, to exclude a merely efficacious presence of the body and blood of Christ in the Holy Supper. We call it a sacramental presence, because the celestial objects in this mystery (the body and blood of Christ) are presented and bestowed through the medium of external sacramental symbols. This sacramental presence is, then, not a figurative, symbolic, or imaginary presence, neither is it a local presence, such as Christ had when He dwelt on earth amongst men; nor yet is it a merely influential, operative, and efficacious presence, resulting from His omnipresence as the God-man, which is described as sitting on the right hand of God, as being the fulness of Him that filleth all in all, as filling all things (Eph. i. 23, iv. 10), and concerning which He says Himself (Matt.

xxviii. 20), 'And, lo, I am with you alway, even unto the end of the world,' and (Matt. xviii. 20), 'Where two or three are gathered together in my name, there am I in the midst of them;' but it is a presence by which Christ communicates Himself to us in a mysterious, supernatural and incomprehensible manner " (H. ZIEGLER). In the Lord's Supper we are His guests, to be made partakers of whatever He therein gives us: for He provides the supper, not we. Hence our formula of administration of the bread is, "Take and eat, this is the body of Christ, given for thee:" and, for the wine, " Take and drink, this is the blood of the New Testament, shed for thy sins." What is required of communicants is truly believing hearts.

21–23. *But behold, the hand of him that betrayeth me is with me on the table. For the Son of man indeed goeth, as it hath been determined: but woe unto that man through whom he is betrayed! And they began to question among themselves, which of them it was that should do this thing.*

See on Matt. xxvi. 21–25; Mark xiv. 18–21; John xiii. 21–30,

Matthew and Mark put the pointing out of the traitor before the account of the institution of the Lord's Supper, and John does not give any account of the latter. It is a question that divides commentators, and is impossible of absolute decision, whether Judas was present at the institution of the Lord's Supper. Luke's account seems to indicate that he was: but many think that Luke, led by his narrative to speak first of the Supper as the great thing into which the Passover had turned, after recording it, returns to some things that took place before it and joins together the pointing out of the traitor; the contention among the Twelve, and the warning to Peter and them all. It is possible, also, that Jesus repeated His declaration about Judas, and that besides what Matthew and Mark relate, as having occurred before the Supper, we have Jesus' further remarks upon His imminent betrayal, spoken after it.

21. **But** marks contrast, a turn in the thought, **behold**, the instrument of my delivery into the hands of my murderous enemies, **the hand of him that betrayeth me**, that has already received (Matt. xxvi. 15) the price of his perfidy, in unblushing effrontery **is with me**, still, as if a friend, **on the table**, receiving and handing to others. As said the Psalmist (xli. 9). "Yea, my own familiar friend, which did eat of my bread, hath lifted up his heel against me." (Comp. John xiii. 18.)

22. **For.** Because. **As . . . determined** in the divine counsel. His way is appointed, even unto death. **But**, all the same, **woe**, untold, everlasting (see Matt. xxvi. 24, Mark xiv. 21) woe, shall be upon His betrayer, who will act in the freedom of his own will, against all the opportunities afforded him in the goodness of God.

23. It suffices Luke to make merely the general statement of their inquiry among themselves **which of them** it possibly was that should **do this thing**, this horrible thing of betraying Jesus!

24. And there arose also a contention among them, which of them is accounted to be greatest.

24. This is not the only intimation and record of **contention** among the twelve about being the **greatest**, who was to have precedence. This is the third time it occurred since the last (third) passover. See Luke ix. 46-48, more fully given in Mark ix. 33-37, where the dispute occurred up in Galilee and a little child was set before them as an object lesson of humility as the foundation of true greatness. See also Matt. xx. 20-28; Mark x. 35-45, where, later, while in Peræa, the ambitious request of James and

John occasioned a fresh breaking out of this dispute, on which occasion the Lord impressed on them the lesson of greatness by service. This later contention, of the text, may have occurred on the road to Jerusalem from Bethany, started by the fact that Peter and John had been sent to make ready the passover, or it may have occurred after arrival in the upper room and in connection with taking their places at the table. Besides Jesus' words of reproof and instruction in the matter, He gave them a most impressive object lesson in rising from the supper table and washing the disciples' feet (recorded only by John, xiii. 1–20).

25, 26. And he said unto them, The kings of the Gentiles have lordship over them: and they that have authority over them are called Benefactors.

But ye *shall* not *be* so: but he that is the greater among you, let him become as the younger; and he that is chief, as he that doth serve.

25. The expectation of the setting up of a visible kingdom by the Lord was probably an exciting occasion of this strife in the disciples' minds. Jesus points out a great difference between earthly kingdoms and the kingdom of heaven. **The kings of the Gentiles,** that is, of the nations of the world, **have lordship over them**, over the nations, their subjects. Such were the governments, east and west, in those days; and such they are now, except where modified by the influence of Christianity. **Are called Benefactors.** A name—($Εὐεργέτης$) often given to Roman Emperors and other princes, and coveted by them.

26. **But ye, not so.** Let them not in this be an example to you. Do not think the kingdom of heaven is to be animated by the principles and rules of governments of this world. **The greater among you, let him** show his title to such a place by humility, **become as the younger,** not seek place but give place. **He that is chief,**

the leader, let him prove this office by becoming **as he that doth serve**, the minister to others. True greatness, as He sees and recognizes it who only is Great, who knows, and whose judgment is perfect and final, consists in unselfish, loving service. True greatness is love. God is love! "Love suffereth long, and is kind; love envieth not; love vaunteth not itself, is not puffed up, doth not behave itself unseemly, seeketh not its own, is not provoked, taketh not account of evil; rejoiceth not in unrighteousness, but rejoiceth with the truth; beareth all things, believeth all things, hopeth all things, endureth all things. Love never faileth" (1 Cor. xiii. 4-8).

27. For whether is greater, he that sitteth at meat, or he that serveth? is not he that sitteth at meat? but I am in the midst of you as he that serveth.

27. Here Jesus instances His own example, "and the servant is not greater than his lord," "the disciple than his master." Jesus acknowledges the social distinction that **he that sitteth at meat is greater** than **he that serveth**. Nor did He interfere with social distinctions. But he showed an example that, observed by all, would take away any sting there may be in these distinctions. I, who indeed am the greater, **am in the midst of you,** mere men, sinful men, in many respects weak men, **as he that serveth.** The particular present act, setting this forth, was His washing their feet, but His whole life showed that He "came not to be ministered unto, but to minister." He commends this way as the way to become truly like Him, truly great. So different is the kingdom of God from the kingdoms of the world. Forget not to be *ministers*—whether technically so called, or not.

A chief trouble in the church is that so many "ministers" are miscalled and are found continually seeking their own, so dishonoring their calling and perverting positions of honor and trust to self-seeking and vain glory. And hence much strife (James iv. 1).

28-30. But ye are they which have continued with me in my temptations: and I appoint unto you a kingdom, even as my Father appointed unto me, that ye may eat and drink at my table in my kingdom; and ye shall sit on thrones judging the twelve tribes of Israel.

28. Here Jesus turns from His gentle reproach of their improper ambition to an acknowledgment of their general fidelity and suffering with Him, and to inspiring declarations concerning the future. Did He cast them down, and put them to service? Here He lifts them up and points them to glory. **But ye are they,** peculiar in the world, **which have continued with me,** my friends, in sympathy and love, **in my temptations.** So He characterizes His active ministry, touched with the feeling of our infirmities, tempted not once only, but all along from the wilderness to the cross, in all points like as we are.

29. **And I,** the Lord or Master, **appoint unto you.** This word "appoint" is in the Greek radically the same as the word covenant or testament, used in the institution of the Lord's Supper. It indicates a real "apportioning, giving over, bequeathing in an institution—in short, a testament" (STIER). LANGE says, "Through an institution, the sacrament." **Even as my Father appointed unto me.** The Master and the disciples are here made equally recipients of God's gift and appointment. What is that which is appointed, bequeathed, covenanted? A **kingdom.** "Your striving is for dominion and power, after the manner of the world; behold I give you *a kingdom*, an infinitely higher authority than *the kings of the Gentiles* have, no other than that which the Father hath given me. I lift you into *co-agents* with me. Thus is it afterwards. —In my kingdom ye shall eat and drink and judge with

me. All of them alike, without distinction in equal dignity, so that no envious contention could find place there.—Judas, the unfaithful one, however, was already excluded by verse 28, similarly to Matt. xix. 28. This kingdom of the Lord is now for the present *over* and *within* all the kingdoms of the world—that kingdom, viz., in which, having become members of his body through the participation of his blood, his disciples in the power of his spirit and of his love serve while they rule. But *one day* it will alone remain, after the fall of all other thrones and dignities " (STIER).

30. The same devout and distinguished commentator just quoted regards the **eat and drink at my table** as referring primarily to the eating and drinking at the Lord's Supper and not a mere conformity to the Jewish notion of the kingdom of God as a social feast. **And ye shall sit on thrones.** STIER regards this as containing " a mystery of the future manifestation." He says further, " The apostles indeed even now exercise dominion through the authority of their writings. But only certain of them; and it would be wrong to limit so massive a promise to a particular number of them. The ' sitting upon thrones ' is not spoken as if for children, who must have figures for everything; but when once ' the twelve apostles of the Lamb ' (not ' of Israel ') in the kingdom of reality rule over glorified humanity with Christ, as spiritual powers—the *thrones* also, according to the relations of the glorified state, will be real enough" (comp. 1 Cor. vi. 2, 3). That which *is to come* is not so clear as that which *has come*. By faith we look at the unseen, and wait to better know and understand.

31, 32. Simon, Simon, behold, Satan asked to have you, that he might sift you as wheat : but I made supplication for thee that thy faith fail not: and do thou, when once thou hast turned again, stablish thy brethren.

31. Between the former verses and these many harmonists place the washing of the disciples' feet, the pointing out of the traitor and the institution of the Lord's Supper. **The Lord** here calls His disciple by his natural name **Simon,** rather than by his spiritual name Peter, because what He foretells will proceed from the prevalence of the old, natural man. Observe the reality and personality here given to **Satan.. Asked to have you.** Comp. Job i. and ii., and observe that this prince of darkness can go only so far as he is allowed. **To sift you as wheat,** to toss you to the winds. The **you** is plural, and refers to all the disciples.

32. **But I made supplication for thee** (singular number, referring specially to Peter) as peculiarly needing intercession, **that thy faith fail not,** though shaken so. And believing, knowing His prayer would be answered and Peter rescued, Jesus adds, comfortingly, **when thou hast turned again** (notice the active voice of this verb), back from thy temporary fall, **stablish thy brethren,** become a strength to them. So he did.

33, 34. And he said unto him, Lord, with thee I am ready to go both to prison and to death. And he said, I tell thee, Peter, the cock shall not crow this day, until thou shalt thrice deny that thou knowest me.

See on Matt. xxvi. 33-36; Mark xiv. 29-31; John xiii. 37, 38.

33, 34. Peter was sincere in his protestation of unswerving fidelity: but he did not know himself as the Lord knew him. Here only in Luke does Jesus call this disciple **Peter,** his divinely given (John i. 42) spiritual name, used, perhaps, as a strength and comfort in view of the just spoken " Simon, Simon," etc., of ver. 31. In all this Jesus showed His knowledge of the heart and of the future, even to details. Time was marked by the cock crowing.

35-37. And he said unto them, When I sent you forth without purse, and wallet, and shoes, lacked ye anything? And they said, Nothing. And he said unto them, But now, he that hath a purse, let him take it, and likewise a wallet: and he that hath none, let him sell his cloke, and buy a sword. For I say unto you, that this which is written must be fulfilled in me, And he was reckoned with transgressors: for that which concerneth me hath fulfilment.

35-37. The general sense of these verses is that there is to be a significant *change* in the apostles' situation, calling for different modes of action. **When I sent you forth** is contrasted with **but now**. Then, without apparent resources and usual equipments, they nevertheless **lacked nothing** for accomplishing their mission. But this method was temporary and introductory. The Lord is about to be taken from them. What is written in Is. liii. 12, summarizing that significant chapter, **must be fulfilled** in Him. **That which concerneth me hath fulfilment**, completion, an end. Thereafter the disciples in fulfilling their mission must use **purse, wallet**, and even **sword**, all necessary human agencies of efficacy and defence, used in the spirit of the Master and in subjection to Him. Whilst principles remain the same, times and methods change. The disciples seem to be warned to do their utmost and not rely entirely, or too much, on supernatural agencies. In quoting Is. liii. 12 Jesus showed He knew the Scriptures and their application to Himself and all that was coming upon Him.

We too are under the like necessities and trials with these first disciples when Jesus was no longer visibly among them; and we are to meet them according to the principles here laid down.

38. And they said, Lord, behold, here are two swords. And he said unto them, It is enough.

38. Misunderstanding Him as though He spake of defence of Himself and them against what He predicted, they reported **two swords**, short swords worn at the girdle, as at hand, to which He replied, with a gentle touch of irony, ending the subject, **It is enough !**

39-42. And he came out, and went, as his custom was, unto the mount of Olives; and the disciples also followed him. And when he was at the place, he said unto them, Pray that ye enter not into temptation. And he was parted from them about a stone's cast; and he kneeled down and prayed, saying, Father, if thou be willing, remove this cup from me; nevertheless not my will, but thine, be done. And there appeared unto him an angel from heaven, strengthening him. And being in an agony he prayed more earnestly: and his sweat became as it were great drops of blood falling down upon the ground. And when he rose up from his prayer, he came unto the disciples, and found them sleeping for sorrow, and said unto them, Why sleep ye? rise and pray, that ye enter not into temptation.

See on Matt. xxvi. 30, 36-46; Mark xiv. 26, 32-42; John xviii. 1.

While they lingered in the large upper room of Jesus' friend, the Lord held those interesting and comforting discourses reported by John (xiv.-xvi.) and offered that great intercessory prayer (John xvii.).

39. **His custom.** See xxi. 37.

40. **The place.** Gethsemane. As far as He would go that night. The place where Jesus often resorted with His disciples (John xviii. 2). Matthew and Mark give more details, and say more of Jesus' own praying at this time. Luke here, as well as at ver. 46, notes His admonition to His disciples to **pray.** Who, in the face of this, can doubt or deny the propriety, the right, or the power of prayer? **That ye enter not into temptation.** The temptation would certainly come. Prayer would not prevent its coming, but thereby they might be strengthened so as to be able to bear it (1 Cor. x. 13). Thus they might avoid entering into temptation so as to be held and over-

come by it. Here is our great Saviour's method of anticipating and meeting temptation. By converse with God we receive grace for grace.

> " Prayer makes the Christian's armor bright,
> Restraining prayer we cease to fight."

41. The word translated **was parted** properly indicates violence: here it was the violence of Jesus' emotions that moved Him to go forward **about a stone's cast,** only a little way, to commune alone with God. He **kneeled down,** a posture corresponding to the sorrow of His soul (Matt. xxvi. 37, 38)—Matthew says He " fell on His face," which probably followed His kneeling down— **and prayed,** doing what He had warned the disciples to do, teaching by example as well as precept. Hear Him, the man divine, bearer of our sins, assaulted by Satan, who left Him in the wilderness only until occasion (Luke iv. 13) would offer again to compass His fall.

42. **Father,** says the Son, the only-begotten, He in whom the Father was ever well pleased, **Father, if thou be willing**—Matthew and Mark have it, "if it be possible : " if it had been possible, God would have been willing: He had come into the world saying, " Lo, I come to do thy will, O my God ; " now He prays conditionally. **Remove this cup from me.** The God-man's cry for deliverance. **Nevertheless,** notwithstanding my anguish and intense desire, **not my will, but thine, be done.** How often He declared He had no will contrary to that of His Father! So now, in the bitterest hour of His trial, He shows Himself " without blemish " of any want of harmony with God's purpose and plan. So He had taught the adopted ones to pray, " Thy will be done."

43. Here was an answer to Jesus' prayer. One of God's holy ministers to men, **an angel from heaven ap-**

peared unto him, in testimony that His prayer was heard and that He was dear to God, **strengthening him,** strengthening His human spirit, bringing Him moral support, and also strengthening His body through the influence of the mind. Here was heaven's testimony, which had been accorded Him all through His earthly pilgrimage. " Which things angels desire to look into" (1 Pet. i. 12).

44. But Jesus' case was desperate. He was **in an agony** that is indescribable and inappreciable by us. His mind so operated on His body that **his sweat became as it were great drops of blood falling down to the ground.** This was at or after midnight on a cold (John xviii. 18) night. Through the body, the house of the soul, His anguish was manifesting itself in an intensity that produced a bloody sweat. (For this must not be jejunely interpreted of the size or thickness of the drops of sweat. They were characterized by real blood, the physician Luke says.) Yet no one had laid hands on Him, and there was no manifest cause for any of these sorrows. Whence came they? Why did Jesus suffer so? Surely it was not a vivid apprehension of the pains of crucifixion which He knew He would suffer on the morrow; for men, and even women and children, have been known to look forward courageously, unfalteringly toward as great physical suffering. There is no reasonable explanation of this agony in the garden except that which the Scriptures give, that Jesus, the Lamb of God, was bearing the sin of the world (John i. 29, 36), as our last lesson said, " was reckoned among the transgressors," and was making " his soul an offering for sin " (Is. liii. 10), " made sin for us " (2 Cor. v. 21). And **he prayed more earnestly.** The other Evangelists represent Him as coming once and again to where Peter, James and John

were, and returning again to pray the same words. Hebrews v. 7 calls these utterances of Jesus "prayers and supplications with strong crying and tears;" says, too, that He "was heard in that he feared" (for His godly fear), and "yet, though he was a son, he learned obedience by the things which he suffered." The cup and the hour did *not* pass from Him without His drinking and enduring all that they brought. He had put in the condition "if it be possible:" it was *not* possible. "Without the shedding of blood"—"the life is in the blood" (Gen. ix. 4; Levit. xvii. 11, 14)—"there is no remission" of sins. Unfathomable as it may be by us, there must be sacrifice for sin; the why or the how is not so important for our realization as the *fact*. As far as mere physical, external power was concerned it was, of course, entirely possible for God to save Jesus—for Jesus to save Himself (comp. John xviii. 3-6)—from death. However, it is not written God is Power, but "God is Love." Jesus, therefore, must suffer, to become what He came to be, and what His name signifies, the *Saviour* of mankind. What a dreadful thing *sin* is, that it was *not possible* for Jesus to be spared His agony and death and yet sin be forgiven! What a feeble sense of sin most of us have! The answer to His prayer took the form of "an angel from heaven strengthening him," and so God said to Paul (2 Cor. xii. 9), "My grace is sufficient for thee:" and *so He says to us in every time of trouble*. These two instances of Jesus and Paul are remarkable ones, illustrating that we do not always get just what we ask for, especially when our requests are for exemption from temporal evils, but yet we are heard and receive grace to bear what cannot be removed. Jesus prayed thrice and Paul prayed thrice, and then they submitted, to bear what could not be removed. So we may pray and pray again; therein we will receive strength, but not necessarily just what we ask. But we should never *demand* anything of God!

45. **Sleeping for sorrow.** It is a psychological fact that their state of feeling might easily induce sleep in minds like theirs and at such an hour of night. The same disciples were sleepy on the mount of Transfiguration. The flesh is weak, indeed. Think of the God-man, the Master, pouring out His heart's blood in the agony of His effort to save mankind—while the disciples, even the chosen ones, sleep again and again within sight and sound of the Redeemer's agony! Poor human nature!

46. **Why sleep ye?** Sorrow may be great, weakness may be depressing: but these are not to be yielded to: **rise,** shake off lethargy, wake, **and pray:** for there is great need, because of great danger.

47-53. While he yet spake, behold, a multitude, and he that was called Judas, one of the twelve, went before them; and he drew near unto Jesus to kiss him. But Jesus said unto him, Judas, betrayest thou the Son of man with a kiss? And when they that were about him saw what would follow, they said, Lord, shall we smite with the sword? And a certain one of them smote the servant of the high priest, and struck off his right ear. But Jesus answered and said, Suffer ye thus far. And he touched his ear, and healed him. And Jesus said unto the chief priests, and captains of the temple, and elders, which were come against him, Are ye come out, as against a robber, with swords and staves? When I was daily with you in the temple, ye stretched not forth your hands against me: but this is your hour, and the power of darkness.

See on Matt. xxvi. 47-56; Mark xiv. 43-52; John xviii. 2-12.

47. **Went before them.** Peculiar to Luke, Judas is plainly with Jesus' enemies now; the treachery of his heart is now acting itself out. Judas is showing what he is, and fulfilling the Lord's prediction concerning him, given more than once. What is the traitor now going to do? **To kiss him!** That was the sign or token he had

given them. "Whomsoever I shall kiss, that is he." Ah, a Judas kiss, the emblem of love turned to a device of treason! According to the other Evangelists, he succeeded in defiling Jesus' cheek with his poisoned kisses. Luke merely relates Jesus' fine rebuke, showing His knowledge and dignity, **Judas, betrayest thou the Son of man with a kiss?**

49-51. Now the other disciples **saw what would follow.** The events taking place fast explained things Jesus had said to them before. Mysteries were clearing up through mysteries then taking place. What shall the disciples do? What can they do? Who will direct them now? **Lord, shall we smite with the sword?** they perplexedly cry, and straightway **one of them,** Peter, made a cut at the assailing crowd, **and cut off** Malchus' **right ear.** Peter meant it well; but when Jesus, a few hours before (see ver. 36), bade them provide themselves with purse and scrip and sword, He did not mean it for His defence. Legions of angels (Matt. xxvi. 53) were at His call, if He desired them. So the Lord, saying to those that had bound and were holding Him, **Suffer ye thus far,** and motioning as though to reach the wounded man, when they allowed Him the freedom of His arm as He desired, **touched his ear,** Malchus' ear, **and healed him,** exhibiting His love and healing power upon His enemies, and showing that He came not to destroy men's lives but to save them. This miracle seems to have made no impression on the heart of Malchus or of the crowd. They were bent on the one thing—to destroy Jesus.

52, 53. Luke alone represents the **chief priests and the elders** as among the crowd and as chiefly addressed in Jesus' words of keen remonstrance for the method they took and the false impression it naturally produced. **Daily,** openly, unarmed, undefended, **I was with you, in** the temple, the chief place of resort, and **ye stretched not forth your hands** to take me. Yet now ye bring the temple guard and search for me in this lone place under cover of the night! True enough, they wanted badly to lay hands on Him, but were afraid of the people. **But this is your hour,** He adds, remembering the Scriptures and all things concerning Himself that must be fulfilled. In all their proceedings there was nothing unexpected to Him who knew the Scriptures so well and yielded Himself up so willingly, in harmony with the testimony of those Scriptures concerning Himself.

And the power—the word used denotes delegated or conceded authority—**of darkness.** Some interpret this, literally, of the then midnight hour; others give it the ethical sense. As God is light, and all that is opposed to God is set forth as darkness, we must see here an acknowledgment of the temporary triumph, allowed by God, of all the powers of evil.

54. And they seized him, and led him *away*, and brought him into the high priest's house. But Peter followed afar off.

54. All the accounts, especially in connection with the statement in John xviii. 6, show that Jesus allowed Himself to be taken at their will. He was neither surprised, nor outwitted, nor overpowered. "He *gave himself* a ransom for all." They took Him to **the high priest's house.** John says they took Him first to Annas, father-in-law of Caiaphas the high priest, who had previously been high priest. It is not improbable that they lived in the same house. Annas seems to have given Jesus an informal examination, recorded in John xviii. 19–23, and then to have handed Him over to Caiaphas, who, along with many of the members of the Sanhedrin, gave Him a more formal examination, but yet not a legal one, since

no legal meeting of the Sanhedrin could be held before sunrise. Matthew and Mark report the informal examination and hint at the other, which was only a repetition of the former, whilst Luke relates more fully the formal examination and condemnation. Peter's denial, then, occurred in the time between the close of Annas' examination and the close of Caiaphas' examination before the morning rose. Some think there was only one examination, i. e. after daybreak, reported by Matthew and Mark by anticipation. The other view is better.

But Peter, who at first fled with the other apostles, **followed afar off,** at what he considered a safe distance. John appears to have returned from flight quicker and closer than Peter, as we read in John xviii. 15, 16. He entered in with Jesus into the court of the high priest, where he was known, and through him it was that Peter who was standing at the gate was admitted. On Peter's denial comp. Matt. xxvi. 58, 69-75; Mark xiv. 54, 66-72; John xviii. 15-18, 25-27.

55. And when they had kindled a fire in the midst of the court, and had sat down together, Peter sat in the midst of them.

55. These were the servants belonging to the establishment, and the officers under the Sanhedrin. There they all were gathered **in the midst of the court** or quadrangle around which the house was built, where they **had kindled a fire** that cool morning early in April. There they were sitting chatting around the fire and **Peter** in among them, listening rather than saying anything, busy with his thoughts.

56, 57. And a certain maid seeing him as he sat in the light *of the fire*, and looking stedfastly upon him, said, This man also was with him. But he denied, saying, Woman, I know him not.

56, 57. Women are curious—so are men! **Now a cer-**

tain maid, belonging to the establishment, scrutinizing Peter carefully, as he sat **in the light** of the fire, came up with the serious charge, **This man also was with him.** Peter was startled and quickly **denied** the impeachment, saying, **Woman, I know him not,** or rather, colloquially, "I don't know him, woman." Peter here took counsel of his fears. What he said was out of his lips almost before he knew it.

58. And after a little while another saw him, and said, Thou also art *one* of them. But Peter said, Man, I am not.

58. Presently **another,** this time a man, observing him and quickly concluding who he was, boldly charged, **Thou also art one of them,** one of these followers of Jesus. Peter thought to get off as well as before, and with some confusion and haste said, **Man, I am not.** Matthew speaks of another woman, and Mark (Revision) of the same maid again, as pointing Peter out to the bystanders, and say that he had moved out toward the door, into the forecourt, away from the fire, where he would be less observed; and Mark refers to the crowing of a cock about that time. No doubt Peter felt very much alone in that company, and on the defensive against all of them, who seemed, he thought, to be watching him.

59–62. And after the space of about one hour another confidently affirmed, saying, Of a truth this man also was with him : for he is a Galilæan. But Peter said, Man, I know not what thou sayest. And immediately, while he yet spake, the cock crew. And the Lord turned, and looked upon Peter. And Peter, remembered the word of the Lord, how that he said unto him, Before the cock crow this day, thou shalt deny me thrice. And he went out and wept bitterly.

59. There was not much respite for Peter. **About one hour** afterwards Satan came on with a fiercer attack.

Had Peter been strengthening himself in God meanwhile? It does not seem so. **Now another**, a man, supported by the by-standers, who had probably been talking the matter over, **confidently**, despite previous denials, **affirmed** that Peter surely belonged to Jesus' party, and gave as corroborative evidence, **for he is a Galilæan.**

60, 61. Peter replied again, **Man, I know not what thou sayest.** But when a kinsman of Malchus, whose ear Peter had cut off at the arrest, said, "Did not I see thee in the garden with him?" and when one and another affirmed that it was so, then Peter even began to curse and to swear to his denial (Matt., Mk.). **And immediately,** before the words were all off his lips, **the cock crew** again, and just then **the Lord,** who was probably in a room opening on the court or on a porch leading down to it, surrounded by His fierce accusers, **turned and looked upon Peter.** What a look of pitying compassion as well as reproof that must have been! Peter saw it and **remembered** the warning Jesus had so lately given him and the prophecy of his denial, now so minutely fulfilled.

62. **And he went out** of the court **and wept bitterly.** But his tears could not recall his words or undo his denial and his fall. Peter's downfall began with *self-confidence* and *unwatchfulness.* "Men fall in private long before they fall in public. The tree falls with a great crash, but the decay which accounts for it is often not discovered till it is down on the ground" (RYLE). Some will lie to get out of difficulty, and think it no harm; but one lie leads on to another, and he who denies his *Christian principle* therein denies Christ. External position does not secure our safety, but internal union with Christ. One apostle out of twelve became a traitor; another denied his Lord. It would, however, be false

logic to say that, therefore, there are no true disciples and religion is vanity and nothing.

> 63-65. And the men that held *Jesus* mocked him, and beat him. And they blindfolded him, and asked him, saying, Prophesy: who is he that struck thee? And many other things spake they against him, reviling him.

63-65. The account now returns to Jesus. Those who **held Jesus** at this time were Jewish officers, who sympathized with their rulers. They **mocked** Him in various ways. (Comp. Matt. xxvi. 67, 68 ; Mark. xiv. 65.) They **beat him,** boxing Him on the ear, slapping Him in the face, and even spat in His face. O holy, innocent, gentle Jesus, what shameful indignities put upon thee! The sinless one made sin for us! **And they blindfolded him,** mockingly bidding him **prophesy,** tell out, who struck Him at different times. All this was awful enough ; but Luke says there were **many other things** that entered into this shameless **reviling** of the meek and lowly, the pure and holy One.

> 66-69. And as soon as it was day, the assembly of the elders of the people was gathered together, both chief priests and scribes ; and they led him away into their council, saying, If thou art the Christ, tell us. But he said unto them, If I tell you, ye will not believe : and if I ask *you,* ye will not answer. But from henceforth shall the Son of man be seated at the right hand of the power of God.

66-69. **As soon as it was day** the Sanhedrin could hold a lawful session, and now they had their **assembly** to legally (in form) do what they had already determined on. Luke seems here to give us but the conclusion and sum of this proceeding. **If thou art the Christ, tell us.** What they wanted was to get an expression from Jesus' own lips which they could construe as blasphemy. Matthew reports that the high priest, alarmed at Jesus' silence and fearing he would not get the desired expression, put Him on oath " by the living God " (Matt. xxvi. 63).

Jesus knew them well, and their purpose. **If I tell you, ye will not believe ;** for ye are not seeking the truth, but to condemn me ; and ye have steadily refused to believe all the testimonies of heaven, earth and hell already given to me. **And if I ask,** that is, *question* **you, ye will not answer.** Jesus here charged them with not being honest and sincere, and with pretending to an examination into truth while they were seeking only a predetermined result. **But,** whatever you may do or think or say, **from henceforth,** rather, from this present time, from now on, **the Son of man,** even I, now apparently so helpless before you, in your toils, **shall be seated at the right hand of the power of God**—equal in power and glory. Yes, the Son of man, the God-man, will from now on appear what He is, and His position will vindicate His claim.

Matthew and Mark report Him also as telling them they will see Him "coming on the clouds of heaven."

70, 71. And they all said, Art thou then the Son of God? And he said unto them, Ye say that I am. And they said, What further need have we of witness? for we ourselves have heard from his own mouth.

70. Then, seeing He was so near a categorical reply, so near to exactly what they wanted, **they all said** with one accord, pressing upon Him for an answer, **Thou, then, art the Son of God ?** (He had called Himself, as usual, the Son of man, while claiming to be the Son of the Highest.) Jesus then replied, **Ye say that I am ;** that is, You are right, I am !

"In the days of His happier ministry, when they would have taken Him by force to make Him a king, He had kept His title of Messiah utterly in the background ; but now, at this awful decisive moment, when death was near,—when, humanly speaking, nothing could be gained, everything *must* be lost, by the avowal,—there thrilled through all the ages the solemn answer, 'I am'" (FARRAR).

71. If Jesus had denied what they asked Him, He would have been false like them. And now when He plainly told the truth about Himself, they construe it into blasphemy, and seek no **further witness.** The truth of God they turn into a lie. They judged Him worthy of death.

CHAPTER XXIII.

1. And the whole company of them rose up, and brought him before Pilate.

Comp., in connection with the first five verses, Matt. xxvii. 1, 2, 11-14; Mark xv. 1-5; John xviii. 28-38.

1. What Jesus' enemies were determined on was His death. Blasphemy by their law was punishable with death (Lev. xxiv. 16). But the Romans, now in power in Palestine, had reserved to themselves the right of inflicting the death penalty. Therefore, to accomplish their purpose, Jesus' enemies must go to **Pilate**, then Roman Procurator (Governor) of Judæa. Pilate was now at his official residence in Herod's palace in Jerusalem. Thither they went to secure legal sentence of death against Him.

2. And they began to accuse him, saying, We found this man perverting our nation, and forbidding to give tribute to Cæsar, and saying that he himself is Christ a king.

2. Arrived there **they began to accuse him**. But their accusation of blasphemy will avail nothing with Pilate. The Romans did not recognize the God of Israel, or count among crimes anything said or done against Him. So the Jews must resort to some other charge. Pilate would not take up such a general charge as that He was "an evil-doer." So they cunningly trump up a political charge. **We found this** one, this fellow (they will not even honor Him with His name), **perverting**, distracting, **our nation** (here they charge Him with what they them-

selves were doing—a not uncommon procedure even now among partisans and violent men), **and forbidding to give tribute to Cæsar** (which was the most galling thing they had to do, and deliverance from which, from almost any source, they would have welcomed with joy). They had, indeed, failed to get Him to compromise Himself with the Romans on this very matter (Luke xx. 20–26), and this charge was an unmixed lie. **Saying that he himself is Christ a king.** There was some truth in this, but it was so stated, and so combined with the preceding charge, as to produce a false impression, and was a malicious misrepresentation. When the people wanted to take Him and make Him such a king as they now suggested (John vi. 15), He withdrew from them. His late triumphal entry into Jerusalem illustrated the kind of king He was and professed to be: but that was open and before the Romans and they took no umbrage at it. But Pilate must guard Cæsar's interests, to protect his own.

3. And Pilate asked him, saying, Art thou the King of the Jews? And he answered him and said, Thou sayest.

3. John gives a much fuller account. Luke simply gives the question and answer, in which Jesus boldly affirms that He is the king of the Jews. The first two evangelists tell also that the chief priests and elders laid many accusations against Him, to which Jesus made no reply whatever, and remained equally silent when Pilate called His attention to them. (Comp. Is. liii. 7.) The Roman Procurator was struck with wonder at his prisoner; he had never encountered the like.

4. And Pilate said unto the chief priests and the multitudes, I find no fault in this man.

4. Here was his deliberate judgment—**I find no fault in this man.** The several accounts show that Pilate

formally expressed this judgment no less than four times, and that he in every way showed his belief of Jesus' innocence.

5. But they were the more urgent, saying, He stirreth up the people, teaching throughout all Judæa, and beginning from Galilee even unto this place.

5. Jesus' accusers began to fear they would be foiled after all, and **they were the more urgent** in the suit against Him. **He stirreth up the people,** they say, falsely again: for though multitudes attended and followed Jesus, there never was any attempt at a political stir, which was here meant, but everything to the contrary. **Teaching.** Yes, this was true, but all His teaching tended to order and better conduct among all classes. Their accusation here is a side-light on the extent of Jesus' ministry and influence. **Throughout all Judæa, beginning from Galilee.** "Not without hostile intentions have the Jews named Galilee, since the hatred of the Procurator against the Galileans and against Herod was well known to them; they hope therewith to engage him the more against our Saviour, as a Galilean" (VAN OOST.). Comp. Luke xiii. 1.

6, 7. But when Pilate heard it, he asked whether the man were a Galilæan. And when he knew that he was of Herod's jurisdiction, he sent him unto Herod, who himself also was at Jerusalem in these days.

6, 7. If such was their design they were disappointed in it. **He sent him to Herod** as Tetrarch of Galilee—most persons think, to get rid of a troublesome case; others suggest, in the hope of getting a favorable opinion from Herod, to strengthen his own judgment of "no fault in him," or, at least, to get some further light in the matter. **Herod was at Jerusalem in these days** of the Feast, as a Jew in religion.

8. Now when Herod saw Jesus, he was exceeding glad: for he was of a

long time desirous to see him, because he had heard concerning him; and he hoped to see some miracle done by him.

8. Remember what sort of man this Tetrarch was. He was a Herod—and that is saying a good deal. It was he who so shamelessly abandoned his own wife for his brother Philip's wife. At her fiendish instigation he had cut off John the Baptist's head, and, conscious of guilt, was presently startled at what he heard about Jesus, and cried out, "It is John the Baptist; he is risen from the dead; and therefore mighty works do show forth themselves in him" (Matt. xiv. 2). See Luke ix. 7–9. That now **he was exceeding glad** to see Jesus only illustrates his curiosity. **Some miracle done by him.** Herod looked upon Jesus as a wonder-worker. " Jesus was to entertain him, as a mighty magician, divert him, or perhaps foretell luck to his egotistic superstition; anything else he sought not of Him" (LANGE).

9, 10. And he questioned him in many words: but he answered him nothing. And the chief priests and the scribes stood, vehemently accusing him.

9, 10. So Herod **questioned him in many words.** The nature of his questions is not given; but they were not heart questions, evidently. Herod was none concerned for his soul. Doubtless his questions were prompted by curiosity. **But he answered him nothing.** Jesus did not deign him a word: He never satisfied mere curiosity, by either word or work. Nor could the vehemence of the Jewish authorities move the Innocent to a single word in reply. "As a sheep before her shearers is dumb, so he opened not His mouth " (Is. liii. 7). Speaking silence!

11. And Herod with his soldiers set him at nought and mocked him, and arraying him in gorgeous apparel sent him back to Pilate.

11. A pretty business for **Herod with his soldiers,** to

set at nought, mock, deride an innocent, seemingly helpless prisoner! Royal and soldierly conduct, indeed! "The priests accuse the Saviour, the courtiers mock him. With the first it is hatred, with the others contempt that strikes the key. Scoffing is here the vengeance of insulted pride, and reveals itself in a peculiar form" (VAN OOST.). He **arrayed him in a gorgeous robe** [ἐσθῆτα λαμπράν] —not the purple robe afterwards put on Him by the Roman soldiers (Matt. xxvii. 28; Mark xv. 17; John xix. 2, 5); but probably a shining white one (as the same words signify in xxiv. 4 and Acts x. 30), the Jewish royal color, and **sent him back to Pilate.** Thus little did he do to protect his subject; thus much to humiliate and insult and give Him over to the Romans. "He could and ought rather to have dismissed him. Therefore in sending back the innocent to Pilate, he involved himself in Pilate's guilt. Acts iv. 27" (BENGEL).

12. And Herod and Pilate became friends with each other that very day: for before they were at enmity between themselves.

12. The cause of the previous **enmity** between these two rulers is not certainly known. It may have been the massacre of Galileans mentioned in Luke xiii. 1; it may have been a disputed point of jurisdiction, in which each of them seems to yield to the other by the sending of Jesus back and forth. "This result, however, appears at any rate remarkable enough to the delicate psychologist, Luke, not to be passed by unmentioned. In view of the general publicity of this unexpected reconciliation, this remark affords at the same time an indirect but yet a very strong proof of the truth of the event related" (VAN OOST.). **That very day they became friends.**

13-16. And Pilate called together the chief priests and the rulers and the people, and said unto them, Ye brought unto me this man, as one that perverteth the people; and behold, I, having examined him before you, found no fault in this man touching those things whereof ye accuse him: No, nor yet Herod; for he sent him back unto us: and behold, nothing worthy of death hath been done by him. I will therefore chastise him, and release him.

13, 14. The Roman Procurator, much to his perplexity, still had Jesus on his hands. The decision of the case reverts again to him. He, therefore, **called together** not only the Jewish authorities, but **the people** also, to state to them his decision. He evidently wanted to keep on the good side of the Jews. He outlined the situation, stating that they were the prosecutors—**Ye brought to me this man,** and the crime alleged—**as one that perverteth the people** (see ver. 2), a disturber of the peace, an inciter of insurrection: then the examination and its results—**Behold, I,** who indeed am most solicitous to prevent such things and am entirely competent to judge of them, **having examined him,** and that, **before you** (as well as privately, John xviii. 33–38), **found no fault** in Him such as alleged.

15, 16. Now he added the judgment of Herod to his own—**he sent him back** without any sentence, and clearly **nothing worthy of death hath been done by him.** " He hath done no violence, neither was any deceit in his mouth" (Is. liii. 9). **I will therefore chastise him and release him.** But why, O judge, chastise an innocent man, one so oft pronounced innocent by thyself? Ah, here Pilate shows his weakness, leans to policy, and shows he does not want to hurt the Jews' feelings too much, enough to make them still more hostile to him. Had Pilate been *a man* he would have said, " The prisoner is dismissed !"

Ver. 17, which reads, in parentheses, in the " Authorized Version," " For of necessity he must release one unto them at the feast," is found in many ancient authorities, and is so inserted in the margin of the "Revised Version," but is excluded from the text. What it states is, however, a fact. A custom had grown up, which came to have the authority of an unwritten law, of releasing a prisoner, of the Jews' choice, at the passover. It may have been a symbolic setting forth of the passover idea—release from bondage, release from sin, free grace. Pilate, as Matthew and John both show, now had recourse to this custom, thinking *the people* would, of course, prefer Jesus to the other notable prisoner then in bonds, as they would not be influenced by the envy which he clearly saw influenced their chief priests and other rulers. Probably at this stage of the proceedings the word from Pilate's wife (Matt. xxvii. 19) was brought, urging him to keep hands off "that just man." Meanwhile the chief priests and elders used the opportunity to persuade the crowd to prefer Barabbas and call for his release.

18, 19. But they cried out all together, saying, Away with this man, and release unto us Barabbas: one who for a certain insurrection made in the city, and for murder, was cast into prison.

18, 19. **But, unexpectedly to the Procurator, they cried out all together,** the people along with their rulers, **Away with this man**—" He was despised and rejected of men, and as one from whom men hide their face he was despised" (Is. liii. 3)—**and release unto us Barabbas.** The Evangelist explains who this Barabbas was; that **for an insurrection and for murder** he was held a prisoner. (See also ver. 25.) He was a double criminal, guilty by both Roman and Jewish law. He had done what the chief priests had falsely charged against Jesus. But they plead *for* him and *against* Jesus. Anything to get rid of Jesus! (Comp. Matt. xxvii. 15–26; Mark xv. 6–15; John xviii. 39, 40.)

20, 21. And Pilate spake unto them again, desiring to release Jesus; but they shouted, saying, Crucify him, crucify him.

20. **Again** Pilate **spake** for Jesus, **desiring to release** Him. But what a spectacle—a man in authority, knowing the right, having declared the right, representative of a great world-power whose boast was the protection it gave its citizens, a man whose very position made him the defender of the innocent, the strength of the weak, and yet now almost begging of the multitude to let him do the right!

21. But they saw his timidity, they knew their man, and now **they shouted** their deprecation of his purpose and their will concerning Jesus, **saying, Crucify, crucify him!** They were like wild beasts close on to their prey. Pilate's hesitation made them only the more defiant; they will make the Roman Procurator do the will of the Jews this time at all events!

Where at this time are all those who, six days before, so enthusiastically shouted, " Hosanna; blessed be the king that cometh in the name of the Lord," etc.? Ah, they were now in the background; another crowd now has sway, and it is headed by the rulers and, therefore, has more sway. That was their hour, this is the hour of the power of darkness, that is using the Sanhedrin and the persuaded multitudes as its instruments. Jerusalem was full of multitudes upon multitudes at this passover time.

22. And he said unto them the third time, Why, what evil hath this man done? I have found no cause of death in him: I will therefore chastise him and release him.

22. **The third time,** and even oftener, as John xix. 4-16 shows, Pilate pronounces a judgment of acquittal, and shows he *ought* to release Him, but also at the same time shows his desire to please the Jews by proposing, as

a compromise, to **chastise him**, and this in the same breath with the question, **Why, what evil hath this man done?** The "why" here is a translation of the Greek γάρ, which is used for illustration and confirmation; it is not an interrogative, but an inferential word.

No cause of death in him. No: He "died for us;" the cause was in us. " The Lord of glory dies for men."

<small>23. But they were instant with loud voices, asking that he might be crucified. And their voices prevailed.</small>

23. **They were instant,** urgent, they lay upon him, **with loud voices** of excitement and determination, **asking that he might be crucified.** Neither Jesus' character, known everywhere, nor His works, equally famous and always beneficent, nor the Roman's voice were listened to by this howling mob, but only their wilful prejudice. **And their voices prevailed.** " Him," said Peter (Acts ii. 23), speaking to the " men of Israel," " being delivered up by the determinate counsel and foreknowledge of God, ye by the hands of lawless men did crucify and slay:" and, again addressing them, (Acts iii. 13) said, " Whom ye delivered up, and denied before the face of Pilate, when he had determined to release him. But ye denied the Holy and Righteous One, and asked for a murderer to be granted unto you." So in a prayer of the early church they said (Acts iv. 27, 28), " For of a truth in this city against thy holy servant Jesus, whom thou didst anoint, both Herod and Pontius Pilate, with the Gentiles and the peoples of Israel, were gathered together to do whatsoever thy hand and thy counsel foreordained to come to pass."

<small>24. And Pilate gave sentence that what they asked for should be done.</small>

24. Here the man who began by showing a craven timidity, who went on to *compromise*, at last yielded en-

tirely and his **sentence** was not for justice and right, nor for the convictions of his own judgment and conscience, but for **what they asked.** The court submitted to the mob. And has it not been so since Pilate's day, when weak, truculent men have sat in the place of God? The man has been handed down to unenviable notoriety, and his false and wicked judgment remembered constantly among the best people of earth, in those words of the Creed, " Suffered under Pontius Pilate."

25. And he released him that for insurrection and murder had been cast into prison, whom they asked for; but Jesus he delivered up to their will.

25. "The righteous for the unrighteous, that he might bring us to God" (1 Pet. iii. 18). And not only was Barabbas then **released** from man's prison, but every sinner who will penitently plead Jesus as his Redeemer, was released from the bondage of sin and the eternal prison of despair.

26-32. And when they led him away, they laid hold upon one Simon of Cyrene, coming from the country, and laid on him the cross, to bear it after Jesus.
And there followed him a great multitude of the people, and of women who bewailed and lamented him. But Jesus turning unto them said, Daughters of Jerusalem, weep not for me, but weep for yourselves, and for your children. For behold, the days are coming, in which they shall say, Blessed are the barren, and the wombs that never bare, and the breasts that never gave suck. Then shall they begin to say to the mountains, Fall on us; and to the hills, Cover us. For if they do these things in the green tree, what shall be done in the dry?
And there were also two others, malefactors, led with him to be put to death.

26. See on Matt. xxvii. 32; Mark xv. 21.

After Jesus is peculiar to Luke. Some suggest that, possibly, Simon may have carried one end of the cross after Jesus who was bearing the other. (See John xix. 17.)

27. The **great multitude** was a natural accompaniment of such an occasion and scene, especially in the then over-crowded city. Among them were all sorts of people, friends and foes (mostly these) of Jesus and the indifferent rabble. Among them, in considerable numbers, were **women** of the city (see next verse) who, according to their natural tenderness of feeling, leaning to mercifulness, possibly believing that Jesus was getting unjustly treated, **bewailed and lamented him** to such an extent as to be noticed amid the general din. It is sweet to notice that, though woman brought sin into the world, she is never, in the sacred history, noted as reproaching the Saviour, whom she also brought into the world!

28. **Jesus** noted it. **Turning unto them** with a chivalry divine, He addressed them. **Daughters of Jerusalem.** This shows who they were, and distinguishes them from the ministering women from Galilee. **Not for me.** Self-forgetful still, thoughtful for others while going to His own execution. God is love. **But weep for yourselves, and for your children.** Words of warning, followed by prophecy. Comp. His own tears (xix. 41–44) over Jerusalem. This is the only place in the record where Jesus bade men weep. "The same lips whose gracious breath had dried so many tears, now cries on the way to the cross: *Weep*—for yourselves and your children" (DRASEKE). See in Matt. xxvii. 25 the people's imprecation on themselves.

29. **Days are coming** upon Jerusalem, this generation and their children, the awful woes of which shall reverse men's judgment of who are **blessed.** Then home shall be undone and the sweetest joys of life be counted bitterness: then, in view of the awful judgments at hand and impending, **the barren** and sterile, the childless, shall be counted blessed!

30. At that time people shall even make their suit to dumb and heartless nature, to escape the terrors of men. Reference is to the destruction of Jerusalem. Comp. Rev. vi. 12-17, descriptive of the great day of the wrath of Him that sitteth on the throne and of the Lamb.

31. This is an aphorism of *a fortiori* argument (Comp. Jer. xlix. 12; Ezek. xx. 47; Prov. xi. 31; 1 Pet. iv. 17, 18). **The green tree** is not naturally for burning, whereas **the dry** is. Jesus, the innocent, the sinless, is not the natural and proper object of judgment, but sinners, especially those of Jerusalem, are. If now **these things**, as then going on, were done to Him, what would be done to Jerusalem and its inhabitants by the Romans—and by the angels of judgment to incorrigible sinners at the last day? "If they do these things in me, fruitful, always green, undying through the divinity—what will they do to you, fruitless and robbed of all life-giving righteousness?" (THEOPHYLACT.)

32. **Two others** (ἕτεροι), different from Him in that they were **malefactors**, evil-doers, "robbers." (See xxii. 37 and Is. liii.)

33-38. And when they came unto the place which is called The skull, there they crucified him, and the malefactors, one on the right hand and the other on the left. And Jesus said, Father, forgive them; for they know not what they do. And parting his garments among them, they cast lots. And the people stood beholding. And the rulers also scoffed at him, saying, He saved others; let him save himself, if this is the Christ of God, his chosen. And the soldiers also mocked him, coming to him, offering him vinegar, and saying, If thou art the King of the Jews, save thyself. And there was also a superscription over him, THIS IS THE KING OF THE JEWS.

See on Matt. xxvii. 33-37; Mark xv. 22-26; John xix. 16-27.

33. The traditional site is near the "Church of the Holy Sepulchre," in the northwest part of the city: but

recent investigations point to a knoll, resembling a **skull** in its contour, outside the Damascus gate, on the northeast, as the true site.

34. It may have been while they were fastening Jesus to the cross that He said, **Father, forgive them; for they know not what they do.** Luke alone records it. This is the first of the seven words from the cross, and at the same time expresses the whole meaning of the crucifixion—that *sinners might be forgiven!* Such is the continual prayer the cross of Jesus pours into the Father's ear! Moreover, here Jesus exemplified the spirit which He taught (Matt. v. 44, 45; comp. Rom. v. 8). This prayer was made for Romans and Jews, representatives of *mankind* in this act of crucifixion. "They know not what they do" was not a *ground* for forgiveness, but an argument for mercy. They *ought* to have known better than they did. So far as the soldiers were concerned they were mere executioners, and not responsible for the act otherwise.

35. **And the people stood beholding,** just as they now do at a public execution. **And the rulers also,** the Jewish religious authorities, forgetting alike justice, mercy and dignity, **scoffed at** the crucified one, in their blind madness fulfilling the Scriptures (Ps. xxii. 7, 8), and thus becoming a testimony to their victim as being the Christ. **He saved others.** Yes, that they could not deny. Everywhere were living evidences of His saving power. But, with extreme malignity, they brought this up as a taunt in contrast with what seemed His present weakness —**let him save himself!** But that He could not do, if He were to carry out His eternal purpose of *saving others.* Voluntarily He took the place of these *others*, and if they are to be saved He must suffer; and therefore came He forth from the bosom of the Father, and **the chosen**

became **the Christ of God** (*anointed* Prophet, Priest and King) of our redemption. Thus their very ridicule has become a historical proof of Jesus' being that which they mocked Him for professing to be.

36, 37. The rough and heartless **soldiers also** readily joined in jeers at the poor sufferer, **coming to him, offering him vinegar,** that is, the sour wine which they were accustomed to drink, and which, perhaps, they were then taking in connection with their lunch as they watched by the cross. And, taking up the Jewish rulers' cry of **Save thyself,** they taunted both Him and them by calling Him **King of the Jews,** as the title over His head named him.

38. The slight variations in the wording of the title over Jesus' head may be accounted for from the fact that it was written in three different languages and would not be expressed in them precisely alike.

39. And one of the malefactors which were hanged railed on him, saying, Art not thou the Christ? save thyself and us.

39. It was not enough that soldiers, Sanhedrin, bystanders, the gaping crowd, mocked Jesus' agony. **One of the malefactors,** on the cross by His side, either from hope or from hardened bravado, joined in and **railed on him.** What a scene! Stand by and learn something of the true nature of sin! Behold mankind! **Art thou not the Christ?** (Then) **save thyself and us.**

Crucified amid malefactors. Derided, mocked, railed on. Yet having done nothing amiss. How can it be accounted for, but that He was "made sin on our behalf?" (2 Cor. v. 21.)

40–43. But the other answered, and rebuking him said, Dost thou not even fear God, seeing thou art in the same condemnation? And we indeed justly; for we receive the due reward of our deeds: but this man hath done nothing amiss. And he said, Jesus, remember me when thou comest in thy kingdom. And he said unto him, Verily I say unto thee, To-day shalt thou be with me in Paradise.

40. **But the other**—though from the accounts of Matthew and Mark it seems he too at first joined in the derision—now repentant, **answered, rebuking** his fellow. They were all in an awful plight. Soon their spirits would go to God. **Dost thou not even fear God,** then? The human tribunal has judged us, and we are paying the last possible penalty it can inflict. But there is yet the judgment of God, to which we are going. Wilt thou, then, thus wantonly revile one **in the same condemnation** with thyself?

41. **And we indeed justly** have been condemned. Here is his penitent acknowledgment. Jesus was listening to it. "Confess your faults one to another that ye may be healed." **But this man hath done nothing amiss.** One voice alone lifted up for Jesus on the cross! Had this robber known before of Jesus' life and teachings? Had he, perhaps, heard something of the trial, and learned how hard a time the malignant Jews had to get Him condemned? Somewhere and somehow he has learned about Jesus, and here testifies to Him.

42. Then turning his head to the central figure, to Jesus Himself, he cried, **Jesus, remember me when thou comest in** (not "into") **thy kingdom.** This robber was a Jew, and knew of an expected Messiah. He may have heard "the kingdom of heaven" preached by John and Jesus and their disciples as *nigh;* he finds himself beside one crucified as "King of the Jews," and for no other crime; his ideas of the kingdom are probably incorrect and very crude; but he ventures his hopes on this Jesus as King, yet to triumph, and begs remembrance in that unknown future. It is remarkable faith. Here, then,

repentance appears in its double sense of turning *from sin* and *to Christ*—it is evangelical penitence. " If we confess our sins, he is faithful and righteous to forgive us our sins, and to cleanse us from all unrighteousness."

43. So Jesus answered, **Verily I say unto thee**—speaking like a king, though dying on the cross—**To-day** (already, without long waiting for the coming kingdom) **shalt thou be with me in Paradise.** Where was that? Not the place to which He ascended bodily after the resurrection. (See John xx. 17; Acts i. 9-11.) The *word* paradise is Greek, derived from the Persian, and was applied to kings' courts and grounds, places of beauty and delight. It is used in the Septuagint for garden, in Gen. ii. 8, where we read that *God planted a paradise in Eden.* The word occurs but three times in our Bible; here and in 2 Cor. xii. 4, and Rev. ii. 7. The *idea* of paradise in the common popular belief was that of a far-off land of rest and peace, a region of the world of the dead. The patriarchs Abraham, Isaac, and Jacob were there, ready to receive their faithful descendants. To recline with Abraham and Isaac and Jacob, to be in Abraham's bosom (Luke xvi. 23, compare John xiii. 23, 25), was the Jews' mode of expressing the blessedness of the future state. In such blessedness, with Jesus, the dying robber is assured by the Saviour he shall be that very day. The souls of believers do at death immediately enter into rest. " Hades," or the place of departed spirits, embraced all the dead, believing and unbelieving; but between the two there is a " great gulf fixed." (See Luke xvi. 19-28. Comp. 1 Pet. iii. 18-20.)

But where would the other malefactor go? Into the spirit world, indeed ; but not into " paradise ;" not to be with Jesus. He cried for temporal deliverance (ver. 39), and, while acknowledging (in words at least) Christ, at the same time railed on Him in the spirit of his unchanged, natural heart; this one, acknowledging his sins as well as Christ, called upon Him for eternal salvation, and, as he looked, so he lived! (John iii. 14, 15; Numb. xxi. 8, 9). He was a brand snatched from the burning.

Speaking of the penitent robber's case, PROF. KENDRICK says, "It is the gospel's pledge of mercy to the sinner *in extremis*. The divine record contains *but* one such example; but it contains *one; but* one, to save us from despair." Remember, there was one dying sinner there unsaved, right by the cross of Jesus.

44-46. *And it was now about the sixth hour, and a darkness came over the whole land until the ninth hour, the sun's light failing: and the veil of the temple was rent in the midst. And when Jesus had cried with a loud voice, he said, Father, into thy hands I commend my spirit: and having said this, he gave up the ghost.*

See on Matt. xxvii. 45-53; Mark xv. 33-38; John xix. 28-30.

44. It satisfies the original language to suppose the **darkness** covered only Judæa or Palestine, though secular history speaks of it as having been noticed in Egypt. **The sun's light failing,** is Luke's explanation of it. This could not have been an ordinary eclipse, for this can occur only at new moon, whereas this was at the time of full moon. The darkness was supernatural, whatever agencies God may have used in producing it. It was an object lesson, setting forth the horror of the creation at such treatment of the Creator. So also there was a shudder of the earth, the Crucified's handiwork sympathizing with its Lord.

46. During the darkness an oppressive, awful silence seems to have settled upon all—oh, how oppressed with the world's sins Jesus' heart must have been—till toward its close He **cried with a loud voice,** that cry of abandon-

ment, unparalleled in the world's history, which marked His most real death, which is separation from God, the offering of His soul (Is. liii. 10)—" My God, my God, why hast thou forsaken me?" Quickly following this came the other voices from the cross, the last, recorded by Luke, also in a loud voice, such voice showing His physical strength comparatively unimpaired. The centurion noted this loud outcry and speedy death thereupon as something unusual (Mark xv. 39). Though He had said, "My God, my God, why hast thou forsaken me?" now He says **Father.** "His soul," remarks *Godet*, "has recovered full serenity. Not long ago He was struggling with the divine sovereignty and holiness. Now the darkness is gone; He has recovered His light—His Father's face. It is the first effect of the completion of redemption, the glorious prelude of the resurrection." **Into thy hands I commend my spirit.** The last words from the cross, and these Scripture words. (See Ps. xxxi. 5.) Who, after this, will have the hardihood to say there is no immortal spirit, but that man is altogether *material*. The *unseen* is as *real* as the *seen*. (Comp. Eccles. xii. 7 and Acts vii. 59.) Thereupon **he gave up the ghost.** All this is one word in the Greek, and may be expressed in our one word "expired." The verb is active. Surely it was not the wounds in His hands and feet that caused His death. Remember that *loud voice!* The thieves had to have their legs broken to hasten their death. Pilate wondered that Jesus was *already* dead. But the soldiers, good authority on such a subject, assured him of the fact. Physicians who have studied the subject say the flow of water and blood which followed the drawing of the soldier's spear from Jesus' side could have come only from the pericardium, or sack in which the heart is enclosed, and indicates a previous *bursting of the heart*, and this is held to have been the *physical cause* of Jesus' death. Such effect might well have followed the burden of the world's sins, and been a consequence of the accumulating agony. (See on John xix. 35.) Jesus' will, by which He *offered Himself* in the first place, sustained Him till He could say, "It is finished," and then He yielded and expired.

"All we who were baptized into Christ Jesus were baptized into his death." "Even so reckon ye also yourselves to be dead unto sin." (See Rom. vi. 1–23.)

47. And when the centurion saw what was done, he glorified God, saying, Certainly this was a righteous man.

47. **When the centurion** who had had supervision of the crucifixion of Jesus and the robbers, **saw what was done.** He had also been present at the trial, a close observer, apparently, of everything that had passed and was transpiring. Mark (xv. 39) mentions the fact "that he so gave up the ghost" as greatly impressing the centurion. Comp. Mark xv. 44, 45. **He glorified** God by the testimony and confession he then made. What he said is given variously by the several Evangelists. **Certainly this was a righteous man.** Then He was all He professed to be. The centurion had heard Him charged at the trial with professing to be the Son of God (John xix. 7). The centurion now professes his belief that He was this. Lange notes the triumvirate of Roman soldiers bearing testimony to Christ—the centurion in Capernaum (Matt. viii. 5–10), the one here mentioned, and Cornelius at Cæsarea (Acts. x).

48, 49. And all the multitude that came together to this sight, when they beheld the things that were done, returned smiting their breasts. And all his acquaintance, and the women that followed with him from Galilee, stood afar off, seeing these things.

48. These **multitudes,** crowds that gathered about this spectacle of an execution, **beheld** more than they had anticipated in **the things that were done.** With signs of amazed apprehension, **smiting their breasts,** in oriental style, they were returning to their various abodes, unsatisfied.

49. **All his acquaintance,** unable to do anything for Him, like stricken deer, had to be content with a position **afar off.** "Lover and friend hast thou put far from me, and mine acquaintance into darkness" (Ps. lxxxviii. 18). Among them were the Galilean **women,** among whom, for a while at least and on occasion pressing nearer to the cross (comp. John xix. 25-27), was His mother. See Simeon's prophecy, Ch. ii. 34, 35, fulfilled.

50-56. And behold, a man named Joseph, who was a councillor, a good man and a righteous (he had not consented to their counsel and deed), *a man* of Arimathæa, a city of the Jews, who was looking for the kingdom of God: this man went to Pilate, and asked for the body of Jesus. And he took it down, and wrapped it in a linen cloth, and laid him in a tomb that was hewn in stone, where never man had yet lain. And it was the day of the Preparation, and the sabbath drew on. And the women, which had come with him out of Galilee, followed after, and beheld the tomb, and how his body was laid. And they returned, and prepared spices and ointments.

See on Matt. xxvii. 57-61; Mark xv. 42-47; John xix. 38-42.

50, 51. **A good,** excellent, **man** and **righteous,** just, as his conduct showed in not consenting to the Sanhedrin's **counsel,** plot (shown in Matt. xxvi. 3-16; Luke xxii. 2-6), **and deed,** correspondent therewith. Neither numbers nor plausible representations could sway this true man from what was right. We need such men now in counsels of both church and state.

52, 53. Timid, not without reason, he now did the bold thing of claiming Jesus' body, and, with the aid of

Nicodemus gave it decent, customary burial in his own rock-hewn tomb, which happily happened to be near at hand, and, fittingly, **where never man had yet lain.** (Comp. John xix. 41.) In like manner Luke notes of the ass on which Jesus rode into the city the first day of that week, that " no man ever yet sat " on it.

54. The word rendered **drew on** here is the same that is used for " began to dawn " (*margin*); but it is generally understood here of the beginning of the Sabbath day that evening.

55, 56. **The women,** named by other evangelists, the well-known ministrants from Galilee, composed the sad, short funeral train. They carefully observed everything thereabouts, **and how his body was laid,** revolving in their minds what they would do. **They prepared spices and ointments** to complete His proper burial, ready for the earliest dawn of the first day, but **on the Sabbath they rested according to the commandment.** According to Mark (xvi. 1) these spices were bought " when the Sabbath was passed," i. e. after 6 o'clock in the evening. This is the more likely, as it was probably as late as that when the women left the sepulchre, and the Sabbath would have already begun.

CHAPTER XXIV.

1. But on the first day of the week, at early dawn, they came unto the tomb, bringing the spices which they had prepared.

1. Thus **the first day of the week** became its crowning day, "the best of all the seven." **At early dawn** those devoted Christian women were up and going toward the **tomb.** Their drawing to Jesus, even though dead (as they thought), was intense. Yet they had observed the Sabbath. **Bringing the spices** of which the last verse of preceding chapter tells. 'Tis well to be "fore-handed" for Jesus' service, even though our preparations may afterwards be found to have been unnecessary.

2. And they found the stone rolled away from the tomb.

2. The stone used to close sepulchres was generally very large and heavy. These women were ignorant of the seal that had been put on this stone the day before. It was unexpected, and naturally startling, that they **found the stone rolled away,** as they got nearer. It was on this discovery that one of them, Mary Magdalene, jumping to the conclusion that Jesus' body had been carried elsewhere by some unknown party, immediately turned back and hastened to report this to Peter and John (John xx. 2).

3. And they entered in, and found not the body of the Lord Jesus.

3. **Entered.** This shows the tomb's large size. But they **found not** what they sought, **the body of the Lord**

Jesus. How bewildered they must have been! What has happened? Where is He? Who has been here? Can they not have the poor privilege of performing the last sad rites upon the body of the blessed Jesus?

> 4-7. And it came to pass, while they were perplexed thereabout, behold, two men stood by them in dazzling apparel: and as they were affrighted, and bowed down their faces to the earth, they said unto them, Why seek ye the living among the dead? He is not here, but is risen: remember how he spake unto you when he was yet in Galilee, saying that the Son of man must be delivered up into the hands of sinful men, and be crucified, and the third day rise again.

4, 5. Perplexed indeed they were, utterly at a loss to account for the situation that confronted them. And when now **two men stood by them in dazzling apparel** their breath almost left them, so **affrighted** were they. See them stand with **bowed down faces to the earth!** They had seen great things in Jesus' life and ministry; they had seen many wonderful miracles; but what is this, and who are these? It must have been with voices most sweet that the dazzling messengers from heaven, upon whom the women could not look, for their glory, said to the trembling friends of Jesus, **Why seek ye the living among the dead?** See, they call Him whose body the women had come to embalm "the living." Matthew and Mark mention but one angel, the spokesman; but this by no means denies the two.

6, 7. He is not here—that they had already noticed, but it was news to them as joyful as startling when the angels further said, **He is risen!** But should this have been to them the unexpected? Had not Jesus told them He would rise again? **Remember**, said the angels to them, **how he spake unto you when he was yet in Galilee,** before His steadfast setting of His face toward Jerusalem to meet His hour. Always, to His solemn foretellings of His coming sufferings and death He had added, **and the third day rise again.** But as they from ardent affection, had not been able to take literally these prophecies of sufferings and death, so they had forgotten that about His resurrection. They had been so taken up with what Jesus was and did that they could not realize the dark side of His mission, the things He must suffer in order to become what He came to be, the author of eternal salvation. Since His arrest they had only sorrow and consternation.

8, 9. And they remembered his words, and returned from the tomb, and told all these things to the eleven, and to all the rest.

8, 9. But now, with these remarkable facts confronting them, and reminded by the angels, **they remembered his words,** and they came like a revelation to them; they flooded the tomb and the past three days with light; they made glad their before sorrowing hearts; and with what thrilling pleasure they now went and **told all these things to the eleven, and to all the rest!** No one loves a messenger of evil tidings, and yet every one likes to tell "the news:" but the tidings the women now brought were of the kind that we often call "too good to be true."

10, 11. Now they were Mary Magdalene, and Joanna, and Mary the *mother* of James: and the other women with them told these things unto the apostles. And these words appeared in their sight as idle talk: and they disbelieved them.

10, 11. So it seemed to these who heard this great news; for **these words,** of Jesus' resurrection, **appeared in their sight as idle talk,** women's tales! That the apostles themselves were slow to believe the resurrection of Jesus and that they afterwards were firmly convinced of it, shows that the proofs thereof must have been complete.

The first disciples were unbelieving, that we might be strong in faith. For **Joanna**, etc., see viii. 2, 3. From the other narratives we learn that the women here spoken of did not all come at the same time with their report, but one after another, Mary Magdalene, who, as mentioned above, first turned back in grief over what she imagined was a rifling of the tomb, having brought the first report of having *seen* Him. (Comp. Mark xvi. 9.)

Comp., on preceding verses, Matt. xxviii. 1-10; Mark xvi. 1-8; John xx. 1, 2.

12. But Peter arose, and ran unto the tomb; and stooping and looking in, he seeth the linen cloths by themselves; and he departed to his home, wondering at that which was come to pass.

12. Naturally **Peter** made haste to see for himself, and at **the tomb** saw evident proof not only of Jesus' absence, but, in the disposition of **the linen cloths** which had been wrapped by Joseph and Nicodemus around the dead body, of an orderly going on His part and that He had not been taken away or stolen but had " risen " indeed. He went off by himself **wondering at that which was come to pass.** Peter was put into an unusually reflective state of mind and sought to be alone awhile. It was probably in this time that Jesus appeared to him, as recorded in 1 Cor. xv. 5, and was reported to and by the other apostles and disciples, as mentioned in ver. 34. One report came in on the heels of another, and that day was an exciting and wonderful one to the first Christians and an ominous, apprehensive one to the Jewish rulers. " Now is Christ risen from the dead." The last enemy is potentially destroyed. For this Jesus came (Heb. ii. 14, 15). See a fuller account of this visit to the sepulchre in John xx. 3-10.

13, 14. And behold, two of them were going that very day to a village named Emmaus, which was threescore furlongs from Jerusalem. And they communed with each other of all these things which had happened.

13, 14. **Two of them.** Not of the apostles (see ver. 33), but of His disciples. The name of one of them is given in ver. 18; we have no means of knowing who the other was. Among many conjectures one is that our author himself was one of the two. His account reads enough like that of an eye-witness. **Were going.** Our lesson finds them on the road. **Em'-ma-us** means "warm water," and may have been the site of warm springs. It was **three-score furlongs,** or seven and a half miles, distant from Jerusalem. It was probably westward, though its site is not now certainly known. Very naturally these two were talking together of the late stirring events at Jerusalem.

15, 16. And it came to pass, while they communed and questioned together, that Jesus himself drew near, and went with them. But their eyes were holden that they should not know him.

15, 16. While they were thus engaged, and so absorbed as scarcely to notice anything going on around them, some one **drew near and went** (was journeying) **with them.** They paid little attention to Him, not knowing that it was **Jesus himself.** Mark (xvi. 12) says it was "in another form" from that in which He appeared to Mary Magdalene; and here we are told **their eyes were holden** (restrained) **that they should not know him.** It was so ordered in God's Providence that they should not yet know Him. There was a great purpose of love in this.

Are not our eyes often holden by the blindness of our hearts? Do not fail to read 2 Kings vi. 13–17; and comp. Ps. xxxiv. 7.

17, 18. And he said unto them, What communications are these that ye have one with another, as ye walk? And they stood still, looking sad.

And one of them, named Cleopas, answering said unto him, Dost thou alone sojourn in Jerusalem and not know the things which are come to pass there in these days?

17. Nor did they know His voice when He entered into the conversation and inquired **what these communications** (words, discussions) were in which they were so absorbed, and which made them evidently **so sad**. He asked this to draw them out and prepare them for His instructions. Awakened now to the fact that another person was walking with them and amazed at such a question, **they stood still** in astonishment. This is just what men would naturally do, strikingly correct psychologically.

18. **One of them**, of whom we know nothing further than his name, which is not the same as *Clopas* of John xix. 25, answered Him with surprise, **Dost thou alone sojourn in Jerusalem, and not know?** "Thou" is emphatic. "Sojourn" means to reside in a place as a stranger. Hast thou dwelt so apart from men as to be thus unacquainted with notorious events? Or, Dost thou alone sojourn at Jerusalem and not know? Everybody knows these things: how in the world dost thou so strangely inquire? **The things which are come to pass there in these days** were not done in a corner. All the city was moved by them; the darkness and earthquake must have impressed all; and there must have been talk enough everywhere throughout the crowded city about these things, and three days had not passed since the crucifixion.

19, 20. And he said unto them, What things? And they said unto him, The things concerning Jesus of Nazareth, which was a prophet mighty in deed and word before God and all the people: and how the chief priests and our rulers delivered him up to be condemned to death, and crucified him.

19, 20. Desiring to have them express themselves, He said, **What things?** Now let us, listening to this colloquy, remember that the questioning stranger was the centre of all the things inquired about, and that these sad disciples were unconsciously talking to their Master about Himself. They called Him **Jesus of Nazareth,** as though they had about given up the idea that He was from heaven and above all; yet they cannot doubt that He was **a prophet, so mighty** had He been **in deed and word before God,** who testified to Him in these very wonders of teaching and doing, and before **all the people,** who had opportunity to see, hear and prove. But though the people were largely in His favor, won by His sayings and doings, **the chief priests and our rulers,** they add as the second well known thing, **delivered him** to the Romans **to be condemned to death,** and, through them, **crucified him.** Stranger, surely you must have heard of these things!

21-24. But we hoped that it was he which should redeem Israel. Yea and beside all this, it is now the third day since these things came to pass. Moreover certain women of our company amazed us, having been early at the tomb; and when they found not his body, they came, saying, that they had also seen a vision of angels, which said that he was alive. And certain of them that were with us went to the tomb, and found it even so as the women had said: but him they saw not.

21-24. But **we** were hoping **that it was he which should redeem,** was about to redeem, **Israel.** We were hoping this was our Messiah; but now it **is the third day** since His crucifixion, and our hope has been fading completely away. Yet it is not entirely dead; we are dumfounded by what **certain women of our company** (of us) have reported. They **were early at the tomb** this morning, but **found not his body** there where it had been laid; and, further, they reported having **seen a vision of**

angels, which said that he was alive and for that reason was not to be found in the sepulchre. Whereupon some of our number **went to the tomb,** to see for themselves, **and found it** empty, **even so as the women had said,** and evidence there also to confirm the idea that He was alive, having risen from the dead. **But him they saw not.** These two had not yet heard of His appearing to Mary Magdalene, and to the other women, and to Peter. This last sentence of their story reveals the sad perplexity of their hearts, which nothing but a sight of the object of their hopes will completely relieve.

<small>25, 26. And he said unto them, O foolish men, and slow of heart to believe in all that the prophets have spoken! Behoved it not the Christ to suffer these things, and to enter into his glory?</small>

25. Now came the stranger's time to speak, and His tone has changed from inquiry to one of confidence and rebuke, as He begins to address them. **O foolish men,** men *without understanding.* **Slow of heart,** sluggish in disposition, **to believe.** Their want of faith arose from their natural heart. Our whole nature, including head and heart, was damaged by the fall; it needs renewal, to become wholly believing and obedient. They were slow to believe **all that the prophets have spoken.** The very things that have staggered your faith and almost destroyed your hope, were minutely set forth by the prophets of old.

26. **Behoved it not,** was it not necessary for **the Christ,** Messiah of the prophets, **to suffer these things** which now you are so sad over? Look at them aright, and you will find them the very establishment of your hopes, and out of what seems to you defeat you will find victory and triumph. **And to enter into his glory?** Through suffering to glory, through humiliation to the Name above every name, through the cross to His crown, **is**

the way marked out in the prophets for the Christ of God.

27. And beginning from Moses and from all the prophets, he interpreted to them in all the scriptures the things concerning himself.

27. **And beginning from Moses,** the first writer in the Bible and the giver of the Law, and going on to **all the prophets,** the second great division of the Hebrew Scriptures, **he interpreted to them in all the scriptures the things concerning himself**—although as yet they did not know that it was Himself of whom He was speaking. Jesus had said, " Think not that I am come to destroy the law or the prophets; I am not come to destroy, but to fulfil;" and now He showed these two how these Scriptures had been fulfilling in the events they deplored. The spirit of prophecy is its testimony to Jesus (Rev. xix. 10). He had said to the Jews concerning the Scriptures, " They are they that testify of me."

Observe that He who was the Truth did not hesitate to quote " Moses and all the prophets " as real and credible witnesses to Himself. See also ver. 44.

28, 29. And they drew nigh unto the village, whither they were going : and he made as though he would go further. And they constrained him, saying, Abide with us: for it is toward evening, and the day is now far spent. And he went in to abide with them.

28, 29. The walk had proved short in view of the excellent company and discourse by the way, and now they **drew nigh unto the village,** Em′-ma-us, whither they were going. Jesus had gone that way to meet these disciples, not to go to that place. Therefore **he made as though**—showed by His actions that—**he would go further.** This is very natural and plain. **And they constrained him**—were urgent in their persuasions—**saying, Abide with us**—come, stop with us in the village. They so enjoyed His company and were so quickened (ver. 32) by His words; they used the argument of the time of day; it was **toward evening.** Whether they refer to the first evening, which began at 3 o'clock, or the second, which began at 6 o'clock, we cannot tell. At all events they could say, **the day is far spent.** So they pressed upon the welcome stranger, **and he went to abide with them,** " Not Mary Magdalene, nor Peter, nor John, nor the whole college of apostles, had as yet received such a favor as this vouchsafed those two disciples—the one to be unnamed, and the other but a name " (WHEDON). But what transpired at our Lord's previous appearance to Peter we do not know.

30, 31. And it came to pass, when he had sat down with them to meat he took the bread, and blessed it, and brake, and gave to them. And their eyes were opened, and they knew him; and he vanished out of their sight.

It was not long before the evening meal was served; **he sat down with them to meat,** their guest by invitation, but, lo, **he took the bread,** acting as host and as He had been wont to do among His disciples, and **blessed,** gave thanks, as He had been wont, **and brake and gave to them.** Perhaps as He did so they saw in His hands the print of the nails. At all events, during this act the restraining influence spoken of in ver. 16 became inoperative, the veil was taken away from their senses and hearts; **their eyes were opened, and they knew him.** It was Jesus Himself! But their opened eyes were not allowed longer to gaze upon Him. The purpose of His appearing to them was fulfilled, **and he vanished out of their sight** in a supernatural way, disappearing without the usual getting up and going. Yet, lo, He was gone! Thus still further was their conviction confirmed that it was their risen Lord. Then they had opportunity to talk to each other about Him. We see no reference here to the Lord's Supper. Roman Catholic Expositors would fain make this a celebration of the Lord's Supper in one kind, to support their heresy.

32. And they said one to another, Was not our heart burning within us, while he spake to us in the way, while he opened to us the scriptures?

32. **Was not our heart burning within us?** How strange the influence of words, the vehicles of thought, upon the human soul! How powerful the influence of truth upon the heart! We speak of "burning words." True hearts are not cold, but burn, when Jesus talks with them. **While he opened to us the scriptures.** This is the way to reach and warm the heart; open to it the Scriptures. That is effective preaching; that is teaching to purpose.

33, 34. And they rose up that very hour, and returned to Jerusalem, and found the eleven gathered together, and them that were with them, saying, The Lord is risen indeed, and hath appeared to Simon.

33, 34. The experience of these disciples of the Lord was too great and good to keep to themselves even a short time. **That very hour they rose up and returned to Jerusalem,** now with quickened steps and lighter hearts. Their sadness had been turned to gladness, and they must tell it. But the news had got there before them; **the eleven gathered together** with other disciples, anticipated them with **The Lord is risen indeed,** there's no doubt about it, **and hath appeared to Simon.** We do not have any particulars of this appearance. Paul (1 Cor. xv. 5) puts first in his list of Jesus' manifestations of Himself " that he appeared to Cephas." Poor Peter, haunted by the recollection of that look that Jesus gave him upon his threefold denial of Him the Friday before, must have rejoiced to see the face of the risen Lord triumphant in love. Though the eleven had counted the reports of the women idle tales, they could not doubt Peter's confirmation of Jesus' resurrection.

35-37. And they rehearsed the things that happened in the way, and how he was known of them in the breaking of the bread. And as they spake these things, he himself stood in the midst of them, and saith unto them, Peace be unto you. But they were terrified and affrighted, and supposed that they beheld a spirit.

35-37. The two just from Emmaus **rehearsed** their experience **in the way,** and told about **the breaking of the bread** by which He became known to them. We can see them listening so intently to this narrative, when, all of a sudden, unannounced, and despite the closed doors (John xx. 19, 26), there **he himself,** Jesus, **stood in the midst of them.** Coming thus supernaturally, they took Him for **a spirit,** thought it was His ghost, and **were terrified and affrighted.** In this they were just like people now. Ever since the fall visitors from the other world have frightened those to whom they have appeared, even though they came saying, "Fear not," just as Jesus here said, **Peace be unto you.** They all saw Him; they all heard Him; and there He stood! (Comp. Mark xvi. 14; John xix. 19-23.)

38-40. And he said unto them, Why are ye troubled? and wherefore do reasonings arise in your heart? See my hands and my feet, that it is I myself: handle me, and see; for a spirit hath not flesh and bones, as ye behold me having. And when he had said this, he shewed them his hands and his feet.

38-40. Unlike "ghosts," Jesus began in natural tones, recognizable by them all, to talk with them and to act in a thoroughly human way. **Why are ye troubled?** said He, just as a few days before He had said, "Let not your heart be troubled, neither let it be fearful." **Wherefore do reasonings,** questionings, **arise in your heart?** We might answer for them—because of unbelief, because of ignorance, because of sin. However, the fact that they were so hard to persuade of it, proves still more strongly for us the truth of Jesus' resurrection. Then Jesus called them to a further and fuller exercise of their senses. **See my hands and my feet,** with the marks of nails that so lately pierced them. **Handle me, and see** the reality, the objectiveness, the substantiality of my presence. **A spirit hath not flesh and bones,** but ye here **behold me having** these, as before my death. What clear evidence of "the resurrection of the body!" The Son of God took upon Him human nature, which is composed not of spirit or soul only, but of body and soul or spirit. Jesus was true man not only before His death, but also after His resurrection, and is so now also, in glory.

41-43. And while they still disbelieved for joy, and wondered, he said unto them, Have ye here anything to eat? And they gave him a piece of a broiled fish. And he took it, and did eat before them.

41-43. They **still disbelieved,** not from perversity and opposition, but **for joy :** what was passing before them was "too good to be true;" it was all like a dream or a vision. They **wondered,** *could it be true?* Then Jesus condescended to give them another proof of His real bodily presence. **Have ye here anything to eat?** said He. Disembodied spirits do not eat. Then **they gave** and **he took,** making a transaction between two parties, each as much "in the body" as the other, **a piece of a broiled fish,** an article of man's diet, and **and he did eat before them.** This was particularly realistic. And whilst it showed Jesus to be there "in the body," it also may throw some light on Scripture statements that speak of eating and drinking in the kingdom of God, as, e. g., in Matt. xxvi. 29; Mark xiv. 25. In Acts x. 41, Peter, preaching to Cornelius and the Gentiles, speaks of the witnesses of Jesus risen as those "who did eat and drink with him after he rose from the dead."

44. And he said unto them, These are my words which I spake unto you, while I was yet with you, how that all things must needs be fulfilled, which are written in the law of Moses, and the prophets, and the psalms, concerning me.

44. **These** things I tell you now, in the light of my resurrection, are no new things, but **my words which I spake unto you** before, all along those years, **while I was yet with you.** A summary of these things is found in the latter part of this verse and in vers. 46, 47. Jesus here speaks as though He were already gone from them, anticipating His ascension: and His words illustrate that He was not with His disciples during the forty days between His resurrection and ascension in just the same manner and relations that characterized His being with them before. He was already in His state of exaltation, which began with His descent into hell. He was not now fulfilling what was written in the Scriptures concerning Himself; that was "finished," as He cried upon the cross: but He was now teaching them and preparing them for His ascension and the Spirit's coming. But it is all in the one line of the work of Redemption. He had told them before (see especially Matt. xvi. 21, xvii. 22, 23; Luke xviii. 31–34) **that all things must be fulfilled which are written** concerning Him. These things are written in the sacred Scriptures of the Old Testament, which where divided by the Jews into **the law of Moses, and the prophets,** with which latter Jesus here couples **the psalms,** which are so full of references and prophecies concerning Himself, some of them reading even like history, though written long before the events to which they prophetically refer. **Concerning me.** "For the

testimony of [to] Jesus," said the angel of the Revelation (Rev. xix. 10) to John, "is the spirit of prophecy."

"As the angels in the sepulchre had referred back to the words of Jesus, verses 6-8, so does the Lord Himself here refer back to them : it was a continued conviction of the identity of their former and their present Lord—only in a higher degree, and with reference to His *spiritual personality*" (STIER).

45-47. Then opened he their mind, that they might understand the scriptures; and he said unto them, Thus it is written, that the Christ should suffer, and rise again from the dead the third day ; and that repentance and remission of sins should be preached in his name unto all the nations, beginning from Jerusalem.

45. (Comp. ver. 31 ; Acts xvi. 14; Ps. cxix. 18.) *How* the Lord **opened their mind** on this occasion we cannot tell. The statement, however, shows the influence the divine mind has and may exert over the human mind. The purpose and result of this present mind-opening was **that they might understand the scriptures.** (See vers. 25-27.) D. BROWN sees in this statement "Christ's immediate access to the human spirit and absolute power over it, to the adjustment of its vision, and its permanent rectification for spiritual discernment" and "that the apostolic manner of interpreting the Old Testament, in the Acts and Epistles, has the direct sanction of Christ Himself." We see that the apostles heard and observed much that they at the time did not undersand, which things afterwards became plain to them. So it may be in our day, in teaching the young especially : immediate understanding is not always necessary or to be expected.

46. **Thus it is written.** How often Jesus said this ! What constant respect He paid to the holy Scriptures ! He was their fulfilment. (See Matt. iv. 4, 7, 10 ; v. 17, 18 ; xxvi. 24, 53-56.) **That the Christ should suffer.** See

the value of the article here, omitted in the Authorized Version. None seem to have understood that the Messiah prophesied in the Old Testament was to be a suffering Saviour, **and rise again from the dead the third day,** a conqueror different from all others and greater than all others, leading "captivity captive!".

47. There was also a great future to all this work of the Messiah. It was also written, and He opened their minds to see it, **that repentance** on man's part, a change of mind and heart, involving a turning from sin and Satan to God in Christ, **and remission,** forgiveness, **of sins** on God's part, **should be preached,** proclaimed for the obedience of faith, **in his name,** in Christ's name, **unto all the nations** of mankind. **Beginning from Jerusalem** and with the Jews, it was not to be restricted to them, but to flow from Zion to all peoples that on earth do dwell. "Salvation is of the Jews" (John iv. 22), but is not for the Jews only, but for "whosoever will!" Hence it must **be preached** to all. Here, together with the great commission (Matt. xxviii. 18–20), is our authorization for missions, and the Church's work is set forth in co-operation with Him "who willeth that all men should be saved and come to the knowledge of the truth" (1 Tim. ii. 4).

"The name of Jesus opens the door for repentance and remission of sins," says RIEGER. "By the *passion* of Christ," says STIER, contrasting Old Testament and New Testament preaching of repentance, "repentance is now preached in its evangelical strength; by His *resurrection* forgiveness is offered and pledged. The New Testament preaching of repentance is itself a Gospel. For, the message of grace does not merely bring 'the *incentive* to repentance, and the promise of forgiveness:' God *gives* to those who hear and believe repentance unto life (Acts xi. 18). The union of these two words, repentance and remission, is full of encouragement to the weak in faith." Hence it is both a scriptural and a helpful order that after our Confession of Sin we have the Declaration of Grace; and we really believe "the forgiveness of sins."

48, 49. Ye are witnesses of these things. And behold, I send forth the promise of my Father upon you: but tarry ye in the city, until ye be clothed with power from on high.

48. **Ye are witnesses.** There may be witnesses of a thing, and again, witnesses *to* a thing. In both senses these disciples, especially the apostles, were witnesses **of these things.** They were witnesses of the facts of Christ's life, teachings, works, death and resurrection (and presently of His ascension), and they were to be witnesses to the people of the purpose and effect of these things, whilst they preached repentance and remission of sins.

"It is not the Lord's will to appoint and send forth orators or enthusiasts, or even simple teachers—and this He shows at the very outset in the typical character of His first Apostles—but, before all and in all, *witnesses*" (STIER). Christianity deals with *facts*, of which there are sufficient witnesses. Moreover, also, every one "in whose heart the Spirit has glorified and sealed the life and the word of Jesus" is a witness to these things. Moreover we give our testimony directly and indirectly, by our lives, our lips, our influence, our gifts. Every one who has his heart full of these things will find a way of *testifying* to them.

49. **And behold** there is something yet to look forward to. **I send forth the promise of my Father** (Joel ii. 28-32) **upon you.** There were yet divine facts for them to witness. The outpouring of the Holy Spirit is what is here referred to. **I send—ye tarry.** Wait on God. He is

the Lord. Follow His leading. **Until ye be clothed, endued, with power from on high.** He had already opened their minds to understand the Scriptures: but they need a still further power to enable them to be His witnesses to all nations, namely, the power of the Holy Ghost. He had, indeed, "breathed on them" and said, "Receive ye the Holy Ghost." But there was to be a further and more striking manifestation of the power from on high—but not until Jesus Himself was taken up from them. We find the fulfilment of this in Acts ii. See the Nicene Creed and what it says concerning the Holy Ghost.

50, 51. And he led them out until *they were* over against Bethany: and he lifted up his hands, and blessed them. And it came to pass, while he blessed them, he parted from them, and was carried up into heaven.

50. Here we come to the final act. For Luke summarily closes his gospel history, saying nothing here of the forty days' sojourn on earth of the risen Jesus. Comp. Acts. i. 1-11. The scene was the Mount of Olives, **over against Bethany.** We do not know the time of day it was. **He lifted up his hands,** a significant gesture, **and blessed them.** What did He say? It is not recorded. Was it the customary and only appointed blessing of the Old Testament, found in Numbers vi. 24-26? Shall we ask also, was there anything in this blessing, or was it a mere form?

51. It was **while he blessed them,** lovely attitude, comforting remembrance, that **he parted from them,** supernaturally and with infinite ease and grace, **and was carried up into heaven,** not in a whirlwind or accompanied by chariots of fire or horses of fire, but just as He was, until "a cloud received him out of their sight" (Acts i. 9; Eph. iv. 10).

52, 53. And they worshipped him, and returned to Jerusalem with great joy: and were continually in the temple, blessing God.

52, 53. First **they worshipped him,** acknowledging Him to be Lord and God: and He accepted that worship. Then they **returned to Jerusalem,** to wait as He (ver. 49) had instructed them. They were filled **with great joy,** despite His personal, visible withdrawal from them. Their eyes were opened, their minds enlightened, they understood the Scriptures as never before, **and were continually in the temple,** God's house, **blessing God,** praising God. This was at the times of worship, the morning and evening sacrifices. In the Acts we learn that they gathered also in the already consecrated upper chamber, and "with one accord continued steadfastly in prayer." So they waited for the promised Holy Ghost.

www.ingramcontent.com/pod-product-compliance
Lightning Source LLC
Chambersburg PA
CBHW022109300426
44117CB00007B/644